Module A

DIPLOMA IN FINANCIAL MANAGEMENT

Subject Area 2

PERFORMANCE MANAGEMENT

Study text

This Study Text

BPP is an **approved provider** of training materials for the ACCA's DipFM qualification.

In this July 2008 edition

- The syllabus and study guide, cross-referenced to the Text

- Comprehensive syllabus coverage, reviewed by the examiner.

- Plenty of activities, examples and quizzes to demonstrate and practise techniques

- Full index

- Layout designed to be easy on the eye and easy to use

FOR EXAMS FROM DECEMBER 2008

STUDY TEXT

First edition 2001
Eighth edition July 2008

ISBN 9780 7517 5301 1 (previous ISBN 9780 7517 4278 7)

British Library Cataloguing-in-Publication Data
A catalogue record for this book
is available from the British Library

Published by

BPP Learning Media Ltd
BPP House, Aldine Place
London W12 8AA

www.bpp.com/learningmedia

Printed in the United Kingdom

We are grateful to the Association of Chartered
Certified Accountants for permission to reproduce past
examination questions. The answers to past
examination questions have been prepared by BPP
Learning Media Ltd.

Your learning materials, published by BPP Learning
Media Ltd, are printed on paper sourced from
sustainable, managed forests.

Contents

How to use this study text

This is the eighth edition of the BPP Learning Media study text for the Diploma in Financial Management Module A, subject area 2 *Performance Management*. It has been specifically written to cover the Syllabus and Study Guide, and has been fully reviewed by the examiner.

To pass the examination you need a thorough understanding in all areas covered by the syllabus and study guide.

Recommended approach

(a)   To pass you need to be able to answer questions on **everything** specified by the syllabus and study guide. Read the text very carefully and do not skip any of it.

(b)   Learning is an **active** process. Do **all** the activities as you work through the text so you can be sure you really understand what you have read.

(c)   After you have covered the material in the Interactive Text, work through the questions in the Practice and Revision Kit for Module A.

(d)   Before you take the exam, check that you still remember the material using the following quick revision plan.

    (i)   Read through the chapter learning objectives. Are there any gaps in your knowledge? If so, study the section again.

    (ii)   Read and learn the key terms.

    (iii)   Read and learn the key learning points, which are a summary of each chapter.

    (iv)   Do the quick quizzes again. If you know what you're doing, they shouldn't take long.

This approach is only a suggestion. You or your college may well adapt it to suit your needs.

Remember this is a **practical** course.

(a)   Try to relate the material to your experience in the workplace or any other work experience you may have had.

(b)   Try to make as many links as you can to subject area 1 of Module A, and also to Module B.

Further question practice

Practice and Revision Kit

A substantial further bank of questions including past exam questions is available in the BPP Learning Media Practice and Revision Kit for this module.

i-Pass CD Rom

BPP Learning Media's i-Pass product is an invaluable aid to revision. We produce one each for Module A and Module B. These interactive CD Roms provide numerous multiple choice and data response questions for each of the two subject areas in the module. Ideal for question practice and revision, they are designed to test knowledge and perfect exam technique.

Revision

Revision is made easier with BPP Learning Media's Passcards. These are pocket sized revision cards, corresponding to each chapter of the study text and covering the essential key points of the topics. The perfect solution for revision on the move.

You can order all these products by using the form at the back of this book, or telephone 0845 0751 100 or on line at www.bpp.com/learningmedia

Help yourself study for your DipFM exams

Exams for professional bodies such as ACCA are very different from those you have taken at college or university. You will be under **greater time pressure before** the exam – as you may be combining your study with work. There are many different ways of learning and so the BPP Learning Media Study Text offers you a number of different tools to help you through. Here are some hints and tips: they are not plucked out of the air, but **based on research and experience**. (You don't need to know that long-term memory is in the same part of the brain as emotions and feelings - but it's a fact anyway.)

The right approach

1 The right attitude

Believe in yourself	Yes, there is a lot to learn. Yes, it is a challenge. But thousands have succeeded before and you can too.
Remember why you're doing it	Studying might seem a grind at times, but you are doing it for a reason: to advance your career.

2 The right focus

Read through the Syllabus and Study guide	These tell you what you are expected to know and are supplemented by Exam focus points in the Text.
Study the Exam Paper section	Past papers are likely to be good guides to what you should expect in the exam.

3 The right method

The whole picture	You need to grasp the detail - but keeping in mind how everything fits into the whole picture will help you understand better. <ul><li>The **Introduction** of each chapter puts the material in context.</li><li>The **Syllabus content**, **Study guide** and **Exam focus points** show you what you need to **grasp**.</li></ul>
In your own words	To absorb the information (and to practise your written communication skills), it helps to **put it into your own words**. <ul><li>**Take notes.**</li><li>Answer the **questions** in each chapter. You will practise your written communication skills, which become increasingly important as you progress through your DipFM exams.</li><li>Try **'teaching' a subject** to a colleague or friend.</li></ul>
Give yourself cues to jog your memory	The BPP Study Text uses **bold** to **highlight key points**. <ul><li>Try **colour coding** with a highlighter pen.</li><li>Write **key points** on cards.</li></ul>

4   **The right review**

Review, review, review	It is a **fact** that regularly reviewing a topic in summary form can **fix it in your memory**. Because **review** is so important, the BPP Study Text helps you to do so in many ways.
	• **Chapter roundups** summarise the 'Fast forward' key points in each chapter. Use them to recap each study session.
	• The **Quick quiz** is another review technique you can use to ensure that you have grasped the essentials.
	• Go through the **Examples** in each chapter a second or third time.

Developing your personal Study Plan

BPP's **Learning to Learn Accountancy** book emphasises the need to prepare (and use) a study plan. Planning and sticking to the plan are key elements of learning success.

There are four steps you should work through.

Step 1   **How do you learn?**

First you need to be aware of your style of learning. The BPP **Learning to Learn Accountancy** book commits a chapter to this **self-discovery**. What types of intelligence do you display when learning? You might be advised to brush up on certain study skills before launching into this Study Text.

BPP's **Learning to Learn Accountancy** book helps you to identify what intelligences you show more strongly and then details how you can tailor your study process to your preferences. It also includes handy hints on how to develop intelligences you exhibit less strongly, but which might be needed as you study accountancy.

Are you a **theorist** or are you more **practical**? If you would rather get to grips with a theory before trying to apply it in practice, you should follow the study sequence on page (vii). If the reverse is true (you like to know why you are learning theory before you do so), you might be advised to flick through Study Text chapters and look at examples, case studies and questions (Steps 8, 9 and 10 in the **suggested study sequence**) before reading through the detailed theory.

Step 2   **How much time do you have?**

Work out the time you have available per week, given the following.

• The standard you have set yourself
• The time you need to set aside later for work on the Practice & Revision Kit and Passcards
• The other exam(s) you are sitting
• Very importantly, practical matters such as work, travel, exercise, sleep and social life

Hours

Note your time available in box A.   A [   ]

Step 3   **Allocate your time**

- Take the time you have available per week for this Study Text shown in box A, multiply it by the number of weeks available and insert the result in box B.   B ☐

- Divide the figure in box B by the number of chapters in this text and insert the result in box C.   C ☐

Remember that this is only a rough guide. Some of the chapters in this book are longer and more complicated than others, and you will find some subjects easier to understand than others.

Step 4   **Implement**

Set about studying each chapter in the time shown in box C, following the key study steps in the order suggested by your particular learning style.

This is your personal **Study Plan**. You should try and combine it with the study sequence outlined below. You may want to modify the sequence a little (as has been suggested above) to adapt it to your **personal style**.

BPP's **Learning to Learn Accountancy** gives further guidance on developing a study plan, and deciding where and when to study.

Suggested study sequence

It is likely that the best way to approach this Study Text is to tackle the chapters in the order in which you find them. Taking into account your individual learning style, you could follow this sequence for each chapter.

Key study steps	Activity
Step 1 **Topic list**	Note the topics covered in the chapter. Each numbered topic is a numbered section in the chapter.
Step 2 **Introduction**	This gives you the big picture in terms of the context of the chapter. The content is referenced to the Study Guide, and Exam Guidance shows how the topic is likely to be examined. In other words, it sets your objectives for study.
Step 3 **Knowledge brought forward boxes**	In these we highlight information and techniques that it is assumed you have 'brought forward' with you from your earlier studies. If there are topics which have changed recently due to legislation for example, these topics are explained in more detail.
Step 4 **Fast forward**	Fast forward boxes give you a quick summary of the content of each of the main chapter sections. They are listed together in the roundup at the end of each chapter to provide you with an overview of the contents of the whole chapter.
Step 5 **Explanations**	Proceed methodically through the chapter, reading each section thoroughly and making sure you understand.
Step 6 **Key terms and Exam focus points**	• Key terms can often earn you *easy marks* if you state them clearly and correctly in an appropriate exam answer (and they are highlighted in the index at the back of the Text). • Exam focus points state how we think the examiner intends to examine certain topics.
Step 7 **Note taking**	Take brief notes, if you wish. Avoid the temptation to copy out too much. Remember that being able to put something into your own words is a sign of being able to understand it. If you find you cannot explain something you have read, read it again before you make the notes.

Key study steps	Activity
Step 8 **Examples**	Follow each through to its solution very carefully.
Step 9 **Case studies**	Study each one, and try to add flesh to them from your own experience. They are designed to show how the topics you are studying come alive (and often come unstuck) in the real world.
Step 10 **Questions**	Make a very good attempt at each one.
Step 11 **Answers**	Check yours against ours, and make sure you understand any discrepancies.
Step 12 **Chapter roundup**	Work through it carefully, to make sure you have grasped the significance of all the fast forward points.
Step 13 **Quick quiz**	When you are happy that you have covered the chapter, use the Quick quiz to check how much you have remembered of the topics covered and to practise questions in a variety of formats.
Step 14 **Question practice**	Either at this point, or later when you are thinking about revising, make a full attempt at the suggested Question(s). If you have bought i-Pass, use this too.

Short of time: Skim study technique?

You may find you simply do not have the time available to follow all the key study steps for each chapter, however you adapt them for your particular learning style. If this is the case, follow the **skim study** technique below.

- Study the chapters in the order you find them in the Study Text.

- For each chapter:

  - Follow the key study steps 1-3

  - Skim-read through step 5, looking out for the points highlighted in the fast forward boxes (step 4)

  - Jump to step 12

  - Go back to step 6

  - Follow through steps 8 and 9

  - Prepare outline answers to questions (steps 10/11)

  - Try the Quick quiz (step 13), following up any items you can't answer

  - Do a plan for the Question (step 14), comparing it against our answers

  - You should probably still follow step 7 (note-taking), although you may decide simply to rely on the BPP Learning Media Passcards for this.

Moving on...

However you study, when you are ready to embark on the practice and revision phase of the BPP Effective Study Package, you should still refer back to this Study Text, both as a source of **reference** (you should find the index particularly helpful for this) and as a way to **review** (the Fast forwards, Exam focus points, Chapter roundups and Quick quizzes help you here).

And remember to keep careful hold of this Study Text – you will find it invaluable in your work.

Syllabus

Aim

To develop a good understanding of knowledge required and techniques available to enable managers to measure and manage business performance within their organisation. Both financial and non-financial measures of performance are included in this paper.

Objectives

On completion of this paper candidates should be able to:

- Understand how performance measures should be linked to overall organisation strategy

- Prepare budgets and use them to control and evaluate organisational performance

- Identify and apply techniques that aid decision making

- Identify and implement appropriate costing systems and business control systems

- Identify and apply techniques to evaluate decisions in relation to: costing, pricing, product range, marketing strategy, purchasing and production strategies

- Identify and apply non-financial performance measures, and understand the inter-relationships between different performance measures

- Explain the behavioural and organisational consequences of using performance measurement and performance management techniques

- Identify and apply techniques for evaluating the performance of divisions

- Identify and explain issues that may cause performance not to meet expectations

- Demonstrate the ability to communicate in a range of formats

Position within the syllabus

Candidates are expected to have a good knowledge of basic accounting principles from subject area 1. Knowledge from subject areas 3 and 4 will be helpful but not essential.

Syllabus content

The syllabus considers Performance Management from three broad and overlapping perspectives, namely: planning and decision making, measuring performance, and managing performance. There are also some general issues.

			Chapter where covered in Text
1	**General issues for performance management**		
	(a)	Mission statements, objectives and targets	1
	(b)	Responsibility centres	1
	(c)	Information systems and costing systems to provide appropriate information	1, 2, 3
	(d)	Overall organisation strategy and how performance measurement and management should enable strategy to be realised.	1
2	**Planning and decision making**		
	(a)	Preparing budgets, including fixed and flexible budgets, cash budgets	3, 4
	(b)	Budgets in different contexts, including: manufacturing, sales, service industries	3
	(c)	Alternative approaches to budgeting and planning	4
	(d)	Decision making techniques required to determine plans that will maximise performance	5, 6
	(e)	Pricing policies and techniques for setting prices	7
	(f)	Strategic planning and operational planning	4
	(g)	The future of budgets and alternatives to budgeting	4
	(h)	Costing data for decision making, and use of activity-based costing data	2
	(i)	Transfer pricing policies and practices.	8
3	**Performance measurement**		
	(a)	Financial measures of performance	9, 10, 11, 12
	(b)	Critical success factors and key performance indicators	12
	(c)	Non-financial performance measures	12
	(d)	Balanced scorecard	12
	(e)	Benchmarking	12
	(f)	Divisional performance measures.	13
4	**Performance management**		
	(a)	Purchasing and production management	14, 15
	(b)	Activity-based management and business process re-engineering	15
	(c)	Techniques for ensuring value-for-money, particularly re not-for-profit organisations	15
	(d)	Techniques to ensure continuous improvement	15
	(e)	Use of performance measurement techniques to manage performance	16
	(f)	Management of divisional performance, including transfer pricing issues	16

		Chapter where covered in Text
(g)	Behavioural and organisational consequences of performance measures, particularly budgeting and other accounting system data	16
(h)	Understanding of practical issues that may affect an organisation's ability to manage performance effectively	16
(i)	Incentive schemes linked to performance measures.	16

Excluded topics

No issues relating to performance management are specifically excluded.

Key areas of the syllabus

The key topics include:

- Decision making techniques to enable managers to maximise performance
- Budgeting and standard costing techniques to assess performance
- Costing systems and use of the data produced, including activity-based costing
- Techniques to aid performance evaluation of divisions
- Techniques to manage the performance of purchasing, production and sales functions
- Behavioural and organisational consequences of performance measurement
- Practical issues that affect a firm's ability to manage performance effectively
- Non-financial performance indicators,

Study Guide

General issues

1   **General issues for performance management**

    Syllabus reference 1a, 1b

    • Explain the purposes of and inter-relationships between mission statements, strategy, corporate objectives and targets

    • Discuss the importance of relating performance measurement and performance management to the overall mission, strategy and objectives of the organisation

    • Describe the nature of responsibility centres, such as investment centres, profit centres, cost centres, revenue centres

    • Identify and discuss different organisational structures

    • Explain the benefits and drawbacks of decentralisation and how such drawbacks can be overcome.

2   **Information systems and strategy**

    Syllabus reference 1c, 1d

    • Describe and evaluate different types of information systems that provide the information required for performance management

    • Explain the features of resource planning systems and management information systems (MIS)

    • Describe the role of costing systems, and evaluate their strengths and weaknesses

    • Describe the links between overall corporate strategy and performance management within an organisation,

Planning and decision making

3   **Preparing budgets**

    Syllabus reference 2a, 2b

    • Prepare budgets for a range of purposes including sales, production and purchases, expenses and the master budget

    • Explain the differences between fixed and flexible budgets

    • Prepare a cash budget

    • Prepare budgets for different types of organisations, such as manufacturing, service companies, not-for-profit organisations

    • Interpret the information included in the budgets

    • Critically appraise the assumptions used in preparing budgets.

4   **Beyond basic budgeting**

    Syllabus reference 2c, 2f, 2g

    • Distinguish between strategic planning and operational planning

    • Explain and evaluate the appropriateness of different budgeting approaches, such as zero-based budgets and activity-based budgets

- Evaluate the critique of budgeting, 'beyond budgeting'
- Evaluate alternatives to budgeting,

5 Decision making techniques I

Syllabus reference 2d(i)

- Distinguish fixed and variable costs, and combinations of these two costs
- Explain the assumption of linearity and the limitations of this assumption
- Demonstrate understanding of the Cost-Volume-Profit (CVP) model
- Prepare breakeven charts, profit-volume charts and margin-of-safety calculations, and interpret the information prepared
- Comment on the limitations of CVP analysis and other factors that may need to be considered with CVP information.

6 Decision making techniques II

Syllabus reference 2d(ii), d(iv)

- Define and distinguish between relevant costs, sunk costs and opportunity costs
- Explain the concept and use of incremental costs
- Use an incremental cost approach to decision making, particularly for make-buy decisions and additional/special orders
- Explain and illustrate the impact of limiting factors/scarce resources in decision making
- Prepare simple calculations to determine the optimal mix of products where there are limiting factors (simplex calculations will not be required).

7 Decision making techniques III

Syllabus reference 2d(iv), f, h

- Demonstrate simple techniques for decision making under uncertainty, such as conservatism, sensitivity analysis, 'maximin-minimax'
- Demonstrate the use of probability estimates and expected values in decision making under uncertainty
- Comment on the strengths and weaknesses of the techniques mentioned above.

8 Pricing policies

Syllabus reference 2e

- Identify and discuss market conditions that will affect the choice of pricing policies, including price elasticity
- Discuss different pricing policies and strategies with which they would be appropriate, for example: skimming and penetration policies
- Calculate prices using various techniques such as: full cost-plus, variable cost-plus, variable cost, and explain when different techniques might be appropriate
- Explain the operation of target costing, apply to examples
- Discuss the implications of different pricing techniques, for example marginal cost for certain short-run pricing decisions
- Evaluate the implications of activity-based costs for pricing.

9   **Transfer pricing**

Syllabus reference 2i

- Identify the circumstances where transfer pricing will be required, and the issues that will arise, particularly in relation to the nature of divisionalisation

- Explain the 'general rule' for transfer pricing and discuss its application

- Discuss the different techniques for setting transfer prices and evaluate their applicability in different situations and divisionalised structures including: market-based prices, marginal cost transfers, cost-plus prices and negotiated prices

- Discuss the impact of transfer prices on divisional performance assessment.

10   **Activity-based costing I**

Syllabus reference 2h

- Discuss the ways in which costing data is used in decision making

- Explain the concept of 'different costs for different purposes' and discuss the issues that arise from this

- Outline the background to the development of activity-based costing

- Calculate simple activity-based costs and compare with traditional volume-based costing methods.

11   **Activity-based costing II**

Syllabus reference 2h

- Explain the different uses to which activity-based cost data can be applied

- Demonstrate the use of activity-based cost data for make/buy and outsourcing decisions

- Demonstrate the use of activity-based cost data for product continuance decisions

- Demonstrate the use of activity-based cost data for customer profitability analysis and decisions

- Discuss other relevant factors that need to be considered in conjunction with cost data

- Discuss the problems of implementing and using activity-based techniques and discuss how these problems might be minimised.

Performance measurement

12   **Budgeting and standard costing**

Syllabus reference 3a(i), 3a(ii)

- Demonstrate the use of budgets to measure performance

- Evaluate actual results compared to budget and calculate budget variances

- Explain process of setting standard costs, and use of standard costs to set targets

- Calculate standard cost variances and prepare operating statements

- Evaluate performance using standard cost variances

- Identify possible causes of variances

- Recommend action using standard cost variance analysis

- Discuss the relevance of the original budget, and its assumptions, when interpreting standard cost variances.

13 **Measures of shareholder value**

Syllabus reference 3a(iii)

- Explain the importance of the shareholder value concept, and discuss its limitations, for example in comparison with stakeholder approaches

- Explain and apply the common methods for measuring shareholder value, such as: profit, return on assets, return on sales, Economic Value Added (EVA®)

- Discuss problems of implementing shareholder value measures and approaches to minimise these problems.

14 **Critical success factors and non-financial performance indicators (NFPIs)**

Syllabus reference 3b, 3c

- Discuss the implications of the growing emphasis on NFPIs, and the benefits their use might bring to an organisation

- Discuss the interaction of NFPIs and financial measures of performance

- Identify and comment on NFPIs in relation to: employee performance, quality, customers, supply chain etc.

- Explain the concept of critical success factors (CSFs)

- Discuss the relation between critical success factors and strategic targets

- Discuss the problems that may arise in implementing and using NFPIs and CSFs for measuring performance.

15 **Balanced scorecard and benchmarking**

Syllabus reference 3c, 3d

- Explain the development of the balanced scorecard as proposed by Kaplan and Norton

- Explain the main features of the balanced scorecard and the interaction between the different perspectives

- Discuss the implementation of a balanced scorecard, the selection of measures to be used, and who should own the implementation process

- Evaluate the benefits and problems that might arise from using a balanced scorecard

- Explain the concept and potential benefits of benchmarking performance measures

- Discuss the problems of implementing and using benchmarking techniques and action to overcome such problems

- Discuss the relationship between balanced scorecard and benchmarking.

16 **Divisional performance measures I**

Syllabus reference 3f

- Discuss the general issues in relation to assessing the performance of divisions, especially the importance of the nature of divisions

- Calculate the basic divisional performance measures: accounting profit, return on investment, residual income, controllable profit, and cash flows

- Discuss the strengths and weaknesses of the above measures and the conditions where each measure would be appropriate.

17   **Divisional performance measures II**

   Syllabus reference 3f, 4f

- Explain the development of economic value added (EVA®)
- Discuss the strengths and weaknesses of EVA®
- Discuss the problems of implementing EVA® and actions to overcome such problems
- Discuss the relationship between financial measures of divisional performance and non-financial measures
- Discuss the issues that arise when divisions are assessed, including problems that arise from using a range of different performance measures
- Comment on the issues that arise in relation to assessing divisional performance and the performance of the divisional management and make suggestions for improvements
- Discuss the inter-relationship between divisional performance measures and transfer pricing
- Discuss the action needed by management to ensure divisions operate effectively in line with the whole organisation's objectives.

Performance management

18   **Performance in operational and production management**

   Syllabus reference 4a

- Outline the key elements of operations management, including: procurement, logistics, production management, and quality management
- Distinguish between functional operational structures, matrix structures and process-based structures
- Discuss production issues, such as 'lean manufacturing; 'focus factories', 'flow-line production', 'cell production', and discuss the implications for performance management
- Explain the problems that may arise in the transition between different production systems
- Explain the basic features of MRP and MRP II systems
- Explain the basic features of optimised production technology (OPT) and theory of constraints, and contrast with MRP systems
- Discuss the information that is available from production planning systems and its use in managing performance.

19   **Supply chain management and e-procurement**

   Syllabus reference 4a(i) and 4a(ii)

- Explain the basic features of the supply chain, including: environmental factors, technology, suppliers, production (of goods or services), customers and logistics
- Discuss strategies and measures that have been used to improve performance in the supply chain
- Discuss measures that can be used to control and improve supply chain performance, and comment on issues that can arise
- Explain the changes in procurement procedures that have taken place using electronic data transfer and the internet
- Discuss measures that can be used to control and improve e-procurement performance.

20   Out-sourcing, joint ventures and partnerships

Syllabus reference 4a(v)

- Discuss the changes in the nature of the supplier relationship in recent years

- Explain the benefits and weaknesses of out-sourcing

- Discuss measures that can be used to determine whether out-sourcing would improve performance and measures that could be used to control this process once implemented

- Discuss the benefits and weaknesses of joint ventures and partnerships between supplier and customer

- Discuss measures that can be used to determine whether a joint-venture or partnership would improve performance and measures that could be used to ensure continued improvement through such relationships.

21   Just-in-time

Syllabus reference 4a(iii)

- Explain the just-in-time production and just-in-time purchasing philosophy, including the kanban system

- Discuss operational issues that arise as a result of implementing just-in-time

- Discuss financial consequences, in the short-term and medium-term, of implementing just-in-time procedures

- Discuss measures that can be used to control and improve production and procurement performance if just-in-time procedures are implemented.

22   Target costing and kaizen costing

Syllabus reference 4a(iv), 4d

- Explain the basic features of target costing and contrast these with traditional cost-plus costing procedures

- Discuss the cost reduction objectives of target costing

- Explain techniques that can be used to ensure continuous improvement in performance

- Discuss the features of kaizen costing and how these may help to manage performance.

23   Activity-based management

Syllabus reference 4b

- Explain the main features of activity-based management (ABM)

- Contrast ABC with ABM

- Discuss the benefits that may arise from using ABM and the problems that may be encountered in its use

- Explain the concept of value-added (VA) and non value-added (NVA) activities

- Discuss the problems that may arise with the implementation of the VA/NVA distinction.

24   Business process re-engineering

Syllabus reference 4b

- Explain the main features of business process re-engineering (BPR)

- Discuss whether and how BPR could improve performance

- Discuss Hammer's contention that BPR will only realise its full potential if carried out for the whole organisation

- Discuss the problems that might arise in adopting BPR and possible approaches to minimise the problems
- Discuss the evidence that BPR has only been successful in a minority of implementations
- Contrast BPR with ABM.

25 Behavioural and organisation issues

Syllabus reference 4e, g

- Explain how performance measures interact with performance management, particularly the issue of 'what you measure is what you get'
- Explain how performance measures and targets can be used to motivate individuals and discuss the problems that may arise
- Discuss whether and how participation in the target-setting process may improve performance
- Discuss the role of organisational culture and the style of management in managing performance.

26 Value-for-money and not-for-profit organisations

Syllabus reference 4c

- Explain the concept of value-for-money
- Distinguish not-for-profit organisations from commercial organisations, in particular in relation to their mission and objectives
- Explain techniques for ensuring value-for-money that may be particularly appropriate for not-for-profit organisations, such as: effectiveness audits, VFM audits, programme budgeting techniques
- Discuss the role of motivation and rewards in not-for profit organisations.

27 Practical difficulties

Syllabus reference 4h

Explain the practical difficulties that may affect an organisation's ability to manage performance effectively including:

- actions of competitors, including new entrants
- price movements
- foreign exchange movements
- labour disputes
- supply problems
- rapid technological change.

28 Incentive schemes

Syllabus reference 4i

- Explain the role of incentive schemes in encouraging high levels of performance from staff
- Outline different forms of incentive scheme, such as: individual, unit and company-wide, and different elements within a scheme, such as: cash bonuses, shares and options
- Discuss the strengths and weaknesses of different incentive schemes
- Discuss problems that may occur with incentive schemes.

Note. When studying for this paper, it will be necessary to discuss examples from a wide variety of organisations, in particular: manufacturing companies, service companies, multinational companies, financial services companies, and not-for-profit organisations

Reading list

The reading list below is issued by the examiner, and offers suggestions for additional reading. This BPP Learning Media Study Text has been reviewed by the examiner, and comprehensively covers the entire syllabus.

The subject matter of this paper is drawn from management accounting and operations management. As a result there is no single text that adequately covers the whole syllabus. Various titles are recommended below with some comments to direct students to a text that will meet their need. Note that in all these texts students will have to be selective as they cover more than the Performance Management syllabus.

- A. Atkinson & R. Kaplan
  Advanced Management Accounting
  Prentice Hall

  Covers many of the accounting topics and managerial techniques

- D. Russell, A. Patel & G. Wilkinson-Riddle
  Cost Accounting: an essential guide
  Prentice Hall

  Brief treatment of budgeting, standard costs and ABC

- Colin Drury
  Management Accounting for Business Decisions
  Thomson Learning

  Deals well with the calculations and detailed management accounting issues

- P. Atrill and E. McLaney
  Management Accounting for Non-Specialists
  Prentice Hall

  Basic overview of the management accounting material

- S. Brown, R. Lamming, J. Bessant, P. Jones
  Strategic Operations Management
  Butterworth-Heinemann

  Covers the non-accounting aspects in a concise and readable manner.

- L. J. Krajewski & L. P. Ritzman
  Operations Management – Strategy and Analysis
  Addison-Wesley

  Covers the non-accounting aspects

The examination

The examination for each module will cover the two subject areas in that module. The examination for Module A will cover both 'Interpretation of Financial Statements' (subject area 1) and 'Performance Management' (subject area 2) topics.

The structure of the examination for Module A will be as follows.

Section A

20 multiple choice questions (10 covering subject area 1 and 10 covering subject area 2) of 2 marks each.

Section B

3 written questions of 20 marks each - covering subject area 1.

Section C

3 written questions of 20 marks each - covering subject area 2.

Candidates will be required to attempt all questions in Section A, one question from Section B, one question from Section C and one final question from either Section B or C.

The time allowed will be 15 minutes reading and planning time (during which you are not allowed to write in the answer booklet) followed by 3 hours writing time.

The structure of the Module B examination follows the same format, but will cover financial strategy and risk management.

The pass mark for each examination is 50%.

Analysis of past papers

The following analysis shows the topics which have been covered in the written sections of the pilot paper and the exams set to date.

	Marks
June 2008	
Pricing	20
Value for money in a not-for-profit organisation	20
Consideration of different marketing/operational policies	20
December 2007	
Budgeted profits calculation and discussion	20
Performance measurement systems	20
Transfer pricing	20
June 2007	
Traditional budgeting problems and how to overcome them	20
Profit contribution calculations	20
Activity based costing	20
December 2006	
Mission statement and performance measurement	20
Production decision	20
Pricing policy	20

Projects

General

Candidates are required, as part of their assessment, to submit a project for each module of the Diploma in Financial Management qualification.

The Module A project is a 5,000 word project which covers both Interpretation of Financial Statements (subject area 1) and Performance Management (subject area 2).

The nature of the projects is such that they will not require extensive research and can be completed without reference to sensitive work situations. The projects will relate to the subject matter of the individual papers, and candidates who have studied the syllabus of each paper should be able to have a good attempt at the projects. Each project should be approximately 5,000 words in length, including appendices, but excluding the bibliography. The assignments will involve a mixture of calculation and narrative. The project will be an integrated assignment covering the two subject areas together; there will not be separate assignments.

The BPP Learning Media Project textbook will help you prepare for the Project element of Module A. You can order by calling 0845 0751 100 (within the UK) +44 (0)20 8740 2211 (from overseas) or by visiting www.bpp.com/learningmedia

P
A
R
T

A

General issues for performance management

1

Introduction to performance management

Introduction

This chapter sets the scene for the whole of your studies of performance management. If performance is to be 'managed', this implies that managers have some idea of the direction in which the organisation should be progressing; we therefore start by looking at the types of plans and targets that might be set for an organisation.

The remainder of the chapter introduces several of the essential topics in performance management that will be expanded on in later chapters of the text.

Learning objectives

On completion of this chapter you will be able to:

Syllabus reference

- explain the meaning and purpose of a mission statement, objectives and targets   1
- explain the roles of performance measurement and management in ensuring   1
  that an organisation's overall strategy is realised
- explain in broad terms how performance management systems differ for   1
  responsibility centres and process-based organisations
- describe the roles of information technology and costing systems in   1, 2
  performance management

1 Mission, objectives and targets

1.1 The purpose of an organisation: mission statements

The **mission** of an organisation is the reason for its existence. Some organisations issue mission statements.

Organisations develop **objectives** (quantified as **targets**) for the achievement of its mission and long-term goals. The strategic objectives for a commercial organisation should include one or more financial objectives.

Key term

Mission 'describes the organisation's basic function in society, in terms of the products and services it produces for its clients' (Mintzberg). The mission of an organisation is the reason for its existence.

Case Study

The Co-op

The Co-operative movement in the UK is a good example of the role of mission. The Co-operative Wholesale Society and Co-operative Retail Society are business organisations, but their mission is not simply profit. Rather, as they are owned by their suppliers/customers rather than external shareholders, they have always, since their foundation, had a wider social concern.

The Co-op has been criticised by some analysts on the grounds that it is insufficiently profitable, certainly in comparison with supermarket chains such as Tesco. However, the Co-op has explicit **social** objectives. In some cases it will retain stores which, although too small to be as profitable as a large supermarket, provide an important social function in the communities which host them.

Judging the Co-op's performance as a retailer on the conventional basis of profitability would ignore its social objectives.

The mission of a company will include the aim of creating wealth for its shareholders, but a financial purpose is not itself sufficient to explain why an organisation exists, or what it is trying to achieve.

1.2 Mission statements

Mission statements are formal statements of an organisation's mission. They might be reproduced in a number of places (e.g. at the front of an organisation's annual report, on publicity material, in the chairman's office, in communal work areas and so on). There is no standard format, but they should possess certain characteristics:

- **Brevity** - easy to understand and remember
- **Flexibility** - to accommodate change
- **Distinctiveness** - to make the firm stand out.

For example, some years ago the pharmaceuticals firm Glaxo expressed its mission by stating that it was 'an integrated research-based group of companies whose corporate purpose is to create, discover, develop, manufacture and market throughout the world, safe, effective medicines of the highest quality which will bring benefit to patients through improved longevity and quality of life, and to society through economic value.'

Similarly, the British Film Institute has expressed its mission in the following terms: 'The BFI is the UK national agency with responsibility for encouraging and conserving the arts of film and television. Our aim is to ensure that the many audiences in the UK are offered access to the widest possible choice of cinema and television, so that their enjoyment is enhanced through a deeper understanding of the history and potential of these vital and popular art forms.'

1.3 Mission and planning

Although a mission statement might be seen as a set of abstract principles, it can play an important role in the planning process.

(a)   Plans should outline the fulfilment of the organisation's mission.

(b)   Evaluation and screening. Mission also acts as a yardstick by which plans are judged. For example, the mission of an ethical investment trust would preclude investing in tobacco firms. Mission also helps to ensure consistency in decision-making.

(c)   Implementation of strategy. Mission also affects the implementation of a planned strategy, in the culture and business practices of the firm.

Problems with 'mission' are:

Problem	Comment
Ignored in practice	The inherent danger of a stated mission is that it will be ignored, and an organisation may pursue objectives that are not consistent with its stated mission.
Public relations	Sometimes, a mission statement is merely for public consumption, not for internal decision making.
'Post hoc'	Missions are sometimes produced to *rationalise* the existence of the organisation to a particular audience. In other words, mission does not drive the organisation. Rather, what the organisation actually does is assumed to be a mission.
Full of generalisations	A mission statement may be full of 'worthy' generalisations, such as 'best', 'quality', and 'major'. If so, the mission statement is in danger of becoming no more than just a wish list.

1.4 Objectives

Objectives (or goals) are aims for achievement. They may be expressed in general terms, such as:

(a)   the objective of becoming one of the two leading global providers of a range of products or services in a particular market

(b)   the objective of achieving strong annual growth in sales and profits, so as to increase the wealth of the company's shareholders

(c)   the objective of remaining at the forefront of technological developments in the industry

Objectives should be consistent with the organisation's mission. They may relate to matters such as profitability or return on capital employed, market share, quality of products or services, and customer satisfaction.

1.5 Targets

Targets are quantified objectives (although in practice some organisations use the terms 'targets' and 'objectives' interchangeably). Targets can be thought of as measurable goals for achievement, usually within a specified time frame, and may be aims for either the long-term or short-term.

- Objectives and targets **orientate the activities** of the organisation towards the fulfilment of the organisation's mission, in theory if not always in practice.
- The objectives and targets for a **business** must include **profitability**.
- Targets (quantified objectives) can also be used as standards **for measuring the performance** of the organisation and departments in it.

1.6 Primary and secondary objectives

Some objectives are more important than others. There is a **primary corporate objective** (restricted by certain constraints on corporate activity) and other **secondary objectives** which are strategic objectives which should combine to ensure the achievement of the primary corporate objective.

(a)   For example, if a company sets itself an objective of growth in profits, as its primary objective, it will then have to develop strategies by which this primary objective can be achieved.

(b)   Secondary objectives might then be concerned with sales growth, continual technological innovation, customer service, product quality, efficient resource management (e.g. labour productivity) or reducing the company's reliance on debt capital.

1.7 Long-term and short-term objectives

Objectives may be long-term or short-term.

(a)   A company that is suffering from a recession in its core industries and making losses in the short term might continue to have a primary objective in the long term of achieving a steady growth in earnings or profits, but in the short term, its primary objective might switch to survival.

(b)   Secondary objectives will range from short-term to long-term. Planners will formulate secondary objectives within the guidelines set by the primary objective, after selecting strategies for achieving the primary objective.

 | Question | Mission

Using the organisation in which you work, investigate the organisation's mission, the planning that the company employs to achieve that mission and the objectives and targets that the company sets. (There is no answer to this activity.)

1.8 Example

A company's primary objective might be to increase its earnings per share from 30c to 50c in the next five years.

(a)   **Strategies** for achieving the objective might be selected.
- Increase profitability in the next twelve months by cutting expenditure.
- Increase export sales over the next three years.
- Develop a successful new product for the domestic market within five years.

(b)   **Secondary objectives** might then be re-assessed.
- Improve labour productivity by 10% within twelve months.
- Improve customer service in export markets with the objective of doubling the number of overseas sales outlets in selected countries within the next three years.
- Invest more in product-market research and development, with the objective of bringing at least three new products to the market within five years.

 Case Study

On Easter Sunday 1997, the UK saw the launch of a new commercial TV station, Channel 5 (C5). The following objectives were relevant.

(a) *Primary objectives* - profit for its various shareholders.

(b) *Secondary objectives*

C5 sells advertising time. The rates it can charge are often determined by audience share. To satisfy advertisers, C5 had to have *audience-share objectives*.

(c) Audience-share objectives affect various operational aspects of the business.

(i) *Coverage.* C5 had to ensure that enough of the population could receive C5.

(ii) *Availability.* Before the launch, video recorders in several million UK households had to be re-tuned. Up to 11 million households were believed to be affected by interference from the new station. Re-tuning problems delayed the initial launch of the channel. This was a *short-term*, but critical, *operational objective*.

(iii) *Programming.* Finally, audience-share targets set priorities for programming.

1.9 Non-profit seeking organisations

FAST FORWARD

One possible definition of a **non-profit seeking organisation** is that its first objective is to be involved in non-loss operations to cover its costs, profits only being made as a means to an end.

Although most people would 'know one if they saw it', there is a surprising problem in clearly defining what counts as a non-profit seeking organisation.

Bois has suggested that non-profit seeking organisations are defined by recognising that their first objective is to be involved in **non-loss operations** in order to cover their costs and that profits are only made as a means to an end (such as providing a service, or accomplishing some socially or morally worthy objective).

Key term

A **non-profit seeking organisation** is '… an organisation whose attainment of its prime goal is not assessed by economic measures. However, in pursuit of that goal it may undertake profit-making activities.'
(*Bois*)

This may involve a number of different kinds of organisation with, for example, differing legal status – charities, statutory bodies offering public transport or the provision of services such as leisure, health or public utilities such as water or road maintenance.

 Case Study

Oxfam operates more shops than any commercial organisation in Britain, and these operate at a profit. The Royal Society for the Protection of Birds operates a mail order trading company which provides a 25% return on capital, operating very profitably and effectively.

1.10 Objectives and non-profit seeking organisations

> The range of **objectives** of non-profit seeking organisations is as wide as the range of non-profit seeking organisations.

A major problem with many non-profit seeking organisations, particularly government bodies, is that it is extremely **difficult to define their objectives** at all. In addition they tend to have **multiple objectives**, so that even if they could all be clearly identified it is impossible to say which is the overriding objective.

Question   Objectives

What objectives might the following non-profit seeking organisations have?

(a) An army   (d) A political party
(b) A local council   (e) A college
(c) A charity

Answer

Here are some suggestions.

(a) To defend a country
(b) To provide services for local people (such as the elderly)
(c) To help others/protect the environment
(d) To gain power/enact legislation
(e) To provide education

More general objectives for non-profit seeking organisations include:

- Surplus maximisation (equivalent to profit maximisation)
- Revenue maximisation (as for a commercial business)
- Usage maximisation (as in leisure centre swimming pool usage)
- Usage targeting (matching the capacity available, as in a public hospital)
- Full/partial cost recovery (minimising subsidy)
- Budget maximisation (maximising what is offered)
- Producer satisfaction maximisation (satisfying the wants of staff and volunteers)
- Client satisfaction maximisation (the police generating the support of the public)

It is difficult to judge whether **non-quantitative objectives** have been met. For example, assessing whether a charity has improved the situation of those benefiting from its activities is difficult to research. Statistics related to product mix, financial resources, size of budgets, number of employees, number of volunteers, number of customers serviced and number and location of facilities are all useful for this task.

The primary objectives of commercial manufacturing and service organisations are likely to be fairly similar and centre on satisfying shareholders. The **range of objectives** of non-profit seeking organisations is as **wide as the range of non-profit seeking organisations**.

2 Strategy

> **Strategies** are plans for achieving objectives and targets. Strategies are formulated for the organisation as a whole, and for individual aspects of the organisation's operations.
>
> **Shorter-term plans** are formulated within the framework of the longer-term objectives and strategies. Most organisations prepare annual **budgets**, which are plans for the entire organisation, expressed in financial terms.

Key terms

A strategy is a course of action adopted in order to achieve a stated objective or target.

(a)   Corporate strategy is concerned with what types of business the organisation should be operating in.

(b)   Functional or operating strategies are for specific areas of operations. An organisation may have strategies for marketing, production, quality enhancement, research and development, finance, human resources development, information systems enhancement, and so on.

(c)   Strategies are formulated in tiers or layers. Within an overall marketing strategy, for example, there may be strategies for advertising, direct selling, customer targeting, market research, sales growth, product pricing, and so on.

Planning should be intended to ensure that an organisation achieves its objectives, in both the long and the shorter term. Shorter-term plans should be formulated within the framework of longer-term plans (strategic plans) and objectives. Typically, an organisation will carry out periodic strategic reviews, and will also prepare regular annual plans (budgets) that should be consistent with the longer-term strategic plan. Shorter-term 'operational plans' are then formulated within the framework of strategic plans and the annual budget.

The 'planning cycle' refers to the continuous review and reformulation of plans for the future. Budgeting, for example, is planning within an annual planning cycle. An essential element in the planning cycle is **control**. Managers should be made responsible for ensuring, as far as possible, that planning targets are achieved, or even exceeded.

The 'control cycle' refers to the process of:

(a)   formulating a plan, such as a strategic plan or budget

(b)   implementing the plan, and making particular managers responsible for putting particular aspects of the plan into effect

(c)   monitoring and measuring actual performance

(d)   comparing actual performance against the plan

(e)   taking control measures, where the comparison suggests that results should have been better, and improvements or corrective action is necessary

(f)   re-assessing, where the comparison suggests that the existing plans are unrealistic, and producing, where appropriate, new plans and planning targets

Formulating plans within the framework of strategic planning, together with performance measurement and management, therefore provide a means of enabling an organisation to achieve its strategic objectives.

•   **Planning**

    Management **plans for both the short term and the long term**. A long-range plan is necessary in order to anticipate any future needs or opportunities that require action to be taken, either now or in the near future. For example, management may need to consider building a new production facility, to meet anticipated increased demand for a product. Management should constantly be **thinking ahead**. They should **never be surprised by any gradual developments**. Planning therefore involves **converting the organisation's long-term objectives into a succession of short-term plans**. One such short-term plan is the annual budget.

- **Controlling**

  Control is exercised by **comparing actual performance with the short-term plans** so that deviations from these short-term plans can be identified and corrective action taken. If the control process indicates that the long-term objectives are not achievable, the objectives can be changed before any serious damage to the company's future occurs.

- **Organising**

  Organising is the establishment of a **framework within which necessary activities can be performed**. For example, the designation of a member of staff to be responsible for a particular activity and the **definition of managers' responsibilities and lines of authority**. It requires the breakdown of the organisation into **manageable sections** such as departments and the **co-ordination of activities** in these sections.

- **Motivating**

  Managers need to influence employees to act in such a manner that will help achieve the organisation's objectives.

- **Decision making**

  Management is decision taking. Managers of all levels within an organisation take decisions.

  – Decisions taken at the strategic level set or change the objectives or strategic targets of an organisation. They include decisions about the selection of products and markets, the required levels of company profitability and the purchase or disposal of subsidiary companies or major non-current assets.

  – Tactical-level decisions are concerned with the efficient and effective use of an organisation's resources (sometimes referred to as the '4Ms': men, materials, machines and money). Tactical-level decisions therefore include setting budgets for the next period for sales, production and inventory levels, and setting measures of performance by which departmental results can be gauged.

  – Operational-level decisions are concerned with ensuring that specific tasks are carried out effectively and efficiently. They might include decisions concerning the allocation of particular staff to particular tasks and jobs or the action to take in respect of customer complaints.

Question
Decisions

What strategic-level, tactical-level and operational-level decisions might an organisation take in relation to sales?

Answer

Here is our suggestion. Your answer could be somewhat different.

(a) At the strategic level, senior management may decide that the company should increase sales by 5% per annum for at least five years. This would be a strategic objective or target.

(b) At the tactical level, the sales director and senior sales managers may decide to increase sales by 5% in the next year, with some provisional planning for future years. This would involve making decisions about direct sales resources, advertising, sales promotion and so on. Sales quotas could be assigned to each sales territory.

(c) At the operational level, the manager of a sales territory may make a decision regarding the weekly sales targets for each sales representative.

3 Performance measurement and performance management

FAST FORWARD

Managers have to **plan, control, organise** and **make decisions**. **Performance measurement** is a system for comparing actual results against plans. **Performance management** involves using information from performance measurement to take new planning decisions or control actions to improve the future performance of the organisation. Performance measurement and management, within a planning framework, should help to ensure that the strategic objectives of the organisation are pursued and achieved.

Although it is convenient to think of a company or other organisation as a single unit, in reality it is an association of many individuals. Objectives and strategy are decided by the board of directors in a company, and are converted into plans and activities by management and employees.

(a) *Performance measurement* is a general term for systems and methods of setting targets for achievement that are consistent with the organisation's strategic and operational goals, and comparing actual results with the target. The nature of performance targets varies. They might be long-term or short-term, and financial or non-financial. Targets also vary according to the nature of the business and its operations, and according to the management responsibility structure.

(b) *Performance management* is a general term for systems and methods for improving performance.

Performance measurement systems and performance management initiatives are an integral part of planning and control systems and decision-making within an organisation. They provide a means by which an organisation can translate its overall objectives and strategies into long-term and short-term plans, for reviewing the implementation of the plans (actual performance) and for monitoring progress towards the achievement of objectives.

4 Responsibility centre and process-based organisations

FAST FORWARD

Performance measurement and management systems should identify aspects of performance that individual managers should be held accountable for, and that they should be able to control. A reporting system might be based on a system of **responsibility centres** or strategic business units.

Within an organisation, there should be a control structure for planning and monitoring performance.

Key term

> A **responsibility centre-based organisation** is divided into a number of responsibility centres or strategic business units (SBUs). Each responsibility centre has its own planning objectives and targets, and its management is responsible (and accountable) for the achievement of those targets.

A responsibility centre structure is only effective, however, if the centre's management have effective control over the resources and factors necessary for achieving the centre's objectives. It would be inappropriate to make management responsible for achieving stated objectives when key planning and control decisions are outside their authority and control. Authority and responsibility should go hand-in-hand.

Key term

> A **process-based organisation** is one in which operations consist of a number of processes, and the work done by different departments is inter-related. For example, work done in one department might be fed through to another department, with the full process consisting of the work done by the two departments together.

A responsibility centre-based organisation would be inappropriate for process-based organisations. A process is a 'collection of activities that takes one or more kinds of input and creates an output that is of value to the customer'.

In a process-based organisation, managers are held responsible for the performance of a process, or a part of a process, rather than responsible for a discrete business unit.

The nature of performance measurement and management differs according to the type of organisation structure. For example, in a responsibility centre-based structure, the centre's management would be responsible for the production of a group of products or the provision of a particular range of services to customers, and would also be responsible for sales, marketing and distribution, and probably also for capital expenditure decisions for the centre. In a process-based organisation in contrast, different managers might be responsible for production and for sales and marketing (since production and sales and marketing are two stages in a process of delivering products to the customer).

In the following chapters, different methods of performance measurement and management are described. The method that might be most appropriate for any organisation may depend on whether the organisation has a responsibility centre structure or a process-based structure.

5 Information for control: IT systems

FAST FORWARD
Performance measurement and management systems have been enhanced by developments in **information and communications technology**.

Information is vital for performance measurement and management. The evolution of information technology in recent years has greatly improved the ability of organisations to develop sophisticated performance measurement systems.

(a) Organisations are able to process large amounts of data, and in a large variety of ways.
(b) Performance reports can be made available to management more regularly, and possibly on demand.
(c) Performance information can be made more widely available to management, for example through a corporate intranet.

A distinction is made between **data** and **information**.

(a) **Data** is the raw material for data processing. Data relates to facts, events and transactions and so forth.
(b) **Information** is data that has been processed in such a way as to be meaningful to the person who receives it.

5.1 Example

An example demonstrates the difference. Companies providing a consumer product or service need to find out about consumer opinion, and might employ market research organisations to do so. In a typical market research survey, a number of researchers ask a sample of the public (or the target market) to answer a number of questions relating to the product.

Individually, a completed questionnaire does not tell the company very much, only the views of one individual consumer. The **data** from the individual questionnaires has to be brought together, processed and analysed. The processed output is the **information** that the company's management will use in decision making.

5.2 Management information

Management information is information used by managers to help control the business. Information must possess certain qualities to be valuable and worth having.

• Information should be **relevant** for its purpose.
• It should be **complete** for its purpose.

- It should be sufficiently **accurate** for its purpose.
- It should be **clear** to the manager using it.
- The manager using it should have **confidence** in it.
- It should be **communicated** to the appropriate manager.
- It should not be excessive: its **volume** should be **manageable**.
- It should be **timely** (in other words communicated at the most appropriate time).

It should be provided at a cost which is less than the value of the benefits it provides.

IT systems can improve the quality of management in a variety of ways. Information should be more complete, because IT systems can process large quantities of data. Information can be made available quickly, and so should improve 'timeliness'. The availability of off-the-shelf software should also mean that information is available at a cost that is justified by the benefits it provides to management.

5.3 Modular IT systems and enterprise resource planning (ERP)

Historically, management information and data processing systems, particularly in larger organisations, have evolved as a number of separate stand-alone systems for different departments.

For example, the production department might have a computerised system for production scheduling, the warehousing department might have a separate system for inventory records, the accounting department might have a system for financial and management accounting, the human resources department might have a system for personnel records, and so on.

Developments in information and communications technology are having a big impact. Database software allows enormous quantities of data to be held in a single source, that can be accessed by many different users via an intranet or the Internet. This has created the potential for integrating information systems into a single organisation-wide system, so that everyone can access whatever information he or she needs.

For example, a customer might telephone the sales department or the accounts department to ask about the progress of an order and the likely delivery date. With an integrated information system, an immediate answer can be provided. The sales or accounts person can simply look up the status of the order on the company database, instead of having to refer the customer to someone in production or the warehouse department for an answer.

A single database or 'information hub' for an entire organisation is often known as an **enterprise resource planning (ERP) system**.

Organisations with an ERP system could well gain competitive advantage over rivals who still use modular systems, by making more use of their data and producing better management information.

ERP systems have been extended outside the boundaries of the organisation, and some companies use a shared database with suppliers and business customers in a web-based 'supply chain management' system. Supply chain management and ERP are explained in greater detail in Chapters 15 and 14 respectively.

The developments in information technology have also made it easier for organisations to decentralise their operations by taking out tiers of middle management and delegating authority and responsibility to individuals who are closer to actual operations. This creates a 'flatter' organisation with fewer management levels between top management and the operational level. The expansion of global businesses, for example, would not have been easily possible without information technology and delegation of authority to local managers.

Although information systems provide non-financial as well as financial information, accounting and costing systems have traditionally been, and continue to be, a major source of management information for performance measurement.

(a)   **Accounting systems** are used to keep detailed records of financial transactions of the organisation, such as sales and expenditures, receipts and payments and records of assets and liabilities. This information is sometimes known collectively as the 'ledger accounting system' or 'ledger accounts'. It provides the basic data, if needed, for obtaining detailed information for management about costs and profits.

(b)   Some organisations have a **costing system**, in addition to their main ledger accounts. A costing system is an information system for establishing the costs of the products that an organisation makes, or the services it provides and possibly also particular activities that it engages in.

(c)   Most organisations prepare an **annual financial plan**, or budget. This is often a spreadsheet model, although large organisations use much more complex planning models. The budget remains an important planning model for companies, even when strategic plans are reviewed regularly. Company performance is often judged by the stock market in terms of what the company hopes to achieve over the course of the next financial year, and whether budgeted expectations have been met in the current year. Management bonuses are also often linked to achievements during the course of the financial year.

Although management information systems extend far beyond costing systems and budgeting systems, costing and management accounting remain an important element and contribute significantly to performance measurement and performance management.

5.4 Resource planning

Resource planning involves allocating the resources (and identifying potential resources) of the undertaking in order that the defined and agreed corporate objectives may be achieved. At operational level, there are four stages in resource planning.

(a)   Establishing currently available and currently obtainable resources (by category) and details of any which are not available or readily obtainable – making a resource audit.

(b)   Estimating what resources would be needed to pursue a particular strategy and deciding whether there would be enough resources to pursue it successfully.

(c)   Assigning responsibilities to managers for the acquisition, use and control of resources.

(d)   Identifying all constraints and factors exerting an influence on the availability and use of resources (internal and external environments).

Resource plans can be prepared in detail providing organisations know what they need to achieve.

(a)   **Critical success factors (CSFs)** 'are those factors on which the strategy is fundamentally dependent for its success'.

(b)   **Key tasks** are what must be done to ensure each critical success factor is achieved.

(c)   **Priorities** indicate the order in which tasks are achieved.

6 Information systems

6.1 Types of information system

FAST FORWARD

Different **types of information systems** exist with different characteristics – reflecting the different roles they perform.

Key terms

A **structured decision** uses a well-defined process to solve a typically repetitive situation. The data used in making the decision is known with certainty and a standardised approach is used to make the decision. For example an order for additional inventory can be triggered where the current inventory level falls below the predetermined reorder level or a customer order can be rejected if this order would take the customer's credit balance above the predetermined credit limit.

An **unstructured decision** is complex and no standard solution exists to resolve the situation. Some of the elements of the decision are ill-defined or unknown. Decision makers have to use their judgement to decide between the options that are known. For example the board of a company have to decide on the appropriate strategic direction for their business.

A **semi-structured decision** lies between the structured and unstructured decision, combining elements of both. There is some agreement as to the data and evaluation method to be used, but some judgement is also required. For example it might be agreed that additional warehouse space is necessary, but the selection of the location and the rent or buy decision will require judgement by management.

6.1.1 Executive Information Systems (EIS)

Key term

An **Executive Information System (EIS)** pools data from internal and external sources and makes information available to senior managers in an easy-to-use form. EIS help senior managers make strategic, unstructured decisions.

An EIS should provide senior managers with easy access to key **internal** and **external** information. The system summarises and tracks strategically critical information, possibly drawn from internal MIS and DSS, but also including data from external sources eg competitors, legislation, external databases such as Reuters.

Executive Information Systems are sometimes referred to as **Executive Support Systems** (ESS). An ESS/EIS is likely to have the following **features**.

- Flexibility
- Quick response time
- Sophisticated data analysis and modelling tools

A model of a typical EIS follows.

An Executive Information System (EIS)

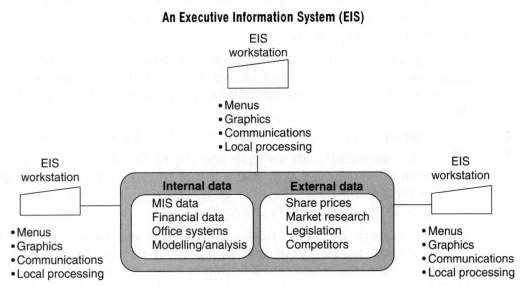

6.1.2 Management Information Systems (MIS)

Key term

Management Information Systems (MIS) convert data from mainly internal sources into information (eg summary reports, exception reports). This information enables managers to make timely and effective decisions for planning, directing and controlling the activities for which they are responsible.

An MIS provides regular reports and (usually) online access to the organisation's current and historical performance.

MIS usually transform data from underlying transaction processing systems into summarised files that are used as the basis for management reports.

MIS have the following characteristics:

- Support **structured** decisions at operational and management control levels
- Designed to report on **existing** operations
- Have little analytical capability
- Relatively **inflexible**
- Have an **internal** focus

6.1.3 Decision Support Systems (DSS)

Key term

> **Decision Support Systems (DSS)** combine data and analytical models or data analysis tools to support semi-structured and unstructured decision making.

DSS are used by management to assist in making decisions on issues which are subject to high levels of uncertainty about the problem, the various **responses** which management could undertake or the likely **impact** of those actions.

Decision support systems are intended to provide a wide range of alternative information gathering and analytical tools with a major emphasis upon **flexibility** and **user-friendliness**.

DSS have more analytical power than other systems enabling them to analyse and condense large volumes of data into a form that aids managers make decisions. The objective is to allow the manager to consider a number of **alternatives** and evaluate them under a variety of potential conditions.

6.1.4 Expert systems

Expert systems are a form of DSS that allow users to benefit from expert knowledge and information. The system will consist of a **database** holding specialised data and **rules** about what to do in, or how to interpret, a given set of circumstances.

For example, many financial institutions now use expert systems to process straightforward **loan applications**. The user enters certain key facts into the system such as the loan applicant's name and most recent addresses, their income and monthly outgoings, and details of other loans. The system will then:

(a) **Check the facts** given against its database to see whether the applicant has a good credit record.

(b) **Perform calculations** to see whether the applicant can afford to repay the loan.

(c) **Match up other criteria**, such as whether the security offered for the loan or the purpose for which the loan is wanted is acceptable, and to what extent the loan applicant fits the lender's profile of a good risk (based on the lender's previous experience).

A decision is then suggested, based on the results of this processing. This is why it is now often possible to get a loan or arrange insurance **over the telephone**, whereas in the past it would have been necessary to go and speak to a bank manager or send details to an actuary and then wait for him or her to come to a decision.

7 Costing systems and management accounting

FAST FORWARD

> Information about **costs, revenues and profits** is an important element of all performance measurement and management systems.
>
> **Management accounting** is concerned with the collection of data, its analysis and processing into information, and the interpretation and communication of that information so as to assist management with planning, control and decision making.

Many organisation plans are stated in financial terms. In particular, annual budgets are plans for the entire organisation expressed in money terms.

The major objectives of a commercial organisation will include one or more financial objectives, such as growth in return on capital employed or profitability.

Performance measurement systems should therefore include systems for establishing the **costs** and the **profits** from operations, and the cost and profitability of the products or services provided by the organisation to its customers.

Information about the cost of an organisation's output can also be used to analyse the **efficiency** of resource utilisation.

Costing systems vary from organisation to organisation, and are a key element in performance measurement. Various aspects of costing systems, and different costing techniques, will be explained in subsequent chapters.

Providing costing information to operational management is one of the functions of the management accountant.

(a)   The management accountant helps in the planning process and decision-making processes, by providing information, primarily about costs and revenues.

(b)   The management accountant supplies performance reports that compare actual performance with planned performance, highlighting those activities which are not conforming to plan.

The CIMA (Chartered Institute of Management Accountants) *Official Terminology* defines management accounting.

Key term

> **Management accounting** is the process of identification, measurement, accumulation, analysis, preparation, interpretation and communication of information used by management to plan, evaluate and control within an entity and to assure appropriate use of, and accountability for, its resources. Management accounting also comprises the preparation of financial reports for non-management groups such as shareholders, creditors, regulatory agencies and tax authorities.

The *Official Terminology* also describes the **core activities of management accounting**.

- **Participation in the planning process** at both strategic and operational levels. This involves the establishment of policies and the formulation of plans and budgets which will subsequently be expressed in financial terms.
- The initiation of, and the **provision of guidance for, management decisions**. This involves the generation, analysis, presentation and interpretation of appropriate relevant information.
- Contributing to the **monitoring and control** of performance through the provision of reports on organisational (and organisational segment) performance, including comparisons of actual with planned or budgeted performance, and their analysis and interpretation.

Management accounting is therefore concerned with the collection of data (from both internal and external sources), its analysis and processing into information, and the interpretation and communication of that information so as to assist management with planning, control and decision making.

Question   Functions of management accounting

Wilton, MacDonald, Pearce & Co, a medium-sized firm of architects, are about to absorb Butcher, Fowler & Partners, a similar sized firm. They have engaged you as management accountant. Part of your duties will be to review the management accounting function of the combined practice. You have an appointment tomorrow morning with the senior partner to discuss this issue.

Required

Jot down notes to use in tomorrow's meeting covering the functions of management accounting, with particular reference to Wilton, MacDonald, Pearce & Co.

Answer

Management accounting involves providing and interpreting internal accounting information for managers to use for the following purposes.

(a)   **Planning the organisation's activities in the short, medium and long term**
      The management accounting system should provide information that will allow management to establish longer-term objectives for the enlarged organisation, and for preparing shorter-term financial plans (in particular, budgets) within the framework of longer-term goals.

(b) **Controlling the activities of the organisation**

Management will have to learn to control a larger business. They will therefore need control reports so that they can compare actual results against plans or budgets. A system must be established for preparing control reports, possibly on the basis of individual responsibility centres within the firm. Performance appraisal systems can use both financial and non-financial information (eg the percentage of contracts tendered for, that are won by the firm).

(c) **Making decisions**

For example, information will be needed for making financial decisions, such as pricing architectural contracts for tendering purposes.

7.1 Management accounting compared with financial accounting

Financial accounting is an aspect of accounting dealing largely with maintaining financial records (the 'ledger accounts'), and the production of general purpose financial statements for various user groups, including shareholders. Management accounting is concerned with the provision of information (largely of a financial nature) for an organisation's management, where the information is provided for a specific decision-making, planning or control purpose.

The following table summarises the main differences between management accounting and financial accounting.

Management accounting	Financial accounting
A management accounting system produces information that is used within an organisation, by managers and employees.	A financial accounting system produces information that is used by parties external to the organisation, such as shareholders, banks and creditors.
Management accounting helps management to record, plan and control activities and aids the decision-making process.	Financial accounting provides a record of the performance of an organisation over a defined period and the state of affairs at the end of that period.
There is no legal requirement for an organisation to use management accounting.	Limited companies are required by the law of most countries to prepare financial accounts.
Management accounting can focus on specific areas of an organisation's activities. Information may aid a decision rather than be an end-product of a decision.	Financial accounting concentrates on the organisation as a whole, aggregating revenues and costs from different operations. Financial accounts are an end in themselves.
Management accounting information may be monetary or alternatively non-monetary.	Most financial accounting information is of a monetary nature.
Management accounting provides both an historical record and a future planning tool.	Financial accounting presents an essentially historical picture of past operations.
No strict rules govern the way in which management accounting operates. The management accounts and information are prepared in a format that is of use to managers.	Financial accounting must operate within a framework determined by law and by accounting standards (eg, IASs and IFRSs). In principle the financial accounts of different organisations can be easily compared.

8 Organisational structures

8.1 Tall and flat organisations

FAST FORWARD

Recent trends have been towards **delayering** organisations of levels of management. In other words, **tall organisations** (with many management levels, and narrow spans of control) are turning into **flat organisations** (with fewer management levels, wider spans of control) as a result of technological changes and the granting of more decision-making power to front line employees.

The span of control concept has implications for the length of the **scalar chain**.

Key terms

> **Span of control**: the number of subordinates responsible to a superior.
>
> **Scalar chain**: the chain of command from the most senior to the most junior.
>
> A **tall organisation** is one which, in relation to its size, has a large number of levels of management hierarchy. This implies a *narrow* span of control.
>
> A **flat organisation** is one which, in relation to its size, has a small number of hierarchical levels. This implies a *wide* span of control.

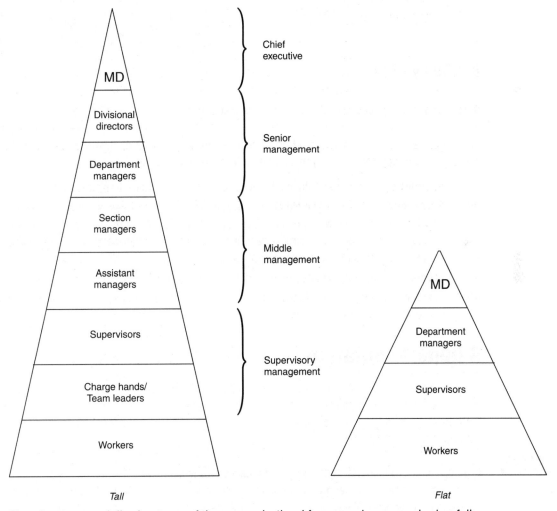

Tall   *Flat*

The advantages and disadvantages of these organisational forms can be summarised as follows.

Tall organisation

For	Against
Narrow control spans	Inhibits delegation
Small groups enable team members to participate in decisions	Rigid supervision can be imposed, blocking initiative
A large number of steps on the promotional ladders – assists management training and career planning	The same work passes through too many hands Increases administration and overhead costs Slow decision making and responses, as the strategic apex is further away

Flat organisation

For	Against
More opportunity for delegation	Requires that jobs *can* be delegated. Managers may only get a superficial idea of what goes on. If they are overworked they are more likely to be involved in crisis management
Relatively cheap	Sacrifices control
In theory, speeds up communication between strategic apex and operating core	Middle managers are often necessary to convert the grand vision of the strategic apex into operational terms

8.2 Delayering

Key term

Delayering is the reduction of the number of management levels from bottom to top.

Many organisations are delayering. Middle line jobs are vanishing. Organisations are increasing the average span of control, reducing management levels and becoming flatter.

(a) **Information technology** reduces the need for middle managers to process information.

(b) **Empowerment**. Many organisations, especially service businesses, are keen to delegate authority down the line to the lowest possible level. Front-line workers in the operating core are allowed to take decisions, in order to increase responsiveness to customer demands. This perhaps removes the need for some middle management jobs.

(c) **Economy**. Delayering reduces managerial/supervisory costs.

(d) **Fashion**. Delayering is fashionable: if senior managers believe that tall structures are inherently inflexible, they might cut the numbers of management levels.

9 Departmentation

In most organisations, tasks and people are grouped together in some rational way: on the basis of specialisation, say, or shared technology or customer base. This is known as **departmentation**. Different patterns of departmentation are possible, and the pattern selected will depend on the individual circumstances of the organisation.

FAST FORWARD

Organisations can be **departmentalised** on a **functional** basis (with separate departments for production, marketing, finance etc), a **geographical** basis (by region, or country), a **product** basis (eg worldwide divisions for product X, Y etc), a **brand** basis, or a **matrix** basis (eg someone selling product X in country A would report to both a product X manager and a country A manager). Organisation structures often feature a variety of these types, as **hybrid** structures.

9.1 Geographic departmentation

Where the organisation is structured according to geographic area, some authority is retained at Head Office but day-to-day operations are handled on a **territorial** basis (eg Southern region, Western region). Many sales departments are organised territorially.

There are **advantages** to geographic departmentation.

(a) There is **local decision-making** at the point of contact between the organisation (eg a salesperson) and its customers, suppliers or other stakeholders.

(b) It may be **cheaper** to establish area factories/offices than to service markets from one location (eg costs of transportation and travelling may be reduced).

But there are **disadvantages** too.

(a) **Duplication** and possible loss of economies of scale might arise. For example, a national organisation divided into ten regions might have a customer liaison department in each regional office. If the organisation did all customer liaison work from head office (centralised) it might need fewer managerial staff.

(b) **Inconsistency** in methods or standards may develop across different areas.

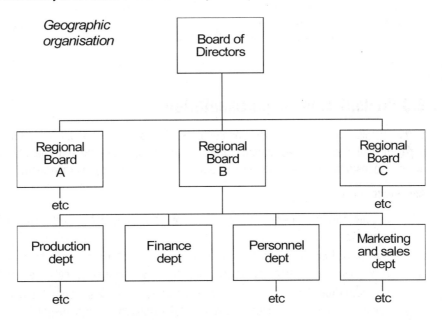

9.2 Functional departmentation

Functional organisation involves grouping together people who do similar tasks. Primary functions in a manufacturing company might be production, sales, finance, and general administration. Sub-departments of marketing might be market research, advertising, PR and so on.

Advantages include:

(a) **Expertise is pooled** thanks to the division of work into specialist areas.

(b) It **avoids duplication** (eg one management accounts department rather than several) and enables economies of scale.

(c) It **facilitates** the recruitment, management and development of functional specialists.

(d) It suits **centralised** businesses.

Disadvantages include:

(a) It focuses on internal **processes** and **inputs**, rather than the **customer** and **outputs**, which are what ultimately drive a business. Inward-looking businesses are less able to adapt to changing demands.

(b) **Communication problems** may arise between different functions, which each have their own jargon.

(c)   **Poor co-ordination**, especially if rooted in a tall organisation structure. Decisions by one function/department involving another might have to be referred upwards, and dealt with at a higher level, thereby increasing the burdens on senior management.

(d)   Functional structures create **vertical barriers** to information and work flow. Management writer Tom Peters suggests that customer service requires 'horizontal' flow between functions – rather than passing the customer from one functional department to another.

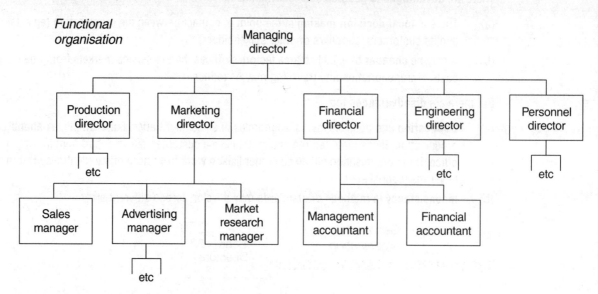

Functional organisation

9.3 Product/brand departmentation

Some organisations group activities on the basis of **products** or product lines. Some functional departmentation remains (eg manufacturing, distribution, marketing and sales) but a divisional manager is given responsibility for the product or product line, with authority over personnel of different functions.

Advantages include:

(a)   **Accountability.** Individual managers can be held accountable for the profitability of individual products.

(b)   **Specialisation**. For example, some salespeople will be trained to sell a specific product in which they may develop technical expertise and thereby offer a better sales service to customers.

(c)   **Co-ordination.** The different functional activities and efforts required to make and sell each product can be co-ordinated and integrated by the divisional/product manager.

Disadvantages include:

(a)   It **increases the overhead costs** and managerial complexity of the organisation.

(b)   Different product divisions may **fail to share resources** and customers.

A **brand** is the name (eg 'Persil') or design which identifies the products or services of a manufacturer or provider and distinguishes them from those of competitors. (Large organisations may produce a number of different brands of the same basic product, such as washing powder or toothpaste.) Branding brings the product to the attention of buyers and creates brand **recognition**, **differentiation** and **loyalty**: often customers do not realise that two 'rival' brands are in fact produced by the same manufacturer.

(a)   Because each brand is packaged, promoted and sold in a distinctive way, the need for specialisation may make brand departmentation effective. As with product departmentation, some functional departmentation remains but brand managers have responsibility for the brand's marketing and this can affect every function.

(b)   Brand departmentation has similar advantages/disadvantages to product departmentation.

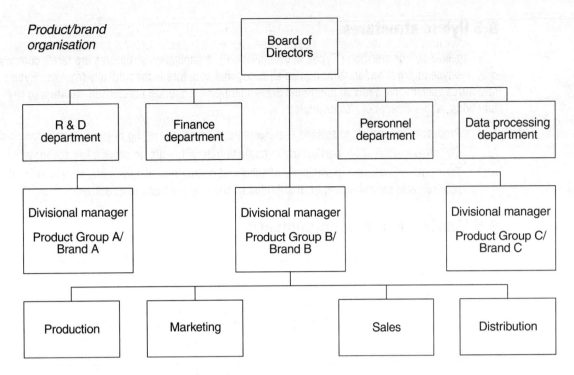

Product/brand organisation

9.4 Customer departmentation

An organisation may organise its activities on the basis of types of customer, or market segment.

(a) Departmentation by customer is commonly associated with **sales departments** and selling effort, but it might also be used by a jobbing or contracting firm where a team of managers may be given the responsibility of liaising with major customers (eg discussing specifications and completion dates, quality of work, progress chasing etc).

(b) Many businesses distinguish between **business** customers and **consumers**.

Question   Types of organisation

Looking at the 'Product/Brand Organisation' chart following Section 9.3 above, what types of organisation can you identify, and why are these appropriate for their purposes? What *added* type of organisation might this firm use, and in what circumstances?

Answer

- At the head office level, there is *functional* organisation. This enables standardisation of policy and activity in key 'staff' or support functions shared by the various divisions.
- At divisional level, there is *product/brand* organisation. This allows the distinctive culture and attributes of each product/brand to be addressed in production processes and marketing approach.
- For each product/brand, there is *functional* organisation, enabling specialist expertise to be directed at the different activities required to produce, market and distribute a product.
- This firm may further organise its marketing department by *customer*, if its customer base includes key (high-value, long-term) customer accounts with diverse service needs, for example.
- It may further organise its sales and distribution departments by *geographical area*, if the customer base is internationally or regionally dispersed: local market conditions and values, and logistical requirements of distribution, can then be taken more specifically into account.

9.5 Hybrid structures

As suggested by our question ('Types of organisation'), organisation structures are rarely composed of only one type of organisation, although an all-functional structure is theoretically feasible. 'Hybrid' structures may involve a mix of functional departmentation, ensuring specialised attention to key functions, with elements of (for example):

(a)   Product organisation, to suit the requirements of brand marketing or production technologies.

(b)   Customer organisation, particularly in marketing departments, to service key accounts.

(c)   Territorial organisation, particularly of sales and distribution departments, to service local requirements for marketing or distribution in dispersed regions or countries.

9.6 Matrix and project organisation

Where hybrid organisation 'mixes' organisation types, **matrix** organisation actually *crosses* functional and product/customer/project organisation.

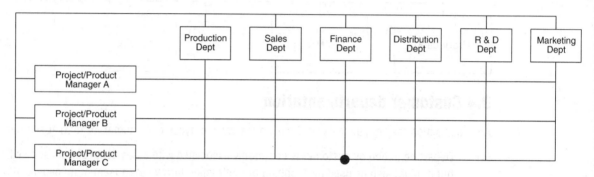

The employees represented by the dot in the above diagram, for example, are responsible to:

*   The finance manager for their work in accounting and finance for their functional department; and

*   To the project manager C for their work on the project team: budgeting, management reporting and payroll relevant to the project, say.

Advantages of matrix organisation include:

(a)   Greater **flexibility** of:

(i)   **People**. Employees develop an attitude geared to accepting change, and departmental monopolies are broken down.

(ii)   **Workflow and decision-making**. Direct contact between staff encourages problem solving and big picture thinking.

(iii)   **Tasks and structure**. The matrix structure may be readily amended, once projects are completed.

(b)   Inter-disciplinary co-operation and a mixing of skills and expertise, along with improved communication and co-ordination.

(c)   Motivation and employee development: providing employees with greater participation in planning and control decisions.

(d)   Market awareness: the organisation tends to become more customer/quality focused.

(e)   Horizontal workflow: bureaucratic obstacles are removed, and department specialisms become less powerful.

There are **disadvantages**, however.

(a)   **Dual authority** threatens a **conflict** between functional managers and product/ project/area managers.

(b)   An individual with two or more bosses may suffer stress from **conflicting demands** or **ambiguous roles**.

(c)   **Cost**: product management posts are added, meetings have to be held, and so on.

(d)   **Slower decision making** due to the added complexity.

10 Decentralisation and divisionalisation

10.1 Divisionalisation

FAST FORWARD

In a **divisional structure** some activities are **decentralised** to business units or regions.

Key term

> **Divisionalisation** is the division of a business into autonomous divisions, regions or product businesses, each with its own revenues, expenditures and capital asset purchase programmes, and therefore each with its own profit and loss responsibility.

Each division of the organisation might be:

- A subsidiary company under the holding company
- A profit centre or investment centre within a single company

Successful divisionalisation requires certain key conditions.

(a) Each division must have **properly delegated authority**, and must be held properly accountable to head office (eg for profits earned).

(b) Each unit must be **large enough** to support the quantity and quality of management it needs.

(c) The unit must not rely on head office for excessive **management support**.

(d) Each unit must have a **potential for growth** in its own area of operations.

(e) There should be scope and challenge in the job for the management of each unit.

(f) If units deal with each other, it should be as an 'arm's length' transaction. There should be no insistence on preferential treatment to be given to a 'fellow unit' by another unit of the overall organisation.

The benefits and drawbacks of divisionalisation may be summarised as follows.

Advantages	Disadvantages
Focuses the attention of management below 'top level' on business performance.	In some businesses, it is impossible to identify completely independent products or markets for which separate divisions can be set up.
Reduces the likelihood of unprofitable products and activities being continued.	Divisionalisation is only possible at a fairly senior management level, because there is a limit to how much discretion can be used in the division of work. For example, every product needs a manufacturing function and a selling function.
Encourages a greater attention to efficiency, lower costs and higher profits.	There may be more resource problems. Many divisions get their resources from head office in competition with other divisions.
Gives more authority to junior managers, and so grooms them for more senior positions in the future (planned managerial succession).	
Reduces the number of levels of management. The top executives in each division should be able to report directly to the chief executive of the holding company.	

10.2 Centralisation and decentralisation

FAST FORWARD

A **centralised** organisation is one in which authority is concentrated in one place.

We can look at centralisation in two ways.

(a) **Geography**. some functions may be centralised rather than 'scattered' in different offices, departments or locations.

So, for example, secretarial support, IT support and information storage (filing) may be centralised in specialist departments (whose services are shared by other functions) rather than carried out by staff/equipment duplicated in each departmental office.

(b) **Authority**. Centralisation also refers to the extent to which people have to refer decisions upwards to their superiors. Decentralisation therefore implies increased delegation, empowerment and autonomy at lower levels of the organisation.

10.3 Benefits and drawbacks of decentralisation

FAST FORWARD

Centralisation offers greater control and co-ordination; **decentralisation** offers greater flexibility.

The table below summarises some of the arguments in favour of centralisation and decentralisation.

Benefits of decentralisation	Drawbacks of decentralisation
Avoids overburdening top managers, in terms of workload and stress.	Decisions are not made at one point and may not be coordinated properly.
Improves motivation of more junior managers who are given responsibility.	Junior managers may not have all the facts to make correct decisions.
Greater awareness of local problems by decision makers. (Geographically dispersed organisations are often decentralised on a regional/area basis for this reason.)	Local decisions may not be in interests of whole group.
Greater speed of decision making, and response to changing events, since no need to refer decisions upwards. This is particularly important in rapidly changing markets.	Local management may lack experience and make wrong decisions.
Helps develop the skills of junior managers: supports managerial succession.	May be cheaper to not decentralise and have fewer managers.
Separate spheres of responsibility can be identified: controls, performance measurement and accountability are better.	Responsibility can be identified even with centralised operations.
Communication technology allows decisions to be made locally, with information and input from head office if required.	Needs sophisticated, expensive systems to coordinate local decisions.

The drawbacks to decentralisation, identified in the table above, can be overcome as follows:

- It is the responsibility of the holding company's board of directors to ensure that **co-ordinated decisions** are taken across the group, regardless of the level of decentralisation in the group. Co-ordination will be more difficult in a decentralised group, but that simply means that the bound must work harder to discharge its responsibility properly.

- The **computerisation of management information** systems in recent years has enabled managers to have access to any facts they wish to know about a decision they are taking. The problem is often that managers have access to too much information rather than too little.

- Again it is the responsibility of the holding company's board to ensure **goal congruence of decision making across the group**. Ideally systems should be structured so that local managers are motivated to take decisions which happen to be in the best interests of the group as a whole.
- Local management may certainly lack **experience**, but it is the role of decision support systems to help them make the current decisions.
- It may indeed be **cheaper** to not decentralise, but it is up to the holding company board to weigh up the costs and benefits of decentralisation.
- **Unclear limits of responsibility** in a decentralised organisation will only be the case when the holding company board has failed to specify responsibilities carefully enough. It is perfectly possible for managers in a decentralised group to know what their responsibilities and duties are.
- The **need for co-ordination systems** has been described above, but the plummeting cost of IT systems over the last ten or so years means that such systems need no longer be prohibitively expensive.

11 Summary: the decision-making process

The decision-making process has six steps.

- Identify objectives
- Search for alternative courses of action
- Collect data about the alternative courses of action
- Select the appropriate course of action
- Implement the decision
- Compare actual and planned outcomes and take corrective action as necessary

There are three broad perspectives to performance management:

(a) planning and decision-making
(b) measuring performance
(c) managing performance (control)

The following steps, describing what is sometimes known as the 'decision-making process', describe the processes of planning, performance measurement and control.

Step 1 **Identify objectives**

The organisation's goals or objectives must be defined to ensure that managers are able to assess which of the courses of action available is the most appropriate for the organisation. The objectives of many profit-making organisations include the maximisation of profit and so the decision option chosen should reflect this. Non-profit-making organisations such as hospitals and charities are likely to have an objective based on providing the most effective services with the resources available.

Exam focus point

The December 2006 exam included a scenario requiring the development of a mission statement, and a reorganisation of an existing structure that would focus on quality, emphasise responsibilities and provide a more structured approach to performance measurement.

Step 2 **Search for alternative courses of action**

The next step is to find a number of possible courses of action that enable the objectives to be achieved. A profit-making organisation might need to consider:

- Developing new products to sell in existing markets
- Developing new products to sell in new markets
- Developing new markets in which to sell existing products

Step 3	**Collect data about the alternative courses of action**
	The type of data that needs collecting will depend on the type of decision. If the decision is concerned with the long-term future of the organisation, the manager will need to collect data about the environment in which the organisation operates and about the organisation's capabilities. If the decision is more concerned with the short-term future of the organisation (such as deciding on the selling price for a product), data on the selling price of competitors' products will have to be collected.
Step 4	**Select the appropriate course of action**
	The course of action which best satisfies the organisation's objectives should be selected.
Step 5	**Implement the decision**
Step 6	**Compare actual and planned outcomes and take any necessary corrective action if the planned results have not been achieved**
	The final stage in the process involves comparing actual results with planned and taking control action required.

Techniques for planning, decision-making, measuring performance and applying control over performance, are the subject of the remainder of this text.

12 Reporting formats

In exam questions and the DipFM projects you may be asked to produce your answer in a specific format, most commonly a letter, a memo, an e-mail or a formal report.

We include here some notes on the format that you should use for each of these requirements.

12.1 Letters

You are most likely to use a letter when communicating with someone **outside your organisation.**

Letters should be polite, accurate, clear, logical and concise; and should give appropriate references. Spelling and punctuation should, of course, be impeccable! Also, if your company has a house-style, your letter should conform to that.

12.2 Example: a letter

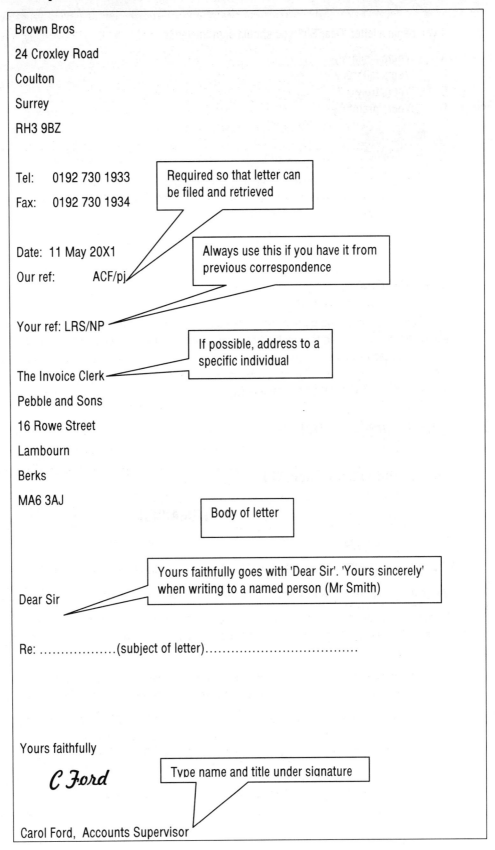

Brown Bros

24 Croxley Road

Coulton

Surrey

RH3 9BZ

Tel: 0192 730 1933

Fax: 0192 730 1934

Date: 11 May 20X1

Our ref: ACF/pj

Your ref: LRS/NP

The Invoice Clerk

Pebble and Sons

16 Rowe Street

Lambourn

Berks

MA6 3AJ

Dear Sir

Re: ....(subject of letter)....................................

Yours faithfully

C Ford

Carol Ford, Accounts Supervisor

Required so that letter can be filed and retrieved

Always use this if you have it from previous correspondence

If possible, address to a specific individual

Body of letter

Yours faithfully goes with 'Dear Sir'. 'Yours sincerely' when writing to a named person (Mr Smith)

Type name and title under signature

Question

If you begin a letter 'Dear Sir', you should sign the letter

A   Yours sincerely
B   Yours faithfully
C   Yours truly
D   Yours gratefully

Answer

B   Yours faithfully is the formal ending if the recipient's name is not used. A would be used if the recipients name had been referred to, e.g. 'Dear Mr Jackson'. C and D are not generally used in business letters.

12.3 Memos

Key term

> The **memorandum** or **memo** performs internally the same function as a letter does in communication externally. It can be used for any kind of communication that is best conveyed in writing such as reports, brief messages or notes.

Memos need less detail than a formal letter.

12.4 Example: a memo

Forrest Fire Extinguishers Ltd

MEMORANDUM

To: All Staff   **Ref:** PANC/mp

From: D B Gavaskar, Managing Director   **Date:** 13 January 20X0

Subject: Overtime arrangements for January/February   Main theme

I would like to remind you that thanks to Pancake Day on and around 12 February, we can expect the usual increased demand for small extinguishers. I am afraid this will involve substantial overtime hours for everyone.

Reason for writing

In order to make this as easy as possible, the works canteen will be open all evening for snacks and hot drinks. The works van will also be available in case of transport difficulties late at night.

I realise that this period puts pressure on production and administrative staff alike, but I would appreciate your co-operation in working as many hours of overtime as you feel able.

Copies to: All staff

No need to sign off

Finish by stating clearly what is required of recipient in response

Question

A memorandum is

A   Signed by the person sending it
B   Generally used for the communication of short messages between different organisations
C   Not used if important information is to be communicated
D   For any written communication within an organisation

D	A memo can be used for internal communication of information that is presented in writing, so B and C are incorrect. A is incorrect as it does not have to be signed.

12.5 E-mails

If available, you can use **e-mails** in the same way as a memo, or for external communications where signatures are unnecessary. An e-mail would therefore not be suitable for confirming a contract, but you can use it to respond to a price query.

12.6 Reports

It is highly likely that you will have to use a report format in the DipFM projects. Further detailed guidance on the writing of reports is given in the BPP Learning Media Project Text. See the inside front cover of this book for details.

FAST FORWARD

Standard reports are a regular part of the management information system.

Ad-hoc reports deal with a one-off issue or problem.

A formal **report** may be needed where a comprehensive investigation has taken place.

ELEMENTS OF A FORMAL REPORT	
Title	Subject of report
Terms of reference	Clarify what has been requested
Introduction	Who the report is from and to
	How the information was obtained
Main body	Divided into sections with sub-headings to aid reader
	Logical order
Conclusions	Summarises findings
Recommendations	Based on information and evidence
	May be combined with conclusion
Signature	Of writer
Executive summary	Saves time for managers receiving a long report
	No more than one page

One example of a short formal report is shown on the next page.

12.7 Example: short formal report

REPORT ON PROPOSED UPDATING OF COMPANY POLICY MANUAL

To: Board of Directors, BCD Ltd
From: J Thurber, Opus Management Consultants
Status: Confidential
Date: 3 October 20X8

I   INTRODUCTION AND TERMS OF REFERENCE

This report details the results of an investigation commissioned by the Board on 7 September 20X8. We were asked to consider the current applicability of the company's policy manual and to propose changes needed to bring it into line with current practice.

II   METHOD

The following investigatory procedures were adopted:

1   Interview all senior staff regarding use of the policy manual in their departments
2   Observe working practices in each department

III   FINDINGS

The manual was last updated 10 years ago. From our observations, the following amendments are now needed:

1   The policy section on computer use should be amended. It deals with safe storage of disks, which is no longer applicable as data is now stored on a server. Also, it does not set out the company's e-mail policy.

2   The company's equal opportunities policy needs to be included.

3   The coding list in the manual is now very out of date. A number of new cost centres and profit centres have been set up in the last 10 years and the codes for these are not noted in the manual.

4   There is no mention of the provisions of the Data Protection Act as they relate to the company.

IV   CONCLUSIONS

We discovered upon interviewing staff that very little use is made of the policy manual. When it has been amended as above, it can be brought back into use, and we recommend that this should be done as soon as possible.

Signed J Thurber, Opus Management Consultants

A formal report like this will of course be **word-processed**.

Question	Communication methods

In each of the cases below, select the form of communication which will generally be the most appropriate.

1   A complaint to a supplier about the quality of goods supplied.

      A   Letter
      B   Memo
      C   Formal report
      D   E-mail

2   A query to a supervisor about the coding of an invoice.

    A   E-mail
    B   Memo
    C   Face-to-face
    D   All of the above are equally suitable if available

3   An investigation into the purchasing costs of your company.

    A   Letter
    B   Memo
    C   Formal report
    D   E-mail

4   Notification to customers of a change of the company's telephone number.

    A   Letter
    B   Memo
    C   E-mail
    D   All of the above are equally suitable if available

5   Reply to an e-mail.

    A   Letter
    B   Memo
    C   E-mail
    D   Face-to-face

6   Query to the sales department about an expenses claim.

    A   Memo
    B   E-mail
    C   Telephone
    D   All of the above are equally suitable if available

Answer

1   A
2   D
3   C
4   A
5   C
6   D

Key learning points

- The **mission** of an organisation is the reason for its existence. Some organisations issue mission statements.

- Organisations develop **objectives** (quantified as **targets**) for the achievement of its mission and long-term goals. The strategic objectives for a commercial organisation should include one or more financial objectives.

- **Strategies** are plans for achieving objectives and targets. Strategies are formulated for the organisation as a whole, and for individual aspects of the organisation's operations.

- **Shorter-term plans** are formulated within the framework of the longer-term objectives and strategies. Most organisations prepare annual **budgets**, which are plans for the entire organisation, expressed in financial terms.

- Managers have to **plan, control, organise** and **make decisions. Performance measurement** is a system for comparing actual results against plans. **Performance management** involves using information from performance measurement to take new planning decisions or control actions to improve the future performance of the organisation. Performance measurement and management, within a planning framework, should help to ensure that the strategic objectives of the organisation are pursued and achieved.

- Performance measurement and management systems should identify aspects of performance that individual managers should be held accountable for, and that they should be able to control. A reporting system might be based on a system of **responsibility centres** or strategic business units.

- Performance measurement and management systems have been enhanced by developments in **information and communications technology**.

- Information about **costs, revenues and profits** is an important element of all performance measurement and management systems.

- **Management accounting** is concerned with the collection of data, its analysis and processing into information, and the interpretation and communication of that information so as to assist management with planning, control and decision making.

- **Divisionalisation and decentralisation**

    - Centralisation offers greater control and arguably makes managing the company easier. Decentralisation offers greater flexibility.

    - Divisionalisation separates the organisation into more manageable parts.

- The **decision-making process** has six steps.

    - Identify objectives
    - Search for alternative courses of action
    - Collect data about the alternative courses of action
    - Select the appropriate course of action
    - Implement the decision
    - Compare actual and planned outcomes and take corrective action as necessary

Quick quiz

1 The mission of a company might be to achieve a 20% growth in profits each year for the next five years. True or false?

2 The strategy of a company might be to achieve a 20% growth in profits each year for the next five years. True or false?

3 The strategy of a company might be to focus on the provision of premium products to customers that earn a high profit ratio, as a means of improving the company's overall profitability and return on capital. True or false?

4 The objective of *all* organisations is the maximisation of profit. True or false?

5 What is ERP?

Answers to quick quiz

1 False. Achieving a 20% growth in profits each year is a target for achievement (a quantified objective for the organisation).

2 False. This is a target (objective), not a strategy for achieving the target.

3 True. A strategy is a plan for achieving a target or objective.

4 False. Profit maximisation is the objective of a lot of profit-making organisations but non-profit-making organisations in particular will have different objectives.

5 An enterprise resource planning system. This is an integrated database and information system, accessible to everyone in the organisation via Internet or intranet.

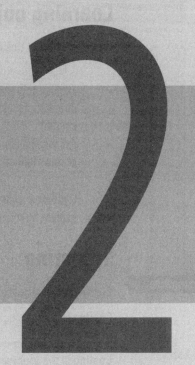

Costing systems for performance management

Topic list
1 Costing
2 Measuring cost
3 Direct costs and indirect costs (overheads)
4 Fixed costs and variable costs
5 Absorption costing
6 Over- and under-absorption
7 Activity-based costing
8 Marginal cost and marginal costing
9 Conclusion: costing methods

Introduction

Managers need to know the costs incurred in producing the organisation's products and services, in order to make accurate decisions about those products and services. In this chapter you will learn about both the traditional method of absorption costing and the more modern (and more accurate) method of activity-based costing (ABC).

Learning objectives

On completion of this chapter you will be able to:

Syllabus reference

- explain how the costs of a product or service might be measured as the sum of direct costs and indirect costs, and understand the features of absorption costing

  2, 5

- explain the distinction between fixed costs and variable costs, and the relevance of this distinction for establishing the costs of a product or service

  5

- explain the rationale for activity-based costing (ABC), and how it differs from traditional absorption costing

  10, 11

- explain how costs and profitability are measured using marginal costing

  6

1 Costing

FAST FORWARD

Costing is the process of determining the costs of products, services or activities.

Costing systems must be flexible enough to provide different costs for different purposes.

Key term

Costing is the process of determining the costs of products, services or activities.

Given the definition of cost accounting we have adopted above, **use of costing methods** to provide information (such as the estimated cost of job X) is part of **cost accounting. Use of that information** (such as whether or not to proceed with job X given estimated costs) is part of **management accounting.**

In this text we will be looking at how to use various costing methods and considering how to use the resulting information.

1.1 The importance of flexibility

The costing systems used by an organisation need to provide information for a **wide variety of purposes** in a **wide range of organisations** (including not-for-profit organisations).

1.1.1 Flexibility and decision making

Management face a wide variety of decisions on an hourly, daily, weekly and monthly basis.

(a) **Routine planning decisions**, for example, budgeting. Budgeting decisions commonly analyse fixed and variable costs, together with revenues, over a one-year period. They are also often concerned with how to make the best use of scarce resources.

(b) **Short-run problem decisions**, typically, unforeseen 'one-off' special decisions of a non-recurring nature, where the costs and benefits are all obtained within a relatively short period. For example, should a contract be accepted or rejected? What price should be quoted in the tender for a contract?

(c) **Investment or disinvestment decisions**, for example should an item of equipment be purchased? Should a department be shut down? Decisions of this nature often have long-term consequences.

(d) **Longer-range decisions**, meaning decisions made once and reviewed infrequently, but which are intended to provide a continuing solution to a continuing or recurring problem. They include decisions about selling and distribution policies (such as whether goods should be sold through middlemen or direct to customers? What type of customer should the sales force attempt to attract? What should the company's discount policies be? Should a new product or service be launched?)

(e)   **Control decisions**, for example, should disappointing performance be investigated, given that the benefits expected must exceed the costs from investigation and control?

It should be clear from the examples given that the management accountant will frequently be involved in providing information for business decisions of all kinds. Costing systems therefore need to be sufficiently flexible to provide the required information.

1.1.2 Flexibility and performance evaluation

Performance evaluation entails setting targets, recording actual performance and comparing this to target performance. This sounds straightforward enough, doesn't it? The **identification of appropriate performance measures** to affect the appropriate behavioural response is often **difficult,** however, and **costing systems** are often **unable to provide** the target and actual **information.** For example, if divisional management are appraised using a profit figure which includes non-controllable costs at division level and apportioned group costs and/or the costing system is unable to provide a figure for controllable profit, a negative motivational impact is likely. We consider these issues more fully throughout the text.

What should now be clear is that **costing systems** need to be **flexible** enough to provide **different costs for different purposes.**

2 Measuring cost

The purpose of a costing system is to provide information about the costs of activities within an organisation, and the costs of the goods produced and sold or the services provided by the organisation.

Establishing the cost of a product or service will help management to:

(a)   Prepare **cost budgets** for the future, based on costs incurred in the past, or **forecast** what costs are likely to be in the future

(b)   **Establish the profitability** of the product or service

(c)   **Compare actual costs with budgeted costs**, to establish whether actual costs are suitably under control

(d)   Possibly, make certain decisions, such as setting prices for the product or service at a margin or mark-up above cost

(e)   Possibly, to reward managers for good performance, for example if actual profits exceed budgeted profits

2.1 Cost units

Key term

A **cost unit** is a unit of a product or service (or activity) for which costs are measured.

A cost unit may be a standard item, such as a can of baked beans or a litre of cooking oil. A cost unit is not always a single item. It might be a batch of an item. Examples of cost units are an individual job or contract, a batch of 1,000 pairs of shoes, or a tonne of bricks. A doctor or dentist operating a practice might want to establish the cost per surgery hour. Other examples of cost units are a passenger mile (in other words, the average cost of transporting a passenger for a mile) and a patient night (the average cost of an overnight stay of a patient in a hospital bed).

2.2 Cost of a manufactured unit

The cost of manufactured products is typically measured as the sum of its **production cost**, plus a unit cost of sales and distribution, plus a unit cost of administration. The requirement to identify the production cost per unit arises because items of finished goods in inventory (and part-finished work-in-progress) are valued at production cost in the balance sheet of the business.

2.3 Cost centres

Key term

> **Cost centres** are the essential 'building blocks' of a costing system. They act as a collecting place for certain costs before they are analysed further.

A cost centre might be a place or physical location, such as a department (e.g. the stores department, the repairs and maintenance department, the production scheduling department, the IT department, and so on). On the other hand, a cost centre might be an individual person, such as the company solicitor. It might be a group of people, all contributing to the same function, such as the accounts staff, say, or the research laboratory staff. Alternatively, a cost centre might be an item of equipment, such as a machine which incurs costs because it needs to be oiled, maintained and operated.

Cost centres may vary in nature, but what they all have in common is that they **incur costs**. It is therefore logical to **collect costs** initially under the headings of the various different cost centres that there may be in an organisation. Then, when we want to know how much our products cost, we simply find out how many cost units have been produced and share out the costs incurred by that cost centre amongst the cost units.

2.4 Profit centres

Some organisations measure performance on a **profit centre basis**. Cost centres only have costs attributed to them. Profit centres, on the other hand, also receive credit for the revenues associated with those costs. For example, an organisation with two departments each making a different product will allocate the revenues from each product to the department where each product is made. This ensures that the organisation has some idea as to the relative profitability of each product.

Key term

> A **profit centre** is similar to a cost centre but is accountable for both costs *and* revenues.

Profit centre managers should normally have control over how revenue is raised and how costs are incurred. Not infrequently, several cost centres will comprise one large profit centre.

3 Direct costs and indirect costs (overheads)

FAST FORWARD

> Costing systems are used to measure the cost of products, services and activities, and to establish their profitability. Costs can be measured as the sum of **direct costs** and **indirect costs** (overheads). Costs may also be measured as the sum of variable costs and fixed costs.

A distinction is made between **direct** and **indirect** costs.

3.1 Direct costs

Key terms

- A **direct cost** is a cost that can be traced in full to the cost unit or cost centre (product, service, or department) that is being costed.

- **Direct material** is all material becoming part of the product (unless used in negligible amounts and/or having negligible cost), or consumed in the provision of a service.

- **Direct wages** are all wages paid for labour (either as basic hours or as overtime) expended on the work of making the product or providing the service. Direct wages are the costs of the employees involved directly in the work, and exclude the labour costs of support staff. The direct wages and salaries cost of a department consist of the wages and salaries of the individuals employed in the department.

- **Direct expenses** are any expenses which are incurred on a specific product, other than direct material cost and direct wages.

Examples of direct expenses may be:

- the cost of special designs, drawings or layouts for a specific job
- the hire of tools or equipment for a particular job
- maintenance costs of tools, fixtures, fittings and so on, incurred on a specific job or contract

3.2 Indirect costs (overheads)

Indirect costs, more commonly known as overheads, are all costs that are not direct costs.

Key term

> An **overhead** is the cost incurred in the course of making a product, providing a service or running a department, but which cannot be traced directly and in full to the product, service or department.

Overheads consist of the following:

- indirect materials
- indirect labour
- indirect expenses

Unit costs therefore consist of the following items.

Materials	=	Direct materials	+	Indirect materials
+		+		+
Labour	=	Direct labour	+	Indirect labour
+		+		+
Expenses	=	Direct expenses	+	Indirect expenses
Total cost	=	Direct cost	+	Overhead

An **absorption costing** system or **full costing** system is used to measure the cost of items (products or services), as the sum of direct costs plus overheads. 'Absorption' of overheads means assigning overhead costs to cost items (products or services).

A common way of categorising overheads is between

(a) production (or factory) overhead
(b) administration overhead
(c) selling and distribution overhead

Key terms

> - **Production (or factory) overhead** includes all indirect material costs, indirect wages and indirect expenses incurred in the factory from receipt of the order until its completion.
>
> - **Administration overhead** is all indirect material costs, wages and expenses incurred in the direction, control and administration of an undertaking.
>
> - **Selling overhead** is all indirect materials costs, wages and expenses incurred in promoting sales and retaining customers.
>
> - **Distribution overhead** is all indirect material costs, wages and expenses incurred in making the packed product ready for despatch and delivering it to the customer.

Examples of production overhead include the following.

(a) **Indirect materials** that cannot be traced in the finished product, such as consumable stores like cleaning materials.

(b) **Indirect wages**, meaning all wages not charged directly to a product. These include the wages or salaries of non-productive personnel in the production department, such as supervisors.

(c) **Indirect expenses** (other than material and labour) not charged directly to production typically include rent, rates and factory insurance of a factory, and depreciation charges for plant and machinery.

In traditional costing systems, all administration costs and most selling and distribution costs are treated as indirect costs (overheads) for products or services.

Examples of administration overhead are as follows.

(a)   Depreciation of office buildings and machinery.

(b)   Office salaries, including salaries of administrative directors, secretaries and accountants.

(c)   Rent, rates, insurance, lighting, cleaning and heating of general offices, telephone and postal charges, bank charges, legal charges, audit fees.

Examples of selling overhead are as follows.

(a)   Costs of printing and stationery, such as catalogues and price lists.

(b)   Salaries of sales representatives and sales department staff.

(c)   Advertising and sales promotion, market research.

(d)   Rent, rates and insurance of sales offices and showrooms, bad debts and collection charges, cash discounts allowed, after-sales service.

Sales commission that is calculated as a percentage of the value of sales should be treated as a **direct selling cost**.

Distribution costs are usually treated as overheads, because of the difficulty in tracing specific costs directly to individual cost units. Examples of distribution overhead are as follows.

(a)   Cost of packing cases.

(b)   Wages of packers, drivers and despatch clerks.

(c)   Freight and insurance charges, rent, rates, insurance and depreciation of warehouses, depreciation and running expenses of delivery vehicles.

3.3 Components of 'full cost'

In 'traditional' costing systems, the unit cost of production has been calculated as the sum of the following items.

	$
Direct materials	X
Direct labour	X
Direct expenses (possibly)	X
Production overhead	X
Full production cost	X
Administration overhead	X
Selling and distribution overhead	X
Full cost of sale	X

In many organisations, overhead costs are a substantial proportion of the total unit cost of a product.

4 Fixed costs and variable costs

FAST FORWARD

Costs that are partly-fixed and partly-variable can be segregated into their fixed cost and variable cost elements using the **high-low method**.

In addition to analysing costs as direct or indirect, they can also be categorised as fixed costs or variable costs, according to whether they change with variations in the 'level of activity' (production and sales volume, etc.).

Key terms

- A **fixed cost** is an item of cost relating to a particular period of time and which, within certain activity levels, is unaffected by changes in the level of activity during that time period.

- A **variable cost** is a cost that tends to vary, in total amount, with the level of activity.

Some examples of fixed costs and variable costs are as follows.

(a) Direct material costs are **variable costs** because the total cost of direct materials rises as more units of a product are manufactured.

(b) Sales commission is often a fixed percentage of sales revenue, and so is a **variable cost** that varies with the level of sales.

(c) Telephone call charges are likely to increase if the volume of business expands, and so they are likely to be a **variable overhead cost.**

The rental cost of business premises is a constant amount, at least within a stated time period, and so is a **fixed cost**.

Within a normal range of activity levels (i.e. those activity levels that would be expected to occur over a number of periods under normal circumstances) the variable cost per unit of an item is usually a constant amount. For example, the variable cost of a product might be, say, $6 per unit. The total variable cost will rise as output rises. The total variable cost of 500 units, for example, would be $3,000 and the total variable cost of 600 units would be $3,600.

Within a normal range of activity levels, the total amount of a fixed cost remains the same, regardless of the activity level. However, the fixed cost per unit of output falls as the activity level rises within a given time period.

For example, suppose that the cost of a unit of product is $8 for direct materials, $6 for direct labour (which is regarded as a variable cost, consisting of one hour of labour time at $6 per hour) and $1 for variable overhead. Fixed costs are $50,000 a year.

(a) If annual output is 5,000 units, the cost per unit will be $15 of variable costs ($8 + $6 + $1) and $10 of fixed overhead per unit ($50,000/5,000), making $25 per unit in total (full cost).

(b) However, if annual output is higher, say 10,000 units, the cost per unit will still be $15 of variable costs ($8 + $6 + $1) but the fixed overhead cost per unit will only be $5 ($50,000/10,000), making just $20 per unit in total (full cost).

4.1 Direct and indirect costs, and fixed and variable costs

Variable costs are often direct costs, but variable cost is *not* just another name for a direct cost. The distinctions that can be made are as follows.

(a) Costs are either variable or fixed, depending upon whether they change when the volume of production changes.

(b) Costs are either direct or indirect, depending upon how easily they can be traced to a specific unit of production.

Question   Fixed and variable costs

Are the following likely to be fixed or variable costs?

(a) Cost of telephone calls made
(b) Cost of rental of telephone system
(c) Annual salary of the chief accountant
(d) Managing director's subscription to the Institute of Directors
(e) Cost of materials used to pack every 20 units of product X into a box

Answer

(a) Variable cost. Call charges vary with the number and duration (and time of day) of calls, but are also likely to vary with the general volume of activity in the organisation, e.g. with the volume of production output. Where an organisation agrees fixed call charges for a period with the telecommunications service provider, call charges will be a fixed cost.

(b) Fixed cost
(c) Fixed cost

(d)   Fixed cost
(e)   Variable cost

4.2 Semi-variable costs

Some items of cost are known as **semi-variable** costs (or **semi-fixed** costs or **mixed** costs). These costs combine a fixed element and a variable element.

Key term

> A **semi-variable or semi-fixed cost, or mixed cost,** is a cost containing both fixed and variable components and so is partly affected by changes in the level of activity.

Examples of semi-variable costs include the following.

(a)   Electricity and gas bills
  - Fixed cost = standing charge
  - Variable cost = charge per unit of electricity used

(b)   Sales representatives' salaries
  - Fixed cost = basic salary
  - Variable cost = commission on sales made

(c)   Costs of running a car
  - Fixed cost = road tax, insurance
  - Variable costs = petrol, oil, repairs (which vary with miles travelled)

4.3 Separating semi-variable costs into a fixed and a variable element

Semi-variable costs can be segregated into a fixed-cost element and a variable cost per unit of activity. A technique for doing this is known as the '**high-low method**'. To apply this technique, we need two figures for total costs:

(a)   the total cost at one level of activity
(b)   the total cost at another level of activity

The total cost will be lower at the lower activity level and higher at the higher activity level. Since fixed costs are the same at both activity levels, the **difference** in the two costs must be the **variable cost** of the difference in the activity levels.

For example, suppose that the total monthly production overhead costs of an organisation have been measured at $78,000 when output was 4,800 units and $81,600 when output was 5,700 units. The fixed costs per month and the variable overhead cost per unit can be calculated as follows.

		$
(High)	Total cost of 5,700 units	81,600
(Low)	Total cost of 4,800 units	78,000
(Difference)	Variable cost of 900 units	3,600
	Variable cost per unit ($3,600/900)	$4

		$
Total cost of 5,700 units		81,600
Less: Variable cost of 5,700 units	($4 per unit)	22,800
Fixed costs		58,800

Note that the same result would have been obtained if the data for 4,800 units was used.

Question

Costs: high-low method

Sandstorm is a firm of gas boiler maintenance engineers. Its indirect costs are thought to be partly variable, with the variable cost element depending on the number of hours worked by maintenance engineers each month.

It has been established that costs were $57,600 in a month when 22,000 engineer hours were recorded, and $54,800 in a month when 20,600 engineer hours were recorded.

Required

Using the high-low method, estimate the fixed costs per month and variable cost per engineer hour.

Answer

		$
(High)	Total cost of 22,000 hours	57,600
(Low)	Total cost of 20,600 hours	54,800
(Difference)	Variable cost of 1,400 hours	2,800
	Variable cost per hour ($2,800/1,400)	$2

		$
Total cost of 22,000 hours		57,600
Variable cost of 22,000 hours	($2 per hour)	44,000
Fixed costs		13,600

4.4 Stepped costs

Another type of cost is a **stepped cost.** This type of cost is fixed over a certain range of activity, but if the activity level rises above or below a certain level, the total cost of the item will rise or fall to a new fixed level. In other words, the cost rises or falls by a step. For example, the cost of warehouse rental might be fixed up to a certain volume of output each month, but if output rises above this level, the organisation might have to rent additional warehouse space, raising 'fixed costs' to a new level.

4.5 Controllable costs and uncontrollable costs

Key terms

- A **controllable cost** is a cost which can be influenced by management decisions and actions.

- An **uncontrollable cost** is any cost that cannot be affected by management within a given time span.

It is sometimes assumed wrongly, that direct costs should be controllable, whereas indirect costs are likely to be uncontrollable. This is not the case. Direct costs might be uncontrollable in the short term (e.g. direct labour costs for a work force paid fixed wages). Some indirect costs, on the other hand, might be controllable, through cost-cutting measures.

5 Absorption costing

Overhead is the cost incurred in the course of making a product, providing a service or running a department, but which cannot be traced directly and in full to the product, service or department. The main groupings of overhead costs are production overhead, administration overhead, selling and distribution overhead.

Overheads may be dealt with by **absorption** costing, **activity-based** costing or **marginal** costing.

The main reasons for using absorption costing are for inventory valuations, pricing decisions and establishing the profitability of different products.

Allocation, apportionment and **absorption** are the three stages of calculating the costs of overheads to be charged to manufactured output.

Apportionment is a procedure whereby indirect costs (overheads) are spread fairly between cost centres.

Overhead absorption is the process whereby costs of cost centres are added to unit, job or process costs. Overhead absorption is sometimes called **overhead recovery.**

Absorption costing is a method of measuring the cost of products, services or activities. The objective of absorption costing is to **include in the total cost of a product an appropriate share of** the organisation's **total overhead.** By an appropriate share we mean an amount that reflects the amount of time and effort that has gone into producing a unit or completing a job.

The 'full cost' or 'fully-absorbed cost' of an item therefore consists of:

(a)   the direct costs of the item, plus
(b)   a fair share of overhead

In many absorption costing systems, **only production overheads** are added to product costs. Administration overheads and sales and distribution overheads are treated as separate expenses in the income statement.

Suppose that a company makes and sells 100 units of a product each week. The direct cost per unit is $6 and the unit sales price is $10. Production overhead costs $200 per week and administration, selling and distribution overhead costs $150 per week. The weekly profit could be calculated as follows.

	$	$
Sales (100 units × $10)		1,000
Direct costs (100 × $6)	600	
Production overheads	200	
Administration, selling, distribution costs	150	
		950
Profit		50

In absorption costing, production overhead costs will be added to each unit of product manufactured and sold.

	$ per unit
Direct cost per unit	6
Production overhead ($200 per week for 100 units)	2
Full factory cost	8

The weekly profit would be calculated as follows.

	$
Sales	1,000
Less factory cost of sales (100 × $8)	800
Gross profit	200
Less administration, selling, distribution costs	150
Net profit	50

If an organisation produced a single standard product (or provided a single standard service) then the overhead cost per unit would be calculated by dividing the total overhead costs among the total units produced.

In practice, firms produce a variety of products or services, or single products in different sizes, and a fair method of sharing overhead costs between the products or services needs to be established.

5.1 Reasons for absorption costing

Before describing absorption costing in more detail, it may be useful to consider the reasons why absorption costing might be used. The reasons for using absorption costing have traditionally been identified as follows.

(a) **Inventory valuations**. Inventory in hand must be given a value. It is usual for inventory to be valued at a full cost, inclusive of production overheads. Absorption costing is **recommended for financial reporting** by the International Accounting Standard on inventories (IAS 2). IAS 2 deals with financial accounting systems and not with internal management accounting systems. The management accountant is (in theory) free to value inventories by whatever method seems best. However, where companies integrate their financial accounting and cost accounting systems into a single system of accounting records, the valuation of closing inventories will be determined by IAS 2, and at full cost.

(b) **Assessing profitability**. An organisation needs to ensure that it earns sufficient revenues to cover all its costs, including indirect costs, and make a profit. By charging all products or services with a fair share of overheads, management can assess whether the profitability of individual products or services is sufficient.

(c) **Pricing decisions**. Many companies attempt to fix selling prices by calculating the full cost of production or sales of each product, and then adding a margin for profit. For example, a firm may price an item by adding a standard margin of, say, 25% to the full cost. **'Full cost plus pricing'** can be particularly useful for companies that do jobbing or contract work, where each job or contract is different, so that a standard unit sales price cannot be fixed. Without using absorption costing, a full cost is difficult to ascertain.

5.2 Absorption costing procedures

There are three stages in measuring the amount of overhead costs to be charged to manufactured output. These are **allocation**, **apportionment** and **absorption**.

(a) The first stage in absorption costing in manufacturing is to charge all production overheads to the departments that are directly engaged in production work. This is the purpose of allocation and apportionment.

 (i) **Allocation** is the process of assigning costs to cost centres. An allocated overhead is an indirect cost that is fully attributable to a particular cost centre.

 (ii) **Apportionment** means 'sharing out'. Not all indirect costs can be allocated directly to production departments, and so they are shared out between departments on a fair basis.

(b) Next, the overheads charged to the production departments in this way are added to ('absorbed into') the cost of products worked on by that department. An 'absorption rate' is established for adding overheads to product costs.

5.3 Example: overhead apportionment

A simplified example might help to illustrate the absorption costing method.

A manufacturing company produces a range of electronic products at a plant. The plant has two production departments, department A and department B, and most products are worked on in both departments before despatch to customers.

Production overheads for a particular period are as follows:

Item of cost	Total cost $
Directly attributable to department A	43,700
Directly attributable to department B	60,300
Factory depreciation	3,000
Repairs and maintenance	15,000
Stores	22,000
Factory office	24,000
Equipment insurance	5,000
Heating and lighting	4,000
Canteen	21,000
Total	198,000

Other information is as follows.

	Department A	Department B
Value of plant and machinery	$200,000	$300,000
Machine hours worked	3,600	900
Direct labour hours worked	6,000	18,000
Number of employees	40	80
Value of materials requisitioned from stores	$150,000	$50,000
Floor area (square metres)	18,000	27,000

How might the production overhead costs be charged to units of production?

Solution

In this example, some overhead costs have been directly allocated to each production department, but other costs are 'shared' by the two departments, and cannot be allocated in full to either department. These costs must be apportioned between the two departments on a fair basis.

There are no rules about selecting a basis for apportionment. In this example, it would seem 'fair' to apportion the cost of depreciation of the factory building on the basis of floor area taken up by each department, and to apportion the costs of the canteen on the basis of the number of employees in each department. Other costs might be apportioned in any of several ways. Possible apportionments are shown in the table below.

Cost item	Basis of apportionment	Total cost $	Dept A $	Dept B $
Allocated costs		104,000	43,700	60,300
Factory depreciation	Floor area	3,000	1,200	1,800
Repairs and maint.	Machine hrs worked	15,000	12,000	3,000
Stores	Materials requis'd	22,000	16,500	5,500
Factory office	Direct labour hours	24,000	6,000	18,000
Equipment insurance	Value of plant	5,000	2,000	3,000
Heating and lighting	Floor area	4,000	1,600	2,400
Canteen	Employee numbers	21,000	7,000	14,000
Total dept overhead		198,000	90,000	108,000

The calculations are not set out in detail. As an example, the repairs and maintenance cost of $15,000 has been shared between the departments on the basis of machine hours worked. The ratio of machine hours is 3,600:900 or 4:1, and the overhead cost has been apportioned between the two departments on this basis, i.e. $12,000: $3,000.

5.4 Overhead absorption

Having established an overhead cost for each production department, the next step is to calculate a rate for absorbing the overhead costs into the cost of production.

> **Overhead absorption** is the process whereby overhead costs allocated and apportioned to production cost centres are added to unit, job or process costs. Overhead absorption is sometimes called **overhead recovery.**

An organisation may use a different absorption rate for each production department, or a single 'factory-wide' absorption rate.

(a)   Where separate absorption rates are used for each production department, the overhead cost for each department is established. This is done by means of overhead allocation and apportionment, as illustrated above.

(b)   The total overhead for each department is then divided by the activity level for each department, to obtain a rate of overhead absorption per unit of activity. Typically, activity is measured in terms of direct labour hours worked (to obtain an overhead rate per labour hour) or machine hours operated (to obtain an overhead rate per machine hour).

The overhead is then added to the cost of each cost unit by **applying** the absorption rate. If overhead is absorbed at, say $2 per labour hour, then a cost unit that takes 3 labour hours to produce absorbs 3 × $2 = $6 in overheads.

5.5 Example: absorption

In the example above, the overhead costs of department A were measured as $90,000 and the overheads of department B were $108,000.

If overheads were absorbed on a labour hours basis, the absorption rate for each department would be as follows.

	Department A	Department B
Overheads	$90,000	$108,000
Direct labour hours	6,000 hours	18,000 hours
Absorption rate	$15 per direct labour hour	$6 per direct labour hour

Suppose that a product with a direct materials cost of $160 and a direct labour cost of $240 manufactured, and takes 10 hours of direct labour work in department A and 20 hours of direct labour work in department B. The full cost of the product would be:

	$	$
Direct materials		160
Direct labour		240
Department A overhead (10 hours × $15)	150	
Department B overhead (20 hours × $6)	120	
Total production overhead		270
Full production cost		670

It is worth noting that a different basis for overhead absorption would result in a different full product cost. Using the same example, suppose that overheads were absorbed on a machine hour basis, rather than a direct labour hour basis, and that the product needed 3 hours of machine time in department A and 2 hours of machine time in department B.

If overheads were absorbed on a machine hours basis, the absorption rate for each department would be as follows.

	Department A	Department B
Overheads	$90,000	$108,000
Machine hours	3,600 hours	900 hours
Absorption rate	$25 per machine hour	$120 per machine hour

The full cost of the product would be:

	$	$
Direct materials		160
Direct labour		240
Department A overhead (3 hours x $25)	75	
Department B overhead (2 hours x $120)	240	
Total production overhead		315
Full production cost		715

5.6 The arbitrary nature of absorption costing

Even when a company is trying to be 'fair', there is a great lack of precision about the way an absorption basis is chosen. This is because:

(a)   the basis for apportioning shared costs between production departments is not 'scientific'

(b)   there is also an element of arbitrariness in the choice of activity (direct labour hours or machine hours etc.) as the basis for establishing an overhead absorption rate.

This arbitrariness is one of the main criticisms of absorption costing, and if absorption costing is to be used (because of its other virtues) then it is important that the methods used are kept under regular review. Changes in working conditions should, if necessary, lead to changes in the way in which work is accounted for.

6 Over- and under-absorption

FAST FORWARD

Predetermined overhead absorption rates are normally used, based on budgeted figures.

The 'actual' full cost of production is therefore made up of the following.

- Direct materials
- Direct labour
- Direct expenses
- Overheads (based on the predetermined overhead absorption rate)

Under- or **over-absorption** of overheads occurs because the predetermined overhead absorption rates are based on forecasts (estimates).

If an organisation has estimated fixed and variable production overheads, it may calculate a **separate absorption rate** for each.

One problem with absorption costing is that the overhead cost per unit will depend on the volume of output or activity during a period. As output volume increases in a given period, the fixed overhead cost per unit will fall.

Suppose for example that a company manufactures a single product that has a direct cost of $5 per unit, and that indirect costs, all fixed, are $2,400 each month. Suppose that output in January, February and March are 600 units, 400 units and 800 units respectively. The full cost per unit in each month would be as follows:

Output		Variable cost per unit	Fixed cost per unit	Full unit cost
		$	$	$
January	600 units	5	4	9
February	400 units	5	6	11
March	800 units	5	3	8

The unit cost ranges between $8 and $11, all because of the volume of output in the month, raising questions about the 'fairness' or 'realism' of the costing method.

A firm might prefer to apply a constant overhead rate to all output throughout the course of a financial year, but if actual overhead expenditure is used, it would have to wait until the year end to establish what unit overhead costs are.

An alternative approach to overhead absorption, which is commonly used by firms that have an absorption costing system, is to apply overhead costs at a **predetermined** or **standard rate**. This rate is derived from the budget, ie from budgeted overhead expenditure and the budgeted volume of activity for the year.

Using the predetermined absorption rate, the actual cost of production can be established as follows.

	Direct materials
plus:	Direct labour
plus:	Direct expenses (if any)
plus:	Overhead (based on the predetermined overhead absorption rate)
equals:	'Actual' full cost of production

6.1 Example: using a predetermined recovery rate

P budgeted to make 10,000 units of a product called Jasmine at a cost of $3 per unit in direct materials and $4 per unit in direct labour. The sales price would be $12 per unit, and production overheads were budgeted to amount to $20,000. A unit basis of overhead recovery is in operation.

During the period 12,000 units were actually produced and sold (for $12 each) and the actual cost of direct materials was $38,000 and of direct labour, $45,000. Overheads incurred came to $21,000.

What was the cost of sales of product Jasmine, and what was the profit? Ignore administration, selling and distribution overheads.

Solution

The cost of production and sales is the actual direct cost plus the cost of overheads, absorbed at a predetermined rate as established in the budget. In our example, the overhead recovery rate would be $2 per unit produced ($20,000 ÷ 10,000 units).

The actual cost of sales is calculated as follows.

	$
Direct materials (actual)	38,000
Direct labour (actual)	45,000
Overheads absorbed (12,000 units × $2 per unit)	24,000
Full cost of sales, product Jasmine	107,000
Sales of product Jasmine (12,000 units × $12)	144,000
Profit, product Jasmine	37,000

The actual overheads incurred, $21,000, are not the same as the overheads absorbed into (ie included in) the cost of production and hence charged against profit. Absorbed overheads were $24,000. Nevertheless, in normal absorption costing $24,000 is the 'correct' cost. The discrepancy between actual overheads incurred, and the overheads absorbed, which is an inevitable feature of absorption costing, is accounted for at the end of the accounting period, as the **under-absorption** or **over-absorption** of overhead.

In this example, $24,000 has been added to the cost of production as overhead, but actual spending was only $21,000. There has been an over-absorption of overheads by $3,000, which has added to costs and so reduced the reported profits on the product. The over-absorbed overhead should therefore be added back to profits, to establish the actual profit for the period.

6.2 Why does under- or over-absorption occur?

The rate of overhead absorption is based on two estimates, an estimate of overhead expenditure and an estimate of production volume. Either one or both of these estimates may not turn out to be what actually occurs. Overheads incurred will therefore almost inevitably be either greater than or less than overheads absorbed into the cost of production. Let's consider an example.

Suppose that the estimated overhead in a production department is $80,000 and the estimated activity is 40,000 direct labour hours. The overhead recovery rate (using a direct labour hour basis) would be $2 per direct labour hour.

Actual overheads in the period are, say $84,000 and 45,000 direct labour hours are worked.

	$
Overhead incurred (actual)	84,000
Overhead absorbed (45,000 × $2)	90,000
Over-absorption of overhead	6,000

In this example, the cost of produced units or jobs has been charged with $6,000 more than was actually spent. An adjustment to reconcile the overheads charged to the actual overhead is necessary and the over-absorbed overhead will be accounted for as an adjustment to the income statement at the end of the accounting period.

The overhead absorption rate is predetermined from estimates of overhead cost and the expected volume of activity. Under- or over-recovery of overhead will therefore occur in the following circumstances.

(a) Actual overhead costs are different from the estimates.

(b) The actual activity volume is different from the estimated activity volume.

(c) Both actual overhead costs and actual activity volume are different from the estimated costs and volume.

6.3 Example: under-/over-absorption

W has a budgeted production overhead of $60,000 and a budgeted activity of 20,000 direct labour hours and therefore a recovery rate of $3 per direct labour hour. Calculate the under-/over-absorbed overhead, and the reasons for the under/over absorption, in the following circumstances.

(a) Actual overheads cost $57,000 and 20,000 direct labour hours are worked.

(b) Actual overheads cost $60,000 and 18,500 direct labour hours are worked.

(c) Actual overheads cost $57,000 and 18,500 direct labour hours are worked.

Solution

(a)

	$
Actual overhead	57,000
Absorbed overhead (20,000 × $3)	60,000
Over-absorbed overhead	3,000

Here there is over-absorption because although the actual and estimated direct labour hours are the same, actual overheads cost less than expected and so too much overhead has been charged against profit.

(b)

	$
Actual overhead	60,000
Absorbed overhead (18,500 × $3)	55,500
Under-absorbed overhead	4,500

Here there is under-absorption because although estimated and actual overhead costs were the same, fewer direct labour hours were worked than expected and hence insufficient overheads have been charged against profit.

(c)

	$
Actual overhead	57,000
Absorbed overhead (18,500 × $3)	55,500
Under-absorbed overhead	1,500

The reason for the under-absorption is a combination of the reasons in (a) and (b).

Question

Under-/over-absorbed overhead

WCX makes a variety of products, and uses a factory-wide absorption rate for calculating production overhead costs of output. This overhead rate is based on budgeted production expenditure and budgeted direct labour hours in the production departments.

In 20X4, budgeted production overheads, all fixed costs, were $380,000 and 47,500 direct labour hours were budgeted.

During 20X4, actual production amounted to 52,000 direct labour hours, and overhead expenditure was $405,000.

Required

What was the under- or over-absorbed overhead for the year, and to what extent was this attributable to differences between budgeted and actual (a) overhead spending and (b) the volume of activity?

Answer

Budgeted overhead expenditure	$380,000	
Budgeted direct labour hours	47,500	
Absorption rate per direct labour hour	$8	

		$
Absorbed overhead	(52,000 × $8)	416,000
Actual overhead		405,000
Over-absorbed		11,000

	$		hours
Budgeted expenditure	380,000	Budgeted hours	47,500
Actual expenditure	405,000	Actual hours	52,000
Expenditure difference	25,000	Difference	4,500
		At $8 per hour	$36,000

There has been an over-absorption of overhead by $11,000, which means that too much overhead has been charged to the cost of production. An upward adjustment should therefore be made to profits for the period to correct the over-charging. The over-absorption is caused by a higher volume of activity than budgeted, resulting in over-absorption of $36,000, offset by higher overhead spending than budgeted of $25,000.

7 Activity-based costing

FAST FORWARD

Activity-based costing is an alternative to absorption costing. It involves the identification of the factors (**cost drivers**) which cause the costs of an organisation's major activities.

Key terms

> **Activity based costing (ABC)** is an approach to the costing and monitoring of activities which involves the tracing of resources to activities, and activities to end products or services, based upon usage measured via cost drivers.
>
> A **cost driver** is a factor that causes a change in the cost of an activity.

7.1 Traditional absorption costing: the quality of cost information

Traditional absorption costing was developed for manufacturing operations in the early 1900s, when the largest items of expense were direct labour costs. Overhead costs were comparatively low, and overhead spending was heavily influenced by direct labour activities. In such an environment, labour-hour based absorption costing provided fairly reliable and valuable information about product costs and profitability.

In a modern business environment, where advanced manufacturing technology is used, the situation is very different. The machine has replaced direct labour, and production overhead expenses are a much higher proportion of total production costs. There have also been large increases in administration and selling and marketing expenses. Direct labour may account for as little as 5% of total product costs.

There has been an increase in the cost of 'support functions' or 'service functions', such as set-up costs, production scheduling, inspection costs, the cost of logistics (transportation and storage), despatch, order handling, data processing and customer service.

However, the amount of work done in many support activities that incur overhead costs is not necessarily related to production volume, nor to direct labour hours of work. In many cases, low-volume (and possibly low-value) products make use of a large amount of resources and time in these support areas. For example:

(a)   Where order handling is a major support operation, the time and resources used in handling a small order might be almost as great, and sometimes greater, than the time and resources needed to process a large order.

(b)   Where the costs of setting up a production run are a major overhead activity, a small production run might need more set-up time and resources than a large standard production run.

(c)   Where packing and despatch are a major overhead activity, the costs of handling non-standard items for despatch might be much greater than the costs of packing and despatching standard items.

Given all these changes, it is perhaps not so surprising that traditional absorption costing information has lost most of its relevance. A system of costing that allocates overhead costs to cost items (products or services) on the basis of production volume or output level (e.g. on the basis of direct labour hours) cannot be relied on to provide a reliable or meaningful assessment of costs. Cost information needs to help a company to maintain or improve its competitive position, by showing which of its products or services are really the most profitable, and which operations are losing money. Traditional absorption costing simply does not provide this information, and something better is needed.

Activity-based costing (ABC) is a concept for overcoming the weaknesses of traditional absorption costing, by trying to attribute costs to the products or services via the activities that caused those costs to be incurred. It has an advantage over traditional costing systems because it allocates overhead costs to programmes and activities in a way that reflects the factors influencing those costs.

7.2 An ABC system in outline

To implement ABC, an organisation must first of all look at all its overhead costs, and try to *identify the main activities* that result in costs being incurred. These are the activities that use up resources. There are no standard rules as to what these major activities should be and they will differ in each organisation. The activities identified in this way need not be confined to a single department, but might be carried out in a number of different departments.

Examples of resource-consuming activities might be the processing of a customer order, procurement, quality inspection, set-up, despatch, warehousing, and so on.

Instead of collecting overhead costs for a service department or an overhead cost centre, an organisation collects the overhead costs for **activity pools** or **cost pools**. There is a separate activity pool for each major resource-consuming activity. For each activity pool, there should be a **cost driver**. A cost driver is a unit of activity that results in the consumption of resources, and so leads to costs being incurred.

Examples of cost drivers are as follows.

Activity	Cost driver
Ordering	Number of orders
Materials handling	Number of materials receipts
Production scheduling	Number of production runs (or set ups)
Despatch	Number of despatches

There are no standard rules about what the cost driver should be for a particular activity, and an organisation should select the cost driver that seems most appropriate for each of its activity pools. Cost drivers might be production-oriented, such as the production cycle time, the number of orders, the number of production runs or batches of output, the number of machine hours operated or the number of inspections. Alternatively, cost drivers might be related to the cost of providing service to customers, such as the number of changes to order specifications or the characteristics of a customer's order.

For each activity pool or cost pool, a *cost per unit of cost driver* is then calculated. The costs in an activity pool are then assigned to products and services on the basis of:

Units of cost driver × Cost per unit of cost driver.

This is similar to the absorption of overheads, using an absorption rate, in traditional costing. However, the cost driver represents the factor that has the greatest influence on the behaviour of costs in the activity pool. For example, if a particular product requires 60% of quality control inspections and there is a cost pool for inspection costs, the product should attract 60% of the total costs of quality inspections.

Suppose for example that processing customer orders is a major activity for which there is a cost pool, and that the cost driver for this activity is the number of orders processed. The total costs for the cost pool might be, say, $200,000, and the company might process 1,000 orders in the year. The cost of order processing would therefore be $200 per order. A product for which there are 80 orders in a year would be charged $16,000 for order processing costs.

7.3 Example

A company manufactures two products, P and Q. The manufacturing process is highly-automated. The following information relates to production in one year.

	Product P	Product Q
Number of units produced	500,000	20,000
Number of batches	500	200
Batch size	1,000 units	100 units
Average number of orders per batch	2	3
Direct materials cost per unit	$5	$10
Direct labour time per unit	0.05 hours	0.05 hours
Direct labour cost per hour	$10	$10
Machine hours per unit	0.08 hours	0.25 hours
Number of set-ups per batch	2	4

Annual overhead costs:

	$	Annual volume
Set-up costs	900,000	1,800 set-ups
Order processing costs	880,000	1,600 orders
Handling costs	630,000	700 batches
Other production overheads	450,000	45,000 machine hours
		26,000 direct labour hours

The total production overhead costs for the year are $2,860,000.

A system of ABC is used.

Set-up costs are charged to products on the basis of a cost per set-up.

Order processing costs are charged on the basis of a cost per order.

Handling costs are charged on the basis of a cost per batch.

Other production overheads are assigned to product costs on a machine hour basis.

The cost per unit for each cost driver is calculated as follows.

Cost pool	Total cost $	Activity level	Cost per unit of cost driver
Set-up	900,000	1,800 set-ups	$500 per set-up
Order processing	880,000	1,600 orders	$550 per order
Handling	630,000	700 batches	$900 per batch
Other costs	450,000	45,000 machine hours	$10 per m/c hour

Product costs are now calculated as follows.

Activity	Total	Product P	Product Q
Set-ups	1,800	1,000	800
Orders	1,600	1,000	600
Batches	700	500	200
Machine hours	45,000	40,000	5,000

	Total	Product P 500,000 units	Product Q 20,000 units
	$	$	$
Direct materials	2,700,000	2,500,000	200,000
Direct labour	260,000	250,000	10,000
Set-up costs	900,000	500,000	400,000
Order processing costs	880,000	550,000	330,000
Handling costs	630,000	450,000	180,000
Other overheads	450,000	400,000	50,000
Total costs	5,820,000	4,650,000	1,170,000
Cost per unit		$9.30	$58.50

If this company had used traditional absorption costing instead of ABC, the production overheads would possibly have been absorbed into production costs on a direct labour hour basis. The overhead recovery rate per direct labour hour would have been $110 per direct labour hour (2,860,000/26,000 hours). The production overhead cost for one unit of each product would have been 0.05 hours × $110 per hour = $5.50.

The costs of each product would then have been as follows.

	Product P $	Product Q $
Direct materials	5.0	10.0
Direct labour	0.5	0.5
Production overhead	5.5	5.5
	11.0	16.0
Units produced	500,000	20,000
Total cost	$5,500,000	$320,000	$5,820,000

The total production costs would have been the same as with ABC, $5,820,000, but the costs have been assigned to the two products differently. With ABC, Product Q receives a higher charge for overhead costs, because of the smaller batch sizes, the larger number of orders per batch, the larger number of set-ups per batch and the larger number of machine hours required for each unit.

7.4 ABC and traditional absorption costing compared

Companies using ABC consider it to be a method of obtaining more relevant and accurate information about the costs of products, processes, services and activities. Traditional absorption costing systems allocate overhead costs to products based on the attributes of a single activity, such as direct labour hours worked or machine hours operated. The allocation of overheads therefore varies directly with production volume. In contrast, ABC focuses on the activities required to make a product or provide a service, based on the consumption or use of those activities.

The unit costs of production are likely to be very different using ABC compared to traditional absorption costing, but this might not be the case every time. For example, the cost of constructing a cupboard might be estimated using traditional costing and ABC as follows.

Traditional absorption costing		_ABC_	
	$		$
Materials	20	Materials	20
Labour	30	Cut wood	15
Overhead	30	Paint	10
	80	Erect	20
		Inspect	15
			80

In this example, using ABC does not change the cost of the cupboard, but it shows how the resources have been consumed and the costs incurred by activities. Arguably, this provides a more useful, practical insight into the way in which costs are incurred. If the company wanted to reduce costs, traditional absorption costing data might suggest the need to reduce direct labour costs. ABC might suggest that combining the erection of the cupboard with inspection might be a way of reducing costs.

7.5 ABC and long-run variable costs

Some activity costs might be variable costs, in the sense that if the volume of activity is reduced or increased, the total costs of the activity will also fall or rise proportionately. But this may not be the case in the short-run; for example, if the cost of processing an order is estimated at $400 using ABC, the actual cost of handling an additional 10 orders is unlikely to be $4,000. This is because many overhead costs are fixed in the short term.

However, it is argued that in the longer term, all costs are variable. By focusing on activities that use up resources and so incur costs, ABC could provide useful information to help management to control overhead costs over the longer term. Traditional absorption costing cannot do this because there is no relationship between product overhead costs and the consumption of resources.

It can certainly be argued that ABC, by assigning costs to products on the basis of activities and resources consumed, provides helpful information about the economic cost of products, and which products are more profitable than others.

The concept of activity costing has been extended by some companies into budgeting methods (activity-based budgeting) and the re-engineering of business activities (activity-based management and business process re-engineering). These techniques are described later.

Exam focus point

The examiner has said that 'candidates must be aware of how and why ABC can be used effectively, not just be able to perform the simple calculations'.

A question in the December 2002 exam required a numerical comparison between product costs using ABC and the more traditional 'volume based allocation system'. It then considered the impact of the costing system used upon pricing policy, which required a discussion as to whether costs were being appropriately recovered within a particular pricing structure. ABC was examined again in December 2003, in a question requiring both calculations and discussion of the issues. In December 2004, ABC was examined with the calculation of individual product costs under ABC and production decisions to be made based on those costs. In December 2005, ABC was examined once more with a requirement to calculate individual product costs under ABC. In June 2007, candidates were asked to calculate product costs using ABC and to discuss its benefits.

7.6 Drawbacks to ABC

The main disadvantages of ABC are the cost of establishing and maintaining an ABC system, and the possible complexity of the system.

An ABC system is more expensive to set up and maintain than a traditional absorption costing system, because activities have to be monitored and measured. The system should also be reviewed regularly to ensure that there is a continuing relationship between expenditure and the activities and cost drivers that have been selected.

The analysis of activities and costs can also be taken to excessive detail, by looking at the costs of activities within broader activities. For example, purchasing activities might be a major cost item, and an ABC cost per purchase order might be calculated for the purchasing costs pool. However, purchasing activities could be analysed further, and costs established for sub-activities such as processing a purchase requisition from the warehouse department, finding a supplier for a new component or sub-assembly, putting a purchase order out to tender and chasing late deliveries from suppliers. A different cost driver could be selected for each sub-activity.

The point to note is that to prevent an ABC system from becoming too expensive to operate, it is probably necessary to keep the cost pools and cost drivers down to a fairly small and manageable number.

Question | ABC costing

A high-technology company manufactures a range of products, that includes product A and product B. Product A is made in standard batch sizes of 300 units, and product B is made in standard batch sizes of 100 units. Direct production costs and other cost information is as follows.

	Product A	Product B
Production run (size)	300 units	100 units
Direct materials cost per unit	$27.50	$40
Direct labour time per unit	0.25 hours	0.5 hours
Direct labour cost per hour	$10	$10
Number of set-ups per batch	5	2
Machine hours per unit	0.5 hours	0.5 hours

Overhead costs are as follows.

	Total annual costs	Annual volume of activity
Set-up costs	$1,500,000	2,500 set-ups
Handling costs	$1,000,000	1,000 batches (production runs)
Other production overheads	$2,000,000	200,000 machine hours

A system of ABC is used. Set-up costs are charged to products on the basis of a cost per set-up, and handling costs are charged on the basis of a cost per batch/production run. Other production overheads are absorbed on a machine hour basis.

Required

Using ABC methodology, calculate the cost per unit of product A and the cost per unit of product B.

Answer

Overhead item	Annual cost	Activity level	O'hd recovery rate
Set-up costs	$1,500,000	2,500 set-ups	$600 per set-up
Handling costs	$1,000,000	1,000 batches	$1,000 per batch
Other	$2,000,000	200,000 machine hours	$10 per m/c hour

		A		B
Batch size		300 units		100 units
		$		$
Direct materials	(300 × $27.50)	8,250	(100 × $40)	4,000
Direct labour	(300 × 0.25 × $10)	750	(100 × 0.5 × $10)	500
Set-up cost	(5 × $600)	3,000	(2 × $600)	1,200
Handling cost		1,000		1,000
Other overheads	(300 × 0.5 × $10)	1,500	(100 x 0.5 × $10)	500
Full production cost		14,500		7,200
Cost per unit		$48.33		$72.00

8 Marginal cost and marginal costing

Absorption costing is most often used for routine profit reporting and must be used for financial accounting purposes. **Marginal costing** provides better management information for planning (budgeting) and decision making.

Marginal cost is the variable cost of one unit of product or service. **Contribution,** which is an important measure in marginal costing, is the difference between sales revenue and the marginal or variable cost of sales. In marginal costing, **fixed production costs are treated as period costs** and are written off as they are incurred.

Key terms

Marginal costing is an alternative method of costing to absorption costing. In marginal costing, only variable costs are charged as a cost of sale. Sales revenue minus the variable cost of sales equals **contribution**, which is the contribution towards covering fixed costs and making a profit. Fixed costs are treated as a period cost, and are charged in full to the income statement of the accounting period in which they are incurred. Closing inventories of work in progress or finished goods are valued at marginal (variable) production cost.

Marginal cost is the cost of a unit of a product or service which would be avoided if that unit were not produced or provided. The marginal cost per unit is also called the variable cost per unit.

The marginal production cost per unit of an item usually consists of:

- direct materials
- direct labour
- variable production overheads

However, there may also be some direct production expense per unit.

Direct labour costs might be excluded from marginal costs when the work force is a given number of employees on a fixed wage or salary. Even so, it is not uncommon for direct labour to be treated as a variable cost, even when employees are paid a basic wage for a fixed working week. If in doubt, you should treat direct labour as a variable cost unless given clear indications to the contrary.

The **marginal cost of sales** consists of the marginal production cost of units sold plus the variable selling costs, which would include items such as sales commission, and possibly some variable distribution costs.

8.1 Contribution

Key term

Contribution is the difference between sales revenue and the marginal cost of sales.

Contribution is of fundamental importance in marginal costing, and the term 'contribution' is really short for 'contribution towards covering fixed overheads and making a profit'.

8.2 The principles of marginal costing

The principles of marginal costing are as follows.

(a) For any given period of time, fixed costs will be the same, for any volume of sales and production (provided that the level of activity is within the 'relevant range'). Therefore, by selling an extra item of product or service the following will happen.

- Revenue will increase by the sales value of the item sold.
- Costs will increase by the variable cost per unit.
- Profit will increase by the amount of contribution earned from the extra item.

(b) Similarly, if the volume of sales falls by one item, the profit will fall by the amount of contribution earned from the item.

(c) Profit measurement should therefore be based on an analysis of total contribution. Since fixed costs relate to a period of time, and do not change with increases or decreases in sales volume, it is misleading to charge units of sale with a share of fixed costs.

(d) When a unit of product is made, the extra costs incurred in its manufacture are the **variable production costs**. Fixed costs are unaffected, and no extra fixed costs are incurred when output is increased.

Before explaining marginal costing principles any further, it will be helpful to look at a numerical example.

8.3 Example: marginal costing principles

Bain Painkillers makes a drug called 'Relief', which has a variable production cost of $6 per unit and a sales price of $10 per unit. At the beginning of June 20X1, there were no opening inventories and production during the month was 20,000 units. Fixed costs for the month were $45,000 (production, administration, sales and distribution). There were no variable marketing costs.

Required

Calculate the contribution and profit for June 20X1, using marginal costing principles, if sales were as follows.

(a) 10,000 Reliefs
(b) 15,000 Reliefs
(c) 20,000 Reliefs

Solution

The first stage in the profit calculation must be to identify the variable cost of sales, and then the contribution. Fixed costs are deducted from the total contribution to derive the profit. All closing inventories are valued at marginal production cost ($6 per unit).

	10,000 Reliefs		15,000 Reliefs		20,000 Reliefs	
	$	$	$	$	$	$
Sales (at $10)		100,000		150,000		200,000
Opening inventory	0		0		0	
Variable production cost	120,000		120,000		120,000	
	120,000		120,000		120,000	
Less value of closing inventory (at marginal cost)	60,000		30,000		-	
Variable cost of sales		60,000		90,000		120,000
Contribution		40,000		60,000		80,000
Less fixed costs		45,000		45,000		45,000
Profit/(loss)		(5,000)		15,000		35,000
Profit/(loss) per unit		$(0.50)		$1		$1.75
Contribution per unit		$4		$4		$4

The conclusions to be drawn from this example are as follows.

(a) The **profit per unit varies** at differing levels of sales, because the average fixed overhead cost per unit changes with the volume of output and sales.

(b) The **contribution per unit is constant** at all levels of output and sales. Total contribution, which is the contribution per unit multiplied by the number of units sold, increases in direct proportion to the volume of sales.

(c) Since the **contribution per unit does not change**, the most effective way of calculating the expected profit at any level of output and sales would be as follows.

(i) First calculate the total contribution.

(ii) Then deduct fixed costs as a period charge in order to find the profit.

(d) In our example the expected profit from the sale of 17,000 Reliefs would be as follows.

	$
Total contribution (17,000 × $4)	68,000
Less fixed costs	45,000
Profit	23,000

If total contribution **exceeds fixed costs**, a profit is made.

If total contribution **exactly equals fixed costs**, no profit and no loss is made. This is known as the **breakeven point**.

If total contribution is **less than fixed costs**, there will be a loss.

Question
Marginal costing

Wong makes two products, the Ping and the Pong. Information relating to each of these products for August 20X1 is as follows.

	Ping	Pong
Opening inventory	nil	nil
Production (units)	15,000	6,000
Sales (units)	10,000	5,000
Sales price per unit	$20	$30
Unit costs	$	$
Direct materials	8	14
Direct labour	4	2
Variable production overhead	2	1
Variable sales overhead	2	3

Fixed costs for the month	$
Production costs	40,000
Administration costs	15,000
Sales and distribution costs	25,000

Required

(a) Using marginal costing principles, calculate the profit in August 20X1.

(b) Calculate the profit if sales had been 15,000 units of Ping and 6,000 units of Pong.

Answer

(a)

	$
Contribution from Pings (unit contribution = $20 – $(8 + 4 + 2 + 2) = $4 × 10,000)	40,000
Contribution from Pongs (unit contribution = $30 – $(14 + 2 + 1 + 3) = $10 × 5,000)	50,000
Total contribution	90,000
Fixed costs for the period ($40,000 + $15,000 + $25,000)	80,000
Profit	10,000

(b)   At a higher volume of sales, profit would be as follows.

	$
Contribution from sales of 15,000 Pings (× $4)	60,000
Contribution from sales of 6,000 Pongs (× $10)	60,000
Total contribution	120,000
Less fixed costs	80,000
Profit	40,000

8.4 The value of marginal costing

The main arguments in favour of marginal costing are that:

(a)   it recognises the distinction between fixed costs and variable costs, and the fact that as activity levels rise, only variable costs, not fixed costs, increase

(b)   it recognises that fixed costs are time-related costs ('period costs') and it is therefore appropriate to charge them in full as a cost to the period in which they arise

Recognition of the distinction between fixed and variable costs has some value in profit measurement. Since fixed costs are not absorbed into product costs, marginal costing avoids the need to apply arbitrary bases of apportionment of overheads, or arbitrary bases for overhead absorption. Since fixed costs are a constant amount in each time period, profitability depends essentially on the amount of contribution earned.

Recognition of the distinction between fixed and variable costs, and particularly between fixed and variable overheads, assists managers to prepare more accurate budgets. Marginal costing techniques, even when not used for measuring historical profits, is widely-used in budgeting.

9 Conclusion: costing methods

This chapter has described three costing techniques for measuring product costs and profitability. A company might use any of these techniques for measuring profitability, and for comparing actual profits against the budget.

In addition, marginal costing techniques are applied for budgeting and management decision-making. An activity-based approach might also be adopted for budgeting ('activity-based budgeting').

The chapters that follow on budgeting and decision-making, performance measurement and performance management will call for some understanding of these costing methods.

Key learning points

- Costing systems are used to measure the cost of products, services and activities, and to establish their profitability. Costs can be measured as the sum of **direct costs** and **indirect costs** (overheads). Costs may also be measured as the sum of variable costs and fixed costs.

- Costs that are partly-fixed and partly-variable can be segregated into their fixed cost and variable cost elements using the **high-low method**.

- **Overhead** is the cost incurred in the course of making a product, providing a service or running a department, but which cannot be traced directly and in full to the product, service or department. The main groupings of overhead costs are production overhead, administration overhead, selling and distribution overhead.

- Overheads may be dealt with by **absorption** costing, **activity-based** costing or **marginal** costing.

- The main reasons for using absorption costing are for inventory valuations, pricing decisions and establishing the profitability of different products.

- **Allocation, apportionment** and **absorption** are the three stages of calculating the costs of overheads to be charged to manufactured output.

- **Apportionment** is a procedure whereby indirect costs (overheads) are spread fairly between cost centres.

- Overhead absorption is the process whereby costs of cost centres are added to unit, job or process costs. Overhead absorption is sometimes called **overhead recovery.**

- **Predetermined overhead absorption** rates are normally used, based on budgeted figures.

- The 'actual' full cost of production is therefore made up of the following.

    - Direct materials
    - Direct labour
    - Direct expenses
    - Overheads (based on the predetermined overhead absorption rate)

- **Under-** or **over-absorption** of overheads occurs because the predetermined overhead absorption rates are based on forecasts (estimates).

- If an organisation has estimated fixed and variable production overheads, it may calculate a **separate absorption rate** for each.

- **Activity-based costing** is an alternative to absorption costing. It involves the identification of the factors (**cost drivers**) which cause the costs of an organisation's major activities.

- **Absorption costing** is most often used for routine profit reporting and must be used for financial accounting purposes. **Marginal costing** provides better management information for planning (budgeting) and decision making.

- **Marginal cost** is the variable cost of one unit of product or service. **Contribution,** which is an important measure in marginal costing, is the difference between sales revenue and the marginal or variable cost of sales. In marginal costing, **fixed production costs are treated as period costs** and are written off as they are incurred.

Quick quiz

1 Is a direct cost also a variable cost, and is a variable cost also a direct cost?
2 What is the objective of absorption costing?
3 What is overhead apportionment?
4 In what circumstances might under- or over-absorption of overheads occur?
5 How does activity-based costing differ from absorption costing?
6 In marginal costing, what are period costs?
7 What is contribution?

Answers to quick quiz

1 A direct cost might be a fixed cost. However, it is usual in costing to treat direct costs as variable. Variable costs include direct costs, but some indirect costs are also variable (variable overheads).

2 To add a fair share of overhead costs to cost units (products or services).

3 A stage in the overhead absorption process. Costs that cannot be directly allocated to a cost centre are shared (apportioned) between cost centres on a fair basis.

4 Whenever overhead absorption rates are predetermined, and based on the budget for overhead expenditure and volume of activity. Actual overhead expenditure will differ from the overhead costs absorbed into production costs because of differences between actual and budgeted overhead expenditure, and between actual and budgeted activity levels.

5 By recognising that overhead costs are 'driven' by factors other than direct labour hours or machine hours in the production department. Overheads are therefore added to product costs on the basis of the utilisation of these 'cost drivers'.

6 Fixed costs.

7 Contribution is the difference between sales revenue and the marginal cost (variable cost) of sales.

Planning and decision making

3

Budgeting

Introduction

Now that you know that an essential part of performance management is to establish plans for the future, we start our study of planning by looking at the preparation of traditional budgets, plans expressed in money terms for the forthcoming period.

Learning objectives

On completion of this chapter you will be able to:

Syllabus reference

- describe the various functions that a budget performs in an organisation   3
- explain the budget preparation timetable   3
- prepare budgets for manufacturing and sales together with other functional budgets, and a budgeted income statement   3
- understand how a budget is prepared for service organisations   3
- prepare a cash budget   3
- understand the difference between a fixed budget and flexible budget, and prepare a flexible budget   3
- understand the use of computers in budgeting   3

1 The functions of a budget

FAST FORWARD

A **budget** is a plan for an entire organisation, typically for a one-year period, and covering all the activities of the organisation. The overall budget is often referred to as the master budget. It is usually expressed in financial terms, partly because 'money' is a common language for business activities and partly because a major objective of any organisation is a financial objective (eg profits in the case of commercial organisations and value for money in the case of not-for-profit organisations).

The functions of a **system of budgeting** are as follows.

- To ensure the achievement of the organisation's objectives
- To compel planning
- To communicate ideas and plans
- To co-ordinate activities
- To provide a framework for responsibility accounting
- To establish a system of control ('budgetary control')
- To motivate employees to improve their performance

Key term

A **budget** is an organisation's plan for a forthcoming period, expressed in quantitative terms.

Except for capital expenditure budgets, the budget period is commonly the accounting year (sub-divided into 12 monthly control periods or 13 four-week control periods).

The functions of a budget are as follows.

Function	Detail
Ensure the achievement of the organisation's objectives	A budget sets quantified targets for achievement within the timescale of the budget plan. These targets should be consistent with the organisation's strategic objectives. Budgeting is therefore a means of ensuring that strategic objectives are pursued.
Compel planning	Budgeting **forces management to look ahead**, and plan for the future. Potential problems might be anticipated, and potential opportunities exploited, that might otherwise be missed if a formal planning process did not take place.
Communicate ideas and plans	Budgeting provides a plan of action for the entire organisation, and for communicating targets for achievement. The communication of a budget should ensure that each person affected by the plans is aware of what he or she is supposed to be doing. Communication might be one-way, with managers giving orders to subordinates, or there might be a two-way dialogue.

Function	Detail
Co-ordinate activities	The activities of different departments need to be **co-ordinated** to ensure maximum integration of effort towards **common goals**. This implies, for example, that the purchasing department should base its budget on production requirements and that the production budget should in turn be based on sales expectations.
Provide a framework for responsibility accounting	Budgets require that managers of budget centres are made **responsible** for the achievement of budget targets for the operations under their personal control.
Establish a system of control	Control over actual performance is provided by the comparisons of **actual results against the budget** plan. Departures from budget can then be **investigated** and the reasons for the departures established. Where appropriate, remedial action can be taken.
Motivate employees to improve their performance	The interest and commitment of employees can be retained if there is a system that lets them participate in the planning process and lets them know how well or badly they are performing. The identification of controllable reasons for departures from budget with managers responsible provides an **incentive for improving future performance**.

1.1 Responsibility for the preparation of budgets

Managers responsible for preparing budgets should ideally be the managers who are responsible for implementing the budget plan. For example, the sales manager should draft the sales budget and selling overhead cost centre budget and the purchasing manager should draft the material purchases budget.

Exam focus point

You may well encounter a numerical question on budgeting in the exam, requiring you to produce a detailed budget. However, in the June 2002 paper there was a question on the advantages and drawbacks of budgeting, requiring you to suggest an appropriate budgeting system in a given situation. The June 2003 and December 2007 exams were more traditional budget preparation questions. These contrast with the June 2007 paper which looked at traditional budgeting problems and how to overcome them. The examiner noted on this question the obvious, but frequently ignored, point that candidates must answer the question set and not merely regurgitate lists they have learnt.

2 The budget preparation timetable

FAST FORWARD

The budget preparation process is as follows.

- Communicating details of the budget policy and budget guidelines.
- Determining the factor(s) that restrict output
- Preparation of the sales budget
- Initial preparation of budgets
- Negotiation of budgets with superiors
- Co-ordination and review of budgets
- Final acceptance of the budgets
- Budget review

The **principal budget factor** should be identified at the beginning of the budgetary process, and the budget for this is prepared before all the others.

The procedures involved in preparing a budget will differ from organisation to organisation, but the step-by-step approach described here is indicative of the steps followed by many organisations. The preparation of a budget may take weeks, possibly months, and the management committee responsible for co-ordinating and approving the budget (the 'budget committee') may meet several times before an organisation's budget is finally agreed.

Step 1   **Communicating details of the budget policy and budget guidelines**
The long-term plan is the starting point for the preparation of the annual budget. Managers responsible for preparing the budget must be aware of how their plans for the budget period should be consistent with the organisation's objectives and strategies. For example, if the organisation's current strategy calls for a more aggressive pricing policy, the budget must take this into account. Managers should also be provided with important guidelines for wage rate increases, changes in productivity and so on, as well as information about industry demand and output.

Step 2   **Determining the factor that restricts output**

Key term

> The **principal budget factor** (also known as the **key budget factor** or **limiting budget factor**) is the factor that sets a limit on what the organisation can do within the budget period. Activity might be restricted by limited sales demand, in which case sales are the limiting factor. Alternatively, activity levels may be restricted by a shortage of a key resource, such as skilled labour, capital equipment or cash.

For example, suppose that a company's sales department estimates that it could sell 1,000 units of product X, which would require 5,000 hours of grade A labour to produce. If there are no units of product X already in inventory, and only 4,000 hours of grade A labour available in the budget period, then the company would be unable to sell 1,000 units of X because of the shortage of labour hours. Grade A labour would be a limiting budget factor, and the company's management must choose one of the following options.

- Reduce budgeted sales by 20%.
- Try to increase the availability of grade A labour by 1,000 hours (25%) by recruitment or overtime working.
- Try to sub-contract the production of 1,000 units to another manufacturer at a cost which will generate a profit on the transaction.

Step 3   **Prepare the sales budget**
In most organisations the principal budget factor is sales demand: a company is usually restricted from making and selling more of its products because there would be no sales demand for the increased output at a price which would be acceptable/profitable to the company. The sales budget is therefore normally the primary budget from which the majority of the other 'functional' budgets are derived.

Step 4   **Initial preparation of budgets**
After the sales budget has been drafted, other functional budgets can be prepared. The functional budgets for a manufacturing organisation are likely to be as follows.

Budget	Detail
Finished goods inventory budget	Decides the planned increase or decrease in inventory levels of finished goods.
Production budget	Stated in units of each product and is calculated as the sales budget in units plus the budgeted increase in finished goods inventory or minus the budgeted decrease in finished goods inventories.

Budget	Detail
Budgets of resources for production	**Materials usage budget.** This is a budget for the quantities of materials and components required for production. It is stated in quantities and cost for each type of material used. It should take into account any budgeted losses or materials wastage in production.
	Machine utilisation budget. This is the budget for the operating hours required on each machine or group of machines.
	Labour budget or wages budget. This is a budget for the quantities of direct labour needed to achieve the production budget. It will be expressed in hours for each grade of labour and in terms of cost. It should take into account any budgeted idle time.
Overhead cost budgets	**Production overheads**
	Administration overheads
	Selling and distribution overheads
	Research and development department overheads
Raw materials inventory budget	Decides the planned increase or decrease of the level of inventories of raw materials.
Raw materials purchase budget	Can be prepared in quantities and value for each type of material purchased. This budget can be prepared once the raw material usage requirements are known, and a decision has been taken on planned increases or decreases in the levels of raw materials inventory.
Overhead absorption rate	When the organisation uses absorption costing, predetermined overhead absorption rates can be calculated once the production budget and the overhead cost centre budgets have been prepared.

Step 5 **Negotiation of budgets with superiors**
Budgets are prepared in draft form, discussed with senior managers, and (usually) revised. A functional budget might go through several drafts until it is eventually approved.

Step 6 **Co-ordination of budgets**
It is unlikely that the above steps will be problem-free. The functional budgets must be reviewed in relation to one another. Such a review may indicate that some budgets are out of balance with others and need modifying. Inconsistencies should be identified by a senior manager and brought to the attention of the manager or managers concerned, with a request to revise the budget. The revision of one budget may lead to the revision of all budgets.

Step 7 **Final acceptance of the budget**
When all the budgets are in harmony with one another they are summarised into a master budget consisting of a budgeted income statement, budgeted statement of financial position and cash budget.

Step 8 **Budget review**
The budgeting process does not stop once the budgets have been agreed. Actual results should be compared on a regular basis with the budgeted results. The frequency with which such comparisons are made depends very much on the organisation's circumstances and the sophistication of its control systems but it should occur at least monthly. Management should receive a report detailing the differences and should investigate the reasons for the differences. If adverse differences are within the control of management, corrective action should be taken to bring the reasons for the difference under control and to ensure that such inefficiencies do not occur in the future.

3 Preparing functional budgets

FAST FORWARD

Once prepared, the **functional budgets** must be reviewed to ensure they are consistent with one another. Functional budgets are brought together to prepare a budgeted income statement for the budget period.

Key term

Functional (or **departmental**) **budgets** are the budgets for the various functions and departments of an organisation. They include production budgets, marketing budgets, sales budgets, personnel budgets, purchasing budgets and research and development budgets.

In this section, we shall look at the preparation of a number of functional budgets for a manufacturing organisation.

3.1 Production budget

The **production budget** is a plan for the **quantities** and **costs** for **each product** and product group. It must tie in with the sales and finished goods inventory budgets.

Once the production budget has been finalised, the labour, materials and machine budgets can be drawn up. These budgets will be based on budgeted activity levels, existing inventory positions and projected labour and material costs.

3.2 Example: the preparation of the production budget and direct labour budget

Pearson manufactures two products, P and L, and is preparing its budget for 20X3. Both products are made by the same grade of labour, grade G. The company currently holds 800 units of P and 1,200 units of L in inventory, but 250 of these units of L have just been discovered to have deteriorated in quality, and must therefore be scrapped. Budgeted sales of P are 3,000 units and budgeted sales of L 4,000 units. The company wishes to maintain finished goods inventories at a level equal to three months' sales.

Grade G labour was originally expected to produce one unit of P in two hours and one unit of L in three hours, at an hourly rate of $5.50 per hour. In discussions with trade union negotiators, however, it has been agreed that the hourly wage rate should be raised by 50c per hour, provided that the times to produce P and L are reduced by 20%.

Required

Prepare the production budget and direct labour budget for 20X3.

Solution

The expected time to produce a unit of product P will now be 80% of 2 hours = 1.6 hours, and the time for a unit of product L will be 2.4 hours. The hourly wage rate will be $6, so that the direct labour cost will be $9.60 for P and $14.40 for L (thus achieving a saving for the company of $1.40 per unit of P produced and $2.10 per unit of L).

(a)   *Production budget*

	Product P		Product L	
	Units	Units	Units	Units
Budgeted sales		3,000		4,000
Closing inventories				
(3/12 of 3,000)	750	(3/12 of 4,000)	1,000	
Opening inventories (minus				
inventories scrapped)	800		950	
(Decrease)/increase in inventories		(50)		50
Production		2,950		4,050

(b)   *Direct labour budget*

	Grade G Hours	Cost $
2,950 units of product P	4,720	28,320
4,050 units of product L	9,720	58,320
Total	14,440	86,640

It is assumed that there will be no idle time among grade G labour which, if it existed, would have to be paid for at the rate of $6 per hour.

3.3 Labour budget

A useful concept in budgeting for labour requirements is the standard hour.

> A **standard hour** is the quantity of work achievable at standard performance (the standard rate of efficiency), expressed in terms of a standard unit of work done in a standard period of time.

Budgeted output of different products or jobs in a period can be converted into standard hours of production, and a labour budget constructed accordingly.

Standard hours are particularly useful when management wants to monitor the production levels of a variety of dissimilar units. For example product A may take five hours to produce and product B, seven hours. If four units of each product are produced, instead of saying that total output is eight units, we could state the production level as:
(4 × 5) + (4 × 7) standard hours = 48 standard hours.

3.4 Example: direct labour budget based on standard hours

Canaervon manufactures a single product, the Close, with a single grade of labour. Its sales budget and finished goods inventory budget for month 3 are as follows.

	Units
Sales	700
Opening inventories, finished goods	50
Closing inventories, finished goods	70

The goods are inspected only when production work is completed, and it is budgeted that 10% of finished work will be scrapped.

The standard direct labour hour content of the Close is three hours. The budgeted productivity ratio for direct labour is only 80% (which means that labour is only working at 80% efficiency).

The company employs 18 direct operatives, who are expected to average 144 working hours each in month 3.

Required

(a)   Prepare a production budget.
(b)   Prepare a direct labour budget.
(c)   Comment on the problem that your direct labour budget reveals, and suggest how this problem might be overcome.

Solution

(a)   *Production budget*

	Units
Sales	700
Add closing inventory	70
	770
Less opening inventory	50
Production required of 'good' output	720

Wastage rate 10%

Total production required $\frac{720}{90} \times 100$ 800

(* Note that the required adjustment is 100/90, not 110/100, since the waste is assumed to be 10% of total production, not 10% of good production.)

(b) Now we can prepare the direct labour budget.

Standard hours per unit	3
Total standard hours required = 800 units × 3 hours	2,400 hours
Productivity ratio	80%

Actual hours required $\frac{\text{Standard hours}}{\text{Productivity}}$ = 3,000 hours

(c) If we look at the direct labour budget against the information provided, we can identify the problem.

	Hours
Budgeted hours available (18 operatives × 144 hours)	2,592
Actual hours required	3,000
Shortfall in labour hours	408

The (draft) budget indicates that there will not be enough direct labour hours to meet the production requirements. This problem might be overcome in one, or a combination, of the following ways.

- Reduce the closing inventory requirement below 70 units. This would reduce the number of production units required.
- Persuade the workforce to do some overtime working.
- Perhaps recruit more direct labour if long-term prospects are for higher production volumes.
- Discuss with the workforce (or their union representatives) the following possibilities.
  - Improve the productivity ratio, and so reduce the number of hours required to produce the output.
  - If possible, reduce the wastage rate below 10%.

 Question   **Direct labour budget**

Guild manufactures three products, X, Y and Z. The direct labour requirements for manufacturing these products are as follows.

	Product X per unit	Product Y per unit	Product Z per unit
Grade I labour	2.5 hours	1.5 hours	3.25 hours
Grade II labour	1.75 hours	2.75 hours	2.5 hours

Budgeted production for 20X4 is to make 7,000 units of X, 12,000 units of Y and 5,000 units of Z.

Grade I labour is paid $15 an hour and Grade II labour is paid $12 an hour.

Required

Prepare a direct labour budget, in hours and cost, for the year 20X4.

Product	units		Grade I hours		Grade II hours	Total
X	7,000	(x 2.5)	17,500	(x 1.75)	12,250	
Y	12,000	(x 1.5)	18,000	(x 2.75)	33,000	
Z	5,000	(x 3.25)	16,250	(x 2.5)	12,500	
			51,750		57,750	
Cost per hr			$15		$12	
Total cost			$776,250		$693,000	$1,469,250

3.5 Material purchases budget

A materials purchases budget is a budget for the quantities of materials and components to be purchased during the budget period, and their cost. The budget should be based on materials usage requirements, and any planned increase or decrease in materials inventory levels.

Question   **Material purchases budget**

Taylors manufactures two products, W and S, which use the same raw materials, R and T. One unit of W uses 3 litres of R and 4 kilograms of T. One unit of S uses 5 litres of R and 2 kilograms of T. A litre of R is expected to cost $3 and a kilogram of T $7.

Budgeted sales for 20X2 are 8,000 units of W and 6,000 units of S; finished goods in inventory at 1 January 20X2 are 1,500 units of W and 300 units of S, and the company plans to hold inventories of 600 units of each product at 31 December 20X2.

Inventories of raw material are 6,000 litres of R and 2,800 kilograms of T at 1 January, and the company plans to hold 5,000 litres and 3,500 kilograms respectively at 31 December 20X2.

The warehouse and stores managers have suggested that a provision should be made for damages and deterioration of items held in store, as follows.

Product W :   loss of 50 units
Product S :   loss of 100 units
Material R :   loss of 500 litres
Material T :   loss of 200 kilograms

Required

Prepare a material purchases budget for the year 20X2.

Answer

To calculate material purchase requirements, it is first of all necessary to calculate the budgeted production volumes and material usage requirements.

	Product W		Product S	
	Units	Units	Units	Units
Sales		8,000		6,000
Provision for losses		50		100
Closing inventory	600		600	
Opening inventory	1,500		300	
(Decrease)/increase in inventory		(900)		300
Production budget		7,150		6,400

	Material R		Material T	
	Litres	Litres	Kg	Kg
Usage requirements				
To produce 7,150 units of W		21,450		28,600
To produce 6,400 units of S		32,000		12,800
Usage budget		53,450		41,400
Provision for losses		500		200
		53,950		41,600
Closing inventory	5,000		3,500	
Opening inventory	6,000		2,800	
(Decrease)/increase in inventory		(1,000)		700
Material purchases budget		52,950		42,300
Cost per unit		$3 per litre		$7 per kg
Cost of material purchases		$158,850		$296,100
Total purchases cost			$454,950	

Exam focus point

> The preparation of a material usage budget and a material purchases budget was examined in December 2005.

3.6 Budgets for departments not involved in manufacturing

Budgets are also prepared for those departments and functions not involved directly in manufacturing. An organisation may therefore prepare budgets for some 'production overhead' departments, such as the warehouse, repairs and maintenance unit, production planning unit, and so on. Budgets are also required for activities outside production, such as an administration budget, a marketing budget, a sales overhead budget (advertising budget, sales labour budget and so on), and a research and development budget.

The example below shows a typical marketing cost budget. Notice that only the selling and agency commission varies directly with the level of sales.

ABC: MARKETING COST BUDGET FOR THE YEAR ENDED 31 MAY 20X4

	$'000
Description/detail of cost items	
Salaries and wages of marketing staff	X
Advertising expenses	X
Travelling and distribution costs	X
Market research activities	X
Promotional activities and marketing relations	X
Selling and agency commission ($2^1/2$% of sales)	X
	X

3.7 Co-ordination of functional budgets

It is vital that the functional budgets are prepared in the correct order (for example, the material usage budget should be prepared after the production budget) and that the **overall process is co-ordinated** to ensure that the budgets are all in balance with each other. There is little point in the material usage budget being based on a budgeted production level of 10,000 units if the budgeted production level specified in the production budget is 15,000 units.

3.8 Example: building up the budget

Here is a fairly extensive example of how functional budgets build up, and lead to the preparation of a budgeted income statement. Check the figures carefully, to make sure that you understand how they are all obtained.

Plug Engineering produces two products, N and V. The budget for the forthcoming year to 31 March 20X8 is to be prepared. The sales director has estimated the following.

			N	V
(a)	(i)	Demand for the company's products	3,600 units	4,800 units
	(ii)	Selling price per unit	$90	$108
	(iii)	Closing inventory of finished products at 31 March 20X8	400 units	200 units
	(iv)	Opening inventory of finished products at 1 April 20X7	NIL	NIL

(b) (i) Amount of plant capacity required for each unit of product

	N	V
Machining	15 min	24 min
Assembling	12 min	18 min

(ii) Raw material content per unit of each product

	N	V
Material A	1.5 kilos	0.5 kilos
Material B	2.0 kilos	4.0 kilos

(iii)	Direct labour hours required per unit of each product	6 hours	9 hours

(c) Raw materials

		Material A	Material B
(i)	Closing inventory requirement in kilos at 31 March 20X8	600	1,000
(ii)	Opening inventory at 1 April 20X7 in kilos	1,100	6,000
(iii)	Opening inventory at 1 April 20X7, in $	$1,650	$6,000
(iv)	Budgeted cost of raw materials per kilo	$1.50	$1.00

(d) *Direct labour*

The standard wage rate of direct labour is $6.60 per hour.

(e) *Production overhead*

Production overhead is absorbed on the basis of machining hours, with separate absorption rates for each department. The following overheads are anticipated in the production cost centre budgets.

	Machining department $	Assembling department $
Supervisors' salaries	10,000	9,150
Power	4,400	2,000
Maintenance and running costs	2,100	2,000
Consumables	3,400	500
General expenses	19,600	5,000
	39,500	18,650

Depreciation is taken at 5% straight line on plant and equipment. A machine costing the company $20,000 is due to be installed on 1 October 20X7 in the machining department, which already has machinery installed to the value of $100,000 (at cost). Assembly has machinery that cost $87,000.

(f) *Selling and administration expenses*

	$
Sales commissions and salaries	44,300
Travelling and distribution	33,500
Office salaries	40,100
General administration expenses	32,500
	150,400

(g) There is no opening or closing work in progress and inflation should be ignored.

Required

Prepare the following for the year ended 31 March 20X8 for Plug Engineering.

(a) Sales budget
(b) Production budget (in quantities)
(c) Plant utilisation budget
(d) Direct materials usage budget

(e) Direct labour budget
(f) Factory overhead budget
(g) Computation of the factory cost per unit for each product
(h) Direct materials purchases budget
(i) Cost of goods sold budget
(j) A budgeted income statement

Solution

(a) *Sales budget*

Product	Market demand Units	Selling price $	Sales value $
N	3,600	90.00	324,000
V	4,800	108.00	578,400
			842,400

(b) *Production budget*

	N Units	V Units
Sales requirement	3,600	4,800
Increase in finished goods inventory	400	200
Production requirement	4,000	5,000

(c) *Plant utilisation budget*

Product	Units	Machining Hours per unit	Total hours	Assembling Hours per unit	Total hours
N	4,000	0.25	1,000	0.20	800
V	5,000	0.40	2,000	0.30	1,500
			3,000		2,300

(d) *Direct materials usage budget*

	Material A kg	Material B kg
Required for production:		
N: 4,000 × 1.5 kilos	6,000	-
4,000 × 2.0 kilos	–	8,000
V: 5,000 × 0.5 kilos	2,500	–
5,000 × 4.0 kilos	–	20,000
Material usage	8,500	28,000
Unit cost	$1.50 per kilo	$1.00 per kilo
Cost of materials used	$12,750	$28,000

(e) *Direct labour budget*

Product	Production Units	Hours required per unit	Total hours	Rate per hour $	Cost $
N	4,000	6	24,000	6.60	158,400
V	5,000	9	45,000	6.60	297,000
			Total direct wages		455,400

(f) *Production overhead budget*

	Machining dept $	Assembling dept $
Production overhead allocated and apportioned		
(excluding depreciation)	39,500	18,650
Depreciation costs		
(i) Existing plant		
(5% of $100,000 in machining)	5,000	
(5% of $87,000 in assembly)		4,350

			Product N	Product V
(ii)	Proposed plant (5% of 6/12 × $20,000)		500	
			45,000	23,000
	Total machine hours (see (c))		3,000 hrs	2,300 hrs
	Absorption rate per machine hour		$15	$10

(g) *Cost of finished goods*

			Product N		Product V
			$		$
Direct material	A	1.5 kg × $1.50	2.25	0.5 kg × $1.50	0.75
	B	2.0 kg × $1.00	2.00	4.0 kg × $1.00	4.00
Direct labour		6 hrs × $6.60	39.60	9 hrs × $6.60	59.40
Production overhead					
Machining department		15 mins at $15 per hr	3.75	24 min at $15 per hr	6.00
Assembling department		12 mins at $10 per hr	2.00	18 mins at $10 per hr	3.00
Production cost per unit			49.60		73.15

(h) *Direct material purchases budget*

	A	B
	kg	kg
Closing inventory required	600	1,000
Production requirements	8,500	28,000
	9,100	29,000
Less opening inventory	1,100	6,000
Purchase requirements	8,000	23,000
Cost per unit	$1.50	$1.00
Purchase costs	$12,000	$23,000

(i) *Cost of goods sold budget*

Product	Sales	Cost per unit	Cost of sales
	Units	$	$
N	3,600	49.60	178,560
V	4,800	73.15	351,120
			529,680

(j) Budgeted income statement for year to 31 March 20X8

	Product N	Product V	Total
	$	$	$
Sales	324,000	518,400	842,400
Less cost of sales	178,560	351,120	529,680
Gross profit	145,440	167,280	312,720
Less selling and administration			150,400
Net profit			162,320

Note. There will be no under-/over-absorbed production overhead in the **budgeted** income statement.

4 Budgets for service organisations

The numerical examples in this chapter have shown how budgets are prepared for manufacturing organisations. A similar approach to budgeting is taken by service organisations, although the functional budgets that are prepared will depend on the nature of the services provided by the organisation. There will inevitably be differences in the budgets for a retail organisation, a software company, a provider of electricity, a newspaper publisher or television company and a firm of accountants.

The basic principles in budgeting, however, are the same in service organisations as in manufacturing organisations.

(a) prepare a budget for sales

(b)   prepare a budget of the resources required (materials and supplies, labour, other expenses) to achieve the sales budget

(c)   construct a budgeted income statement from these functional budgets

(d)   prepare a cash budget (see below)

5 Cash budgets

Cash budgets show the expected receipts and payments during a budget period and are a vital management control tool.

Key term

A **cash budget** is a detailed budget of cash inflows and outflows incorporating revenue items (cash received and spent for operational purposes), capital items (capital expenditure, loan repayments, etc) and other items such as dividend payments.

A cash budget is a statement in which estimated future cash receipts and payments are tabulated in such a way as to show the forecast cash balance of a business at defined intervals. For example, in December 20X2 an accounts department might wish to estimate the cash position of the business during the three following months, January to March 20X3. A cash budget might be drawn up in the following format.

	Jan $	Feb $	Mar $
Estimated cash receipts			
From credit customers	14,000	16,500	17,000
From cash sales	3,000	4,000	4,500
Proceeds on disposal of non-current assets		2,200	
Total cash receipts	17,000	22,700	21,500
Estimated cash payments			
To suppliers of goods	8,000	7,800	10,500
To employees (wages)	3,000	3,500	3,500
Purchase of non-current assets		16,000	
Rent and rates			1,000
Other overheads	1,200	1,200	1,200
Repayment of loan	2,500		
	14,700	28,500	16,200
Net surplus/(deficit) for month	2,300	(5,800)	5,300
Opening cash balance	1,200	3,500	(2,300)
Closing cash balance	3,500	(2,300)	3,000

In this example, the accounts department has calculated that the cash balance at the beginning of the budget period, 1 January, will be $1,200. Estimates have been made of the cash that is likely to be received by the business (from cash and credit sales, and from a planned disposal of non-current assets in February). Similar estimates have been made of cash due to be paid out by the business (payments to suppliers and employees, payments for rent, rates and other overheads, payment for a planned purchase of non-current assets in February and a loan repayment due in January).

From these estimates of cash receipts and payments, it is a simple step to calculate any excess of cash receipts over cash payments in each month. In some months cash payments may exceed cash receipts and there will be a deficit for the month; this occurs during February in the above example because of the large investment in non-current assets in that month.

The last part of the cash budget shows how the business's estimated cash balance can then be rolled along from month to month. Starting with the opening balance of $1,200 at 1 January, a cash surplus of $2,300 is generated in January. This leads to a closing January balance of $3,500, which becomes the opening balance for February. The deficit of $5,800 in February throws the business's cash position into overdraft and the overdrawn balance of $2,300 becomes the opening balance for March. Finally, the cash surplus of $5,300 in March leaves the business with a favourable cash position of $3,000 at the end of the budget period.

5.1 The usefulness of cash budgets

The cash budget is an important part of the 'master budget' for an organisation. A commercial organisation must make a profit, but at the same time it needs to ensure that it has sufficient cash to meet its liabilities to pay what it owes. Profits and cash flow are not the same thing.

Preparation of the cash budget can lead to a modification of the other budgets (for sales and production, or capital expenditure) if it shows that there are insufficient cash resources to finance the planned operations.

The cash budget can also give management an indication of potential 'liquidity' problems that could arise and allows them the opportunity to take action to avoid such problems. A cash budget can show four positions. Management will need to take appropriate action depending on the potential position.

Cash position	Appropriate management action
Short-term cash surplus	Pay creditors early to obtain early settlement discount
	Attempt to increase sales by increasing receivables and inventories
	Make short-term investments (eg put cash on deposit)
Short-term cash deficit	Increase payables, ie take longer credit before paying suppliers
	Reduce receivables, ie chase debtors for earlier or prompt payment
	Arrange a bank overdraft
Long-term cash surplus	Make long-term investments
	Replace/update non-current assets
	Consider a special dividend payment to shareholders
Long-term cash deficit	As a matter of urgency, consider the profitability of each part of the organisation's operations. An organisation that foresees a *long-term* cash deficit is likely to be unprofitable
	Raise long-term finance (such as via issue of share capital)
	Consider shutdown/disinvestment opportunities

Exam focus point

> A cash budgeting question in an examination could ask you to recommend appropriate action for management to take once you have prepared the cash budget. Ensure your advice takes account both of whether there is a surplus or deficit and whether the position is long- or short-term. Also your advice should consider the particular situation of the organisation for which the cash budget has been prepared. Exactly this type of question was set in December 2004.

5.2 What to include in a cash budget

A cash budget shows the **expected receipts of cash and payments of cash** during a budget period.

Receipts of cash may come from one or more of the following.

- Cash sales
- Payments by debtors (credit sales)
- The sale of non-current assets
- The issue of new shares or loan stock and less formalised loans
- The receipt of interest and dividends from investments outside the business

Although all of these receipts would affect a cash budget, some of them would not appear in the income statement.

(a) The issue of new shares or loan stock is an item in the statement of financial position.

(b) The cash received from an asset affects the statement of financial position, and the profit or loss on the sale of an asset, which appears in the income statement, is not the cash received but the difference between cash received and the written-down value of the asset at the time of sale.

Payments of cash may be for one or more of the following.

- Purchase of inventories
- Payroll costs or other expenses
- Purchase of capital items
- Payment of interest, dividends or taxation

Not all cash payments are income statement items. For example, payments for the purchase of capital equipment and the payment of sales tax are not items that appear in the income statement.

There are several reasons why the **profit or loss made by an organisation during an accounting period does not reflect its cash flow position.**

- Not all cash receipts affect income as reported in the income statement.
- Not all cash payments affect expenditure as reported in the income statement.
- Some costs in the income statement such as the depreciation of non-current assets **are not cash items** but are costs derived from accounting conventions.
- The **timing of cash receipts and payments** may not coincide with the recording of income statement transactions. For example, a sale might be made on credit in November, and the customer might not pay until February. The sale is treated as an income statement item in November, but it only becomes a cash flow in February, three months later. Similarly, a company might buy an item for re-sale in March and pay for it in April, but the item might not be re-sold (for cash) until July. The cash payment would be in April, but the item will not be a 'cost of goods sold' in the income statement until July.

5.3 Example: cash budget

Peter Blair has worked for some years as a sales representative, but has recently been made redundant. He intends to start up in business on his own account, using $15,000 which he currently has invested with a building society. Peter maintains a bank account showing a small credit balance, and he plans to approach his bank for the necessary additional finance. Peter asks you for advice and provides the following additional information.

(a) Arrangements have been made to purchase non-current assets costing $8,000. These will be paid for at the end of September and are expected to have a five-year life, at the end of which they will possess a nil residual value.

(b) Inventories costing $5,000 will be acquired on 28 September and subsequent monthly purchases will be at a level sufficient to replace forecast sales for the month.

(c) Forecast monthly sales are $3,000 for October, $6,000 for November and December, and $10,500 from January 20X4 onwards.

(d) Selling price is fixed at the cost of inventory plus 50%.

(e) Two months' credit will be allowed to customers but only one month's credit will be received from suppliers of inventory.

(f) Running expenses, including rent but excluding depreciation of non-current assets, are estimated at $1,600 per month.

(g) Blair intends to make monthly cash drawings of $1,000.

Required

Prepare a cash budget for each month of the six months to 31 March 20X4.

Solution

The opening cash balance at 1 October will consist of Peter's initial $15,000 less the $8,000 expended on non-current assets purchased in September. In other words, the opening balance is $7,000. Cash receipts from credit customers arise two months after the relevant sales.

Payments to suppliers are a little more tricky. We are told that cost of sales is 100/150 × sales. Thus for October cost of sales is 100/150 × $3,000 = $2,000. These goods will be purchased in October but not paid for until November. Similar calculations can be made for later months. The initial inventory of $5,000 is purchased in September and consequently paid for in October.

Depreciation is not a cash flow and so is *not* included in a cash budget.

The cash budget can now be constructed.

CASH BUDGET FOR THE SIX MONTHS ENDING 31 MARCH 20X4

	Oct $	Nov $	Dec $	Jan $	Feb $	Mar $
Payments						
Suppliers	5,000	2,000	4,000	4,000	7,000	7,000
Running expenses	1,600	1,600	1,600	1,600	1,600	1,600
Drawings	1,000	1,000	1,000	1,000	1,000	1,000
	7,600	4,600	6,600	6,600	9,600	9,600
Receipts						
Debtors	–	–	3,000	6,000	6,000	10,500
Surplus/(shortfall)	(7,600)	(4,600)	(3,600)	(600)	(3,600)	900
Opening balance	7,000	(600)	(5,200)	(8,800)	(9,400)	(13,000)
Closing balance	(600)	(5,200)	(8,800)	(9,400)	(13,000)	(12,100)

5.4 Cash budgets and an opening statement of financial position

You might be given a cash budget question in which you are required to analyse an opening statement of financial position to decide how many outstanding debtors will pay what they owe in the first few months of the cash budget period, and how many outstanding creditors must be paid.

Suppose that a statement of financial position as at 31 December 20X4 shows the following details.

Due from customers (receivables)	$150,000
Due to suppliers (trade payables)	$60,000

The following information is relevant.

* Customers are allowed two months to pay.
* $1^1/2$ months' credit is taken from trade suppliers.
* Sales and materials purchases were both made at an even monthly rate throughout 20X4.

Let's try to ascertain the months of 20X5 in which the customers will eventually pay and the suppliers will be paid.

(a) Since customers take two months to pay, the $150,000 of receivables in the statement of financial position represents credit sales in November and December 20X4, who will pay in January and February 20X5 respectively. Since sales in 20X4 were at an equal monthly rate, the cash budget should plan for receipts of $75,000 each month in January and February from the receivables in the opening statement of financial position.

(b) Similarly, since payables are paid after $1^1/2$ months, the payables in the statement of financial position will be paid in January and the first half of February 20X5, which means that budgeted payments will be as follows.

	$
In January (purchases in 2nd half of November and 1st half of December 20X4)	40,000
In February (purchases in 2nd half of December 20X4)	20,000
Total payables in the statement of financial position	60,000

(The payables in the statement of financial position of $60,000 represent $1^1/2$ months' purchases, so that purchases in 20X4 must be $40,000 per month, which is $20,000 per half month.)

5.5 Example: a month by month cash budget

From the following information which relates to George and Zola you are required to prepare a month by month cash budget for the second half of 20X5 and to append such brief comments as you consider might be helpful to management.

(a) The company's only product, a vest, sells at $40 and has a variable cost of $26 made up as follows.

Material $20   Labour $4   Overhead $2

(b) Fixed costs of $6,000 per month are paid on the 28th of each month.

(c) Quantities sold/to be sold on credit

May	June	July	Aug	Sept	Oct	Nov	Dec
1,000	1,200	1,400	1,600	1,800	2,000	2,200	2,600

(d) Production quantities

May	June	July	Aug	Sept	Oct	Nov	Dec
1,200	1,400	1,600	2,000	2,400	2,600	2,400	2,200

(e) Cash sales at a discount of 5% are expected to average 100 units a month.

(f) Customers are expected to settle their accounts by the end of the second month following sale.

(g) Suppliers of material are paid two months after the material is used in production.

(h) Wages are paid in the same month as they are incurred.

(i) 70% of the variable overhead is paid in the month of production, the remainder in the following month.

(j) Income tax of $18,000 is to be paid in October.

(k) A new delivery vehicle was bought in June. It cost $8,000 and is to be paid for in August. The old vehicle was sold for $600, the buyer undertaking to pay in July.

(l) The company is expected to be $3,000 overdrawn at the bank at 30 June 20X5.

(m) No increases or decreases in raw materials, work in progress or finished goods are planned over the period.

(n) No price increases or cost increases are expected in the period.

Exam focus point

In June 2006 a budgeting question covered production, materials and a cash budget. The wages were partly fixed up to a certain level and variable above that level.

Solution

Cash budget for July 1 to December 31 20X5

	July $	Aug $	Sept $	Oct $	Nov $	Dec $	Total $
Receipts							
Credit sales	40,000	48,000	56,000	64,000	72,000	80,000	360,000
Cash sales	3,800	3,800	3,800	3,800	3,800	3,800	22,800
Sale of vehicle	600	–	–	–	–	–	600
	44,400	51,800	59,800	67,800	75,800	83,800	383,400
Payments							
Materials	24,000	28,000	32,000	40,000	48,000	52,000	224,000
Labour	6,400	8,000	9,600	10,400	9,600	8,800	52,800
Variable o'head (W)	3,080	3,760	4,560	5,080	4,920	4,520	25,920
Fixed costs	6,000	6,000	6,000	6,000	6,000	6,000	36,000
Income tax				18,000			18,000
Purchase of vehicle		8,000					8,000
	39,480	53,760	52,160	79,480	68,520	71,320	364,720
Receipts less payments	4,920	(1,960)	7,640	(11,680)	7,280	12,480	18,680
Balance b/f	(3,000)	1,920	(40)	7,600	(4,080)	3,200	(3,000)
Balance c/f	1,920	(40)	7,600	(4,080)	3,200	15,680	15,680

Working

Variable overhead

	June $	July $	Aug $	Sept $	Oct $	Nov $	Dec $
Variable overhead production cost	2,800	3,200	4,000	4,800	5,200	4,800	4,400
70% paid in month		2,240	2,800	3,360	3,640	3,360	3,080
30% in following month		840	960	1,200	1,440	1,560	1,440
		3,080	3,760	4,560	5,080	4,920	4,520

Comments

(a) There will be a small overdraft at the end of August but a much larger one at the end of October. It may be possible to delay payments to suppliers for longer than two months or to reduce purchases of materials or reduce the volume of production by running down existing inventory levels.

(b) If none of these courses is possible, the company may need to negotiate overdraft facilities with its bank.

(c) The cash deficit is only temporary and by the end of December there will be a comfortable surplus. The use to which this cash will be put should ideally be planned in advance.

Question

Cash budget

You are presented with the following budgeted cash flow data for your organisation for the period November 20X1 to June 20X2. It has been extracted from functional budgets that have already been prepared.

	Nov X1 $	Dec X1 $	Jan X2 $	Feb X2 $	Mar X2 $	Apr X2 $	May X2 $	June X2 $
Sales	80,000	100,000	110,000	130,000	140,000	150,000	160,000	180,000
Purchases	40,000	60,000	80,000	90,000	110,000	130,000	140,000	150,000
Wages	10,000	12,000	16,000	20,000	24,000	28,000	32,000	36,000
Overheads	10,000	10,000	15,000	15,000	15,000	20,000	20,000	20,000
Dividends		20,000						40,000
Capital expenditure			30,000			40,000		

You are also told the following.

(a) Sales are 40% cash, 60% credit. Credit sales are paid two months after the month of sale.
(b) Purchases are paid the month following purchase.
(c) 75% of wages are paid in the current month and 25% the following month.
(d) Overheads are paid the month after they are incurred.
(e) Dividends are paid three months after they are declared.
(f) Capital expenditure is paid two months after it is incurred.
(g) The opening cash balance is $15,000.

The managing director is pleased with the above figures as they show sales will have increased by more than 100% in the period under review. In order to achieve this he has arranged a bank overdraft with a ceiling of $50,000 to accommodate the increased inventory levels and wage bill for overtime worked.

Required

(a) Prepare a cash budget for each month of the six-month period January to June 20X2.
(b) Comment upon your results in the light of your managing director's comments and offer advice.

Answer

(a)

	January $	February $	March $	April $	May $	June $
Cash receipts						
Cash sales	44,000	52,000	56,000	60,000	64,000	72,000
Credit sales	48,000	60,000	66,000	78,000	84,000	90,000
	92,000	112,000	122,000	138,000	148,000	162,000
Cash payments						
Purchases	60,000	80,000	90,000	110,000	130,000	140,000
Wages 75%	12,000	15,000	18,000	21,000	24,000	27,000
25%	3,000	4,000	5,000	6,000	7,000	8,000
Overheads	10,000	15,000	15,000	15,000	20,000	20,000
Dividends			20,000			
Capital expenditure			30,000			40,000
	85,000	114,000	178,000	152,000	181,000	235,000
b/f	15,000	22,000	20,000	(36,000)	(50,000)	(83,000)
Net cash flow	7,000	(2,000)	(56,000)	(14,000)	(33,000)	(73,000)
c/f	22,000	20,000	(36,000)	(50,000)	(83,000)	(156,000)

(b) The overdraft arrangements are quite inadequate to service the cash needs of the business over the six-month period. If the figures are realistic then action should be taken now to avoid difficulties in the near future. The following are possible courses of action.

(i) Activities could be curtailed.

(ii) Other sources of cash could be explored, for example a long-term loan to finance the capital expenditure and a factoring arrangement to provide cash due from debtors more quickly.

(iii) Efforts to increase the speed of debt collection could be made.

(iv) Payments to creditors could be delayed.

(v) The dividend payments could be postponed (the figures indicate that this is a small company, possibly owner-managed).

(vi) Staff might be persuaded to work at a lower rate in return for, say, an annual bonus or a profit-sharing agreement.

(vii) Extra staff might be taken on to reduce the amount of overtime paid.

(viii) The inventory holding policy should be reviewed; it may be possible to meet demand from current production and minimise cash tied up in inventories.

Presentation is very important when you are preparing budgets. There are often large volumes of calculations and workings and it is easy to omit figures or use the wrong figures. Furthermore, poor presentation makes the information difficult to follow, both for management in a practical situation and for markers in the exam.

6 Fixed and flexible budgets

FAST FORWARD

The **master budget** consists of a budgeted income statement, a budgeted statement of financial position and a cash budget.

A **fixed budget** is a budget for one activity level, which is not changed even if the actual level of activity in the budget period turns out to be different from that originally planned. A **flexible budget** is a budget that is adjusted to allow for changes in the level of activity in the budget period.

The preparation of flexible budgets calls for an understanding of **cost behaviour**.

Flexible budgets might be prepared in advance of the budget period, when the organisation is uncertain about what the actual level of activity will be. Flexible budgets might be prepared in retrospect, once the actual level of activity is known. Retrospective flexible budgets might be used for budgetary control purposes (comparing actual results against what results should have been at that level of activity).

6.1 Fixed budgets

Key term

A **fixed budget** is a budget which is designed to remain unchanged regardless of the volume of output or sales achieved.

The master budget prepared before the beginning of the budget period is known as the **fixed budget**. The term 'fixed' means:

(a) The budget is **prepared on the basis of an estimated volume of production** and an **estimated volume of sales**, but no plans are made for the event that actual volumes of production and sales may differ from budgeted volumes.

(b) When actual volumes of production and sales during a control period (month or four weeks or quarter) are achieved, a fixed budget is **not adjusted (in retrospect) to the new levels of activity**.

The major purpose of a fixed budget is at the planning stage, when it seeks to define the broad objectives of the organisation.

6.2 Flexible budgets

Key term

A **flexible budget** is a budget which, by recognising different cost behaviour patterns, is designed to change as volumes of output change.

Flexible budgets may be used in one of two ways.

(a) **At the planning stage**. For example, suppose that a company expects to sell 10,000 units of output during the next year. A master budget (the fixed budget) would be prepared on the basis of these expected volumes. However, if the company thinks that output and sales might be as low as 8,000 units or as high as 12,000 units, it may prepare **contingency flexible budgets**, at volumes of, say 8,000, 9,000, 11,000 and 12,000 units. There are a number of advantages of planning with flexible budgets.

- It is possible to find out well in advance the costs of lay-off pay, idle time and so on if output falls short of budget.

- Management can decide whether it would be possible to find alternative uses for spare capacity if output falls short of budget (could employees be asked to overhaul their own machines for example, instead of paying for an outside contractor?).

- An estimate of the costs of overtime, subcontracting work or extra machine hire if sales volume exceeds the fixed budget estimate can be made. From this, it can be established whether there is a limiting factor which would prevent high volumes of output and sales being achieved.

(b) **Retrospectively**. At the end of each month (control period) or year, flexible budgets can be used to compare actual results achieved with what results should have been under the circumstances. Flexible budgets are an essential factor in **budgetary control** and overcome the practical problems involved in monitoring the budgetary control system.

- Management needs to be informed about how good or bad actual performance has been. To provide a **measure of performance**, there must be a **yardstick** (budget or standard) against which actual performance can be measured.

- Every business is **dynamic**, and actual volumes of output cannot be expected to conform exactly to the fixed budget. Comparing actual costs directly with the fixed budget costs is meaningless (unless the actual level of activity turns out to be exactly as planned).

- For useful control information, it is necessary to compare actual results at the actual level of activity achieved against the results that should have been expected at this level of activity, which are shown by the flexible budget.

The use of flexible budgets for budgetary control reporting is described in a later chapter.

6.3 Preparing flexible budgets

Flexible budgets apply the principles of marginal costing, and recognise the distinction between fixed and variable costs.

(a) For some items of expense, it might be necessary to recognise semi-variable costs, and split these into their variable cost and fixed cost elements. The high-low method was explained in an earlier chapter.

(b) Some variable unit costs might change if the level of activity rises above a certain level or falls below a certain level. For example, if output rises above a certain level, it might be necessary to pay overtime to some employees, or to recruit casual labour at a different rate of pay. Similarly, if output rises above a certain level, it might be possible to benefit from bulk purchases of materials or supplies, and so pay a lower unit cost.

(c) Some fixed cost items might show 'step cost' characteristics, and rise by a certain amount as the level of activity rises above a particular level.

Question	Cost of electricity

Using the high-low method and the following information, determine the cost of electricity in July if 2,750 units of electricity are consumed.

Month	Cost $	Electricity consumed Units
January	204	2,600
February	212	2,800
March	200	2,500
April	220	3,000
May	184	2,100
June	188	2,200

Answer

			$
(High)	Total cost of 3,000 units		220
(Low)	Total cost of 2,100 units		184
(Difference)	Variable cost of 900 units		36
	Variable cost per unit ($36/900)		$0.04

		$
Total cost of 3,000 units		220
Variable cost of 3,000 units	($0.04 per unit)	120
Fixed costs		100

		$
Budget		
Variable cost of 2,750 units	($0.04 per unit)	110
Fixed costs		100
Total cost, 2,750 units		210

Exam focus point

An exam question may not specifically tell you to use the high-low method to determine the fixed and variable elements of mixed costs. You will have to recognise for yourself that this is the method to be used.

We can now look at a full example of preparing a flexible budget.

6.4 Example: preparing a flexible budget

(a) Prepare a budget for 20X6 for the direct labour costs and overhead expenses of a production department at the activity levels of 80%, 90% and 100%, using the information listed below.

   (i)   The direct labour hourly rate is expected to be $3.75.

   (ii) 100% activity represents 60,000 direct labour hours.

   (iii) Variable costs

Indirect labour	$0.75 per direct labour hour
Consumable supplies	$0.375 per direct labour hour
Canteen and other welfare services	6% of direct and indirect labour costs

   (iv) Semi-variable costs are expected to relate to the direct labour hours in the same manner as for the last five years.

Year	Direct labour hours	Semi-variable costs $
20X1	64,000	20,800
20X2	59,000	19,800
20X3	53,000	18,600
20X4	49,000	17,800
20X5	40,000 (estimate)	16,000 (estimate)

   (v)   Fixed costs

	$
Depreciation	18,000
Maintenance	10,000
Insurance	4,000
Rates	15,000
Management salaries	25,000

(vi)   Inflation is to be ignored.

(b)   Calculate the **budget cost allowance (ie expected expenditure)** for 20X6 assuming that 57,000 direct labour hours are worked.

Solution

(a)

	80% level	90% level	100% level
	48,000 hrs	54,000 hrs	60,000 hrs
	$'000	$'000	$'000
Direct labour	180.00	202.50	225.00
Other variable costs			
Indirect labour	36.00	40.50	45.00
Consumable supplies	18.00	20.25	22.50
Canteen etc	12.96	14.58	16.20
Total variable costs ($5.145 per hour)	246.96	277.83	308.70
Semi-variable costs (W)	17.60	18.80	20.00
Fixed costs			
Depreciation	18.00	18.00	18.00
Maintenance	10.00	10.00	10.00
Insurance	4.00	4.00	4.00
Rates	15.00	15.00	15.00
Management salaries	25.00	25.00	25.00
Budgeted costs	336.56	368.63	400.70

Working

Using the high/low method:

	$
Total cost of 64,000 hours	20,800
Total cost of 40,000 hours	16,000
Variable cost of 24,000 hours	4,800
Variable cost per hour ($4,800/24,000)	$0.20

	$
Total cost of 64,000 hours	20,800
Variable cost of 64,000 hours (× $0.20)	12,800
Fixed costs	8,000

Semi-variable costs are calculated as follows.

		$
60,000 hours	(60,000 × $0.20) + $8,000	20,000
54,000 hours	(54,000 × $0.20) + $8,000	18,800
48,000 hours	(48,000 × $0.20) + $8,000	17,600

(b)   The budget cost allowance for 57,000 direct labour hours of work would be as follows.

		$
Variable costs	(57,000 × $5.145)	293,265
Semi-variable costs	($8,000 + (57,000 × $0.20))	19,400
Fixed costs		72,000
		384,665

6.5 The measure of activity in flexible budgets

The preparation of a flexible budget requires an estimate of the way in which costs (and revenues) vary with the level of activity.

Sales revenue will clearly vary with sales volume, and direct material costs (and often direct labour costs) will vary with production volume. In some instances, however, it may be appropriate to budget for overhead costs as semi-variable costs (part-fixed, part-variable) which vary with an 'activity' which is neither production nor sales volume. Taking production overheads in a processing department as an illustration, the total overhead costs will be partly fixed and partly variable. The variable portion may vary with the direct labour hours worked in the department, or with the number of machine hours of operation. The better measure of activity, labour hours or machine hours, may only be decided after a close analysis of historical results.

The **measure of activity used to estimate variable costs should satisfy certain criteria**.

- The measurement of activity should be **derived from the activity that causes particular costs to vary**.

- The unit of a measured activity should be **independent of variable factors other than its own volume**; for example, if labour hours are the measure of activity, the level of activity should be measured in labour hours, and not the labour cost of those hours (the latter being prone to the effect of a price change).

- The measure of activity should be **stable**, and in this respect, a standard unit of output provides a better measure than actual units. For example, if total costs are assumed to vary with direct labour hours, it would be more appropriate to choose 'standard hours produced' as a measure of activity than 'actual hours worked' because the actual hours may have been worked efficiently or inefficiently, and the variations in performance would probably affect the actual costs incurred.

<table>
<tr><td>**Exam focus point**</td><td>In an exam do not fall into the trap of flexing fixed costs. Do not forget that they remain unchanged regardless of the level of activity.</td></tr>
</table>

Question	Flexible budget

The fixed budget of C for 20X5 is as follows.

Sales and production

	100,000 units	
	$'000	$'000
Sales		2,000
Variable cost of sales		
Direct materials	800	
Direct labour	400	
Variable overhead	200	
		1,400
Contribution		600
Fixed costs		500
Profit/(loss)		100

Sales demand is strong, and management is considering a proposal to increase the budget from 100,000 to 120,000 units.

(a) If output were to be increased above 100,000 units, all the additional output would have to be made by the existing work force in overtime, for which the rate of pay would be 25% above the normal rate.

(b) If output went up to 120,000 units, the company would be able to benefit from a lower purchase price for direct materials. The purchase prices for materials would be 5% less than currently budgeted, for all materials purchased.

(c) If output rose above 100,000 units, fixed costs would rise by $60,000, due to additional accommodation requirements, particularly storage space.

Required

Prepare a flexible budget for output and sales of 120,000 units.

Sales and production	120,000 units	
	$'000	$'000
Sales (x 120%)		2,400
Variable cost of sales		
Direct materials (x 95% of 120%)	912	
Direct labour [400 + (20% of 400 x 1.25)]	500	
Variable overhead (x 120%)	240	
		1,652
Contribution		748
Fixed costs		560
Profit		188

6.6 Factors to consider when preparing flexible budgets

The mechanics of flexible budgeting are, in theory, fairly straightforward. In practice, however, there are a number of **points that must be considered before figures are flexed**.

- The **separation of costs into their fixed and variable elements** is not always straightforward.
- Fixed costs may behave in a **step-line** fashion as activity levels increase/decrease.
- Account must be taken of the **assumptions** upon which the original fixed budget was based. Such assumptions might include the constraint posed by limiting factors, the rate of inflation, judgements about future uncertainty, the demand for the organisation's products and so on.

7 Computers and budgeting

Computers provide invaluable assistance in co-ordinating the production of budgets.

Budgeting used to be a very **time-consuming** task, due to the need for a great number of numerical manipulations to produce a budget, and the likelihood that budgets will go through several drafts before they are finally agreed. It is likely that the budgeting process will encounter problems. Functional budgets will be out of balance with each other and require modification. The revision of one budget may well lead to the revision of all of the budgets. The manual preparation of a master budget and a cash budget in the real world would therefore be daunting.

Computers can recalculate budgets in an instant, and are almost invariably used nowadays in the budgeting process. A computerised system has a number of advantages.

- A computer has the ability to **process larger volumes of data**.
- A computerised system can process data **more rapidly** than a manual system.
- Computerised systems tend to be more **accurate** than manual systems.
- Computers have the ability to **store large volumes** of data in a readily accessible form.
- **Numerous scenarios** can be evaluated quickly.
- Budgets can go through many drafts, if necessary, with a relatively small amount of time needed to revise one draft and prepare a new one.

A computerised budget model is ideal for taking over the manipulation of numbers, leaving staff to get involved in the real planning process.

Budgeting may be computerised using a **program written specifically** for the organisation or one within an accounting package or simply with **spreadsheets**. All these methods of computerisation of the budgeting process will involve a **mathematical model** which represents the real world in terms of financial values. The model will consist of several, or many, interrelated variables, a variable being an item in the model which has a value.

A cash budgeting model, for example, should include all the factors (variables) which have a significant influence on cash flow. Variables would include time taken by debtors to pay what they owe, cash sales and credit sales, other cash expenses, and capital expenditure.

Once the **planning model** has been constructed, the same model can be used week by week, month after month, or year after year, simply by changing the values of the variables to produce new results for cash inflows, cash outflows, net cash flows and cash/bank balance.

A major advantage of budget models is the ability to **evaluate different options** and carry out **'what if' analysis**. By changing the value of certain variables (for example altering the ratio of cash sales to credit sales, increasing the amount of bad debts or capital expenditure, increasing the annual pay award to the workforce and so on) management are able to assess the effect of potential changes in their environment.

Computerised models can incorporate actual results, period by period, and carry out the necessary calculations to produce budgetary control reports.

The use of a model allows the budget for the remainder of the year to be adjusted once it is clear that the circumstances on which the budget was originally based have changed.

7.1 Spreadsheets and budgeting software

Presently most organisations use standard spreadsheet packages for budgeting rather than a specific budgeting package. However, budgeting packages are becoming more powerful and user-friendly. Budgeting packages often look and feel like spreadsheets, but have additional budgeting-specific features such as pre-programmed forecasting capabilities using complex statistical methods. They are less likely to contain errors as the package is less dependent on user-entered formulae than spreadsheets.

Key learning points

- A **budget** is a plan for an entire organisation, typically for a one-year period, and covering all the activities of the organisation. The overall budget might be referred to as the master budget. It is expressed in financial terms, partly because 'money' is a common language for business activities and partly because a major objective of any organisation is a financial objective (eg profits in the case of commercial organisations and value for money in the case of not-for-profit organisations).

- The functions of a **system of budgeting** are as follows.

  - To ensure the achievement of the organisation's objectives
  - To compel planning
  - To communicate ideas and plans
  - To co-ordinate activities
  - To provide a framework for responsibility accounting
  - To establish a system of control ('budgetary control')
  - To motivate employees to improve their performance

- A budget is a **quantified plan of action** for a forthcoming accounting period.

- The **budget preparation process** is as follows.

  - Communicating details of the budget policy and budget guidelines.
  - Determining the factor(s) that restrict output
  - Preparation of the sales budget
  - Initial preparation of budgets
  - Negotiation of budgets with superiors
  - Co-ordination and review of budgets
  - Final acceptance of the budgets
  - Budget review

- The **principal budget factor** should be identified at the beginning of the budgetary process, and the budget for this is prepared before all the others.

- Once prepared, the **functional budgets** must be reviewed to ensure they are consistent with one another. Functional budgets are brought together to prepare a budgeted income statement for the budget period.

- **Cash budgets** show the expected receipts and payments during a budget period and are a vital management control tool.

- The **master budget** consists of a budgeted income statement, a budgeted statement of financial position and a cash budget.

- A **fixed budget** is a budget for one activity level, which is not changed even if the actual level of activity in the budget period turns out to be different from that originally planned. A **flexible budget** is a budget that is adjusted to allow for changes in the level of activity in the budget period.

- The preparation of flexible budgets calls for an understanding of **cost behaviour**.

- Flexible budgets might be prepared in advance of the budget period, when the organisation is uncertain about what the actual level of activity will be. Flexible budgets might be prepared in retrospect, once the actual level of activity is known. Retrospective flexible budgets might be used for budgetary control purposes (comparing actual results against what results should have been at that level of activity).

- **Computers** provide invaluable assistance in co-ordinating the production of budgets.

Quick quiz

1   What are the functions of a system of budgeting?
2   What is meant by the term principal budget factor?
3   How can a shortfall in capacity be overcome, when it is revealed by the budgeting process?
4   Explain the concept of the standard hour.
5   Describe appropriate management action if a cash budget shows a potential long-term surplus.
6   Why might the net cash inflows for an organisation differ from its profit for the period?

Answers to quick quiz

1   To ensure the achievement of the organisation's objectives
    To compel planning
    To communicate ideas and plans
    To co-ordinate activities
    To provide a framework for responsibility accounting
    To establish a system of control
    To motivate employees to improve their performance

2   A principal budget factor is the factor that limits an organisation's performance for a given period.

3   Consideration should be given to overtime, subcontracting, machine hire and/or new sources of materials.

4   A standard hour is the quantity of work achievable at standard performance, expressed in terms of a standard unit of work done in a standard period of time.

5   • Make long-term investments
    • Expand
    • Diversify
    • Replace/update non-current assets

6   Profits and cash flow might differ because:
    • Some cash receipts are not income statement items (cash from sale of non-current assets, new bank loans, etc)
    • Some cash payments are not income statement items (capital expenditure, etc)
    • Some income statement expenses do not create cash flows (depreciation charges)
    • Timing differences. Some items appear in the income statement before or after they give rise to a cash flow. For example, sales on credit: the sale is an income statement item when it occurs, but a cash flow item only when the customer eventually pays.

Further issues with budgets

4

4

4

Topic list
1 Strategic planning, operational planning and budgeting
2 Zero-based budgeting
3 Advantages and limitations of zero-based budgets
4 Using zero-based budgeting
5 Activity-based budgeting (ABB)
6 Rolling budgets
7 The behavioural implications of budgeting
8 Using budgets as targets
9 Beyond budgeting

Introduction

In recent years, many practitioners have voiced dissatisfaction with traditional budgeting as set out in the previous chapter. It seemed to take up a large amount of management time at the start of each year, with little tangible benefit derived from it.

This chapter looks at developments of traditional budgeting that have been proposed to make the process more relevant and more rewarding.

Learning objectives

On completion of this chapter you will be able to:

Syllabus reference

*   explain the importance of the link between strategic planning and operational planning, the consequences of not having such a link, and the role of budgeting in providing such a link   4

*   describe the potential weaknesses of traditional budgeting, and reasons why some organisations have questioned the need for budgets at all   4

*   describe alternative approaches to budgeting that attempt to overcome some of the weaknesses of traditional budgeting, such as zero-based budgeting, activity based budgeting and rolling budgets   4

*   explain the motivational aspects of budgeting, and the possible value of encouraging participation by all employees in the budgeting process   4

1 Strategic planning, operational planning and budgeting

FAST FORWARD

If an organisation is to achieve its strategic objectives, there must be an **effective link between strategic plans and operational plans.** This is a link that budgets should help to provide.

Traditional budgeting has frequently been criticised for failing to provide this link, and for encouraging the continuation of wasteful and inefficient practices and excessive spending. A few organisations have questioned the value of having traditional budgets at all.

Alternatives to traditional budgeting have been developed, such as zero-based budgeting, activity-based budgeting and rolling budgets.

Key terms

Strategic planning is the process of specifying the objectives or targets of the organisation, consistent with the organisation's mission, and formulating plans for the achievement of those objectives. It is the process of deciding:

(a)   where the organisation is trying to get to
(b)   how it should get there, and
(c)   how quickly.

Management control, also called **tactical planning**, is the process by which management converts strategic plans into more detailed and shorter-term plans. It involves making sure that resources are made available at an economic price, and are applied both efficiently and effectively towards the achievement of strategic goals. Planning horizons are medium-term.

Operational control or **operational planning** is the process of ensuring that specific tasks are carried out effectively and efficiently. Planning horizons can range, but are often short-term. Operational planning decisions are made with a view to achieving longer-term planning goals.

1.1 Strategic planning information

Strategic planning decisions are taken at the top level of management, but strategic plans have to be converted into practical 'action plans'. The process of converting strategy into action involves all levels of management. Planning horizons range from long-term to fairly short-term.

For many organisations, the annual budget is the major element of planning. Strategic planning, however, calls for different types of information, and different methods of analysis. Much of the information for strategic planning must come from outside the organisation, and may be non-financial in nature. An organisation should consider, at the strategic level, competitors' actions, and a range of so-called 'PEST' factors (political, environmental, social and technological factors).

Examples of strategic information, and how it might be used, are as follows.

Item	Strategic management information needs
Competitors' costs	What are they? How do they compare with ours? Can we beat our competitors on cost?
Product profitability	What profits or losses are made by each of our products? Why is Product A making good profits whereas Product B is making a loss, even though its quality is just as good? Should we be switching from focus on some products to greater emphasis on others? Should we be targeting particular types of customer with particular types of product or service?
Pricing decisions for new products	Pricing a new product can be critically important for the success or failure of the product launch. Information is needed, possibly from market research, about how the market might respond to a new product at various prices.
The value of market share	An organisation needs to be aware of what it would be worth to increase its share of the market for any of its products. What would be the value of an increase of market share of, say, 1%? Is this a goal worth pursuing?
Future prices	What might product prices be in the future, as the market evolves, and as existing products go through their life cycle?
Future products	How is the market likely to evolve, and what new products are likely to succeed in the market?
Capacity expansion	Should the firm expand its capacity, and if so by how much? Should it diversify into a new area of operations or into a new market?

1.2 Ensuring a link between strategic and operational planning

Achieving longer-term strategic goals will not happen unless there is an effective link between the strategic planning process and the formulation of operational plans. 'If there is no link between strategic planning and operational planning, the result is likely to be *unrealistic plans, inconsistent goals, poor communication and inadequate performance measurement.*' (George Brown, 'Management Accounting and Strategic Management' *ACCA Students Newsletter*, March 1994).

'Management control', of which budgeting is a key element, sits between strategic planning at a senior management level and 'hands-on' management decision-making at the short-term level.

(a)   A primary function of budgeting is therefore to ensure that the organisation's strategic objectives are achieved, or that progress is made towards their achievement. Budgeting can support strategic planning in various ways.

Objective	Comment
Strategic direction	Operations and resource plans, and hence budgets, should be derived from business strategies.
Resource allocation	Resources should be allocated according to the required outputs. Budgets should be directed towards achieving critical success factors.
Continuous improvement	Firms should always seek to improve their performance in relation to customer needs, industry best practice and competitors. Budgets should support continuous improvement.
Goal congruence	Managers must understand the effect of their decisions on the work processes beyond their departmental boundaries.
Add value	The time spent on budgetary activities should be worth more than its cost.

Objective	Comment
Cost reductions	When an organisation's targets include improved productivity, or restoring profitability, cost reductions are likely to be a crucial short-term target. The budget will be the planning mechanism.
Targets and responsibilities	Budgets will set targets for divisions, departments, and sub-sections of departments. Individual managers should be aware of what their personal targets are.

1.3 Problems with budgeting

In practice, budgets and the budgeting process are frequently criticised because they fail to provide a link between strategic and operational planning, and fail to help the organisation to achieve its strategic objectives. The main criticisms are:

(a)   the rigid organisational structure within which budgets are normally formulated, with departmental managers often competing with each other for money and resources, and with departmental interests taking precedence over the wider interests of the organisation

(b)   the inefficient planning techniques in budgeting, that encourage the continuation of existing inefficiencies, and fail to encourage managers to look for performance improvements

(c)   the rigid one-year time frame of the budget, and the lack of flexibility in the planning horizon

Traditional budgets are based on the management structure of the organisation. However, it has been argued that management should think in terms of **processes**, stretching across departmental boundaries, and with the customer at the end of them. Activities should not be looked at in terms of a static organisation structure.

At its worst, the traditional budgeting process commences with management setting a revenue forecast and financial targets. Departmental budgets are then prepared based on last year's costs and year-to-date actual costs, 'plus or minus a bit'. Budgeting is often insufficiently concerned with how resources should be used more efficiently and effectively, or with whether resources can even be obtained more cheaply.

Most budgets are prepared over a **one-year period** to enable managers to plan and control financial results for the purposes of the annual accounts. There is a need for management to satisfy shareholders that their company is achieving good results, and for this reason, the arbitrary one-year financial period is usually selected for budgeting. One-year plans are not necessarily relevant to the business strategy.

As a consequence of criticisms of traditional budgeting:

(a)   alternative methods of budgeting have been developed, and
(b)   some organisations have questioned the value of having budgets at all.

 Case Study

A small number of companies have gone so far as to abolish budgeting as traditionally practised.

(a)   IKEA took the move in 1992 of abolishing its internal budgets. Its chief executive was reported in *The Economist* (November 1994) to have said, 'We realised that our business planning system was getting too heavy; we can use the time saved for doing other things better.'

(b)   Volvo has dropped its once-a-year traditional budgeting process and introduced a new concurrent planning process. This has a permanent focus on objectives and uses key performance indicators, rolling forecasting and short- and long-term 'balanced scorecards'. (These are described in a later chapter.)

Some of the alternative approaches to budgeting are described below.

2 Zero-based budgeting

The principle behind **zero-based budgeting (ZBB)** is that the budget for each cost centre should be made from 'scratch' or zero. Every item of expenditure must be justified in its entirety in order to be included in the next year's budget.

There is a three-step approach to ZBB.

- Define **decision packages**
- Evaluate and **rank** packages
- **Allocate** resources

A 'traditional approach' to budgeting is to base next year's budget on the current year's results plus an extra amount for estimated growth or inflation next year. This approach is known as **incremental budgeting** since it is concerned mainly with the increments in costs and revenues which will occur in the coming period.

Incremental budgeting is a reasonable procedure if current operations are as effective, efficient and economical as they can be, and the organisation and the environment are largely unchanged.

In general, however, it is an **inefficient form of budgeting** as it **encourages slack** and **wasteful spending** to creep into budgets. Past inefficiencies are perpetuated because cost levels are rarely subjected to close scrutiny.

To ensure that inefficiencies are not concealed, alternative approaches to budgeting have been developed. One such approach is **zero-based budgeting (ZBB)**, the use of which was pioneered by *P Pyhrr* in the United States in the early 1970s.

2.1 The principles of zero-based budgeting

ZBB rejects the assumption inherent in incremental budgeting that next year's budget can be based on this year's costs. In a ZBB approach to planning, every aspect of the budget is examined in terms of its cost and the benefits it provides and the selection of better alternatives is encouraged.

Key term

> **Zero-based budgeting** involves preparing a budget for each cost centre from a zero base. Every item of expenditure has then to be justified in its entirety in order to be included in the next year's budget.

2.2 Implementing zero-based budgeting

Implementing ZBB calls for a **questioning attitude** by all those involved in the planning process. Existing practices and expenditures must be challenged and searching questions, such as the following, must be asked.

- Does this activity need to be carried out?
- What would be the consequences if the activity was not carried out?
- Does this activity benefit the organisation?
- Is the current level of provision appropriate?
- Are there alternative ways of providing the function?
- How much should the activity cost?
- Is the expenditure worth the benefits achieved?

There are three stages in a zero-based budgeting process.

Stage 1 **Identify and define decision packages**

A **decision package** is an activity within the organisation that results in costs (or revenues). There is a choice whether the activity should or should not be carried out. If it is carried out, a certain amount of additional costs will be incurred (or, if it ceases to be carried out, certain costs will be avoided). Decision packages can be evaluated. (Is the activity worthwhile?) Decision packages can also be compared with each other and ranked in an order of preference. (If we could do only A or B, which would be preferred?) Managers prepare decision packages for the activities within the budget centre for which they have responsibility.

There are two types of decision package.

(a)   **Mutually exclusive packages** contain **alternative methods of getting the same job done**. The best option among the packages must be selected by comparing costs and benefits and the other packages are then discarded. For example, an organisation might consider two alternative decision packages for the preparation of the payroll: Package 1 might be in-house preparation of the payroll whereas Package 2 could involve the use of an outside agency.

(b)   **Incremental packages divide one aspect of an activity into different levels of effort**. The 'base' package will describe the minimum amount of work that must be done to carry out the activity and the other packages describe what additional work could be done, at what cost and for what benefits.

EXAMPLE

Suppose that a cost centre manager is preparing a budget for maintenance costs. He or she might first consider two mutually exclusive packages. Package A might be to keep a maintenance team of two people per shift for two shifts each day at a cost of $60,000 per annum, whereas package B might be to obtain a maintenance service from an outside contractor at a cost of $50,000. A cost-benefit analysis will be conducted because the quicker repairs obtainable from an in-house maintenance service might justify its extra cost.

If we now suppose that package A is preferred, the budget analysis must be completed by describing the incremental variations in this chosen alternative.

(a)   The 'base' package would describe the minimum requirement for the maintenance work. This might be to pay for one person per shift for two shifts each day at a cost of $30,000.

(b)   Incremental package 1 might be to pay for two people on the early shift and one person on the late shift, at a cost of $45,000. The extra cost of $15,000 would need to be justified, for example by savings in lost production time, or by more efficient machinery.

(c)   Incremental package 2 might be the original preference, for two people on each shift at a cost of $60,000. The cost-benefit analysis would compare its advantages, if any, over incremental package 1.

(d)   Incremental package 3 might be for three people on the early shift and two on the late shift, at a cost of $75,000; and so on.

Question   Packages

What might the base package for a personnel department cover? What might incremental packages cover?

Answer

The base package might cover the recruitment and dismissal of staff. Incremental packages might cover training, pension administration, trade union liaison, staff welfare and so on.

Stage 2 **Evaluate and rank packages**

Each activity (decision package) is evaluated and ranked on the basis of its benefit to the organisation.

The ranking process provides managers with a technique to allocate scarce resources between different activities. Minimum work requirements (those that are essential to get a job done) will be given high priority and so too will work which meets legal obligations. In the accounting department these would be minimum requirements to operate the payroll, purchase ledger and sales ledger systems, and to maintain and publish a set of accounts which satisfies the external auditors.

The ranking process can be lengthy because large numbers of different packages will have been prepared by managers throughout the organisation. In large organisations the number of packages might be so huge that senior management cannot do the ranking unaided. In such circumstances, the following occurs.

(a) Cost centre managers will be asked to rank the packages for their own cost centre.

(b) The manager at the next level up the hierarchy of seniority will consolidate the rankings of his or her subordinates into a single ranking list for the group of cost centres, using the rankings of each cost centre as a guide.

(c) These consolidated rankings will be passed in turn one stage further up the management hierarchy for further consolidation. At higher levels of consolidation, the ranking process might be done by a committee of managers rather than by an individual.

Once a consolidated ranking of packages has been prepared, it should be reviewed to make sure that there is a general agreement that the rankings are reasonable and there are no anomalies in them.

Stage 3 **Allocate resources**

Resources in the budget are then **allocated** according to the funds available and the evaluation and ranking of the competing packages. Packages involving small expenditures can be dealt with by junior managers but senior managers must make decisions involving larger amounts of expenditure. The ZBB process must, however, run through the entire management structure.

3 Advantages and limitations of zero-based budgets

3.1 The advantages of implementing ZBB

Zero-based budgeting has some advantages over traditional budgeting methods.

- It is possible to identify and **remove inefficient or obsolete operations.**
- It forces employees to **avoid wasteful expenditure**.
- It can **increase motivation**, by involving employees in the process of looking for better ways of performing activities.
- It provides a **budgeting and planning tool** for management that responds to changes in the business environment; 'obsolescent' items of expenditure are identified and dropped.
- The **documentation** required **provides** all management with a co-ordinated, in-depth **appraisal of an organisation's operations.**
- It **challenges the status quo** and forces an organisation to examine alternative activities and existing expenditure levels.
- In summary, ZBB should result in a **more efficient allocation of resources** to an organisation's activities and departments.

3.2 The disadvantages of ZBB

The major disadvantage of zero-based budgeting is the **time and energy required** to implement it, particularly on a regular basis. The assumptions about costs and benefits in each package must be continually updated and new packages developed as soon as new activities emerge. The following problems might also occur.

(a) **Short-term benefits** might be **emphasised** to the detriment of long-term benefits.

(b) The **false idea that all decisions have to be made in the budget might be encouraged**. Management must be able to meet unforeseen opportunities and threats at all times, and must not feel restricted from carrying out new ideas simply because they were not approved by a decision package, cost-benefit analysis and the ranking process.

(c) It may be a **call for management skills** both in constructing decision packages and in the ranking process **which the organisation does not possess**. Managers may therefore have to be trained in ZBB techniques so that they can apply them sensibly and properly.

(d) It may be **difficult to 'sell' ZBB to managers as a useful technique** for the following reasons.

- Incremental costs and benefits of alternative courses of action are hard to quantify accurately.
- Employees or trade union representatives may resist management ideas for changing the ways in which work is done.

(e) The organisation's information systems may not be capable of providing suitable incremental cost and incremental benefit analysis.

(f) The ranking process can be difficult. Managers face three common problems.

- A large number of packages may have to be ranked.
- There is often a conceptual difficulty in having to rank packages which managers regard as being equally vital, for legal or operational reasons.
- It is difficult to rank completely different types of activity, especially where activities have qualitative rather than quantitative benefits - such as spending on staff welfare and working conditions - where ranking must usually be entirely subjective.

In summary, perhaps the most serious drawback to ZBB is that it requires a lot of management time and paperwork. One way of obtaining the benefits of ZBB but of overcoming the drawbacks is to apply it selectively on a rolling basis throughout the organisation. This year finance, next year marketing, the year after personnel and so on. In this way all activities will be thoroughly scrutinised over a period of time.

4 Using zero-based budgeting

ZBB can be used by both **profit-making** and **non-profit-making** organisations. It has been popular in the US and Canada but has not been taken up much in the UK.

The procedures of zero-based budgeting do not lend themselves easily to direct manufacturing costs where standard costing, work study and the techniques of management planning and control have long been established as a means of budgeting expenditure.

ZBB is best applied to expenditure incurred in **departments that support** the essential production function. These include marketing, finance, quality control, repairs and maintenance, production planning, research and development, engineering design, personnel, data processing, sales and distribution. In many organisations, these expenses make up a large proportion of the total expenditure. These activities are less easily quantifiable by conventional methods and are **more discretionary** in nature.

ZBB can also be successfully applied to **service industries** and **non-profit-making organisations** such as local and central government departments, educational establishments, hospitals and so on.

ZBB can be applied in any organisation where alternative levels of provision for each activity are possible and where the costs and benefits are separately identifiable.

Some particular uses of ZBB are:

(a) **Budgeting for discretionary cost items**, such as advertising, R & D and training costs. The priorities for spending money could be established by ranking activities and alternative levels of spending or service can be evaluated on an incremental basis. For example, is it worth spending $2,000 more to increase the numbers trained on one type of training course by 10%? If so, what priority should this incremental spending on training be given, when compared with other potential training activities?

(b) **Rationalisation measures.** 'Rationalisation' means cutting back on production and activity levels, and cutting costs. ZBB can be used to make rationalisation decisions when an organisation is forced to make spending cuts. (This use of ZBB might explain any unpopularity it might have among managers.)

5 Activity-based budgeting (ABB)

FAST FORWARD

Activity-based budgeting provides a method of budgeting for 'overhead' costs whereby planned costs are related to the activities performed. Overhead costs are not treated as fixed or variable according to whether they vary with the level of production or sales volume. Instead, costs are assumed to vary with changes in the level of the factor that drives the costs of each support activity.

Key term

Activity based budgeting (ABB) is a method of budgeting based upon an activity framework, using cost driver data in budget setting and variance analysis.

Activity-based budgeting is an approach to budgeting that applies many of the concepts of activity-based costing. It might be particularly relevant, therefore, to high-technology industries, in which processes are more complex, and quality issues are often important.

Like ZBB, activity-based budgeting is particularly applicable to 'support functions', away from the factory floor, such as product design, order handling, quality control, customer service and production planning. It is also applicable to administrative functions, such as personnel and facilities management.

The approach taken in ABB is to recognise that an organisation consists of a number of activities rather than a number of departments, and that costs are incurred by activities. Cost drivers can also be identified for activities. Even within a single department, costs are caused by activities, and vary with the level of that activity.

For example, within the HR department, some costs might be driven by recruitment numbers (the costs of setting up personnel records, medical checks, training arrangements, and so on). If so, a part of the budget for the HR department might be prepared on the basis of the expected number of employees to be recruited in the budget period.

ABB is an alternative to 'traditional' volume-based models for budgeting, in which costs are either fixed or vary with the volume of production and sales. It is an approach to planning aimed primarily at understanding the reason why costs are incurred, and giving planners the opportunity to manage those costs.

Cost budgets can be prepared on the basis of:

(a) the activities performed in the support areas of the organisation
(b) recognising the cost driver for each of those activities
(c) analysing costs as either variable or fixed in relation to changes in the level of that activity
(d) budgeting what the level of activity will be, and
(e) preparing a cost budget for the activity accordingly.

ABB therefore brings a better analysis of costs into budgeting for overhead operations, compared with traditional budgeting systems, where overheads are all treated as fixed unless they vary with output volume.

A further consequence of an activity-based approach might be to identify wasteful spending, ie spending incurred that has no value or purpose in relation to the activities of the organisation. It might also help managers to identify limiting factors, and constraints on activities.

By focusing on activities, activity-based budgeting encourages managers to think about the most economical or efficient way of getting something done. For example, suppose that a resources manager states that he or she needs a new building in which to re-locate a particular operation that is growing in size. It might well be that obtaining an additional building is the best solution. However, by looking at the activity, it might be seen that a better solution is to employ more efficient technology, or to use a more distributive form of doing the work, so that the operation can be performed without the need for the extra space.

Question

Non-value-added

One consequence of the activity based budgeting process might be the identification of 'non-value-added' activities – what do you think this means, and can you give an example of such an activity in, say, a book publishing company?

Answer

A non-value added activity is one that does nothing to enhance the value of the product from the point of view of the consumer, and could be removed without the customer perceiving a fall in quality of the product. So whilst proofreading in a publishing company is a value-added activity (customers would soon notice if it wasn't done), the storage and handling of the inventories of paper for books is not. Cost reduction is best achieved by the minimisation of such activity (for example, by only ordering paper when a print run is about to start – see Just in Time in Chapter 15).

6 Rolling budgets

FAST FORWARD

Rolling budgets (or **continuous budgets**) are budgets which are continuously updated by adding a further period (say a month or a quarter) and removing the earliest period.

Rolling budgets might be used to overcome the problem that a fixed budget might get out of date, and cease to be of relevance or value once the budget period is under way. This is particularly likely to happen to an organisation that operates in a dynamic and continually-changing environment.

Rolling budgets might also be used as a means of ensuring that the budget is not simply a once-a-year exercise, but that the budgeting process is a more frequent and dynamic part of the planning process.

Key term

A **rolling budget** is a budget that is continuously updated by adding a further accounting period (a month or quarter) when the earlier accounting period has expired.

For example, if an organisation prepares a rolling annual budget every three months:

(a)   it might begin by preparing a budget for the period January – December Year 1

(b)   three months later, it will prepare a budget for the year April Year 1 – March Year 2

(c)   three months later, it will prepare a budget for the year July Year 1 – June Year 2

(d)   a further three months later, it will prepare a budget for the year October Year 1 – September Year 2, and so on.

Each rolling budget is for one year, but there are four budgets in the year. As a result, management re-visits its planning decisions four times a year, much more frequently than with traditional annual budgeting.

Rolling budgets should help management to prepare targets and plans that are **more realistic and certain**, by shortening the period between preparing budgets.

Computerised budget models enable rolling budgets to be prepared relatively easily.

6.1 The advantages and disadvantages of rolling budgets

The **advantages** of rolling budgets are as follows.

- By producing budgets more frequently than once a year, there is a better likelihood that the budgets will provide an effective **link between strategic planning and operational planning**. They **reduce the element of uncertainty** in budgeting. Rolling budgets concentrate detailed planning and control on short-term prospects where the degree of **uncertainty is smaller**.

- They force managers to reassess the budget regularly, and to **produce budgets** that are **up-to-date in the light of current events and expectations**. For example, if annual budgets are formulated by adding an allowance for inflation to last year's figures, there is a danger that the annual rate of inflation will be over-estimated so that the budgets will be too high and thus encourage overspending by departments. In contrast, quarterly **budgets prepared on a rolling basis are likely to predict inflation rates more accurately** because shorter-term forecasts are used.

- **Planning and control will be based on a recent plan** instead of a fixed annual budget that might have been made many months ago and which is no longer realistic.

- Realistic budgets are likely to have a **better motivational influence** on managers.

- There is **always a budget which extends for several months ahead**. For example, if rolling budgets are prepared quarterly there will always be a budget extending for the next 9 to 12 months. If rolling budgets are prepared monthly there will always be a budget for the next 11 to 12 months. This is not the case when fixed annual budgets are used.

The **disadvantages** of rolling budgets are as follows.

(a) A system of rolling budgets calls for the routine preparation of a new budget at regular intervals during the course of the one financial year. This involves more time, effort and money in budget preparation.

(b) Frequent budgeting might have an off-putting effect on managers who doubt the value of preparing one budget after another at regular intervals, even when there are major differences between the figures in one budget and the next.

(c) Revisions to the budget might involve revisions to standard costs too, which in turn would involve revisions to inventory valuations. This could mean that a large administrative effort is required in the accounts department every time a rolling budget is prepared to bring the accounting records up to date.

7 The behavioural implications of budgeting

There are basically two ways in which a budget can be set: from the **top down** (**imposed budget**) or from the **bottom up** (**participatory** budget). Many writers refer to a third style (**negotiated**).

Participation in the budgeting process might improve the motivation of employees and junior managers.

7.1 Motivation

Motivation is what makes people behave in the way that they do. It comes from individual attitudes, or group attitudes. Individuals will be motivated by personal desires and interests. These may be in line with the objectives of the organisation, and some people 'live for their jobs'. Other individuals see their job as a chore, and their motivations will be unrelated to the objectives of the organisation they work for.

It will be of enormous benefit to an organisation if the goals of its management and employees are in harmony with the goals of the organisation itself. (This is known as 'goal congruence'.) Motivation – attitudes – could affect performance. Performance may be enhanced if motivation is positive, and performance could be damaged by poor motivation.

7.2 Participation

It has been argued that **participation** by individuals in the budgeting process **will improve their motivation,** and that improved motivation will improve:

(a)   the quality of budget decisions, and
(b)   the efforts of individuals to achieve their budget targets.

7.3 Motivation and the budgeting process

Plans cannot succeed unless they are put into effect. A plan that looks wonderful on paper is of no value if either:

(a)   it is unrealistic, or
(b)   it would be realistic, but only if employees were willing to make an effort to achieve the planning targets.

An important issue in planning is how to get employees to work towards the achievement of the organisation's objectives, particularly since the objectives of the organisation are unlikely to be of much interest to the 'average' employee. It has been argued that the style of management can have an effect on the performance of employees.

There are basically two ways in which a budget can be set: from the **top down** (imposed budget) or from the **bottom up** (participatory budget).

7.4 Imposed style of budgeting

In this approach to budgeting, top management prepares a budget with little or no input from junior managers or operating personnel. The budget is then imposed on the employees who have to work to its targets.

Imposed budgets can be implemented effectively:

- in newly-formed organisations
- in very small businesses
- during periods of economic hardship
- when operational managers lack budgeting skills
- when the organisation's different units require precise co-ordination

Possible **advantages** of senior management imposing a budget are that:

- it might increase the probability that the organisation's strategic plans will be incorporated into planned activities
- it might enhance the co-ordination between the budgets of the various departments or divisions of the organisation
- senior managers are more aware than junior managers or employees of what resources are available to the organisation, particularly in terms of money for extra spending
- budgets should be prepared quickly, because limited negotiations (if any) are required before the budget is agreed

There are also **disadvantages** in imposing a budget.

- It can produce dissatisfaction, defensiveness and low morale amongst employees on whom the budget is imposed. It is hard for people to be motivated to achieve targets set by somebody else.
- Any feeling of team spirit there might have been will probably disappear.
- There may be a feeling that the budget is a punitive device, i.e. that employees will be punished in some way if they fail to achieve the targets.
- Lower-level management initiative may be stifled.

7.5 Participative style of budgeting

In a bottom-up approach to budgeting, budgets are developed by lower-level managers who then submit the budgets to their superiors for discussion and approval. The budgets are based on the lower-level managers' perceptions of what is achievable and what resources would be needed to achieve them.

Participative budgets might be effective in the following circumstances.

- In well-established organisations.
- In very large businesses, where junior managers often have a better understanding of local circumstances than senior management.
- When operational managers have strong budgeting skills.
- When the organisation's different units or divisions act autonomously.

Advantages of participative budgets are as follows.

- Information is gathered from employees most familiar with each department's needs and constraints, strengths and weaknesses.
- Knowledge spread among several levels of management is pulled together.
- Morale and motivation is improved.
- Acceptance of and commitment to organisational goals and objectives by operational managers is likely to be improved.
- In general, they are more realistic and achievable.
- Co-ordination between units is improved.
- Operating managers are more likely to develop operational plans which are consistent with the budget and tie in with the organisation's goals and objectives.
- Senior managers' overview of the organisation is mixed with operational level details.

Participative budgets have **disadvantages**.

- They consume more time than top-down budgets.
- The advantages of managerial participation could be negated if senior management over-ride or ignore planning targets proposed by their juniors. This can lead to dissatisfaction similar to that experienced with imposed budgets.
- Junior managers might be ambivalent about wanting to participate in the budgeting process.
- Managers may set budgets for their departments without trying to co-ordinate their own plans with those of other departments.
- They may encourage managers to introduce 'budgetary slack', by trying to obtain a larger spending budget for their department.
- They can support 'empire building' by subordinates.

7.6 Negotiated style of budgeting

There is a third style of budgeting, a **negotiated style**. Different levels of management often agree budgets by a process of negotiation. In top-down budgeting, operational managers will try to negotiate with their senior managers to reduce the budget targets they consider to be unreasonable or unrealistic. Likewise, in a bottom-up budgeting environment, senior management usually review and revise budgets presented to them, through a process of negotiation with lower level managers. **Final budgets are therefore most likely to lie between what top management would really like and what junior managers believe is feasible**. The budgeting process is hence a **bargaining process**.

8 Using budgets as targets

FAST FORWARD

A lack of employee **motivation** will make it more difficult for an organisation to achieve its objectives.

In certain situations it may be useful to prepare an **expectations budget** and an **aspirations budget**.

Once decided, budgets become targets. As targets, they can motivate managers to achieve a high level of performance. But **how difficult should targets be**? And how might people react to targets of differing degrees of difficulty in achievement?

(a) There is likely to be a **demotivating** effect where an **ideal standard** of performance is set, because adverse efficiency variances will always be reported.

(b) A **low standard of efficiency** is also **demotivating**, because there is no sense of achievement in attaining the required standards.

(c) A budgeted level of attainment could be 'normal': that is, the **same as the level that has been achieved in the past**. Arguably, this level will be **too low**. It might encourage the continuation of current inefficiencies.

It has been argued that **each individual has a personal 'aspiration level'**. This is a level of performance in a task with which the individual is familiar, which the individual undertakes for him or herself to reach. This aspiration level might be quite challenging and if individuals in a work group all have similar aspiration levels it should be possible to incorporate these levels within the official operating standards.

Some care should be taken, however, in applying this.

(a) If a manager's tendency to achieve success is stronger than the tendency to avoid failure, budgets with targets of intermediate levels of difficulty are the most motivating, and stimulate a manager to better performance levels. Budgets which are either too easy to achieve or too difficult are de-motivating, and managers given such targets achieve relatively low levels of performance.

(b) A manager's tendency to avoid failure might be stronger than the tendency to achieve success. (This is likely in an organisation in which the budget is used as a pressure device on subordinates by senior managers). Managers might then be discouraged from trying to achieve budgets of intermediate difficulty and tend to avoid taking on such tasks, resulting in poorer levels of performance than if budget targets were either easy or very difficult to achieve.

It has therefore been suggested that in a situation where budget targets of an intermediate difficulty *are* motivating, such targets ought to be set if the purpose of budgets is to motivate. However, although budgets set for **motivational purposes** need to be stated in terms of **aspirations rather than expectations**, budgets for planning and decision purposes need to be stated in terms of the best available estimate of expected actual performance.

Budgets to motivate, and budgets as realistic targets might therefore be inconsistent with each other. The **solution** might therefore be to have **two budgets**.

(a) A budget for planning and decision making based on reasonable expectations.

(b) A second budget for motivational purposes, with more difficult targets of performance (that is, targets of an intermediate level of difficulty).

These two budgets might be called an **'expectations budget'** and an **'aspirations budget'** respectively.

Key terms

> An **expectations budget** is a budget set on the basis of the most likely outcomes from the process. It is used as a planning tool.
>
> An **aspirations budget** is a budget set on the basis of providing challenging targets to the individuals involved in the process. It is used as a motivational tool.

For example, a salesman might be expected to sell 20,000 units of a product next year at a fixed price of $5 each. His character may be such that he thrives on being given a challenging target, so he may be given a personal sales target of 22,000 units at $5 each. The sales revenue generated by this salesman would be forecast at $100,000 in an expectations budget, but $110,000 in an aspirations budget.

Question — Budgeting process

What points would you raise in a discussion about the behavioural aspects of participation in the budgeting process, and the difficulties you might envisage?

Answer

The level of participation in the budgeting process can vary from zero participation to a process of group decision making. There are a number of behavioural aspects of participation to consider.

(a) *Communication.* Managers cannot be expected to achieve targets if they do not know what those targets are. Communication of targets is made easier if managers have participated in the budgetary process from the beginning.

(b) *Motivation.* Managers are likely to be better motivated to achieve a budget if they have been involved in compiling it, rather than having a dictatorial budget imposed on them.

(c) *Realistic targets.* A target must be achievable and accepted as realistic if it is to be a motivating factor. A manager who has been involved in setting targets is more likely to accept them as realistic. In addition, managers who are close to the operation of their departments may be more aware of the costs and potential savings in running it.

(d) *Goal congruence.* One of the best ways of achieving goal congruence is to involve managers in the preparation of their own budgets, so that their personal goals can be taken into account in setting targets.

Although participative budgeting has many advantages, difficulties might also arise.

(a) *Pseudo-participation.* Participation may not be genuine, but merely a pretence at involving managers in the preparation of their budgets. Managers may feel that their contribution is being ignored, or that the participation consists of merely obtaining their agreement to a budget which has already been decided. If this is the case then managers are likely to be more demotivated than if there is no participation at all.

(b) *Co-ordination.* If participative budgeting is well-managed it can improve the co-ordination of the preparation of the various budgets. There is, however, a danger that too many managers will become involved so that communication becomes difficult and the process becomes complex.

(c) *Training.* Some managers may not possess the necessary skill to make an effective contribution to the preparation of their budgets. Additional training may be necessary, with the consequent investment of money and time. It may also be necessary to train managers to understand the purposes and advantages of participation.

(d) *Slack.* If budgets are used in a punitive fashion for control purposes then managers will be tempted to build in extra expenditure to provide a 'cushion' against overspending. It is easier for them to build in slack in a participative system.

9 Beyond budgeting

FAST FORWARD

In fast moving markets, traditional budgets might be a handicap to efficient management, and some companies have moved **'beyond' budgeting**, decentralising authority and responsibility to front-line managers who measure performance by reference to competition and other benchmarks rather than by reference to budget targets.

Traditional budgeting methods have remained largely unchanged for many years, and are used by many organisations. Zero-based budgeting and activity-based budgeting are methods for improving the way that budgets are prepared, and there have also been vast improvements in the use of information technology, for example, to prepare quarterly or six-monthly rolling budgets.

Part B Planning and decision making | **4: Further issues with budgets** | 111

Traditional budgeting has its severe critics, who argue that the system is too centralised and too rigid, and does not provide a suitable framework for improving performance. An alternative to budgeting, known as '**beyond budgeting**' has been proposed.

The criticism of traditional budgeting is that it is a handicap to company performance. Budgets are a barrier to the devolution of authority to front-line managers and to the implementation of more effective performance management processes (such as the balanced scorecard, which is described in a later chapter). 'The traditional performance management model is too rigid to reflect today's fast-moving economy. Two new approaches – devolution and strategic performance management – have risen in popularity, but they are equally frustrated by unyielding budgeting systems.' (Jeremy Hope and Robin Fraser).

Events in businesses and markets are often fast-moving. Customers are able to switch from one supplier to another quickly, often at the click of a mouse button, and to be successful, companies need to focus on providing customer satisfaction. In rapidly-changing markets, companies need to move from decision-making based on budget forecasts to real-time responses to events, and from centralised co-ordination of decision-making to empowerment for local management.

In dynamic markets, companies cannot plan one year ahead with confidence. It is also difficult to separate strategic planning from day-to-day operations. Traditional budgeting was designed to support centralised, remote decision-making, which can now be too time-consuming, slow and inflexible. Whereas traditional budgets are intended to provide order, control, predictability and co-ordination, this is often not true. In reality, competitors and other benchmarks of performance provide better control than budget targets, and the management of motivation and behaviour provides a better way than budgets of achieving co-operation.

It has been argued that a 'beyond budgeting' model represents the best management practice in the 'information age'. This model is based on:

(a)   Decentralisation and devolving authority, and empowering local managers to make their own decisions on strategy, methods of working, managing resources, responding to customers and self-governance

(b)   The clear communication to local managers of the strategic goals of the organisation and the boundaries within which they have freedom to make their own decisions and act

(c)   Setting clear targets for performance and making local managers responsible for actual results

(d)   Simplified management processes, taking out tiers of middle management to create a 'leaner organisation'.

 Case Study

A number of companies have adopted a beyond budgeting model, but the earliest exponent appears to be the Nordic bank, Svenska Handelsbanken, which abandoned traditional budgeting in the early 1970s. Within this company:

(a)   Authority was devolved to the managers of branches of the bank, and each branch became a profit centre.

(b)   Branch managers were allowed to run their own business with a large degree of freedom and responsibility. For example, they were allowed to decide which products and services to offer individual customers, which central services of the bank to use (and negotiate a price for the service) and how many staff to employ.

(c)   Their ability to act and take well-informed decisions was supported by access to up-to-date on-line information, for example about customers gained and lost, work productivity and the profitability of branches and different categories of customer.

(d)   Branch managers were empowered to make decisions and correct their mistakes. Senior managers would only interfere where absolutely necessary.

Svenska Handelsbanken has been a very successful business, with an impressive profit record. Customer satisfaction was high, because local managers responded to their needs. Costs were low, because cost levels were continually challenged by the local managers rather than protected by the budget system. Credit decisions were devolved to local managers, and possibly because local managers knew their customers, bad debts were very low.

The culture that evolved within the company was one of seeking continuous improvement. There was constructive rivalry between branches, and peer pressure from other branch managers to make improvements. The bank provided league tables of branch performance, which were provided on line for everyone to see.

Employee satisfaction was also high. Handelsbanken succeeded in attracting top-quality graduates as recruits into the bank, attracted by the opportunity to exercise devolved responsibility as local managers.

A key to a beyond budgeting model is delegation of authority and decentralised decision-making. In criticising the traditional budgeting model, Hope and Fraser have written that delegation and co-ordination 'don't make comfortable bedfellows. A constant battle is being waged in most large organisations between the forces of decentralised initiative (usually the losers) and the forces of centralised co-ordination (invariably the winners). The difference is the centralising power of the budgeting system that emphasises coercion rather than co-ordination (you will co-operate, won't you?), focuses on cost reduction rather than value creation, stifles initiative and keeps planning and execution apart, thus reinforcing the separation between thinkers and doers.'

9.1 Ingredients of a beyond budgeting model

The key elements in a beyond budgeting model can be summarised as follows.

(a) The organisation should be governed through shared values and clear boundaries. Local managers should be able to make fast decisions knowing that they are operating within agreed parameters for action.

(b) The organisation should create as many profit centres as possible, and the manager of the profit centre should have freedom to run the centre as his or her own business.

(c) Co-ordination within the organisation should be achieved through market forces. Central service units (ie 'head office' functions) should regard the operating units as their internal customers, who must be serviced and satisfied in the same way as external customers.

(d) Front-line managers should be provided with a fast and open information network. Everyone should receive important information at the same time.

(e) Local managers should be given freedom to act but also the responsibility for delivering results. Front-line managers are expected to perform!

(f) Managers should be given suitable training and support to enable them to think and act decisively.

To create wealth, firms need to exploit the benefits of effective devolution of authority (such as fast decision-making and quick responses) and more effective performance management, supported by a system for providing fast, open and relevant information.

Performance targets for local managers should be set with regard to competitors and other benchmarks. Targets should be stretching, and should be continually adjusted. Setting targets calls for a process for identifying the 'metrics' or indicators of performance that really drive better business performance. The performance targets chosen will include non-financial as well as financial targets, and there will be more targets than traditional budgeting measures of profits, revenues, costs and return on capital. Multiple performance targets might be chosen, possibly using a balanced scorecard approach. (The balanced scorecard is explained in a later chapter.)

Rolling forecasts should be produced regularly, so that local managers can adjust their strategy continually in response to changing conditions and changing expectations. Managers must remain aware of the financial implications of the decisions they make.

Managers should be rewarded on the basis of their relative performance, and their achievement of performance targets (both non-financial and financial).

Traditional budgeting certainly has serious weaknesses, but is still widely practised. A beyond budgeting model seeks to replace budgets with an alternative management system for many of the purposes for which budgets have been used. Budgeting remains, however, an important tool for financial forecasting, and will continue to be used for this purpose.

'With the notable exception of the forecasting of financial outcomes, there are very few elements of the traditional budgeting process which are not performed more rigorously and more effectively within other strategic management processes. These redundant elements of the process can be eliminated and most of the companies that have adopted [a beyond budgeting] approach have done just that.'

Key learning points

- If an organisation is to achieve its strategic objectives, there must be an **effective link between strategic plans and operational plans.** This is a link that budgets should help to provide.

- Traditional budgeting has frequently been criticised for failing to provide this link, and for encouraging the continuation of wasteful and inefficient practices and excessive spending. A few organisations have questioned the value of having traditional budgets at all.

- Alternatives to traditional budgeting have been developed, such as zero-based budgeting, activity-based budgeting and rolling budgets.

- The principle behind **zero-based budgeting (ZBB)** is that the budget for each cost centre should be made from 'scratch' or zero. Every item of expenditure must be justified in its entirety in order to be included in the next year's budget.

- There is a three-step approach to ZBB.

    - Define **decision packages**
    - Evaluate and **rank** packages
    - **Allocate** resources

- **Activity-based budgeting** provides a method of budgeting for 'overhead' costs whereby planned costs are related to the activities performed. Overhead costs are not treated as fixed or variable according to whether they vary with the level of production or sales volume. Instead, costs are assumed to vary with changes in the level of the factor that drives the costs of each support activity.

- **Rolling budgets (continuous budgets)** are budgets which are continuously updated by adding a further period (say a month or a quarter) and removing the earliest period.

- There are basically two ways in which a budget can be set: from the **top down (imposed budget)** or from the **bottom up (participatory** budget). Many writers refer to a third style (**negotiated**).

- Participation in the budgeting process might improve the motivation of employees and junior managers.

- A lack of employee **motivation** will make it more difficult for an organisation to achieve its objectives.

- In certain situations it may be useful to prepare an **expectations budget** and an **aspirations budget**.

- In fast moving markets, traditional budgets might be a handicap to efficient management, and some companies have moved '**beyond' budgeting**, decentralising authority and responsibility to front-line managers who measure performance by reference to competition and other benchmarks rather than by reference to budget targets.

Quick quiz

1   What is incremental budgeting?
2   Name two types of decision package in ZBB.
3   Describe two particular uses of ZBB.
4   How does ABB differ from traditional budgeting?
5   What are rolling budgets (also called continuous budgets)?
6   In what circumstances might imposed budgets be effective?
7   What are key elements of a 'beyond budgeting' approach?

Answers to quick quiz

1   Incremental budgeting involves basing the budget on the current year's results plus an extra amount for estimated growth or inflation.

2   Mutually exclusive packages and incremental packages

3   ZBB can be applied to support expenses, discretionary cost items and rationalisation measures.

4   With ABB, overhead costs are not assumed to vary with the volume of output or sales. Instead, costs of support activities are planned on the basis of expected activity levels for the 'cost driver' for each activity.

5   Rolling budgets are budgets (usually with a 12-month planning period) that are prepared at regular intervals, such as every one, two, three or six months. They encourage more frequent planning reviews.

6   • In newly-formed organisations
     • In very small businesses
     • During periods of economic hardship
     • When operational managers lack budgeting skills
     • When the organisation's different units require precise co-ordination

7   Decentralisation of authority to front line managers with clear boundaries for decision-making. Performance targets set by reference to competition and other benchmarks. Each local manager runs their own 'business'. A fast and open information network. Senior managers interfere only when absolutely necessary. Rewards for managers based on performance, with non-financial as well as financial indicators.

5

CVP analysis

Introduction

Managers need to be able to forecast the expected profits for their organisation at certain levels of costs and sales volumes. The Cost-Volume-Profit (CVP) model is a simple model based on the ideas of marginal costing that enables such forecasts to be achieved.

Learning objectives

On completion of this chapter you will be able to:

		Syllabus reference
•	calculate and explain the breakeven point	5
•	analyse the effect on the breakeven point of changes in sales price and costs	5
•	prepare and explain breakeven charts	5
•	apply CVP analysis to decision-making situations	5
•	describe the advantages and limitations of breakeven analysis for management decision making	5

1 Introduction

FAST FORWARD

CVP analysis has a number of purposes: to provide information to management about cost behaviour for routine **planning** and 'one-off' **decision making**; to determine what volume of sales is needed at any given budgeted sales price in order to **break even**; to identify the 'risk' in the budget by measuring the **margin of safety**; to calculate the effects on profit of changes in variable costs, sales prices, fixed costs, and so on.

Key term

Cost-volume-profit (CVP)/breakeven analysis is the study of the interrelationships between costs, output volume and profit at various levels of activity.

To assist planning and decision making, management should know not only the budgeted profit, but also:

- the output and sales level at which there would be neither profit nor loss (break-even point)
- the amount by which actual sales can fall below the budgeted sales level, without a loss being incurred (the margin of safety)

2 Marginal costs, contribution and profit

A marginal cost is another term for a variable cost. The term 'marginal cost' is usually applied to the variable cost of a unit of product or service, whereas the term 'variable cost' is more commonly applied to resource costs, such as the cost of materials and labour hours.

Marginal costing is a form of management accounting based on the distinction between:

(a) the marginal costs of making and selling goods or services, and

(b) fixed costs, which should be the same for a given period of time, regardless of the level of activity in the period.

Suppose that a firm makes and sells a single product that has a marginal cost of $5 per unit and that sells for $9 per unit. For every additional unit of the product that is made and sold, the firm will incur an extra cost of $5 and receive income of $9. The net gain will be $4 per additional unit. This net gain per unit, the difference between the sales price per unit and the marginal cost per unit, is called **contribution**.

Contribution is a term meaning 'making a contribution towards covering fixed costs and making a profit'. Before a firm can make a profit in any period, it must first of all cover its fixed costs. **Breakeven** is where total sales revenue for a period just covers fixed costs, leaving neither profit nor loss. For every unit sold in excess of the breakeven point, profit will increase by the amount of the contribution per unit.

In the example above of the product selling for $9 and with a variable cost of $5, suppose that fixed costs each month are $60,000. At a contribution of $4 for each unit, the firm would have to sell 15,000 units each month, just to break even. To make a profit, it would have to make and sell more than this quantity.

The mathematics of cost-volume-profit analysis is based largely on this simple arithmetical concept.

	$
Sales	A
Variable cost of items sold	B
Contribution	A – B
Fixed costs	C
Profit	(A – B) – C

3 The breakeven point

The **breakeven point** is the activity level (output and sales level) at which there will be neither profit nor loss.

The breakeven point (BEP) can be calculated arithmetically.

$$\text{Breakeven point} = \frac{\text{Total fixed costs}}{\text{Contribution per unit}} = \frac{\text{Contribution required to break even}}{\text{Contribution per unit}}$$

= Number of units of sale required to break even.

The contribution required to break even is the amount which exactly equals total fixed costs.

3.1 Example: breakeven point

Expected sales	10,000 units at $8 = $80,000
Variable cost	$5 per unit
Fixed costs	$21,000

Required

Compute the breakeven point.

Solution

The contribution per unit is $(8–5)	=	$3
Contribution required to break even	=	fixed costs = $21,000
Breakeven point (BEP)	=	21,000 ÷ 3
	=	7,000 units
In revenue, BEP	=	(7,000 × $8) = $56,000

Sales above $56,000 will result in profit of $3 per unit of additional sales and sales below $56,000 will mean a loss of $3 per unit for each unit by which sales fall short of 7,000 units. In other words, profit will improve or worsen by the amount of contribution per unit.

	7,000 units	7,001 units
	$	$
Revenue	56,000	56,008
Less variable costs	35,000	35,005
Contribution	21,000	21,003
Less fixed costs	21,000	21,000
Profit	0 (= breakeven)	3

3.2 Breakeven point and the contribution to sales ratio

An alternative way of calculating the breakeven point, in terms of sales revenue, is as follows.

The C/S ratio is the ratio of contribution to sales revenue (contribution/sales ratio) and is also sometimes called a profit/volume or P/V ratio.

In paragraph 3 above we saw that the contribution required to break even is the amount which exactly equals fixed costs.

It follows that sales revenue at breakeven point = $\dfrac{\text{Required contribution}}{\text{C/S ratio}}$ = $\dfrac{\text{Fixed costs}}{\text{C/S ratio}}$

In the example in Paragraph 3.1 the C/S ratio is $\dfrac{\$3}{\$8}$ = 37.5%

Breakeven is where sales revenue equals $\dfrac{\$21,000}{37.5\%}$ = $56,000

At a price of $8 per unit, this represents 7,000 units of sales.

The contribution/sales ratio is a measure of how much contribution is earned from each $1 of sales. The C/S ratio of 37.5% in the above example means that for every $1 of sales, a contribution of 37.5c is earned. Thus, in order to earn a total contribution of $21,000 and if contribution increases by 37.5c per $1 of sales, sales must be:

$$\dfrac{\$1}{37.5c} \times \$21,000 = \$56,000$$

Question

Contribution

The C/S ratio of product A is 20%. AB, the manufacturer of product A, wishes to make a contribution of $50,000 towards fixed costs. How many units of product A must be sold if the selling price is $10 per unit?

Answer

$\dfrac{\text{Required contribution}}{\text{C/S ratio}}$ = $\dfrac{\$50,000}{20\%}$ = $250,000

∴ Number of units = $250,000 ÷ $10 = 25,000.

4 The margin of safety

> The **margin of safety** is the difference in units between the budgeted sales volume and the breakeven **sales volume** and it is sometimes expressed as a percentage of the budgeted **sales volume**.

The margin of safety may also be expressed as the difference between the budgeted **sales revenue** and breakeven sales revenue, expressed as a percentage of the budgeted **sales revenue**.

If the margin of safety is expressed as a percentage of the budgeted sales volume or budgeted sales revenue it is referred to as the **margin of safety ratio**. It is an indication of the percentage by which sales can fall before losses are made.

4.1 Example: margin of safety

Homer makes and sells a product which has a variable cost of $30 and which sells for $40. Budgeted fixed costs are $70,000 and budgeted sales are 8,000 units.

Required

Calculate the breakeven point and the margin of safety.

Solution

$$\text{Breakeven point} = \frac{\text{Total fixed costs}}{\text{Contribution per unit}} = \frac{\$70,000}{\$(40-30)}$$

$$= 7,000 \text{ units}$$

Margin of safety   =   8,000 – 7,000 units = 1,000 units

$$\text{Margin of safety ratio} = \frac{1,000 \text{ units}}{8,000 \text{ units}} \times 100\% = 12\tfrac{1}{2}\% \text{ of budget}$$

The margin of safety indicates to management that actual sales can fall short of budget by 1,000 units or 12½% before the breakeven point is reached and no profit at all is made.

Question

Budgeted level of sales

The margin of safety on the production of product L is 200 units and the breakeven point is 400 units. What is the budgeted level of sales?

Answer

Let S be budgeted level of sales

Margin of safety = 200 = S – 400

∴ S = 600 units

5 CVP and decision making

At the **breakeven point**, sales revenue equals total costs and there is no profit.

$$S = V + F$$

where S   = Sales revenue
       V   = Total variable costs
       F   = Total fixed costs

Subtracting V from each side of the equation, we get:

$$S - V = F \text{, that is, } \textbf{total contribution = fixed costs}$$

5.1 Example: breakeven arithmetic

Bluebell makes a product which has a variable cost of $7 per unit.

Required

If fixed costs are $63,000 per annum, calculate the selling price per unit if the company wishes to break even with a sales volume of 12,000 units.

Solution

			$
Contribution required to break even (= Fixed costs)	=	$63,000	
Volume of sales	=	12,000 units	
Required contribution per unit (S – V)	=	$63,000 ÷ 12,000 =	5.25
Variable cost per unit (V)	=		7.00
Required sales price per unit (S)	=		12.25

5.2 Target profits

A similar formula may be applied where a company wishes to **achieve a certain profit** during a period. To achieve this profit, **sales must cover all costs and leave the required profit**.

The target profit is achieved when: S = V + F + P,

> where P = required profit

Subtracting V from each side of the equation, we get:

> S – V = F + P, so

Total contribution required = F + P

5.3 Example: target profits

Whippy makes and sells a single product, for which variable costs are as follows.

	$
Direct materials	10
Direct labour	8
Variable production overhead	6
	24

The sales price is $30 per unit, and fixed costs per annum are $68,000. The company wishes to make a profit of $16,000 per annum.

Required

Determine the sales required to achieve this profit.

Solution

Required contribution = fixed costs + profit
= $68,000 + $16,000 = $84,000

Required sales can be calculated in one of two ways.

(a) $\dfrac{\text{Required contribution}}{\text{Contribution per unit}} = \dfrac{\$84,000}{\$(30-24)}$

= 14,000 units, or $420,000 in revenue

(b) $\dfrac{\text{Required contribution}}{\text{C/S ratio}} = \dfrac{\$84,000}{20\%}$

= $420,000 of revenue, or 14,000 units.

Question	Sales price

Grumpy wishes to sell 14,000 units of its product, which has a variable cost of $15 to make and sell. Fixed costs are $47,000 and the required profit is $23,000.

Required

Calculate the required sales price per unit.

Answer

Required contribution = fixed costs plus profit
= $47,000 + $23,000
= $70,000
Required sales = 14,000 units

	$
Required contribution per unit sold	5
Variable cost per unit	15
Required sales price per unit	20

5.4 Decisions to change sales price or costs

You may come across a problem in which you will be expected to analyse the effect of altering the selling price, or a change in the variable cost per unit or fixed costs for the period. These problems are slight variations on basic breakeven arithmetic. Examples to illustrate typical questions are shown below.

5.5 Example: change in selling price

Fairy bake and sell a single type of cake. The variable cost of production is 15c and the current sales price is 25c. Fixed costs are $2,600 per month, and the monthly profit for the company at current sales volume is $3,000.

The sales manager wishes to raise the sales price to 29c per cake, but considers that a price rise will result in some loss of sales.

Required

Ascertain the minimum volume of sales required each month to justify a rise in price to 29c.

Solution

The minimum volume of demand which would justify a price of 29c is one which would leave total profit at least the same as before, ie $3,000 per month. Required profit should be converted into required contribution, as follows.

	$
Monthly fixed costs	2,600
Current monthly profit	3,000
Current monthly contribution	5,600
Contribution per unit (25c – 15c)	10c
Current monthly sales	56,000 cakes

The minimum volume of sales required after the price rise will be an amount which earns a contribution of $5,600 per month, no worse than at the moment. The contribution per cake at a sales price of 29c would be 14c.

$$\text{Required sales} = \frac{\text{required contribution}}{\text{contribution per unit}} = \frac{\$5,600}{14c}$$

$$= 40,000 \text{ cakes per month.}$$

5.6 Example: change in costs

Brickhill makes a product which has a variable cost of $12 and a sales price of $20 per unit. Fixed costs are $304,000 per annum, and the current volume of output and sales is 39,000 units.

The company is considering whether to try to improve sales volumes. To increase output and sales above 40,000 units, it would have to hire additional equipment, at a cost of $36,000 per annum.

Required

(a) Calculate the current annual profit and the breakeven point without the additional equipment, and calculate the breakeven point with the new equipment.

(b) Determine the number of units that must be produced and sold to achieve the same profit as is currently earned, if the additional equipment is hired.

Solution

The current unit contribution is $(20 – 12) = $8

(a)

	$
Current contribution (39,000 × $8)	312,000
Less current fixed costs	304,000
Current profit	8,000

Breakeven point is $304,000/$8 per unit = 38,000 units.

With the additional equipment, fixed costs will go up by $36,000 to $340,000 per annum. Because fixed costs have gone up 'a step' to a new level, there is a different breakeven point.

The new breakeven point is $340,000/$8 per unit = 42,500 units.

(b)

	$
Required profit (as currently earned)	8,000
Fixed costs	340,000
Required contribution	348,000

Contribution per unit $8

Sales required to earn $8,000 profit ($348,000/$8) = 43,500 units

5.7 Example: comparing the cost of two options

The managing director of a company has a mobile phone. He has been looking at two different tariffs for his phone.

(a)   Tariff A: an annual rental of $400 plus calls charged at 5c per minute
(b)   Tariff B: an annual rental of $250 plus calls charged at 8c per minute

How much would he need to use his phone to be indifferent as to which tariff he pays, and if his estimated annual usage is 9,000 minutes, which tariff would be cheaper?

Solution

This is a break-even problem, but without any sales revenue, only costs. There are two cost structures. If V is the MD's annual usage in minutes, the total cost of each tariff will be:

(a)   Tariff A: 400 + 0.05V
(b)   Tariff B: 250 + 0.08V.

To be indifferent between Tariff A and Tariff B, the cost with each tariff must be the same: 400 + 0.05V = 250 + 0.08V.

This equation can be solved to find a value for V. (0.03V = 150, V = 5,000 minutes.)

The two tariffs would result in the same cost if the managing director used the mobile phone for 5,000 minutes a year. Above this level, Tariff A (5c per extra minute) is cheaper than Tariff B (8c per extra minute). Since the managing director has 9,000 minutes of call charges each year, Tariff A is cheaper (by 4,000 minutes × (8 – 5)c per minute, ie $120).

6 Breakeven charts

FAST FORWARD

Make sure that you understand how to calculate the **breakeven point**, the **C/S ratio**, the **margin of safety** and **target profits**, and can apply the principles of CVP analysis to decisions about whether to change sales prices or costs. You should also be able to construct a **breakeven chart**.

The breakeven point can also be shown graphically using a breakeven chart.

> A **breakeven chart** is a chart showing levels of profit or loss at different sales volume levels.

A breakeven chart has the following axes.

- A **horizontal** axis showing the **sales/output** (in value or units).
- A **vertical axis** showing $ for **sales revenues** and **costs**

The following lines are drawn on the breakeven chart.

- The **sales line**

  - Starts at the origin
  - Ends at the point signifying expected sales

- The **fixed costs line**

  - Runs parallel to the horizontal axis
  - Meets the vertical axis at a point which represents total fixed costs

- The **total costs line**

  - Starts where the fixed costs line meets the vertical axis
  - Ends at the point which represents the following
  - Anticipated sales on the horizontal axis
  - Total costs of anticipated sales on the vertical axis

The **breakeven point** is the **intersection** of the **sales line** and the **total costs line**.

The distance between the breakeven point and the expected (or budgeted) sales, in units, indicates the margin of safety.

6.1 Example: a breakeven chart

The budgeted annual output of a factory is 120,000 units. The fixed overheads amount to $40,000 and the variable costs are 50c per unit. The sales price is $1 per unit.

Required

Construct a breakeven chart showing the current breakeven point and profit earned up to the present maximum capacity.

Solution

We begin by calculating the profit at the budgeted annual output.

	$
Sales (120,000 units)	120,000
Variable costs	60,000
Contribution	60,000
Fixed costs	40,000
Profit	20,000

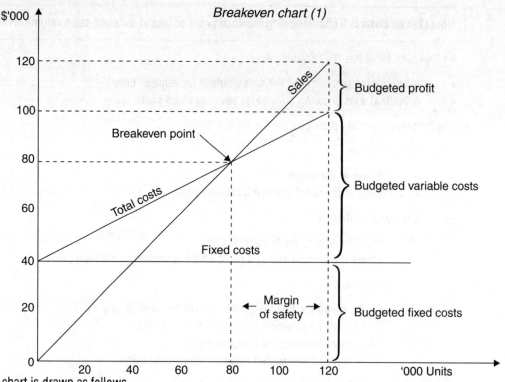

Breakeven chart (1)

The chart is drawn as follows.

(a) The vertical axis represents money (costs and revenue) and the horizontal axis represents the level of activity (production and sales).

(b) The fixed costs are represented by a straight line parallel to the horizontal axis (in our example, at $40,000).

(c) The variable costs are added 'on top of' fixed costs, to give total costs. It is assumed that fixed costs are the same in total and variable costs are the same per unit at all levels of output.

The line of costs is therefore a straight line and only two points need to be plotted and joined up. Perhaps the two most convenient points to plot are total costs at zero output, and total costs at the budgeted output and sales.

(i) At zero output, costs are equal to the amount of fixed costs only, $40,000, since there are no variable costs.

(ii) At the budgeted output of 120,000 units, costs are $100,000.

	$
Fixed costs	40,000
Variable costs 120,000 × 50c	60,000
Total costs	100,000

(d) The sales line is also drawn by plotting two points and joining them up.

(i) At zero sales, revenue is nil.
(ii) At the budgeted output and sales of 120,000 units, revenue is $120,000.

The breakeven point is where total costs are matched exactly by total revenue. From the chart, this can be seen to occur at output and sales of 80,000 units, when revenue and costs are both $80,000. This breakeven point can be proved mathematically as:

$$\frac{\text{Required contribution} = \text{fixed costs}}{\text{Contribution per unit}} = \frac{\$40,000}{50c \text{ per unit}} = 80,000 \text{ units}$$

The margin of safety can be seen on the chart as the difference between the budgeted level of activity and the breakeven level.

6.2 The value of breakeven charts

Breakeven charts are used as follows.

- To **plan** the production of a company's products
- To **market** a company's products
- To give a **visual display** of breakeven arithmetic

Breakeven charts can also be used to **show variations** in the possible **sales price**, **variable costs** or **fixed costs**.

6.3 Example: breakeven charts and variations in selling price

Suppose that a company sells a product which has a variable cost of $2 per unit. Fixed costs are $15,000. It has been estimated that if the sales price is set at $4.40 per unit, the expected sales volume would be 7,500 units; whereas if the sales price is lower, at $4 per unit, the expected sales volume would be 10,000 units.

Required

Draw a breakeven chart to show the budgeted profit, the breakeven point and the margin of safety at each of the possible sales prices.

Solution

Workings	Sales price $4.40 per unit $		Sales price $4 per unit $
Fixed costs	15,000		15,000
Variable costs (7,500 × $2.00)	15,000	(10,000 × $2.00)	20,000
Total costs	30,000		35,000
Budgeted revenue (7,500 × $4.40)	33,000	(10,000 × $4.00)	40,000

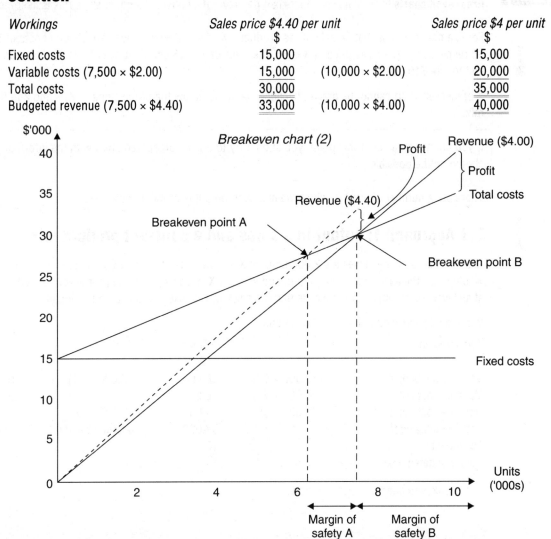

(a) Breakeven point A is the breakeven point at a sales price of $4.40 per unit, which is 6,250 units or $27,500 in costs and revenues.

$$\text{(check: } \frac{\text{Required contribution to break even}}{\text{Contribution per unit}} = \frac{\$15,000}{\$2.40 \text{ per unit}} = 6,250 \text{ units)}$$

The margin of safety (A) is 7,500 units − 6,250 units = 1,250 units or 16.7% of expected sales.

(b) Breakeven point B is the breakeven point at a sales price of $4 per unit which is 7,500 units or $30,000 in costs and revenues.

$$\text{(check: } \frac{\text{Required contribution to break even}}{\text{Contribution per unit}} = \frac{\$15,000}{\$2 \text{ per unit}} = 7,500 \text{ units)}$$

The margin of safety (B) = 10,000 units − 7,500 units = 2,500 units or 25% of expected sales.

Since a price of $4 per unit gives a higher expected profit and a wider margin of safety, this price will probably be preferred even though the breakeven point is higher than at a sales price of $4.40 per unit.

7 Multi product CVP analysis

A very serious limitation of breakeven charts is that they can show the costs, revenues, profits and margins of safety for a single product only, or at best for a **single 'sales mix' of products.**

FAST FORWARD

Breakeven charts for multiple products can be drawn if a constant product sales mix is assumed.

For example suppose that FA sells three products, X, Y and Z which have variable unit costs of $3, $4 and $5 respectively. The sales price of X is $8, the price of Y is $6 and the price of Z is $6. Fixed costs per annum are $10,000.

A breakeven chart cannot be drawn, because we do not know the proportions of X, Y and Z in the sales mix.

Attention!

> If you are not sure about this point, you should try to draw a breakeven chart with the information given. It should not be possible.

There are a number of ways in which we can overcome this problem, however.

7.1 Approach 1: output in $ sales and a constant product mix

Assume that budgeted sales are 2,000 units of X, 4,000 units of Y and 3,000 units of Z. A breakeven chart would make the assumption that output and sales of X, Y and Z are in the proportions 2,000: 4,000: 3,000 at all levels of activity, in other words that the sales mix is 'fixed' in these proportions.

We begin by carrying out some calculations.

Budgeted costs		Costs $		Revenue $
Variable costs of X	(2,000 × $3)	6,000	X (2,000 × $8)	16,000
Variable costs of Y	(4,000 × $4)	16,000	Y (4,000 × $6)	24,000
Variable costs of Z	(3,000 × $5)	15,000	Z (3,000 × $6)	18,000
Total variable costs		37,000	Budgeted revenue	58,000
Fixed costs		10,000		
Total budgeted costs		47,000		

The **breakeven chart** can now be drawn.

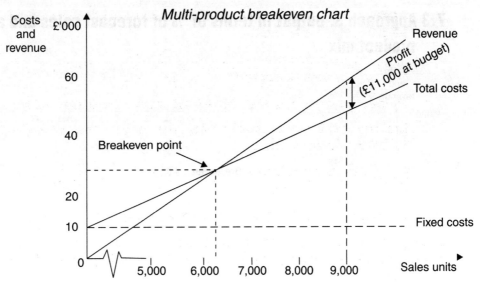

Multi-product breakeven chart

The **breakeven point** is approximately $27,500 of sales revenue. This may either be **read from the chart or computed mathematically**.

(a) The budgeted C/S ratio for all three products together is contribution/sales = $(58,000 – 37,000)/$58,000 = 36.21%.

(b) The required contribution to break even is $10,000, the amount of fixed costs. The breakeven point is $10,000/36.21% = $27,500 (approx) in sales revenue.

The margin of safety is approximately $(58,000 – 27,500) = $30,500.

7.2 Approach 2: products in sequence

The products could be plotted in a particular sequence (say X first, then Y, then Z).

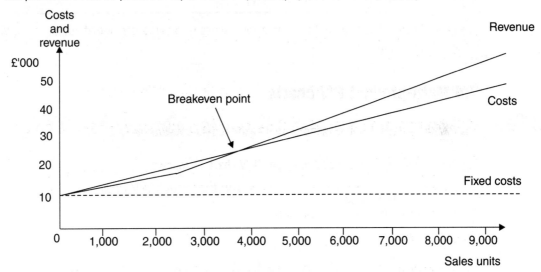

In this case the breakeven point occurs at about 3,800 units of sales (2,000 units of product X and 1,800 units of product Y) and the margin of safety is roughly 2,200 units of Y and 3,000 units of Z.

7.3 Approach 3: output in terms of % of forecast sales and a constant product mix

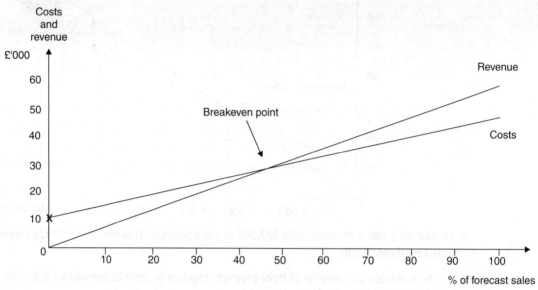

The breakeven point can be read from the graph as approximately 48% of forecast sales ($30,000 of revenue).

Alternatively, with contribution of $(58,000 – 37,000) = $21,000, one percent of forecast sales is associated with $21,000/100 = $210 contribution.

Breakeven point (%) = fixed costs/contribution per 1%
= $10,000/$210 = 47.62%

∴ Margin of safety = (100 – 47.62) = 52.38%

Attention!

> The general point of setting out these three approaches is to demonstrate that output can be viewed in several different ways.

7.4 Multi-product P/V charts

FAST FORWARD

> The **P/V chart** can show information about each product individually.

The same information could be shown on a **P/V chart**, as follows.

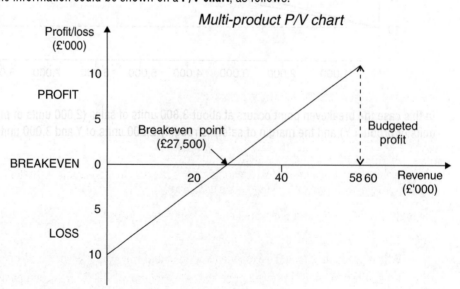

Multi-product P/V chart

An **addition** to the chart would **show further information about the contribution earned by each product individually**, so that their performance and profitability can be compared.

	Contribution $	Sales $	C/S ratio %
Product X	10,000	16,000	62.50
Product Y	8,000	24,000	33.33
Product Z	3,000	18,000	16.67
Total	21,000	58,000	36.21

By convention, the **products are shown individually** on a P/V chart from **left to right**, in **order of the size of their C/S ratio**. In this example, product X will be plotted first, then product Y and finally product Z. A **dotted line** is used to show the **cumulative profit/loss and the cumulative sales** as each product's sales and contribution in turn are added to the sales mix.

Product	Cumulative sales $		Cumulative profit $
X	16,000	($10,000 – $10,000)	–
X and Y	40,000		8,000
X, Y and Z	58,000		11,000

You will see on the graph which follows that these three pairs of data are used to plot the dotted line, to indicate the contribution from each product. The **solid line** which joins the two ends of this dotted line **indicates the average profit** which will be earned from sales of the three products in this mix.

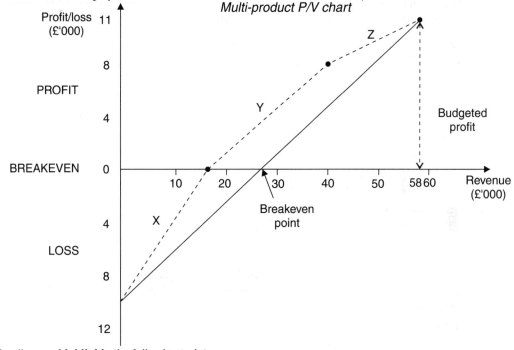

Multi-product P/V chart

The diagram **highlights** the following points.

(a)   Since X is the most profitable in terms of C/S ratio, it might be worth considering an increase in the sales of X, even if there is a consequent fall in the sales of Z.

(b)   Alternatively, the pricing structure of the products should be reviewed and a decision made as to whether the price of product Z should be raised so as to increase its C/S ratio (although an increase is likely to result in some fall in sales volume).

The **multi-product P/V chart** therefore helps to **identify** the following.

(a)   The overall company breakeven point.

(b)   Which products should be expanded in output and which, if any, should be discontinued.

(c)   What effect changes in selling price and sales volume will have on the company's breakeven point and profit.

Question

A company sells three products, X, Y and Z. Cost and sales data for one period are as follows.

	X	Y	Z
Sales volume	2,000 units	2,000 units	5,000 units
Sales price per unit	$3	$4	$2
Variable cost per unit	$2.25	$3.50	$1.25
Total fixed costs	$3,250		

Required

Construct a multi-product P/V chart based on the above information on the axes below.

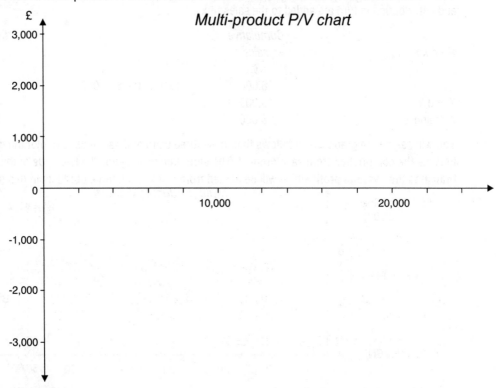

Multi-product P/V chart

Answer

	X	Y	Z	Total
Contribution per unit	$0.75	$0.50	$0.75	$
Budgeted contribution (total)	$1,500	$1,000	$3,750	6,250
Fixed costs				3,250
Budgeted profit				3,000

Product	Cumulative sales $		Cumulative profit $
Z	10,000	($3,750 – $3,250)	500
Z and X	16,000		2,000
Z, X and Y	24,000		3,000

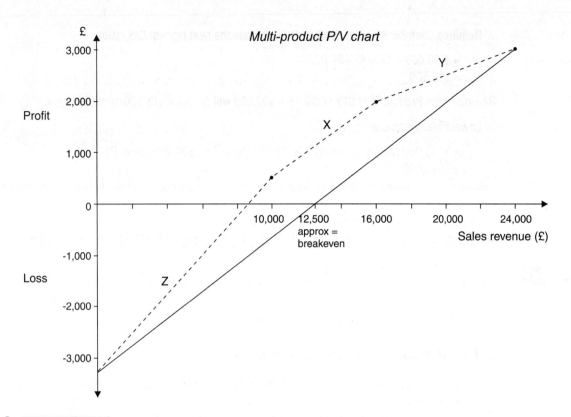

Multi-product P/V chart

Question
Breakeven point and sales value constraints

Sutton produces four products. Relevant data is shown below for period 2.

	Product M	Product A	Product R	Product P
C/S ratio	5%	10%	15%	20%
Maximum sales value	$200,000	$120,000	$200,000	$180,000
Minimum sales value	$50,000	$50,000	$20,000	$10,000

The fixed costs for period 2 are budgeted at $60,000.

Required

Fill in the blank in the sentence below.

The lowest breakeven sales value, subject to meeting the minimum sales value constraints, is $............. .

Answer

The correct answer is $390,000

Breakeven point occurs when contribution = fixed costs

∴ Minimum breakeven point occurs when contribution is $60,000.

Contribution achieved from minimum sales value

		$
M	5% × $50,000	2,500
A	10% × $50,000	5,000
R	15% × $20,000	3,000
P	20% × $10,000	2,000
		12,500

Product P has the highest C/S ratio and so should be produced first (as it earns more contribution per $ of revenue than the others).

Contribution from sales of P between minimum and maximum points = $170,000 × 20% = $34,000

∴ Required contribution from Product R (which has the next highest C/S ratio)

> = \$(60,000 − 12,500 − 34,000)
> = \$13,500

Revenue from Product R of \$13,500/0.15 = \$90,000 will produce \$13,500 of contribution.

∴ Lowest breakeven sales

> = \$130,000 (minimum sales) + \$170,000 (from P) + \$90,000 (from R)
> = \$390,000

8 The advantages and limitations of CVP analysis

FAST FORWARD

Do not forget that CVP analysis does have **limitations**: for example, it is only valid within a 'relevant range' of output volumes; and it measures profitability, but does not consider the volume of capital employed to achieve such profits.

8.1 Limitations of breakeven charts

- A breakeven chart can **only apply to one single product** or a single mix (fixed proportions) of a group of products.
- It is **assumed** that **fixed costs are the same in total** and **variable costs are the same per unit at all levels of output**. This is a simplification.
  - Fixed costs will change if output falls or increases substantially. (Most fixed costs are 'step costs', rising or falling in stepped amounts if output and sales rise above or fall below a given level).
  - The variable cost per unit will decrease where economies of scale are made at higher output volumes, and the variable cost per unit will also eventually rise where diseconomies of scale begin to appear at higher volumes of output (for example the extra cost of labour in overtime working).

A breakeven chart is drawn on the assumption that fixed costs and the variable cost per unit are constant, this is **only correct within the relevant range of output**.

8.2 Advantages of CVP analysis

At its most simple level, CVP analysis assumes a constant variable cost per unit at all levels of output, a constant sales price per unit at all levels of sales, and constant fixed costs at all levels of output. As earlier examples in this chapter have shown, CVP analysis can be used to analyse the effects of changes in the sales price above or below a certain level of output and sales, or changes in the variable costs per unit or the fixed costs per period.

CVP analysis is based on fairly simple logic and simple arithmetic, but it has been found to apply to a number of business situations, and so is a useful planning and decision-making technique.

8.3 Summary: using CVP analysis

In spite of limitations, breakeven analysis is a **useful technique** for managers in planning sales prices, the desired sales mix, and profitability.

Breakeven analysis should be used with a full awareness of its limitations, but can usefully be applied to **provide simple and quick estimates of breakeven volumes or profitability given variations** in sales price, variable and fixed costs within a 'relevant range' of output/sales volumes.

It is not generally applicable to more complex decision-making situations, where an understanding of relevant costs, such as opportunity costs, may be required. Relevant costs and opportunity costs are explained in the next chapter.

Exam focus point

CVP analysis, expected values and decision making issues were all examined in a question in the December 2003 exam. General decision making issues involving three different scenarios for increasing output and revenues, involving an element of budgeting, were examined in December 2006. Profit contribution calculations were examined in June 2007. The examiner noted here that 'As noted in previous questions, the most successful approach was to read the question carefully'. For success in this exam, and indeed any exam, read the question and answer the question set.

Key learning points

- **CVP analysis** has a number of purposes: to provide information to management about cost behaviour for routine **planning** and 'one-off' **decision making**; to determine what volume of sales is needed at any given budgeted sales price in order to **break even**; to identify the 'risk' in the budget by measuring the **margin of safety**; to calculate the effects on profit of changes in variable costs, sales prices, fixed costs, and so on.

- Make sure that you understand how to calculate the **breakeven point**, the **C/S ratio**, the **margin of safety** and **target profits**, and can apply the principles of CVP analysis to decisions about whether to change sales prices or costs. You should also be able to construct a **breakeven chart**.

- Do not forget that CVP analysis does have **limitations**: for example, it is only valid within a 'relevant range' of output volumes; and it measures profitability, but does not consider the volume of capital employed to achieve such profits.

Quick quiz

1   What is the formula for calculating the breakeven point in terms of the number of units required to break even?
2   Give the formula which uses the C/S ratio to calculate the breakeven point.
3   What is the margin of safety?
4   What do the axes of a breakeven chart represent?
5   Give three uses of breakeven charts.
6   What is a profit/volume chart?
7   What does the horizontal axis of the P/V chart represent?
8   What are the limitations of breakeven charts and CVP analysis?

Answers to quick quiz

1. Breakeven point (units) = $\dfrac{\text{Total fixed costs}}{\text{Contribution per unit}}$

2. Sales value at breakeven point = $\dfrac{\text{Fixed costs}}{\text{C/S ratio}} = \dfrac{\text{Required contribution}}{\text{C/S ratio}}$

3. The margin of safety is the difference in units between the budgeted sales volume and the breakeven sales volume.

4. The vertical axis represents money (costs and revenue) and the horizontal axis represents the level of activity (production and sales).

5. Breakeven charts are used as follows.

    - To plan the production of a company's products
    - To market a company's products
    - To give a visual display of breakeven arithmetic

6. The profit/volume chart is a variation of the breakeven chart which provides a simple illustration of the relationship of costs and profit to sales.

7. 'V' on the horizontal axis is volume or value of sales.

8.
    - A breakeven chart can only apply to a single product or a single mix of a group of products.
    - A breakeven chart may be time-consuming to prepare.
    - It assumes fixed costs are constant at all levels of output.
    - It assumes that variable costs are the same per unit at all levels of output.
    - It assumes that sales prices are constant at all levels of output.
    - It assumes production and sales are the same (inventory levels are ignored).
    - It ignores the uncertainty in the estimates of fixed costs and variable cost per unit.

Decision making techniques

Introduction

Management is all about making decisions. This chapter identifies the costs and revenues that are relevant to particular situations, and describes a number of techniques that can be used by managers in specific scenarios to make an appropriate decision.

Learning objectives

On completion of this chapter you will be able to:

Syllabus reference

- describe the concept of relevant costs and its importance for decision making — 6
- describe the nature of cost behaviour, and its relevance for decision making — 5, 6
- understand the concept of opportunity cost, and its relevance for decision making — 6
- apply concepts of relevant costs and opportunity costs to analysing decision problems — 6
- apply concepts of relevant costs and opportunity costs to decision problems involving scarce resources and limiting factors — 6
- apply decision-making techniques, particularly the concept of expected value, to decisions involving uncertainty (probabilities) — 7
- outline the advantages and limitations of using an opportunity cost approach for decision making — 6

1 Introduction: decision making and relevant costs

A large part of accounting is concerned with recording actual revenues and expenditures, and reporting historical profits or losses. For this aspect of accounting, for example in preparing the annual financial accounts of a company, the concepts of variable and fixed costs, and of direct and indirect costs, are not necessary or relevant.

Another major area of accounting is the preparation of budgets and regular plans. For this aspect of accounting, it is necessary to recognise the difference between fixed and variable costs, and that total costs will rise or fall with rises or falls in the level of activity.

Yet another area of management accounting is the analysis of costs and revenue that would occur (or be lost) as a result of making specific 'one-off' decisions. A decision of this type involves making a choice between two or more possible courses of action. Examples of 'one-off' decisions include:

(a) Make-or-buy decisions, ie should an organisation make a component itself, or buy it in from an outside supplier?

(b) Sub-contracting decisions, ie should an organisation do a job itself, or put the work out to a sub-contractor?

(c) Minimum pricing decisions, ie what is the minimum price that should be charged for a special job or item, to ensure that a profit will be made from the sale?

(d) Extra shift decisions, ie should work be increased from one shift a day to two shifts, or from two shifts a day to three shifts?

The common characteristic of 'one-off' decisions is that an organisation is faced with a decision outside the normal planning and decision-making routine, and information about the extra costs and extra revenues (that would arise as a result) is needed to help with making the decision. An understanding of fixed and variable costs is important for decision making, but other aspects of cost behaviour are likely to be relevant too.

The basic principle for decision making is assumed to be that a course of action is worth taking if, as a result, the organisation increases its total profit. A course of action is not worth taking if it would result in a fall in profit, or in a sub-optimal profit being achieved.

To analyse whether or not a course of action would result in higher profit or in an optimal profit being achieved, relevant costs must be used to evaluate the decision.

Examination questions on decision problems with relevant costs can often be identified by the words: 'decide', 'decision', 'advise', 'advice', 'recommend' or 'suggest whether', 'what is the minimum price...?' or 'what is the maximum (cost)...?'

2 Cost behaviour and decision making

Cost behaviour is simply a term referring to the way in which the total cost of an item will change as a result of something new happening, or as a result of the level of activity being increased or reduced. To analyse the consequences of a course of action, it is necessary to estimate what will happen to costs (and revenue) as a result.

Within the normal range of output, costs can usually be assumed to be either variable, fixed or semi-variable. A decision resulting in a higher level of activity would therefore be expected to result in higher total variable costs, but no change in fixed costs.

Costs should be categorised as either fixed or variable in relation to the span of time under consideration. Over a sufficiently **long period of time of several years, virtually all costs are variable.** For example:

- Salaried employees could be released or land and buildings could be sold if demand dropped
- Additional managers could be appointed and land and buildings acquired if demand increased
- Rents could be renegotiated

Within shorter time periods, costs will be either fixed or variable in relation to changes in activity level. The shorter the time period, the greater the probability that a cost will be fixed.

2.1 Step fixed costs

Over a time period of one year, costs associated with providing an organisation's operating capacity (such as the salaries of senior managers) will probably be fixed in relation to changes in activity level. A decision about the level of an organisation's operating capacity will have been made as part of the long-term planning process and so cannot easily be reversed in the short term. For example, machinery would not be sold simply because demand drops in one month.

Spending on some fixed costs can be adjusted in the short term to **reflect changes in activity level**. An example is the salaries of supervisors. If demand drops significantly in the short-term, supervisors might continue to be employed in the hope that the decline is only temporary. If demand fails to pick up, supervisors might eventually be made redundant. On the other hand, if demand increases above a certain critical level, additional supervisors may need to be employed. Thus supervisors' salaries can change in response to changes in demand in a manner described as a **step fixed cost**. Within a given time period, step fixed costs are **fixed within specified activity levels** but increase or decrease by a constant amount at various critical activity levels.

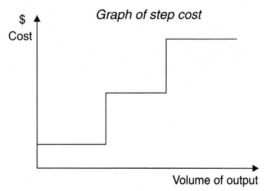

The relationship between cost behaviour and time can be summarised as:

- **Over a given short time period, such as one year, costs will be fixed, variable or semi-variable.**
- **Over longer time periods of several years, all costs will tend to change in response to large changes in activity level.**

3 Relevant costs and non-relevant costs

Accounting information can be used to identify a profit-maximising or cost-minimising decision option. When accounting figures are used for this purpose, **relevant costs** must be used. A relevant cost is a future cash flow arising as a direct consequence of a decision.

Avoidable costs, **differential** costs and **opportunity** costs are all relevant costs.

Non-relevant costs include **sunk** costs, **committed** costs and **notional** (imputed) costs.

Directly attributable fixed costs are relevant costs, general fixed overheads are not.

The costs which should be used for decision making are often referred to as **relevant costs**.

Key term

> A **relevant cost** is a future cash flow arising as a direct consequence of a decision.

Relevant costs are **future costs**.

(a)   A decision is about the future; it cannot alter what has been done already. A cost that has been incurred in the past is totally irrelevant to any decision that is being made 'now'. It is a **sunk cost**.

(b)   Costs that have been incurred include not only costs that have already been paid, but also costs that are the subject of legally binding contracts, even if payments due under the contract have not yet been made. These are **committed costs**.

Relevant costs are **cash flows**. Costs or charges which do not reflect additional cash inflows or spending should be ignored for the purpose of decision making. These include the following.

- **Depreciation**. Depreciation is a means of spreading the cost of a non-current asset over its useful life, and is not a cash flow. The only cash flow is the cash paid to acquire the non-current asset in the first place, and the cash received (if any) from its eventual disposal.

- Any **notional** rent or **notional** interest charged in the accounts.

Relevant costs are those arising as a **direct consequence of a decision**. Costs that will occur whatever decision or course of action is taken can be ignored. Only costs that **will differ** under some or all of the available opportunities should be considered. Relevant costs are therefore sometimes referred to as **incremental costs**. For example, if an employee is expected to have no other work to do during the next week, but will be paid his basic wage (of, say, $200 per week) for attending work, his manager might decide to give him a job which earns only $80. The net gain to the business is $80 and the $200 is irrelevant to the decision, because although it is a future cash flow, **it is a cost that will be incurred anyway**. The business will not want to keep paying the employee $200 each week to do work that earns only $80, but in the short-term, for one week only, it is better to earn an extra $80 than not to earn it.

Relevant costs are therefore future, incremental cash flows.

Other terms can be used to describe relevant costs.

Key term

> **Avoidable costs**. These are costs that would not be incurred if the activity to which they relate did not exist.

One of the situations in which it is necessary to identify avoidable costs is in deciding whether or not to discontinue a product. The only costs that would be saved from shutting down a product line are the **avoidable costs**. These are usually the variable costs and probably also some specific fixed costs. Costs that would be incurred whether or not the product is discontinued are **unavoidable costs.**

Key term

> **Differential cost**. This is the difference in relevant costs between alternative courses of action.

The term **'differential costs'** is used to compare the differences in cost between **two alternative** courses of action, while **'incremental costs'** is used to state the relevant costs when **two or more** options are compared. If option A will cost an extra $300 and option B will cost an extra $360, the differential cost is $60.

In June 2006 a question gave a scenario where some costs had been contracted and some only quoted for. The decision to be made would cause both costs to be less than their contracted/quoted amount.

3.1 Opportunity cost

Opportunity cost is the benefit which has been given up, by choosing one option instead of the next most profitable alternative.

Suppose for example that there are three mutually exclusive options, A, B and C. The net profit from each would be $80, $100 and $70 respectively.

Since only one option can be selected option B would be chosen because it offers the biggest benefit.

	$
Profit from option B	100
Less **opportunity cost** (ie the benefit from the next most profitable alternative, A)	**80**
Differential benefit of option B	20

The decision to choose option B would not be taken simply because it offers a profit of $100, but because it offers a differential profit of $20 in excess of the next most profitable course of action.

3.2 Non-relevant costs

A number of terms are used to describe costs that are **irrelevant for decision making**.

A **sunk cost** is a cost that has already been incurred and hence should not be taken account of in decision making.

Management decisions can only affect the future. In decision making, managers therefore require information about future costs and revenues which would be affected by the decision under review. A sunk cost has been incurred already, and the decision currently under consideration cannot affect it. An example is the cost of goods or materials that have already been purchased. A decision about what to do with these goods or materials should not be influenced by what they originally cost, only by the different possible uses that these materials have in the future.

A **committed cost** is a future cash outflow that will be incurred anyway, whatever decision is taken now about alternative opportunities.

Committed costs may exist because of contracts already entered into by the organisation, which it cannot get out of.

A **notional cost** or **imputed cost** is a hypothetical accounting cost to reflect the use of a benefit for which no actual cash expense is incurred.

Examples in cost accounting systems include the following.

(a)   Notional rent, such as that charged to a cost centre or profit centre of an organisation for the use of accommodation that the organisation owns.

(b)   Notional interest charges on capital employed, sometimes made against a profit centre or cost centre.

3.3 Fixed and variable costs

Unless you are given an indication to the contrary, it is likely that:

- Variable costs will be relevant costs, and
- Fixed costs are irrelevant to a decision.

This need not be the case, however, and you should analyse variable and fixed cost data carefully. Do not forget that 'fixed' costs may only be fixed in the short term.

3.4 Attributable fixed costs

There might be occasions when a fixed cost is a relevant cost, and you must be aware of the distinction between 'specific' or 'directly attributable' fixed costs, and general fixed overheads.

(a)   **Directly attributable fixed costs** are those costs which although fixed within a relevant range of activity level, or regarded as fixed because management has set a budgeted expenditure level, would either:

   (i)   **increase if certain extra activities were undertaken**

   (ii)   **decrease/be eliminated entirely if a decision were taken either to reduce the scale of operations or shut down entirely**

(b)   **General fixed overheads** are those fixed overheads which will be **unaffected by decisions to increase or decrease the scale of operations.** For example an apportioned share of fixed costs which would be completely unaffected by the decisions, such as share of head office charges.

Directly attributable fixed costs are relevant to decision making, **general fixed overheads are not**.

4 Some rules for identifying relevant costs

FAST FORWARD

The total relevant cost of a scarce resource consists of the variable cost of the scarce resource plus the opportunity cost of the contribution forgone by not being able to use the scarce resource for its next most profitable use.

4.1 The relevant cost of materials

The relevant cost of raw materials is **generally** their **current replacement cost**.

The exception to this rule occurs if materials have already been purchased but will not be replaced. The relevant cost of such materials is the **higher of** the following:

*   **Their current resale value**, and
*   **The value they would obtain if they were put to an alternative use.**

If the materials have no resale value and no other possible use, then the relevant cost of using them for the opportunity under consideration would be nil.

You should test your knowledge of the relevant cost of materials by attempting the following exercise.

Question				Relevant cost of materials

Darwin has been approached by a customer who would like a special job to be done, and who is willing to pay $22,000 for it. The job would require the following materials.

Material	Total units required	Units already in inventory	Book value of units in inventory $/unit	Realisable value $/unit	Replacement cost $/unit
A	1,000	0	–	–	6.00
B	1,000	600	2.00	2.50	5.00
C	1,000	700	3.00	2.50	4.00
D	200	200	4.00	6.00	9.00

Material B is used regularly by Darwin, and if units of B are required for this job, they would need to be replaced to meet other production demand.

Materials C and D are in inventory as the result of previous over-buying, and they have a restricted use. No other use could be found for material C, but the units of material D could be used in another job as substitute for 300 units of material E, which currently costs $5 per unit (and of which the company has no units in inventory at the moment).

Required

Calculate the relevant costs of material for deciding whether or not to accept the contract.

(a)   *Material A* is not yet owned. It would have to be bought in full at the replacement cost of $6 per unit.

(b)   *Material B* is used regularly by the company. There are existing inventories (600 units) but if these are used on the contract under review a further 600 units would be bought to replace them. Relevant costs are therefore 1,000 units at the replacement cost of $5 per unit.

(c)   1,000 units of *material C* are needed and 700 are already in inventory. If used for the contract, a further 300 units must be bought at $4 each. The existing inventories of 700 will not be replaced. If they are used for the contract, they could not be sold at $2.50 each. The realisable value of these 700 units is an opportunity cost of sales revenue forgone.

(d)   The required units of *material D* are already in inventory and will not be replaced. There is an opportunity cost of using D in the contract because there are alternative opportunities either to sell the existing inventories for $6 per unit ($1,200 in total) or avoid other purchases (of material E), which would cost 300 x $5 = $1,500. Since substitution for E is more beneficial, $1,500 is the opportunity cost.

(e)   *Summary of relevant costs*

	$
Material A (1,000 × $6)	6,000
Material B (1,000 × $5)	5,000
Material C (300 × $4) plus (700 × $2.50)	2,950
Material D	1,500
Total	15,450

4.2 The relevant cost of using machines

Using machinery will involve some incremental costs, **user costs**. These include repair costs arising from use, hire charges and any fall in resale value of owned assets which results from their use. Depreciation is *not* a relevant cost.

4.3 Example: user costs

Sydney is considering whether to undertake some contract work for a customer. The machinery required for the contract would be as follows.

(a)   A special cutting machine will have to be hired for three months. Hire charges for this machine are $75 per month, with a minimum hire charge of $300.

(b)   All other machinery required in the production for the contract has already been purchased by the organisation on hire purchase terms. The monthly hire purchase payments for this machinery are $500. This consists of $450 for capital repayment and $50 as an interest charge. The last hire purchase payment is to be made in two months' time. The cash price of this machinery was $9,000 two years ago. It is being depreciated on a straight line basis at the rate of $200 per month. However, it still has a useful life which will enable it to be operated for another 36 months.

The machinery is highly specialised and is unlikely to be required for other, more profitable jobs over the period during which the contract work would be carried out. Although there is no immediate market for selling this machine, it is expected that a customer might be found in the future. It is further estimated that the machine would lose $200 in its eventual sale value if it is used for the contract work.

Required

Calculate the relevant cost of machinery for the contract.

Solution

(a) The cutting machine will incur an incremental cost of $300, the minimum hire charge.

(b) The historical cost of the other machinery is irrelevant as a past cost; depreciation is irrelevant as a non-cash cost; and future hire purchase repayments are irrelevant because they are committed costs. The only relevant cost is the loss of resale value of the machinery, estimated at $200 through use. This user cost will not arise until the machinery is eventually resold and the $200 should be 'discounted' to allow for the time value of money. However, discounting is ignored here.

(c) *Summary of relevant costs*

	$
Incremental hire costs	300
User cost of machinery	200
	500

A machine which originally cost $12,000 has an estimated life of ten years and is depreciated at the rate of $1,200 a year. It has been unused for some time, as expected orders did not materialise.

A special order has now been received which would require the use of the machine for two months.

The current net realisable value of the machine is $8,000. If it is used for the job, its value is expected to fall to $7,500. The net book value of the machine is $8,400.

Routine maintenance of the machine currently costs $40 a month. With use, the cost of maintenance and repairs would increase to $60 a month.

Required

Determine the cost of using the machine for the order.

Answer

	$
Loss in net realisable value of the machine through using it on the order $(8,000 – 7,500)	500
Costs in excess of existing routine maintenance costs $(120 – 80)	40
Total marginal user cost	540

A printing company carries out work for a number of clients. One particularly important client has telephoned to ask whether the company will do a special printing job. As a special favour, the customer would like this job to be priced very competitively. The managing director is inclined to respond favourably to the request, in view of the large amounts of routine work the company does for the customer.

The cost estimator has provided the following estimate for the job.

	$
Grade A labour (50 hours at $15 per hour)	750
Grade B labour (10 hours at $20 per hour)	200
Ordinary paper, at cost	450
Special paper, at cost	300
Variable overhead (60 hours at $3 per hour)	180
Fixed overhead (60 hours at $20 per hour)	1,200
	3,080

The following information is also available.

All Grade A labour is paid for a basic 40-hour week. This job could be done mostly in normal working time, and only 10 hours of Grade A overtime would be needed.

Similarly, all Grade B labour is paid for a 40-hour week. Only 5 hours of Grade B overtime would be needed to do the work.

There is no other work for which the Grade A or Grade B labour would be needed.

All overtime is paid at 50% above normal hourly rates.

The ordinary paper to do the work is already in inventory. It is regularly used on many jobs by the company. A 10% increase in the cost of ordinary paper has just been notified by the paper suppliers.

The special paper for the job is already in inventory. It was purchased some months ago for another job, for a customer who suddenly went out of business. There is no other use for the paper, but it could be re-sold to the supplier for $100.

Required

What is the minimum price the company should charge for the job, if it wanted to make no profit but no loss on doing the work? If the managing director decides to charge a 10% mark-up on this minimum price, what price should be quoted to the customer?

Answer

(a) Labour in normal time is a committed cost, and so is irrelevant to a minimum pricing decision. Only overtime hours, paid at 50% over the normal rate, are relevant.

(b) By using ordinary paper for this job, additional paper must be purchased by the company, at a price 10% above the cost of paper in inventory. This replacement price is the relevant cost, because replacement is a direct consequence of the decision to do the special job for the customer.

(c) The relevant cost of the special paper is its opportunity cost, ie its resale value.

(d) It is assumed that variable overhead is a relevant cost, and fixed overhead will be unaffected and so is irrelevant.

(e) *Summary of relevant costs*

	$
Grade A labour (10 hours × $22.50)	225
Grade B labour (5 hours × $30)	150
Ordinary paper ($450 x 110%)	495
Special paper	100
Variable overhead	180
Minimum price	1,150

If the job is priced at 10% above the minimum price, the charge to the customer will be $1,265.

5 The relevant cost of scarce resources: limiting factors

When an organisation provides a range of products or services to its markets, but has a restricted amount of resources available to it, then it will have to make a decision about what **product mix** (or mix of services) it will provide. Its volume of output and sales will be constrained by its limited key resources rather than by sales demand, and so management faces a decision about **how scarce capacity should best be used**. The scarce resource might be a type of material, machine time, cash or a particular labour skill.

Key term

> An organisation has a **scarce resource** if it does not have enough of the resource to undertake every available opportunity for making more contribution towards profit. Thus machine time would be scarce if every machine was being operated at full capacity, without being able to produce enough output to meet sales demand in full.

From an accounting point of view, the assumption is that a firm faced with a problem of scarce resources would select a product or service mix that would maximise overall profitability, and so **maximise** total **contribution**.

When there is just one scarce resource, the technique for establishing the contribution-maximising product mix or service mix is to **rank** the products or services in order of **contribution-earning ability per unit of the scarce resource**.

5.1 Example

Alphabet makes two products, P and Q, for which there is unlimited sales demand at the budgeted sales price of each. A unit of P takes 8 hours to make, and has a variable cost of $36 and a sales price of $72. A unit of Q takes 5 hours to make, and has a variable cost of $24 and a sales price of $48. Both products use the same type of labour, which is in restricted supply. Which product should be made in order to maximise profits?

Solution and discussion

(a)   There is no limitation on sales demand, but **labour** is in restricted supply, and so to determine the profit-maximising production mix, we must rank the products in order of **contribution-earning capability per labour hour**.

	P	Q
	$	$
Sales price	72	48
Variable costs	36	24
Contribution	36	24
Hours per unit	8 hrs	5 hrs
Contribution per labour hour	$4.50	$4.80
Ranking	**2nd**	**1st**

Although units of Product P have the higher unit contribution, product Q is more profitable because it earns a **greater contribution per unit** in each scarce hour of labour time worked. For instance, eight units of product Q (worth 8 × $24 = $192) can be made in the same time as five units of P (worth only 5 × $36 = $180).

(b)   *Other considerations*

A profit-maximising budget would therefore be to produce units of product Q only, within the assumptions made. It is important to remember, however, that other considerations, so far excluded from the problem, might alter the decision entirely.

(i)   Can the **sales price** of either product be **raised**, thereby increasing unit contribution, and the contribution per labour hour, without reducing sales demand? Since sales demand is apparently unlimited, it would be reasonable to suspect that both products are under-priced.

(ii)   To what extent are sales of each product **interdependent**? For example, a manufacturer of knives and forks could not expect to cease production of knives without affecting sales demand for the forks.

(iii)   Would a decision to cease production of product P entirely really have no effect on fixed costs? The assumption that **fixed costs** are unaffected by limiting factor decisions is not always valid, and closure of the production line for either product might result in **fixed cost savings** (for example a reduction in production planning costs, product design costs, or equipment depreciation).

(c)   *Qualitative factors*

There are also qualitative factors to consider.

(i)   Would a decision to make and sell just product Q have a harmful effect on **customer loyalty** and sales demand?

(ii) Is the decision going to affect the long-term plans of the company as well as the short-term? If product P is not produced next year, it is likely that **competitors** will take over the markets vacated by Alphabet. **Labour** skilled in the manufacture of product P will be lost, and a decision in one year's time to re-open manufacture of product P might not be possible.

(iii) **Why is there a shortage of labour?** Are the skills required difficult to obtain, perhaps because the company is using very old-fashioned production methods, or is the company a high-tech newcomer located in a low-tech area? Or perhaps the conditions of work are so unappealing that people simply do not want to work for the company.

Whatever the scarce resource, it is always advisable to ask why it is scarce, and whether the shortage could be overcome. If machine hours are in short supply is this because more machines are needed, or newer, more reliable and efficient machines? If materials are in short supply, what are competitors doing? Have they found an equivalent or better substitute? Is it time to redesign the product?

Exam focus point

This example illustrates the need to be able to think about other factors affecting such decisions in addition to pure financial considerations. A question in the June 2002 exam required a quantitative evaluation of two lease contract options, on a relevant cost basis, but also a discussion of non-financial aspects that should be taken into account in any recommendation for action. Relevant costs and decision making were examined in June 2004.

5.2 Scarce resource and restricted sales demand

When there is a maximum **limit on sales demand** for an organisation's products or services, the products or services should still be ranked in order of contribution-earning ability per unit of the scarce resource. However, the profit-maximising decision will be to produce the **top-ranked products** (or to provide the top-ranked services) **up to the sales demand limit**.

5.3 Example: one scarce resource and limited sales demand

Wantmore manufactures and sells three products, B, S and N, for which budgeted sales demand, unit selling prices and unit variable costs are as follows.

	Product B		Product S		Product N	
Budgeted sales demand	550 units		500 units		400 units	
	$	$	$	$	$	$
Unit sales price		16		18		14
Variable costs: materials	8		6		2	
labour	4		6		9	
		12		12		11
Unit contribution		4		6		3

The company has existing inventories of 250 units of B and 200 units of N, which it is quite willing to use up to meet sales demand. All three products use the same direct materials and the same type of direct labour. In the next year, the available supply of materials will be restricted to $4,800 (at cost) and the available supply of labour to $6,600 (at cost). What product mix and sales mix would maximise the company's profits in the next year?

Solution and discussion

There appear to be **two** scarce resources, direct materials and direct labour. However, this is not certain, and because there is a limited sales demand as well, it might be that there is:

(a) No limiting factor at all, except sales demand – i.e. none of the resources is scarce
(b) Only one scarce resource preventing the full potential sales demand being achieved

Step 1   Begin by establishing **how many scarce resources** there are, and if there are any, which one or which ones they are. In this example we have:

	B Units	S Units	N Units
Budgeted sales	550	500	400
Inventory in hand	250	0	200
Minimum production to meet demand	300	500	200

	Minimum production to meet sales demand Units	Required materials at cost $	Required labour at cost $
B	300	2,400	1,200
S	500	3,000	3,000
N	200	400	1,800
Total required		5,800	6,000
Total available		4,800	6,600
(Shortfall)/Surplus		(1,000)	600

Materials are a limiting factor, but labour is not.

Step 2   The next step is to rank the three products in order of contribution earned per unit of limiting factor/scarce resource (in this case per $1 of direct materials consumed).

	B $	S $	N $
Unit contribution	4	6	3
Cost of materials	8	6	2
Contribution per $1 materials	$0.50	$1.00	$1.50
Ranking	**3rd**	**2nd**	**1st**

Step 3   Product N should be manufactured up to the limit where units produced plus units in inventory will meet sales demand, then Product S second and finally Product B third, until all the available materials are used up.

Ranking	Product	Sales demand less units in inventory Units	Production quantity Units		Materials cost $
1st	N	200	200	(× $2)	400
2nd	S	500	500	(× $6)	3,000
3rd	B	300	175	(× $8)	* 1,400
			Total available		4,800

* Balancing amount using up total available.

Step 4   The profit-maximising budget is as follows.

	B Units	S Units	N Units
Opening inventory	250	0	200
Add production	175	500	200
Sales	425	500	400

	B $	S $	N $	Total $
Revenue	6,800	9,000	5,600	21,400
Variable costs	5,100	6,000	4,400	15,500
Contribution	1,700	3,000	1,200	5,900

5.4 Assumptions in limiting factor analysis

In the previous examples, the following assumptions were made. If any of the assumptions are not valid, then the profit-maximising decision might be different.

(a)   **Fixed costs will be the same** regardless of the decision that is taken, and so the profit maximising and contribution-maximising output level will be the same. This will not necessarily be true, since some fixed costs might be **directly attributable** to a product or service. A decision to reduce or cease altogether activity on a product or service might therefore result in some fixed cost savings, which would have to be taken into account.

(b)   The **unit variable cost is constant**, regardless of the output quantity of a product or service. This implies that:

(i)   the price of resources will be unchanged regardless of quantity; for example, there will be no bulk purchase discount of raw materials

(ii)   efficiency and productivity levels will be unchanged; regardless of output quantity, the direct labour productivity, the machine time per unit, and the materials consumption per unit will remain the same.

(c)   The **estimates** of sales demand for each product, and the resources required to make each product, are **known with certainty.** In the previous example, there were estimates of the maximum sales demand for each of three products, and these estimates were used to establish the profit-maximising product mix. **Suppose the estimates were wrong?** The product mix finally chosen would then either mean that some sales demand of the most profitable item would be unsatisfied, or that production would exceed sales demand, leaving some inventory unsold. Clearly, once a profit-maximising output decision is reached, management will have to **keep their decision under continual review**, and adjust their decision as appropriate in the light of actual results.

(d)   **Units of output are divisible**, and a profit-maximising solution might include fractions of units as the optimum output level. Where fractional answers are not realistic, some rounding of the figures will be necessary.

Exam focus point

In June 2005 limiting factor analysis was examined. It was a largely numerical question but part (b) required consideration of other factors, not just financial, in the making of a decision.

Question   Acceptable offer?

A company has been making a machine to order for a customer, but the customer has since gone into liquidation, and there is no prospect that any money will be obtained from the winding up of the company.

Costs incurred to date in manufacturing the machine are $50,000 and progress payments of $15,000 had been received from the customer prior to the liquidation.

The sales department has found another company willing to buy the machine for $34,000 once it has been completed.

To complete the work, the following costs would be incurred.

(a)   Materials: these have been bought at a cost of $6,000. They have no other use, and if the machine is not finished, they would be sold for scrap for $2,000.

(b)   Further labour costs would be $8,000. Labour is in short supply, and if the machine is not finished, the work force would be switched to another job, which would earn $30,000 in revenue, and incur direct costs of $12,000 and absorbed (fixed) overhead of $8,000.

(c)   Consultancy fees $4,000. If the work is not completed, the consultant's contract would be cancelled at a cost of $1,500.

(d)   General overheads of $8,000 would be added to the cost of the additional work.

Required

Assess whether the new customer's offer should be accepted.

(a) Costs incurred in the past, or revenue received in the past are not relevant because they cannot affect a decision about what is best for the future. Costs incurred to date of $50,000 and revenue received of $15,000 are 'water under the bridge' and should be ignored.

(b) Similarly, the price paid in the past for the materials is irrelevant. The only relevant cost of materials affecting the decision is the opportunity cost of the revenue from scrap which would be forgone – $2,000.

(c) *Labour costs*

	$
Labour costs required to complete work	8,000
Opportunity costs: contribution forgone by losing – other work $(30,000 – 12,000)	18,000
Relevant cost of labour	26,000

(d) The incremental cost of consultancy from completing the work is $2,500.

	$
Cost of completing work	4,000
Cost of cancelling contract	1,500
Incremental cost of completing work	2,500

(e) Absorbed overhead is a notional accounting cost and should be ignored. Actual overhead incurred is the only overhead cost to consider. General overhead costs (and the absorbed overhead of the alternative work for the labour force) should be ignored.

(f) Relevant costs may be summarised as follows.

	$	$
Revenue from completing work		34,000
Relevant costs		
Materials: opportunity cost	2,000	
Labour: basic pay	8,000	
Opportunity cost	18,000	
Incremental cost of consultant	2,500	
		30,500
Extra profit to be earned by accepting the completion order		3,500

6 Make or buy decisions

FAST FORWARD

> In a **make or buy** situation with no scarce resources, the relevant costs are the differences in unit variable costs plus differences in directly attributable fixed costs.
>
> In a situation where a company must **subcontract** work to make up a shortfall in its own in-house capabilities, its total costs will be minimised if those units bought have the lowest extra variable cost of buying per unit of scarce resource saved by buying of all the products in question.

A make or buy decision is about whether an organisation should make a product or whether it should pay another organisation to do so. These are some examples of make-or-buy decisions.

- Whether a company should manufacture its own components, or else buy the components from an outside supplier.

- Whether a construction company should do some work with its own employees, or whether it should sub-contract the work to another company.

- Whether a service should be carried out by an internal department or whether the service should be outsourced to an external organisation.

The 'make' option gives management more direct control over the work. The 'buy' option has the benefit that the external organisation has a specialist skill and expertise in the work. Make or buy decisions should **not be based exclusively on cost considerations**.

6.1 Example: make or buy

Starfish makes four components, W, X, Y and Z, for which costs in the forthcoming year are expected to be as follows.

	W	X	Y	Z
Production (units)	1,000	2,000	4,000	3,000
Unit marginal costs	$	$	$	$
Direct materials	4	5	2	4
Direct labour	8	9	4	6
Variable production overheads	2	3	1	2
	14	17	7	12

Directly attributable fixed costs per annum and committed fixed costs are as follows.

	$
Incurred as a direct consequence of making W	1,000
Incurred as a direct consequence of making X	5,000
Incurred as a direct consequence of making Y	6,000
Incurred as a direct consequence of making Z	8,000
Other fixed costs (committed)	30,000
	50,000

A sub-contractor has offered to supply units of W, X, Y and Z for $12, $21, $10 and $14 respectively.

Required

Decide whether Starfish should make or buy the components.

Solution

The **relevant costs are the differential costs between making and buying**, and they consist of differences in unit variable costs plus differences in directly attributable fixed costs.

	W	X	Y	Z
	$	$	$	$
Unit variable cost of making	14	17	7	12
Unit variable cost of buying	12	21	10	14
	(2)	4	3	2
Annual requirements (units)	1,000	2,000	4,000	3,000
	$	$	$	$
Extra variable cost (saving) of buying p.a.	(2,000)	8,000	12,000	6,000
Fixed costs saved by buying	(1,000)	(5,000)	(6,000)	(8,000)
Extra total cost (saving) of buying	(3,000)	3,000	6,000	(2,000)

The company would save $3,000 per annum by sub-contracting component W (where the purchase cost would be less than the marginal cost per unit to make internally) and would save $2,000 pa by sub-contracting component Z (because of the saving in fixed costs of $8,000).

In this example, relevant costs are the variable costs of in-house manufacture, the variable costs of sub-contracted units, and the saving in fixed costs.

6.2 Qualitative factors to consider

Important further considerations include:

(a)   If components W and Z are sub-contracted, the company will have spare capacity. **How should that spare capacity be profitably used?** Are there hidden benefits to be obtained from sub-contracting? Would the **company's workforce resent the loss of work to an outside sub-contractor,** and might such a decision cause an industrial dispute?

(b)   **Would the sub-contractor be reliable with delivery times**, and would they supply components of the **same quality** as those manufactured internally?

(c)   Does the company wish to be **flexible and maintain better control** over operations **by making everything itself?**

(d)   **Are the estimates of fixed cost savings reliable?** In the case of Product W, buying is clearly cheaper than making in-house. In the case of product Z, the decision to buy rather than make would only be financially beneficial if it is feasible that the fixed cost savings of $8,000 will really be 'delivered' by management. All too often in practice, promised savings fail to materialise!

Question	Accept the job?

An information technology consultancy firm has been asked to do an urgent job by a client, for which a price of $2,500 has been offered. The job would require the following.

(a)   30 hours' work from one member of staff, who is paid on an hourly basis, at a rate of $20 per hour, but who would normally be employed on work for clients where the charge-out rate is $45 per hour. No other member of staff is able to do the work of the member of staff in question.

(b)   The use of 5 hours of mainframe computer time, which the firm normally charges out to external users at a rate of $50 per hour. Mainframe computer time is currently used 24 hours a day, 7 days a week.

(c)   Supplies and incidental expenses of $200.

Should the firm accept the job?

Answer

The opportunity cost of the job would be calculated as follows.

	$
Labour (30 hours × $45)	1,350
Computer time opportunity cost (5 hours × $50)	250
Supplies and expenses	200
	1,800

The opportunity cost of labour and computer time is the normal charge-out rate, of $45 and $50 per hour respectively.

A further addition to cost might be added for 'general overhead' depending on the system of costing being used.

The opportunity cost of the job shows that the firm would increase profits by accepting the job, by $(2,500 − 1,800) = $700.

7 Activity-based costing (ABC) and decision making

7.1 Different uses of activity based costing

We have seen that ABC is a method of absorbing overheads to cost units in a way that reflects the causes of the overheads (the cost drivers) and the way that the different products make use of the overheads.

This technique can make a difference to decisions such as 'make or buy' or product continuance. The general principle is that ABC allocates costs to products in a manner different from traditional absorption costing such that decisions based on traditional techniques may be changed if ABC is used.

7.2 Example: adding or deleting products (or departments)

A company manufactures three products, Pawns, Rooks and Bishops. The present net annual income from these is as follows.

	Pawns	Rooks	Bishops	Total
	$	$	$	$
Sales	50,000	40,000	60,000	150,000
Variable costs	30,000	25,000	35,000	90,000
Contribution	20,000	15,000	25,000	60,000
Fixed costs				
(calculated using absorption costing)	17,000	18,000	20,000	55,000
Profit/loss	3,000	(3,000)	5,000	5,000

The company is concerned about its poor profit performance, and is considering whether or not to cease selling Rooks. It is felt that selling prices cannot be raised or lowered without adversely affecting net income. $5,000 of the fixed costs of Rooks are direct fixed costs which would be saved if production ceased (ie there are some attributable fixed costs). All other fixed costs, it is considered, would remain the same.

By **stopping production of Rooks**, the **consequences** would be a $10,000 fall in profits compared to a loss of $3,000. Therefore the production of Rooks should continue.

	$
Loss of contribution	(15,000)
Savings in fixed costs	5,000
Incremental loss	(10,000)

Question	Shutdown decision

How would the above decision change if Pawns, Rooks and Bishops were manufactured in different departments, variable costs could be split down into the costs of direct materials, labour and overheads, and fixed costs could be analysed into the costs of administrative staff and equipment and premises costs?

Answer

The decision would not change at all unless activity based analysis of overheads were undertaken and unexpected cost patterns were revealed.

Thus for example an analysis of the total fixed costs of $55,000 might reveal that $40,000 was for materials handling which under absorption costing was apportioned equally across the three product ranges. In fact Pawns required not only a much higher proportion of deliveries inwards of small amounts of specialised goods but also many more small production runs and set ups that were very time consuming and used up 75% of the $40,000 cost.

This would clearly alter the allocation of fixed overheads which may well cause Pawns to be unprofitable. If the material handling costs would be saved if production ceased then it may be advisable to discontinue producing Pawns.

7.3 Make or buy

We shall now return to the example Starfish earlier in this chapter. The question is not repeated, but the answer is repeated below so that the effect of ABC on the options to be considered can be examined.

Solution

(a)   The **relevant costs** are the differential costs between making and buying, and they consist of **differences in unit variable costs plus differences in directly attributable fixed costs**. Sub-contracting will result in some **fixed cost savings.**

	W	X	Y	Z
	$	$	$	$
Unit variable cost of making	14	17	7	12
Unit variable cost of buying	12	21	10	14
	(2)	4	3	2
Annual requirements (units)	1,000	2,000	4,000	3,000
	$	$	$	$
Extra variable cost of buying (per annum)	(2,000)	8,000	12,000	6,000
Fixed costs saved by buying	(1,000)	(5,000)	(6,000)	(8,000)
Extra total cost of buying	(3,000)	3,000	6,000	(2,000)

(b)   The company would save $3,000 pa by sub-contracting component W (where the purchase cost would be less than the marginal cost per unit to make internally) and would save $2,000 pa by sub-contracting component Z (because of the saving in fixed costs of $8,000).

(c)   In this example, relevant costs are the variable costs of in-house manufacture, the variable costs of sub-contracted units, and the saving in fixed costs.

7.3.1 Comments on the solution in the light of ABC

As discussed in 7.2 above, a 'realignment' of the fixed costs in the manner discussed above may very quickly cause a change in the decision as to which products to make or buy.

We will not make fresh calculations, but you simply have to understand the effects that recalculating the fixed overheads can have. It is all too easy to be seduced by the idea that marginal costing and contribution analysis make the fixed costs irrelevant to many decisions. Costs that are fixed using absorption costing may turn out to be attributable to specific products and may therefore be avoided if the product is discontinued.

7.4 Customer costs and ABC

The creation of cost pools for activities in **ABC** systems allows organisations to arrange costs in a variety of different ways. Because different customers use different amounts of activities, it is possible to **build up costs for individual customers or groups of customers** on an activity basis so that their **relative profitability** can be assessed.

Examples of the build up of customer costs using an activity based system

Activity	Cost driver
Order taking	Number of orders taken
Sales visits	Number of sales visits
Emergency orders	Number of rushed orders
Delivery	Miles travelled
Product handling	Number of pallets or part-pallets handled
After sales service and support	Number of visits
Product repairs and service	Number of repair visits

Drury cites the case of Kanthal, a Swedish company that sells electric heating elements. Customer-related selling costs represented 34% of total costs. In the past Kanthal had allocated these costs on the basis of sales value when customer profitability studies were carried out. The company then introduced an ABC system in order to determine the resources consumed by different customers.

An investigation identified two cost drivers for the resources used to service different customers.

(a)   **Number of orders placed.** Each order had a large fixed cost, which did not vary with the number of items ordered. A customer ordering 10 items 100 times cost more to service than a customer placing a single order for 1,000 items.

(b)   **Non-standard production items.** These cost more to manufacture than standard items.

A cost per order and the cost of handling standard and non-standard items were calculated and a customer profitability analysis (CPA) carried out on the basis of the previous year's sales. The analysis showed that only 40% of customers were profitable, and a further 10% lost 120% of the profits. In other words, 10% of customers incurred losses equal to 120% of Kanthal's total profits. Two of the most unprofitable customers were actually in the top three in terms of total sales volume but made many small orders of non-standard items.

Unprofitable customers identified by CPA should be persuaded to **alter their buying behaviour** so they become profitable customers. In the Kanthal example above, unprofitable customers should be discouraged from placing lots of small orders and/or from buying non-standard products.

The **activity based approach** also **highlights where cost reduction efforts should be focused**. Kanthal should concentrate on reducing ordering cost and the cost of handling non-standard items.

Activity-based CPA allows an organisation to adopt a more **market-orientated approach** to management accounting.

 Question   CPA

B Ltd manufactures components for the heavy goods vehicle industry. The following annual information regarding three of its key customers is available.

	P	Q	R
Gross margin	$897,000	$1,070,000	$1,056,000
General administration costs	$35,000	$67,000	$56,000
Units sold	4,600	5,800	3,800
Orders placed	300	320	480
Sales visits	80	50	100
Invoices raised	310	390	1,050

The company uses an activity based costing system and the analysis of customer-related costs is as follows.

Sales visits	$420 per visit
Order processing	$190 per order placed
Despatch costs	$350 per order placed
Billing and collections	$97 per invoice raised

Using customer profitability analysis, how would the customers be ranked?

Answer

	P	Q	R
	$'000	$'000	$'000
Gross margin	897.00	1,070.00	1,056.00
Less: customer specific costs			
sales visits (80/50/100 × $420)	(33.60)	(21.00)	(42.00)
order processing (300/320/480 × $190)	(57.00)	(60.80)	(91.20)
despatch costs (300/320/480 × $350)	(105.00)	(112.00)	(168.00)
billing and collections (310/390/1,050 × $97)	(30.07)	(37.83)	(101.85)
	671.33	838.37	652.95
Ranking	2	1	3

7.5 Customer profitability statement

There is no set format, but it would normally be similar to the one below. Note that financing costs have been included.

	$'000	$'000
Revenue at list prices		100
Less: discounts given		8
Net revenue		92
Less: cost of goods sold		50
Gross margin		42
Less: customer specific costs	28	
financing costs:		
credit period	3	
customer specific inventory	2	
		33
Net margin from customer		9

Question

Which customer is the most profitable?

Seth Co supplies shoes to Narayan Co and Kipling Co. Each pair of shoes has a list price of $50 and costs Seth Co $25. As Kipling buys in bulk it receives a 10% trade discount for every order for 100 pairs of shoes or more. Narayan receives a 15% discount irrespective of order size, because that company collects the shoes, thereby saving Seth Co any distribution costs. The cost of administering each order is $50 and the distribution cost is $1,000 per order. Narayan makes 10 orders in the year, totalling 420 pairs of shoes, and Kipling places 5 orders for 100 pairs. Which customer is the most profitable for Seth Co?

Answer

It can be shown that Seth Co earns more from supplying Narayan, despite the larger discount percentage:

	Kipling	Narayan
	$	$
Revenue	25,000	21,000
Less: discount	2,500	3,150
Net revenue	22,500	17,850
Less: cost of shoes	(12,500)	(10,500)
customer transport cost	(5,000)	–
customer administration cost	(250)	(500)
Net gain	4,750	6,850

The difference on a unit basis is considerable.

Number of pairs of shoes sold	500	420
Net gain per pair of shoes sold	$9.50	$16.31
Net gain per $1 of sales revenue	$0.19	$0.33

7.6 Other considerations

It is important to remember, however, that considerations other than cost data might alter a decision entirely.

(a) Can the **sales price** of products be **raised**, thereby increasing unit contribution without reducing sales demand?

(b) To what extent are sales of each product **interdependent**? For example, a manufacturer of knives and forks could not expect to cease production of knives without affecting sales demand for the forks.

(c) **Qualitative factors**

    (i) Would a decision to stop selling one product have a harmful effect on **customer loyalty** and sales demand?

    (ii) Is the decision to stop selling a product going to affect the long-term plans of the company as well as the short-term? It is likely that **competitors** will take over the markets vacated. **Labour** skilled in the manufacture of the product will be lost, and a decision in one year's time to reopen manufacture might not be possible.

    (iii) Are the costs too high because the company is using very old-fashioned production methods, or is the company a high-tech newcomer located in a low-tech area and the company has yet to achieve sufficient economies of scale to bring down unit costs?

8 Uncertainty in decision making

FAST FORWARD

Decisions are generally taken without any certainty as to what the actual outcome will be. A range of likely outcomes may be likely. The approach to decision making under conditions of **uncertainty** depends on the attitude of an organisation and its management to risk. Decision-making should certainly be taken with a proper understanding of the different possible outcomes.

A risk-averse manager might opt for the option that offers the best 'worst result' (the **maximin criterion**).

Some of the **assumptions** that are typically made in relevant costing are as follows.

- **Cost behaviour patterns are known**; if a department closes down, for example, the attributable fixed cost savings would be known.

- The **amount** of fixed costs, unit variable costs, sales price and sales demand are **known with certainty**.

- The **objective** of decision making in the short run is to **maximise 'satisfaction'**, which is **often regarded as 'short-term profit'**.

- The **information** on which a decision is based is **complete and reliable**.

In reality, the future outcome from taking any particular course of action can be estimated. A future outcome might even be probable. However, the future can rarely be predicted with certainty. Managers must recognise that when they make a decision, there will often be an element of risk or uncertainty.

8.1 Risk preference

A **risk seeker** is a decision maker who is interested in the best outcomes no matter how small the chance that they may occur.

A decision maker is **risk neutral** if he or she is concerned with what will be the most likely outcome.

A **risk averse** decision maker acts on the assumption that the worst outcome might occur.

Decision-making information could be presented to managers in such a way as to ensure that they consider **all** the possibilities, including the worst.

8.2 Conservatism in decision making

Conservatism is associated with **risk aversion** and caution. A technique for assisting a risk-averse manager might be to measure the most likely outcome from a decision, and the worst and best possible outcomes. This will show the **full range of possible outcomes** from a decision, and might help the manager to reject certain alternatives because the worst possible outcome might involve an unacceptable amount of loss.

8.3 Example: worst/best possible outcomes

Omelette is trying to set the sales price for one of its products. Three prices are under consideration, and expected sales volumes and costs are as follows.

Price per unit	$4	$4.30	$4.40
Expected sales volume (units)			
Best possible	16,000	14,000	12,500
Most likely	14,000	12,500	12,000
Worst possible	10,000	8,000	6,000

Fixed costs are $20,000 and variable costs of sales are $2 per unit.

Which price should be chosen?

Solution

Price per unit	$4	$4.30	$4.40
Contribution per unit	$2	$2.30	$2.40
Total contribution	$	$	$
Best possible	32,000	32,200	30,000
Most likely	28,000	28,750	28,800
Worst possible	20,000	18,400	14,400

(a) The highest contribution based on **most likely** sales volume would be at a price of $4.40 but arguably a price of $4.30 would be much better than $4.40, since the most likely profit is almost as good, the worst possible profit is not as bad, and the best possible profit is better.

(b) However, only a price of $4 guarantees that the company would **not make a loss,** even if the worst possible outcome occurs. (Fixed costs of $20,000 would just be covered.) A risk averse management might therefore prefer a price of $4 to either of the other two prices.

8.4 The maximin decision rule

The **maximin** decision rule suggests that a decision maker should select the alternative that offers the least unattractive worst outcome. This would mean choosing the alternative that *maxi*mises the *min*imum profits.

8.5 Example: maximin decision rule

A business is trying to decide which of three mutually exclusive projects to undertake. Each of the projects could lead to varying net costs which the business classifies as outcomes I, II, and III. The business has constructed the following payoff table or matrix.

		Net profit in $'000s if outcome turns out to be		
		I (Worst)	II (Most likely)	III (Best)
	A	50	85	130
Project	B	70	75	140
	C	90	100	110

Which project should they undertake? Use the maximin decision rule.

Solution

The maximin decision rule suggests that they should select the 'best worst result' that could happen. This is the decision criterion that managers should 'play safe' and either minimise their losses or costs, or else go for the decision which gives the highest minimum profits. If the business selects project A the worst result is a net profit of 50. Similarly, the worst results for B and C are 70 and 90 respectively. The best 'worst outcome' is 90 and project C would therefore be selected (because this is a better 'worst possible' than either A or B).

The maximin decision rule is also known as the **minimax cost** rule – minimise the maximum costs or losses.

8.6 Criticisms of the maximin decision rule

The maximin decision rule is subject to two major criticisms.

(a) It is **defensive** and **conservative**, being a safety first principle of avoiding the worst outcomes without taking into account opportunities for maximising profits.

(b) It ignores the **probability** of each different outcome taking place. In the previous example, we ignored the fact that outcome II was the most likely outcome.

8.7 Sensitivity analysis

Key term

> **Sensitivity analysis** is a term used to describe any technique whereby decision options are tested for their vulnerability to changes in any 'variable' such as expected sales volume, sales price per unit, material costs, or labour costs.

Here are three useful approaches to sensitivity analysis.

(a) To estimate by **how much costs and revenues would need to differ** from their estimated values before the decision would change.

(b) To estimate whether a decision would change **if estimated costs were x% higher** than estimated, or estimated revenues y% lower than estimated.

(c) To estimate by how much costs and/or revenues would need to differ from their estimated values before the decision maker **would be indifferent** between two options.

The essence of the approach, therefore, is to carry out the calculations with one set of values for the variables and then substitute other possible values for the variables to see how this affects the overall outcome.

(a) Such a **'what if' analysis** can be carried out using a spreadsheet.
(b) **Flexible budgeting** can also be a form of sensitivity analysis.

9 Probabilities and expected values

FAST FORWARD

When probabilities can be estimated for possible outcomes, a weighted average of all the possible outcomes can be calculated. This is an **expected value** or EV.

A risk-neutral organisation and management might decide to take the course of action offering the highest expected value of profit or the lowest expected value of loss.

Although the outcome of a decision may not be certain, there is some likelihood that **probabilities** could be assigned to the various possible outcomes from an analysis of previous experience.

For example, it might be estimated, on the basis of past experience, that the amount of sales that a company's sales team will win at an annual trade fair are as follows:

(a)   0.3 probability of $600,000
(b)   0.5 probability of $700,000
(c)   0.2 probability of $1,000,000

All the probabilities **must add up to 1.0** (which is 100% of possible outcomes).

One way of analysing these estimates is to calculate an 'average' of the different possible outcomes, allowing for the probability that each will occur. This average is called an expected value. It is calculated by multiplying each outcome by its associated probability, and then adding up the resulting numbers.

In the example above, the expected value of sales is as follows.

Outcome: Sales	Probability	Expected value
x	p	px
$		$
600,000	0.3	180,000
700,000	0.5	350,000
1,000,000	0.2	200,000
		730,000

The expected value of probable sales is $730,000. However, the expected value is simply a weighted average of possible outcomes, and actual sales could be much higher or lower than this average figure.

Where a choice has to be made between different decision options, and probabilities are assigned to different possible outcomes, the **expected value** of profit for each of the decision options can be calculated. Management may then choose the decision option that offers the highest expected value, i.e. the option that has the highest expected value of profit, or the lowest expected value of cost.

Choosing the option with the best expected value is not going to guarantee that the best choice will be made. However, it provides a basis for making a decision under conditions of uncertainty.

Exam focus point

In June 2006 expected values were examined. A fairly straightforward calculation was required with a written part asking about the limitations of expected values in the example given in the question.

9.1 Example: expected values

Suppose a manager has to choose between mutually exclusive options A and B, and the probable outcomes of each option are as follows.

Option A			Option B	
Probability	Profit		Probability	Profit
	$			$
0.8	5,000		0.1	(2,000)
0.2	6,000		0.2	5,000
			0.6	7,000
			0.1	8,000

The expected value (EV) of profit of each option would be measured as follows.

	Option A				Option B		
Prob	Profit		EV of profit	Prob	Profit		EV of profit
	$		$		$		$
0.8	× 5,000	=	4,000	0.1	× (2,000)	=	(200)
0.2	× 6,000	=	1,200	0.2	× 5,000	=	1,000
	EV	=	5,200	0.6	× 7,000	=	4,200
				0.1	× 8,000	=	800
					EV	=	5,800

In this example, since it offers a higher EV of expected profit, option B would be selected in preference to A, unless further risk analysis is carried out.

> **Formula to learn**
>
> The **expected value** of an opportunity is equal to the sum of the probabilities of an outcome occurring multiplied by the return expected if it does occur:
>
> $EV = \sum px$
>
> where p is the probability of an outcome occurring and x is the value (profit or cost) of that outcome. $\sum$ means 'the sum of'.

Question   Options

A manager has to choose between mutually exclusive options C and D and the probable outcomes of each option are as follows.

	Option C		Option D	
Probability	Cost	Probability	Cost	
	$		$	
0.30	15,000	0.05	14,000	
0.55	20,000	0.30	17,000	
0.15	30,000	0.35	21,000	
		0.30	24,000	

Both options will produce an income of $30,000. Which should be chosen?

Answer

	Option C			Option D	
Cost	Probability	EV	Cost	Probability	EV
$		$	$		$
15,000	0.30	4,500	14,000	0.05	700
20,000	0.55	11,000	17,000	0.30	5,100
30,000	0.15	4,500	21,000	0.35	7,350
			24,000	0.30	7,200
EV of cost		20,000			20,350

On the basis of expected values, Option C should be chosen, because it has the lowest expected value of cost.

9.2 Limitations of expected values

In the example above, the preference for option B over option A on the basis of expected value is marred by the fact that A's **worst possible** outcome is a profit of $5,000, whereas B might incur a loss of $2,000 (although there is a 70% chance that profits would be $7,000 or more, which would be more than the best profits from option A).

Since the decision must be made **once only** between A and B, the expected value of profit (which is **merely a weighted average** of all possible outcomes) has severe limitations as a decision rule by which to judge preference.

Expected values are more valuable as a guide to decision making where they refer to outcomes which will occur **many times over**. Examples would include the probability that so many customers per day will buy a can of baked beans, the probability that a customer services assistant will receive so many phone calls per hour, and so on. The reliability of expected value calculations depends upon the accuracy of both the values assigned to the various outcomes and the probabilities of those outcomes.

Key learning points

- Accounting information can be used to identify a profit-maximising or cost-minimising decision option. When accounting figures are used for this purpose, **relevant costs** must be used. A relevant cost is a future cash flow arising as a direct consequence of a decision.

- **Avoidable costs**, **differential** costs and **opportunity** costs are all relevant costs.

- Non-relevant costs include **sunk** costs, **committed** costs and **notional** (imputed) costs.

- Directly attributable fixed costs are relevant costs, general fixed overheads are not.

- The total relevant cost of a scarce resource consists of the variable cost of the scarce resource plus the opportunity cost of the contribution forgone by not being able to use the scarce resource for its next most profitable use.

- In a **make or buy** situation with no scarce resources, the relevant costs are the differences in unit variable costs plus differences in directly attributable fixed costs.

- In a situation where a company must **subcontract** work to make up a shortfall in its own in-house capabilities, its total costs will be minimised if those units bought have the lowest extra variable cost of buying per unit of scarce resource saved by buying of all the products in question.

- Decisions are generally taken without any certainty as to what the actual outcome will be. A range of likely outcomes may be likely. The approach to decision making under conditions of **uncertainty** depends on the attitude of an organisation and its management to risk. Decision-making should certainly be taken with a proper understanding of the different possible outcomes.

- A risk-averse manager might opt for the option that offers the best 'worst result' (the **maximin criterion**).

- When probabilities can be estimated for possible outcomes, a weighted average of all the possible outcomes can be calculated. This is an **expected value** or EV.

- A risk-neutral organisation and management might decide to take the course of action offering the highest expected value of profit or the lowest expected value of loss.

Quick quiz

1   Over a sufficiently long period of time, virtually all costs are fixed. True or false?

2   Define opportunity cost.

3   Should you assume that variable costs are relevant costs or non-relevant costs?

4   If materials have already been purchased but will not be replaced, what is their relevant cost?

5   A company could make a component in-house, and estimates that the cost of manufacture would be $14,000 (probability 0.25), $16,000 (probability 0.50) or $25,000 (probability 0.25). It would cost $16,500 to buy the component from an external supplier. On the basis of expected value, should the component be made in-house or purchased externally?

6   List four assumptions typically made in relevant costing.

Answers to quick quiz

1   False. Virtually all costs are variable in the long term.

2   Opportunity cost is the benefit which could have been earned, but which has been given up, by choosing one option instead of another.

3   Relevant costs.

4   The relevant cost will be the higher of their current resale value and the value they would obtain if they were put to an alternative use.

5   EV of in-house manufacture = $17,750. The component should be purchased externally, on the basis of expected value (even though there is a 75% probability that it would be cheaper to manufacture in-house).

6   Some of the assumptions that are typically made in relevant costing are as follows.

  • Cost behaviour patterns are known; if a department closes down, for example, the attributable fixed cost savings would be known.

  • The amount of fixed costs, unit variable costs, sales price and sales demand are known with certainty.

  • The objective of decision making in the short run is to maximise 'satisfaction', which is often regarded as 'short-term profit'.

  • The information on which a decision is based is complete and reliable.

7

Pricing

Introduction

Management must decide on the prices at which products and services will be offered to the market. This chapter considers the matters that managers should bear in mind when making such decisions.

Learning objectives

On completion of this chapter you will be able to:

Syllabus reference

- describe the factors which may influence an organisation's pricing policy, and what pricing policies might be used

8

- understand various techniques for setting prices, in particular cost plus pricing, variable cost plus pricing, marginal or incremental cost pricing and target cost pricing

8

1 Pricing policy

FAST FORWARD

> Pricing policy is just one element in the marketing mix, but it is important that prices should be sufficient to achieve profitability. Pricing policy is influenced by a variety of market factors/demand factors, such as competition in the market, and the life cycle of the product.
>
> **Market penetration pricing** and **market skimming pricing** are pricing policies for new products.
>
> **Differential pricing** involves selling the same product at different prices to different customers.

Price can go by many names. Fares, rent, assessments and fees for example. All profit-making organisations and many non-profit-making organisations face the task of setting a price for their products or services.

In the past, setting a price was regarded as the single most important factor in marketing. In modern marketing philosophy, pricing decisions remain important. However, price is just one element in the marketing mix. Other factors include:

(a) The satisfaction of customer wants and needs by providing products of the right type, quality and image

(b) Targeting particular types of customer (e.g. customers more concerned with product quality or purchasing convenience, rather than customers wanting to buy at the cheapest possible price)

(c) Advertising and sales promotion

(d) The delivery of goods or services at a location or by a delivery method that customers prefer

Although there are many elements in the marketing mix, the pricing of an organisation's products or services is crucial to its profitability.

1.1 Factors affecting pricing policy

Influences on pricing policy include:

Influence	Comment
Price sensitivity	This describes how demand for a product reacts to price changes. Sensitivity to price levels will vary amongst purchasers. Business customers who can pass on the cost of purchases will normally be the least sensitive to price.
	For example, when looking for a hotel to stay in, the business traveller will be more concerned about the level of service and quality of food than about price, since his or her employer will be paying the bill. In contrast, the family on holiday are likely to be very price-sensitive when choosing an overnight stay.
Price perception	Price perception is **the way customers react to prices**.
	For example, customers may react to a price increase by buying more. This could be because they expect further price increases to follow (they are 'stocking up').

Influence	Comment
Quality	In the absence of other information, customers tend to **judge quality by price**. A price change may send signals to customers concerning the quality of the product. A price rise may indicate improvements in quality, a price reduction may signal reduced quality, for example through the use of inferior components. Of two products, the more expensive is usually judged to be of 'better quality'.
Intermediaries	If an organisation distributes products or services to the market through independent intermediaries, the **objectives of these intermediaries complicate the pricing decision**. Such intermediaries are likely to deal with a range of suppliers and their aims concern their own profits rather than those of suppliers. The organisation's pricing policy should take into consideration the attitudes to price of both their immediate customer (the intermediaries) and the end-consumer.
Competitors	In setting prices, an organisation sends out signals to rivals. **Competitors are likely to react to these signals in some way**. In some industries (such as petrol retailing) **pricing moves in unison**; in others, price changes by one supplier may initiate a **price war**, with each supplier undercutting the others.
Suppliers	If an organisation's suppliers **notice a price rise** for the organisation's products, they **may seek a rise** in the price for their supplies to the organisation, on the grounds that it is now able to pay a higher price.
Inflation	In periods of inflation the organisation may need to change prices to reflect increases in the prices of supplies, labour, rent and so on. Such changes may be needed to keep relative (real) prices unchanged.
Economic wealth/incomes	In times of rising incomes or economic affluence, price may be less important to consumers than product quality or convenience of access (distribution). When income levels are falling and/or unemployment levels rising, price will become more important.
Product range	The products made by an organisation might complement each other and customers might buy a range of the supplier's products in one buying decision. With such 'complementary products', pricing is likely to focus on the profit from the whole range rather than the profit on each single product.

A pricing policy may use **loss leaders**: offering one product at a very low price is intended to make consumers buy additional products in the range that carry higher profit margins. An example is selling razors at a loss whilst selling the blades for the razors at a higher profit margin. Another example would be selling the Monday edition of a national newspaper cheaply, to encourage new readers to buy the newspaper more regularly throughout the week. |
| Ethics | Ethical considerations may be a further factor, for example whether or not to exploit short-term shortages through higher prices. |
| Substitute products | Pricing policy might be affected by the existence of substitute products or services to which consumers might switch if the price of the product becomes too high. For example if the price of train travel rises, customers might switch to coach travel or air travel. |

1.2 Product life cycle

Key term

The **product life cycle** is the period over which a product is initially researched and developed, then introduced to the market; its market gradually grows until it reaches maturity, then declines until the product is finally withdrawn from the market and abandoned.

The product life concept is the recognition that most products do not have a limitless life. Some last much longer than others, although not without modifications and enhancements. Some products have a very short life cycle, and 'disappear' soon after they have been launched in the market. The aim of pricing policy should be to set prices through the various stages of a product's life so as to optimise profitability. This may call for a different pricing policy at each stage of the product's life.

The life cycle concept states that a typical product moves through four stages.

(a) **Introduction**

The product is introduced to the market. Heavy **capital expenditure** will be incurred on product development and perhaps also on the purchase of new non-current assets and building up inventories for sale.

On its introduction to the market, the product will begin to earn some revenue, but initially demand is likely to be small. Potential customers will be unaware of the product or service, and the organisation may have to spend further on **advertising** to bring the product or service to the attention of the market.

(b) **Growth**

The product gains a bigger market as demand builds up. Sales revenues increase and the product begins to make a profit. The initial costs of the **investment** in the new product are gradually **recovered**.

(c) **Maturity**

Eventually, the growth in demand for the product will slow down and it will enter a period of relative maturity. It will continue to be profitable. The product may be **modified or improved, as a means of sustaining its demand**.

(d) **Saturation and decline**

At some stage, the market may reach 'saturation point'. Demand will start to fall. For a while, the product will still be profitable in spite of declining sales, but eventually it will become a **loss-maker** and this is the time when the organisation should decide to stop selling the product or service, and so the product's life cycle should reach its end.

Remember, however, that some mature products will **never decline**: staple food products such as milk or bread are the best example. However, even with staple products, innovations may be necessary to sustain market demand (such as new packaging, new methods of delivery to the consumer, and niche products such as organic food or low-calorie food items).

Not all products follow the 'standard' life cycle pattern, but it remains a useful tool when considering decisions such as pricing. The life cycle concept is relevant when considering what pricing policy will be adopted.

1.3 Markets and competition

The price that an organisation can charge for its products will also be influenced by the market in which it operates.

In **established industries** dominated by a few major firms, a price initiative by one firm will usually be countered by a price reaction by competitors. In these circumstances, **prices tend to be stable**.

If a **rival cuts its prices** in the expectation of increasing its market share, a firm has several options.

(a) It will **maintain its existing prices** if the expectation is that only a small market share would be lost, so that it is more profitable to keep prices at their existing level. Eventually, the rival firm may drop out of the market or be forced to raise its prices.

(b) It may maintain its prices but respond with a **non-price counter-attack**. This is a more positive response, because the firm will be securing or justifying its current prices with a product change, advertising, or better back-up services.

(c) It may **reduce its prices**. This should protect the firm's market share so that the main beneficiary from the price reduction will be the consumer.

(d) It may **raise its prices** *and respond with a* **non-price counter-attack**. The extra revenue from the higher prices might be used to finance an advertising campaign or product design changes. A price increase would be based on a campaign to emphasise the quality difference between the firm's own product and the rival's product.

1.4 Price leadership

Given that price competition can have disastrous consequences in conditions of oligopoly, it is not unusual to find that large corporations emerge as price leaders. The price leader **indicates to the other firms in the market what the price will be**, and **competitors then set their prices with reference to the leader's price**.

1.5 New product pricing

When an organisation introduces a new product to the market, a decision has to be made about the price that will be charged. If there are no obvious rival products, the organisation will have a choice about whether to set prices high or low. High prices should provide high unit profits, but lower demand. Low prices will provide lower unit profits, but higher sales volume.

Two pricing policies for new products are therefore **market penetration** pricing and **market skimming**.

1.6 Market penetration pricing

This is a policy of **low prices** when the product is **first launched** in order to obtain sufficient penetration into the market. A penetration policy may be appropriate:

- If the firm wishes to **discourage new entrants** into the market.
- If the firm wishes to **shorten the initial period of the product's life cycle** in order to enter the growth and maturity stages as quickly as possible.
- If there are significant **economies of scale** to be achieved from a high volume of output, so that quick penetration into the market is desirable in order to gain unit cost reductions.
- If **demand is likely to increase as prices fall.**

1.7 Market skimming pricing

In contrast, market skimming involves charging **high prices** when a product is **first launched** and **spending heavily on advertising** and sales promotion to obtain sales. As the product moves into the **later stages** of its life cycle (growth, maturity and decline) **progressively lower prices** will be charged. The profitable 'cream' is thus skimmed off in stages until sales can only be sustained at lower prices.

The aim of market skimming is to gain **high unit profits early** in the product's life. High unit prices make it more likely that **competitors** will enter the market than if lower prices were to be charged.

Such a policy is appropriate:

- Where the **product is new and different**, so that customers are prepared to pay high prices so as to be one up on other people who do not own it. Examples have been DVD players and mobile phones.
- Where the strength of **demand** and the sensitivity of demand to price are **unknown**. It is better from the point of view of marketing to start by charging high prices and then reduce them if the demand is insufficient.
- Where products may have a **short life cycle**, and so need to recover their development costs and make a profit quickly.

Exam focus point

| The June 2003 exam contained a question on pricing policy, with specific reference to market skimming and market penetration. |

1.8 Differential pricing

In certain circumstances the **same product** can be sold at **different prices** to **different customers**. There are a number of bases on which such prices can be set.

Basis	Example
By **market segment**	A cross-channel ferry company would market its services at different prices in England, Belgium and France, for example. Services such as cinemas and hairdressers are often available at lower prices to old age pensioners and/or juveniles.
By **product version**	Many car models have 'add on' extras which enable one brand to appeal to a wider cross-section of customers. The final price need not reflect the cost price of the add-on extras directly: usually the top of the range model would carry a price much in excess of the cost of provision of the extras, as a prestige appeal.
By **place**	Theatre seats are usually sold according to their location so that patrons pay different prices for the same performance according to the seat type they occupy.
By **time**	This is perhaps the most popular type of price discrimination. Railway companies, for example, are successful price discriminators, charging more to rush hour rail commuters whose demand remains the same whatever the price charged at certain times of the day.

Question

Different prices

Can you think of any more examples of products or services which are sold to different customers at different prices on the basis of time?

Answer

Off-peak travel bargains, hotel prices, telephone and electricity charges are examples.

2 Setting prices

FAST FORWARD

A number of techniques may be used to set prices. These include price-setting techniques based on the cost of the item.

The prices that an organisation sets for its products or services should be consistent with its pricing policies.

Prices are often determined by market factors, such as the prices currently charged by competitors, and considerations of how much customers would be prepared to pay for a particular item. Pricing is therefore often market-driven or marketing-driven.

At the same time, an organisation needs to make a profit from the items that it sells, and price-setting should also have regard to costs and profits.

In some cases, particularly contracting work and jobbing work, an organisation may set prices by first of all estimating the likely cost, and then quoting a price at which a suitable profit margin would be earned. Price tenders for contracts are usually set on this basis.

3 Economic factors influencing the price of a product

3.1 The economic analysis of demand

There are two extremes in the relationship between price and demand. A supplier can either **sell a certain quantity, Q, at any price** (as in graph (a)). Demand is totally unresponsive to changes in price and is said to be **completely inelastic**. Alternatively, **demand might be limitless at a certain price** P (as in graph (b)), but there would be no demand above price P and there would be little point in dropping the price below P. In such circumstances demand is said to be **completely elastic**.

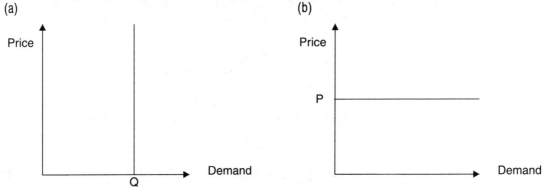

(a)

(b)

A more **normal situation** is shown below. The **downward-sloping** demand curve shows that demand will increase as prices are lowered. Demand is therefore **elastic**.

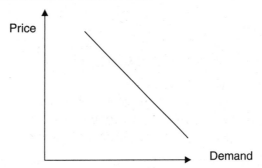

3.2 Price elasticity of demand (η)

Price elasticity is a measure of the extent of change in market demand for a good in response to a change in its price. If **demand is elastic** a reduction in price would lead to a rise in total sales revenue. If demand is **inelastic** a reduction in price would lead to a fall in total sales revenue.

Key term

Price elasticity of demand (η) is a measure of the extent of change in market demand for a good in response to a change in its price. It is measured as:

$$\frac{\text{The change in quantity demanded, as a \% of demand}}{\text{The change in price, as a \% of the price}}$$

Since the demand goes up when the price falls, and goes down when the price rises, the elasticity has a negative value, but it is usual to ignore the minus sign.

3.2.1 Example: Price elasticity of demand

The price of a good is $1.20 per unit and annual demand is 800,000 units. Market research indicates that an increase in price of 10 cents per unit will result in a fall in annual demand of 75,000 units. What is the price elasticity of demand?

Solution

Annual demand at $1.20 per unit is 800,000 units.
Annual demand at $1.30 per unit is 725,000 units.

% change in demand	=	(75,000/800,000) × 100% = 9.375%
% change in price	=	(10c/120c) × 100% = 8.333%
Price elasticity of demand	=	(−9.375/8.333) = −1.125

Ignoring the minus sign, price elasticity is 1.125.

The demand for this good, at a price of $1.20 per unit, would be referred to as **elastic** because the **price elasticity of demand is greater than 1**.

3.3 Elastic and inelastic demand

The value of demand elasticity may be anything from zero to infinity.

Key term

> Demand is referred to as **inelastic** if the absolute value is less than 1 and **elastic** if the absolute value is greater than 1.

(a)   Where demand is inelastic, the quantity demanded falls by a smaller percentage than the percentage increase in price.

(b)   Where demand is **elastic, demand falls** by a **larger percentage than the percentage rise in price**.

Question
Price elasticity of demand

If the price elasticity of demand is zero, which of the following is/are true?

I   Demand is 'perfectly inelastic'
II   There is no change in price regardless of the quantity demanded
III   The demand curve is a vertical straight line
IV   There is no change in the quantity demanded, regardless of any change in price

A   I and III only
B   I and IV only
C   I, II and III only
D   I, III and IV only

Answer

Demand is perfectly inelastic when price changes have no impact on demand. The price elasticity of demand will equal zero only if demand remains unchanged. Statement I is therefore correct.

The price elasticity of demand will equal zero only if demand remains unchanged. If the price remains unchanged, the denominator of the price elasticity of demand equation will have an infinite value. Statement II is therefore incorrect.

If the price elasticity of demand is zero it means that demand never changes and so the graph is a vertical straight line. Statement III is therefore correct.

The price elasticity of demand will equal zero only when demand remains unchanged. Statement IV is therefore correct.

The correct answer is therefore D since statements I, III and IV are correct.

3.4 Elasticity and the pricing decision

In practice, organisations will have only a rough idea of the shape of their demand curve. Data about quantities sold at certain prices over a period of time will be limited and there may be other factors that might have an effect on the demand for a product.

Despite this limitation, an awareness of the concept of elasticity can assist management with pricing decisions.

(a)   In circumstances of **inelastic demand, prices should be increased** because revenues will increase and total costs will reduce (because quantities sold will reduce).

(b)   In circumstances of **elastic demand**, increases in prices will bring decreases in revenue and decreases in price will bring increases in revenue. Management therefore have to **decide** whether the **increase/decrease in costs will be less than/greater than the increases/decreases in revenue**.

Factors that determine the degree of elasticity are as follows.

(a)   The price of the good.

(b)   The price of other goods. For some goods the market demand is interconnected.

   (i)   **Substitutes**. An increase in demand for one version of a good is likely to cause a decrease in demand for others. Common examples are rival brands of the same commodity (such as *Coca-Cola* and *Pepsi-Cola*).

   (ii)   **Complements**. An increase in demand for one is likely to cause an increase in demand for the other, for examples, cups and saucers.

(c)   **Income**. A rise in income gives households more to spend and they will want to buy more goods. Different goods are affected in different ways.

   (i)   Normal goods are those for which a rise in income increases the demand.

   (ii)   Inferior goods are those for which demand falls as income rises (eg cheap wine).

   (iii) For some goods demand rises up to a certain point and then remains unchanged, because there is a limit to which consumers can or want to consume. Examples are basic foodstuffs such as salt and bread.

(d)   Tastes and fashions.

(e)   Expectations. Where consumers believe that prices will rise or that shortages will occur they will attempt to stock up on the product, thereby creating excess demand in the short term.

(f)   Obsolescence. Many products and services have to be replaced periodically.

4 A demand-based approach to pricing

FAST FORWARD

A **demand-based approach to pricing** involves determining a profit-maximising price.

Price theory or demand theory is based on the idea that there is a connection between price, the total quantity demanded by customers, and total revenue and profits. Demand varies with price, and so if an estimate can be made of demand at different price levels, it should be possible to derive either a profit-maximising price or a revenue-maximising price.

To apply this approach to pricing in practice, it is necessary to have realistic estimates of demand at different price levels. Making accurate estimates of demand is often difficult, since price is only one of many variables that influence demand. Even so, some larger organisations (e.g. oil companies) go to considerable effort to estimate the demand for their products or services at differing price levels.

4.1 Example

For example a large transport authority might be considering an increase in bus fares or underground fares. The effect on total revenues and profit of the increase in fares could be estimated from a knowledge of the demand for transport services at different price levels. If an increase in the price per ticket caused a large fall in demand, total revenues and profits would fall. However, if a fares increase would cause relatively little change in demand (e.g. possibly, on commuter routes) a price increase would boost total revenue. Since a transport authority's costs are largely fixed in relation to sales volume (passenger miles), a rise in revenues from fares would boost total profits too.

Many businesses enjoy something akin to a monopoly position, even in a competitive market. This is because they develop a unique marketing mix, for example a unique combination of price and quality. The significance of a monopoly situation is:

(a)   The business does not have to 'follow the market' on price; in other words it is not a 'price-taker', but has more choice and flexibility in the prices it sets.

    (i)   At higher prices, demand for its products or services will be less.
    (ii)   At lower prices, demand for its products or services will be higher.

(b)   There will be a selling price at which the business can maximise its profits.

Question   Maximising contribution

Moose sells a product which has a variable cost of $8 per unit. The sales demand at the current sales price of $14 is 3,000 units. It has been estimated by the marketing department that the sales volume would fall by 100 units for each addition of 25c to the sales price.

Required

Establish whether the current price of $14 is the optimal price which maximises contribution.

Answer

Sales price	Unit contribution	Sales volume	Total contribution
$	$	Units	$
13.00	5.00	3,400	17,000
13.25	5.25	3,300	17,325
13.50	5.50	3,200	17,600
13.75	5.75	3,100	17,825
14.00	6.00	3,000	18,000
14.25	6.25	2,900	18,125
14.50	6.50	2,800	18,200
14.75	6.75	2,700	18,225*
15.00	7.00	2,600	18,200

* Contribution would be maximised at a price of $14.75, and sales of 2,700 units.

The current price is not optimal.

5 Full cost plus pricing

FAST FORWARD

Using **full cost plus pricing**, the sales price is determined by calculating the full cost of the product and adding a percentage mark-up for profit.

Key term

As indicated earlier, pricing decisions must recognise the requirement to make a profit. Some organisations set prices by estimating (in advance) or calculating (after the work has been done) the full cost of the product and adding a percentage mark-up for profit. This approach to setting prices is known as **full cost plus pricing**.

In full cost plus pricing, the full cost may be a fully absorbed *production* cost only, or it may include some absorbed administration, selling and distribution overhead. The full cost might also include some opportunity costs as well, such as the opportunity cost of a production resource that is in short supply, so that 'full cost' need not be the cost as it might be established in the accounts.

A business might have an idea of the percentage profit margin it would like to earn and so might decide on an average profit mark-up as a general guideline for pricing decisions. This would be particularly useful for businesses that carry out a large amount of contract work or jobbing work, for which individual job or contract prices must be quoted regularly to prospective customers.

However, the **percentage profit mark-up** does not have to be fixed, but can be **varied to suit the circumstances**. In particular, the percentage mark-up can be varied to suit demand conditions in the market.

5.1 Problems with full cost plus pricing

There are several problems with full cost plus pricing.

(a)   Cost plus pricing fails to recognise that since demand may be determined by price, there will be a profit-maximising combination of price and demand. A cost plus based approach to pricing will be **unlikely to arrive at the profit-maximising price** for a 'standard' product.

(b)   In most markets, prices must be adjusted to market and demand conditions; the decision cannot simply be made on a cost basis only.

(c)   The calculation of a full cost plus price requires an overhead absorption rate. Output volume, which is a key factor in the fixed overhead absorption rate, must therefore be budgeted. Output volume will depend on demand. An estimate of demand depends on price levels. Successful use of cost plus pricing therefore depends on the budget for output volume being reasonably accurate, and when competition in the market is severe, this might be difficult.

Further disadvantages of full cost plus pricing are:

(a)   It **fails to allow for competition**. A company may need to match the prices of rival firms when these take a price-cutting initiative.

(b)   A full cost plus basis for a pricing decision is a means of ensuring that, in the long run, a company succeeds in covering all its fixed costs and making a profit out of revenue earned. However, in the short term it is **inflexible**.

(i)   A firm tendering for a contract may quote a cost plus price that results in the contract going elsewhere, although a lower price would have been sufficient to cover all incremental costs and opportunity costs.

(ii)   In the short term, rapidly-changing environmental factors might dictate the need for lower (or higher) prices than long-term considerations would indicate.

(c)   Full cost plus prices tend to ignore opportunity costs.

(d)   Where **more than one product is sold** by a company, the **price** decided by a cost plus formula **depends on the method of apportioning fixed costs** between the products. Products taking a higher share of the total overheads will be charged to customers at higher prices.

5.2 Example: full cost plus pricing with more than one product

Giraffe is attempting to decide sales prices for two products, Lyons and Tygers. The products are both made by the same workforce and in the same department. 30,000 direct labour hours are budgeted for the year. The budgeted fixed costs are $30,000 and it is expected that the department will operate at full capacity. Variable costs per unit are as follows.

		Lyons		Tygers
		$		$
Materials		4		4
Labour	(2 hours)	6	(3 hours)	9
Expenses	(1 machine hour)	2	(1 machine hour)	2
		12		15

Expected demand is 7,500 Lyons and 5,000 Tygers.

Required

Calculate the unit prices which give a profit of 20% on full cost if overheads are absorbed on the following bases.

(a)   On a direct labour hour basis
(b)   On a machine hour basis

Solution

(a)   **A direct labour hour basis**

$$\frac{\text{Budgeted fixed costs}}{\text{Budgeted labour hours}} = \frac{\$30,000}{(15,000+15,000)} = \$1$$

Absorption rate $1 per direct labour hour

	Lyons	Tygers
	$	$
Variable costs	12.00	15.00
Overhead absorbed	2.00	3.00
	14.00	18.00
Profit (20%)	2.80	3.60
Price	16.80	21.60

The total budgeted profit would be ((2.80 × 7,500) + (3.60 × 5,000)) = $(21,000 + 18,000) = $39,000.

(b)   **A machine hour basis**

$$\frac{\text{Budgeted fixed costs}}{\text{Budgeted machine hours}} = \frac{\$30,000}{(7,500+5,000)} = \frac{\$30,000}{12,500} = \$2.40$$

Absorption rate $2.40 per machine hour

	Lyons	Tygers
	$	$
Variable costs	12.00	15.00
Overhead absorbed	2.40	2.40
Full cost	14.40	17.40
Profit (20%)	2.88	3.48
Price	17.28	20.88

The total budgeted profit would be $(21,600 + 17,400) = $39,000.

(c)   The different bases for charging overheads result in different prices for both Lyons (difference of 48c per unit) and Tygers (difference of 72c per unit).

It is unlikely that the expected sales demand for the products would be the same at both sales prices. It is questionable whether one (or either) product might achieve expected sales demand at the higher price. In other words, although the budgeted profit is $39,000 whichever overhead absorption method is used, this assumes that budgeted sales would be achieved regardless of the unit price of each product. This is an unrealistic basis on which to make a decision.

5.3 Advantages of full cost plus pricing

Since the size of the profit margin can be varied at management's discretion, a decision based on a price in excess of full cost should ensure that a company working at normal capacity will cover all its fixed costs and make a profit. Companies may benefit from cost plus pricing in the following circumstances.

(a)   When they carry out large contracts which must make a sufficient profit margin to cover a fair share of fixed costs.

(b)   If they must justify their prices to potential customers (for example for government contracts).

(c)   If they find it difficult to estimate expected demand at different sales prices.

It is a **simple, quick and cheap** method of pricing which can be delegated to junior managers. This may be particularly important with jobbing work where many prices must be decided and quoted each day.

Question   **Mark up**

A product's full cost is $4.75 and it is sold at full cost plus 70%. A competitor has just launched a similar product selling for $7.99. How will this affect the first product's mark up?

Answer

Price needs to be reduced to $7.99

Mark-up therefore needs to be $\left(\dfrac{7.99 - 4.75}{4.75} \right) \times 100\% = 68\%$

The mark-up therefore needs to be reduced by 2%.

5.4 Advantages of activity-based costing pricing

Rather than add the profit mark-up to the full cost of the product, one could add the mark-up to the ABC-determined cost of the product. Since ABC costs are more accurate than traditional full costs, this should assist the organisation's recovery of its costs.

The **principal idea** of ABC is to **focus attention on what causes costs to increase,** ie the **cost drivers**.

(a)   The **costs that vary with production volume**, such as power costs, should be traced to products using production **volume-related cost drivers**, such as direct labour hours or direct machine hours.

Overheads which do not **vary** with output but **with some other activity** should be traced to products using **transaction-based cost drivers**, such as number of production runs and number of orders received.

(b)   Traditional costing systems allow overheads to be related to products in rather more arbitrary ways producing, it is claimed, less accurate product costs.

(c)   The result of the above is that ABC, by giving management product costs that more accurately reflect the true cost involved in the production process, enables managers to set more realistic prices than when using the traditional full cost plus model.

Question   **Traditional costing versus ABC**

A company manufactures two products, L and M, using the same equipment and similar processes. An extract of the production data for these products in one period is shown below.

	L	M
Quantity produced (units)	5,000	7,000
Direct labour hours per unit	1	2
Machine hours per unit	3	1
Set-ups in the period	10	40
Orders handled in the period	15	60
Overhead costs		$
Relating to machine activity		220,000
Relating to production run set-ups		20,000
Relating to handling of orders		45,000
		285,000

Required

Calculate the production overheads to be absorbed by one unit of each of the products using the following costing methods.

(a)   A traditional costing approach using a direct labour hour rate to absorb overheads
(b)   An activity based costing approach, using suitable cost drivers to trace overheads to products

Answer

(a)   **Traditional costing approach**

		Direct labour hours
Product L = 5,000 units × 1 hour		5,000
Product M = 7,000 units × 2 hours		14,000
		19,000

∴ Overhead absorption rate   = $\dfrac{\$285,000}{19,000}$

= $15 per hour

Overhead absorbed would be as follows.

Product L	1 hour × $15	=	$15 per unit
Product M	2 hours × $15	=	$30 per unit

(b)   **ABC approach**

		Machine hours
Product L	= 5,000 units × 3 hours	15,000
Product M	= 7,000 units × 1 hour	7,000
		22,000

Using ABC the overhead costs are absorbed according to the **cost drivers**.

	$			
Machine-hour driven costs	220,000	÷	22,000 m/c hours	= $10 per m/c hour
Set-up driven costs	20,000	÷	50 set-ups	= $400 per set-up
Order driven costs	45,000	÷	75 orders	= $600 per order

Overhead costs are therefore as follows.

		Product L		*Product M*
		$		*$*
Machine-driven costs	(15,000 hrs × $10)	150,000	(7,000 hrs × $10)	70,000
Set-up costs	(10 × $400)	4,000	(40 × $400)	16,000
Order handling costs	(15 × $600)	9,000	(60 × $600)	36,000
		163,000		122,000
Units produced		5,000		7,000
Overhead cost per unit		$32.60		$17.43

These figures suggest that product M absorbs an unrealistic amount of overhead using a direct labour hour basis. Overhead absorption should be based on the activities which drive the costs, in this case machine hours, the number of production run set-ups and the number of orders handled for each product.

6 Variable cost plus pricing

Variable cost plus pricing (mark-up pricing) involves adding a profit margin to the marginal cost of production or the marginal cost of sales.

Key term

Instead of pricing products or services by adding a profit margin on to full cost, a business might add a profit margin on to the variable cost or marginal cost of the product (either the marginal cost of production or else the marginal cost of sales). This is **variable cost plus pricing**, sometimes called **mark-up pricing**.

If a company budgets to make 10,000 units of a product for which the variable cost of production is $3 a unit and the fixed production cost is $60,000 a year, it might decide to fix a price by adding, say, $33\frac{1}{3}$% to full production cost to give a price of $9 × $1\frac{1}{3}$ = $12 a unit. Alternatively, it might decide to add a profit margin of, say, 250% on to the variable production cost, to give a price of $3 × 350% = $10.50.

The **advantages** of a marginal cost plus approach:

(a)   It is a **simple and easy** method to use.

(b)   The size of the **mark-up can be varied**, and so, provided that a rigid mark-up is not used, mark-up pricing can be adjusted to reflect demand conditions.

(c)   It draws management attention to contribution and the effects of higher or lower sales volumes on profit. This helps to **create a better awareness of** the concepts and implications of **marginal costing and breakeven analysis**. For example, if a product costs $10 a unit and a mark-up of 150% is added to reach a price of $25 a unit, management should be clearly aware that every additional $1 of sales revenue would add 60c to contribution and profit.

(d)   Mark-up pricing is **convenient where there is a readily identifiable basic variable cost.** Retail industries are the most obvious example, and it is quite common for the prices of goods in shops to be fixed by adding a mark-up (20% or $33\frac{1}{3}$%, say) to the purchase cost. For example, a department store might buy in items of pottery at $3 each, add a mark-up of one third and resell the items at $4.

Drawbacks to marginal cost plus pricing are as follows.

(a)   Although the size of the mark-up can be varied in accordance with demand conditions, it does not ensure that sufficient attention is paid to demand conditions, competitors' prices and profit maximisation.

(b)   It ignores fixed overheads in the pricing decision. However, prices must be high enough to ensure that a profit is made after covering fixed costs. Pricing decisions cannot ignore fixed costs altogether.

Question	Profit margin

A product has the following costs.

	$
Direct materials	5
Direct labour	3
Variable overhead	7

Fixed overheads are $10,000 per month. Budgeted sales for the month are 400 units.

What profit margin needs to be added to marginal cost to breakeven?

To breakeven, total contribution = fixed costs

Let selling price = p

Unit contribution = p − 15

Total monthly contribution = 400 (p − 15)

At breakeven point, 400(p − 15) = 10,000

$$p - 15 = 25$$
$$p = 40$$

Profit margin = $\dfrac{40 - 15}{15} \times 100\% = 166^2/3\%$

7 Opportunity cost approach to pricing (marginal pricing)

FAST FORWARD

An **opportunity cost approach to pricing** involves allowing in the price for the opportunity costs of the resources consumed in making and selling the item. A marginal price or minimum price is the price at which the organisation would be no better or no worse off if it were to make and sell the item.

In some circumstances, particularly when it is working at full capacity, a firm might be willing to charge a price for an item that leaves it no worse off than if it did the next most profitable alternative thing. This is the marginal price or minimum price of an item. Any additional amount on top of the marginal price would give the firm a higher profit.

To estimate the marginal price for an item, it is necessary to take into account the opportunity costs of the resources consumed in making and selling the item.

7.1 Marginal pricing (minimum pricing)

A minimum price is the price that would have to be charged to cover:

(a)   The **incremental costs** of producing and selling the item
(b)   The **opportunity costs** of the resources consumed in making and selling the item.

A minimum price would leave the business no better or worse off in financial terms than if it did not sell the item.

A minimum price is based on relevant costs. It is unlikely to be the price actually charged, because it would not provide the business with any incremental profit. However, calculating the minimum price is useful as it shows:

(a)   An absolute minimum below which the price should not be set
(b)   The incremental profit that would be obtained from any price that is actually charged in excess of the minimum. For example, if the minimum price is $20,000 and the actual price charged is $24,000, the incremental profit on the sale would be $4,000.

If resources are scarce, minimum prices must include an allowance for the opportunity cost of using the resources on the job.

7.2 Example: marginal pricing and opportunity costs

OP has begun to produce a new product, T, for which the following cost estimates have been made.

	$
Direct materials	27
Direct labour: 4 hrs at $5 per hour	20
Variable production overheads: machining, ½ hr at $6 per hour	3
	50

If the company decides to make and sell product T, it will have to switch its machine capacity from making other products, since there is a restriction on total machine time available.

Production fixed overheads are budgeted at $300,000 per month. The overhead absorption rate will be a direct labour rate, and budgeted direct labour hours are 25,000 per month.

Because of the shortage of available machining capacity, the company will be restricted to 10,000 hours of machine time a year for making product T. It is estimated that the company could obtain a minimum contribution of $10 per machine hour on producing items other than product T.

Required

(a)   What is the marginal price for product T?
(b)   If the company wishes to make an additional profit of 20% on top of the marginal price from making product T, what would the price be, and how much additional profit would OP make?

Solution

	$
Direct materials	27.0
Direct labour (4 hours × $5)	20.0
Variable production overheads	3.0
Opportunity cost: contribution forgone from alternative use of machines	
(0.5 hours at $10 per hour)	5.0
Marginal price	55.0

If product T could be sold at a mark-up of 20% on top of its marginal price, the unit price would be $66 ($55 plus 20%). There would be 10,000 machine hours of time spent making product T each year, 20,000 units would be produced and sold, increasing the company's profits by (20,000 × $11) $220,000.

8 Fixed price tenders

FAST FORWARD

> Marginal cost pricing, for example in **fixed price tenders**, involves an analysis of relevant costs. A profit margin (mark-up) is often added to the **minimum price**.

8.1 Special orders

A special order is a **one-off revenue earning opportunity**. These may arise in the following situations.

(a)   When a business has a regular source of income but also has some **spare capacity** allowing it to take on extra work if demanded. For example a brewery might have a capacity of 500,000 barrels per month but only be producing and selling 300,000 barrels per month. It could therefore consider special orders to use up some of its spare capacity.

(b)   When a business has no regular source of income and **relies exclusively** on its **ability to respond to demand**. A building firm is a typical example as are many types of sub-contractors. In the service sector consultants often work on this basis.

The reason for making the distinction is that in situation (a) above, a firm would normally attempt to cover its longer-term running costs in its prices for its regular products. Pricing for special orders need therefore take no account of unavoidable fixed costs. This is clearly not the case for a firm in situation (b), where special orders are the only source of income for the foreseeable future.

The basic approach in both situations is to determine the price at which the firm would break even if it undertook the work; that is, the minimum price that it could afford to charge.

8.2 Example: special order and minimum price

Minimax has just completed production of an item of special equipment for a customer, only to be notified that this customer has now gone into liquidation.

After much effort, the sales manager has been able to interest a potential buyer who might buy the machine if certain conversion work could first be carried out.

(a)   The sales price of the machine to the original buyer had been fixed at $138,600 and had included an estimated normal profit mark-up of 10% on total costs. The costs incurred in the manufacture of the machine were as follows.

	$
Direct materials	49,000
Direct labour	36,000
Variable overhead	9,000
Fixed production overhead	24,000
Fixed sales and distribution overhead	8,000
	126,000

(b)   If the machine is converted, the production manager estimates that the cost of the extra work required would be as follows.

Direct materials (at cost) $9,600

Direct labour

Department X: 6 workers for 4 weeks at $210 per worker per week
Department Y: 2 workers for 4 weeks at $160 per worker per week

(c)   Variable overhead would be 20% of direct labour cost, and fixed production overhead would be absorbed as follows.

Department X: 83.33% of direct labour cost
Department Y: 25% of direct labour cost

(d)   Additional information is available as follows.

    (i)   In the original machine, there are three types of material.

        (1)   Type A could be sold for scrap for $8,000.

        (2)   Type B could be sold for scrap for $2,400 but it would take 120 hours of casual labour paid at $3.50 per hour to put it into a condition in which it would be suitable for sale.

        (3)   Type C would need to be scrapped, at a cost to Minimax of $1,100.

    (ii)   The direct materials required for the conversion are already in inventory. If not needed for the conversion they would be used in the production of another machine in place of materials that would otherwise need to be purchased, and that would currently cost $8,800.

    (iii) The conversion work would be carried out in two departments, X and Y. Department X is currently extremely busy and working at full capacity; it is estimated that its contribution to fixed overhead and profits is $2.50 per $1 of labour.

        Department Y, on the other hand, is short of work but for organisational reasons its labour force, which at the moment has a workload of only 40% of its standard capacity, cannot be reduced below its current level of eight employees, all of whom are paid a wage of $160 per week.

    (iv)   The designs and specifications of the original machine could be sold to an overseas customer for $4,500 if the machine is scrapped.

(v) If conversion work is undertaken, a temporary supervisor would need to be employed for four weeks at a total cost of $1,500. It is normal company practice to charge supervision costs to fixed overhead.

(vi) The original customer has already paid a non-returnable deposit to Minimax of 12.5% of the selling price.

Required

Calculate the minimum price that Minimax should quote for the converted machine if this is the best option. Explain clearly how you have reached this figure and conclusion.

Solution

The minimum price is the price which reflects the opportunity costs of the work. These are established as follows.

(a) Past costs are not relevant, and the $126,000 of cost incurred should be excluded from the minimum price calculation. It is necessary, however, to consider the alternative use of the direct materials which would be forgone if the conversion work is carried out.

	$
Type A	
Revenue from sales as scrap (note (i))	8,000
Type B	
Revenue from sales as scrap, minus the additional cash costs	
necessary to prepare it for sale ($2,400 − (120 × $3.50)) (note (i))	1,980
Type C	
Cost of disposal if the machine is not converted	
(a negative opportunity cost) (note (ii))	(1,100)
Total opportunity cost of materials types A, B and C	8,880

By agreeing to the conversion of the machine, Minimax would therefore lose a net revenue of $8,880 from the alternative use of these materials.

Notes

(i)   Scrap sales would be lost if the conversion work goes ahead.
(ii) These costs would be incurred unless the work goes ahead.

(b) The cost of additional direct materials for conversion is $9,600, but this is an historical cost as inventories already exist. The relevant cost of these materials is the $8,800 which would be spent on new purchases if the conversion is carried out. If the conversion work goes ahead, the materials in inventory would be unavailable for production of the other machine mentioned in item (d)(ii) of the question and so the extra purchases of $8,800 would then be needed.

(c) Direct labour in departments X and Y is a fixed cost and the labour force will be paid regardless of the work they do or do not do. The cost of labour for conversion in department Y is not a relevant cost because the work could be done without any extra cost to the company.

In department X, however, acceptance of the conversion work would oblige the company to divert production from other profitable jobs. The minimum contribution required from using department X labour must be sufficient to cover the cost of the labour and variable overheads and then make an additional $2.50 in contribution per direct labour hour.

Department X: costs for direct labour hours spent on conversion

6 workers × 4 weeks × $210 = $5,040

Variable overhead cost

$5,040 × 20% = $1,008

Contribution forgone by diverting labour from other work

$2.50 per $1 of labour cost = $5,040 × 250% = $12,600

(d) Variable overheads in department Y are relevant costs because they will only be incurred if production work is carried out. (It is assumed that if the workforce is idle, no variable overheads would be incurred.)

Department Y 20% of (2 workers × 4 weeks × $160) = $256

(e) If the machine is converted, the company cannot sell the designs and specifications to the overseas company. $4,500 is a relevant (opportunity) cost of accepting the conversion order.

(f) Fixed overheads, being mainly unchanged regardless of what the company decides to do, should be ignored because they are not relevant (incremental) costs. The additional cost of supervision should, however, be included as a relevant cost of the order because the $1,500 will not be spent unless the conversion work is done.

(g) The non-refundable deposit received should be ignored and should not be deducted in the calculation of the minimum price. Just as costs incurred in the past are not relevant to a current decision about what to do in the future, revenues collected in the past are also irrelevant.

Estimate of minimum price for the converted machine

	$	$
Opportunity cost of using the direct materials types A, B and C		8,880
Opportunity cost of additional materials for conversion		8,800
Opportunity cost of work in department X		
Labour	5,040	
Variable overhead	1,008	
Contribution forgone	12,600	
		18,648
Opportunity cost: sale of designs and specifications		4,500
Incremental costs:		
Variable production overheads in department Y		256
Fixed production overheads (additional supervision)		1,500
Minimum price		42,584

Question

Minimum price

Ship has recently shut down its London factory where it used to make cushions, although all the inventories of raw materials and machinery are still there awaiting disposal. A former customer has just asked whether he could be supplied with one last delivery of 500 cushions. You ascertain the following facts.

(a) There is sufficient covering material in inventory. This originally cost $400 but has a disposal value of $190.

(b) There is sufficient stuffing in inventory. This originally cost $350. It was to have been shipped to the Bristol factory at a cost of $80. The Bristol factory would currently expect to pay $500 for this quantity.

(c) Labour costs would be $450.

(d) A supervisor could be spared from the Bristol factory for the week needed to produce the cushions. His normal wage is $160 and his rail fare and hotel bill in London would amount to $135.

(e) Before the factory was closed, fixed overheads were absorbed at 200% of direct labour cost.

Required

Calculate the minimum price that could be quoted.

The minimum price is estimated from the relevant costs of producing the cushions.

	$
Covering material (the opportunity cost of this material is its scrap value of $190. The original cost is irrelevant because it is a historical cost, not a future cash flow)	190
Stuffing (the opportunity cost of the stuffing is the savings forgone by not sending it to Bristol, net of the transport costs of getting it to Bristol: $(500 – 80))	420
Labour: incremental cost	450
Supervisor's expenses: incremental expense item	135
Minimum price	1,195

The supervisor's basic wage and the overheads are irrelevant to the decision because these are costs that would be incurred anyway, even if the cushions were not produced.

Question

Acceptance or refusal of contract

DDD has decided to price its jobs as follows.

(a)   It calculates the minimum price for the job using relevant costs.
(b)   It adds $5,000 to cover fixed costs.
(c)   It adds a 10% profit margin to the total cost.

A customer who has work to be performed in May says he will award the contract to DDD if its bid is reduced by $5,000.

Required

Assess whether the contract should be accepted.

Answer

Yes or no. Yes, if there is no other work available, because DDD will at least earn a contribution towards fixed costs of 10% of the minimum cost. But no, if by accepting this reduced price it would send a signal to other prospective customers that they too could negotiate such a large reduction.

In setting the price, management must decide **how much profit** it would consider reasonable on the job. A simple cost-plus approach can be used (for example, add 10% to the minimum price) but the company management should **consider the effect that the additional jobs will have** on the activities engaged in by the company and whether these activities will create additional unforeseen costs.

Sometimes an organisation may depart from its typical price-setting routine and 'low-ball' bid jobs. A **low-ball bid** may be a minimum price or it may even be below the minimum price. The rationale behind low-ball bids is to obtain the job so as to have the opportunity to introduce products or services to a particular market segment. This type of bidding cannot be sustained in the long term.

8.3 Qualitative factors

When setting the price management must consider qualitative as well as quantitative issues.

- Will setting a low bid price cause the customer (or others) to feel that a **precedent** has been established for future prices?
- Will the contribution margin on a bid set low enough to acquire the job, **earn a sufficient amount to justify the additional burdens** placed on management or employees by the activity?
- How, if at all, will fixed price tenders **affect the organisation's normal sales**?

- If the job is taking place during a period of low business activity (off-season or during a recession), is management willing to take the business at a **lower contribution or profit margin simply to keep a valued workforce employed?**

8.4 Monitoring costs against fixed prices

Once the tender has been submitted and accepted, management must ensure that actual costs do not exceed the estimated costs, since for every cost overrun profit is eroded. **Actual costs must be monitored. Variances** between actual and estimated costs must be **highlighted and, if significant, investigated.** Control action may be required.

9 Target cost pricing

FAST FORWARD

In **target costing**, an organisation decides what the sales price of the item will be, and the required profit margin. Subtracting the desired profit margin from the target price gives a target cost, which is the cost for the item that the organisation should aim to achieve. The difference between the current cost and the target cost is a **cost gap**, that the organisation should seek to eliminate.

To compete effectively in today's competitive markets, organisations must continually redesign their products, with the result that **product life cycles** have become much shorter. The **planning, development and design stage** of a product is therefore critical to an organisation's cost management process. Many companies have to think about:

(a) How long the life cycle of the product might be

(b) What prices will need to be charged at each stage in the product's life cycle for the product to be successful.

Target costing, and target cost pricing, is an approach to pricing that combines an awareness of market demand conditions and the need for profitability.

Key term

Target cost means a product cost estimate derived by subtracting a desired profit margin from a competitive market price. This may be less than the planned initial product cost, but will be expected to be achieved by the time the product reaches the mature production stage. (CIMA, *Official Terminology*)

Target cost = Market price − Desired profit margin

This approach to pricing and costs requires managers to change the way they think about the relationship between cost, price and profit.

(a) Traditionally, the approach has been to develop a new product, determine what it costs to make, and set a selling price. The product will be profitable if its selling price exceeds its cost.

(b) The target costing approach to new product development is to determine what the market selling price will be at each stage of its life cycle and what the desired profit margin should be. As a result, it is then possible to calculate what the cost of the product must be at each stage of its life cycle, to ensure that the desired profits will be achieved.

The target cost for a product is likely to change over its life cycle. Typically, in the early stages of its life, a higher sales price will be achievable, and so a higher unit production cost is acceptable. However, as the price of a product falls, its target cost must also come down. Decisions made at the planning and design stage for a product can be crucial in making the target cost achievable (e.g. decisions affecting the choice of materials for making the item, or in the choice of the number of product features to build into the product).

The steps for implementing a target costing approach are as follows.

Step 1 Determine a product specification for which an adequate sales volume is expected.

Step 2 Set a selling price at which the organisation will be able to achieve a desired market share.

Step 3   Estimate the required profit based on return on sales or return on investment.

Step 4   Calculate the target cost = target selling price – target profit.

Step 5   Compile an estimated cost for the product based on the anticipated design specification and current cost levels.

Step 6   Calculate the **cost gap**. This is the difference between the product cost that is currently estimated and the target cost that needs to be achieved. Cost gap = estimated cost – target cost.

Step 7   Make efforts to close the cost gap. This is more likely to be successful if efforts are made to 'design out' costs prior to production, rather than to 'control out' costs during the production phase.

Step 8   Negotiate with the customer before making the decision about whether to go ahead with the project.

When a product is first manufactured, its target cost may well be much lower than its currently-attainable cost, which is determined by current technology and processes. Management can then set **benchmarks for improvement** towards the target costs, by improving technologies and processes.

Various techniques of cost reduction can be employed. The objective in each case is to reduce the unit cost of the product without reducing the customer's perception of the product in its intended use. Possible techniques are:

- **Reduce the number of components** – if redundant components can be identified, or the product can be reconfigured more simply while still satisfying the customer, then unit cost can be reduced.
- Using **different materials** – can plastic be used rather than more expensive metal, for example.
- Using **standard components** whenever possible – rather than building one's own components in-house, or paying for a third party to construct components to one's individual specifications, it will almost certainly be cheaper to design the product to incorporate industry-standard components that can be bought in large quantities on the world market where economies of scale have already driven the price down.
- Using **cheaper staff** – As far as possible, a few skilled staff should be used to supervise the work of the many unqualified staff.
- **Training staff** in more efficient techniques – the time of the existing staff can then be used more profitably.
- Acquiring new, more **efficient technology** – often an investment in new technology will enable the same or a greater volume of output to be achieved by fewer employees, who can either be released from employment or who can carry out alternative profitable work for the company.
- **Cutting out non value-added activities** – perhaps the work flow can be redesigned, for example to reduce inventories of part-finished items, or perhaps the product can be redesigned, for example not painting surfaces unseen by the customer, or cutting down on unnecessary packaging.

Exam focus point

The pricing question in the June 2005 exam required a discussion of target cost pricing and cost plus pricing, plus suggestions regarding reaching the target cost and discussion of other relevant pricing policies.

The December 2006 exam included a pricing question that compared variable cost-plus pricing and target cost pricing, asking for techniques of cost reduction.

Key learning points

- Pricing policy is just one element in the marketing mix, but it is important that prices should be sufficient to achieve profitability. Pricing policy is influenced by a variety of market factors/demand factors, such as competition in the market, and the life cycle of the product.

- **Market penetration pricing** and **market skimming pricing** are pricing policies for new products.

- **Differential pricing** involves selling the same product at different prices to different customers.

- A number of techniques may be used to set prices. These include price-setting techniques based on the cost of the item.

- **Elasticity of demand** underlies much of the theory of pricing.

- A **demand-based approach to pricing** involves determining a profit-maximising price.

- Using **full cost plus pricing**, the sales price is determined by calculating the full cost of the product and adding a percentage mark-up for profit. Activity based costing may provide a more accurate cost base for this.

- **Variable cost plus pricing (mark-up pricing)** involves adding a profit margin to the marginal cost of production or the marginal cost of sales.

- An **opportunity cost approach to pricing** involves allowing in the price for the opportunity costs of the resources consumed in making and selling the item. A marginal price or minimum price is the price at which the organisation would be no better or no worse off if it were to make and sell the item.

- Marginal cost pricing, for example in **fixed price tenders**, involves an analysis of relevant costs. A profit margin (mark-up) is often added to the **minimum price**.

- In **target costing**, an organisation decides what the sales price of the item will be, and the required profit margin. Subtracting the desired profit margin from the target price gives a target cost, which is the cost for the item that the organisation should aim to achieve. The difference between the current cost and the target cost is a **cost gap**, that the organisation should seek to eliminate.

Quick quiz

1. Name ten influences (apart from cost) on pricing policy.
2. What are the four stages of the product life cycle?
3. What price is first charged for a product under a policy of market penetration pricing?
4. What are the four bases on which the same product can be sold at different prices to different customers?
5. What technique for pricing is useful for businesses that carry out a large amount of jobbing or contract work?
6. What costs does a minimum price cover?
7. What qualitative issues should management consider when submitting a fixed price quotation?
8. List four ways for closing a cost gap between current cost and target cost.

Answers to quick quiz

1   Price sensitivity, price perception, quality, intermediaries, competitors, suppliers, newness, incomes, product range, ethics, substitute products

2   Introduction, growth, maturity, decline

3   Low prices

4   By market segment, by product version, by place, by time

5   Full cost plus pricing

6
   • The incremental costs of producing and selling the item
   • The opportunity costs of the resources consumed in making and selling the item

7
   • Will setting a low bid price cause the customer (or others) to feel that a precedent has been established for future prices?

   • Will the contribution margin on a bid set low enough to acquire the job, earn a sufficient amount to justify the additional burdens placed on management or employees by the activity?

   • How, if at all, will fixed price tenders affect the organisation's normal sales?

   • If the job is taking place during a period of low business activity (off-season or during a recession), is management willing to take the business at a lower contribution or profit margin simply to keep a valued workforce employed?

8   Reduce the number of components in the product or the number of features in the product, use cheaper materials (eg standard components), use cheaper labour, train staff and improve efficiency, use better technology, cut out features or activities that do not add value.

Transfer pricing

Topic list
1 Transfer pricing: basic principles
2 Profit centres and transfer pricing
3 Problems with transfer pricing
4 Transfers at market price
5 Cost-based approaches to transfer pricing
6 Opportunity cost and transfer pricing
7 The 'general rule'
8 Negotiated transfer prices

Introduction

Where internal transfers of goods or services are made between different units
of the same business, management must decide on the appropriate price at
which such transfers should be charged. This chapter considers the matters
that management should bear in mind when setting such transfer prices.

Learning objectives

On completion of this chapter you will be able to:

Syllabus reference

- understand the purpose of transfer prices   2 (i)
- understand the various ways in which transfer prices may be set, and the   2 (i)
  relative advantages and disadvantages of each method

1 Transfer pricing: basic principles

Key term

> A **transfer price** is 'The price at which goods or services are transferred between different units of the same company.... The extent to which the transfer price covers costs and contributes to (internal) profit is a matter of policy.'
> (CIMA *Official Terminology*)

When there are transfers of goods or services between divisions, the transfers could be made free to the division receiving the benefits. For example, if a garage and car showroom has two divisions, one for car repairs and servicing and the other for car sales, the servicing division will be required to service cars before they are sold. The servicing division could do the work without making any record of the work done. However, unless the cost or value of such work is recorded, management cannot keep a check on the amount of resources (such as time) that has been required for new car servicing. For planning and control purposes, it is necessary that some record of inter-divisional services or transfers of goods should be kept.

Inter-divisional work can be given a cost or charge, and this is its transfer price. The transfer price is revenue to the division providing the goods or service, and a cost to the division receiving the benefit.

Exam focus point

> Transfer pricing was examined in June 2004 and in December 2007.
>
> The question in the December 2007 exam was not a popular question, and was attempted by the fewest candidates. The examiner noted that 'this may be because transfer pricing is regarded as a complex topic. While this may be the case, it can be understood by adopting a logical approach....... a careful and logical approach led to good marks. The main reason that some candidates did not obtain good marks was that their calculations were difficult to follow as calculations were presented with no annotation to indicate what was being calculated.' The conclusion to this is that candidates will be awarded marks for method but only if the marker can recognise what is being calculated.

2 Profit centres and transfer pricing

An organisation might be divided into a number of profit centres. The manager of each profit centre is required to make a profit from the activities for which he or she is responsible, and the performance of the centre is measured in terms of profit (or return on capital).

A profit centre might be a division within the company, or a separate subsidiary company within the group. The activities of a profit centre might be fairly autonomous, and separate from the activities of other profit centres within the organisation. Alternatively, the activities of profit centres might be fairly closely inter-related, with some profit centres providing products or services to others.

When one profit centre provides products or services to another profit centre, its manager will expect to make a profit from these transactions, and so will charge the other profit centre a price for the work that is in excess of the costs it incurred.

An issue that arises in such situations is how to fix a price for the work that is acceptable to both profit centres.

2.1 Example

Suppose that profit centre A supplies goods to profit centre B, and the cost to profit centre A is, say, $10,000. Any price in excess of $10,000 will result in a profit for profit centre A. Now suppose that profit centre B then re-sells the goods for $18,000 without doing any further work on them.

(a)   The total profit to the company is $8,000 ($18,000 – $10,000).

(b)   If the price charged by profit centre A to profit centre B is $12,000, profit centre A will make a profit of $2,000 ($12,000 – $10,000) and profit centre B will make a profit of $6,000 ($18,000 – $12,000).

(c)   If the price charged by profit centre A to profit centre B is $17,000, profit centre A will make a profit of $7,000 ($17,000 – $10,000) and profit centre B will make a profit of $1,000 ($18,000 – $17,000).

The overall profit is the same, whatever price profit centre A charges to profit centre B, but the price charged affects the share of the total profit enjoyed by each profit centre.

The purpose of having a profit centre organisation is to provide an incentive for improving profitability within each part of the organisation. However, setting prices for work done by one profit centre for another is a potential source of disagreement, since profit centres can improve their profits at the expense of another, by charging higher prices.

2.2 Bases for setting a transfer price

A transfer price may be based upon:

(a)   Market price
(b)   A discount to the market price
(c)   Marginal cost, or marginal cost with a gross profit margin on top
(d)   Full cost, or full cost plus a profit margin
(e)   A negotiated price, which could be based on any of (a) to (d) above

If a transfer price is at an amount in excess of cost, a profit centre system is in operation.

3 Problems with transfer pricing

FAST FORWARD

Transfer prices are a way of promoting **divisional autonomy**, ideally without prejudicing the **divisional performance** measurement or discouraging overall **corporate profit maximisation**.

They may be based on **market price** where there is a market.

If not, problems arise with **cost-based** transfer prices because one party or the other is liable to perceive them as unfair.

3.1 Divisional autonomy

Transfer prices are particularly appropriate for **profit centres** because if one profit centre does work for another, the size of the transfer price will affect the costs of one profit centre and the revenues of another.

However, a danger with profit centre accounting is that the business organisation will divide into a number of **self-interested segments**, each acting at times against the wishes and interests of other segments. Decisions might be taken by a profit centre manager in the best interests of his or her own part of the business, but against the best interests of other profit centres and possibly the organisation as a whole.

A task of head office is therefore to try to prevent dysfunctional decision making by individual profit centres. To do this, it must reserve some power and authority for itself and so profit centres **cannot** be allowed to make entirely **autonomous decisions**.

Just how much authority head office decides to keep for itself will vary according to individual circumstances. A **balance** ought to be kept between **divisional autonomy** to provide incentives and motivation, and retaining **centralised authority** to ensure that the organisation's profit centres are all working towards the same target, the benefit of the organisation as a whole (in other words, retaining **goal congruence** among the organisation's separate divisions).

3.2 Divisional performance measurement

Profit centre managers tend to put their own profit **performance** above everything else. Since profit centre performance is measured according to the profit they earn, no profit centre will want to do work for another and incur costs without being paid for it. Consequently, profit centre managers are likely to dispute the size of transfer prices with each other, or disagree about whether one profit centre should do work for another or not. Transfer prices **affect behaviour and decisions** by profit centre managers.

3.3 Corporate profit maximisation

When there are disagreements about how much work should be transferred between divisions, and how many sales the division should make to the external market, there is presumably a **profit-maximising** level of output and sales for the organisation as a whole. However, unless each profit centre also maximises its own profit at this same level of output, there will be inter-divisional disagreements about output levels and the profit-maximising output will not be achieved.

3.4 The ideal solution

Ideally a transfer price should be set at a level that overcomes these problems.

(a)   The transfer price should provide an 'artificial' selling price that enables the transferring division to **earn a return** for its efforts, and the receiving division to **incur a cost** for benefits received.

(b)   The transfer price should be set at a level that enables profit centre performance to be **measured 'commercially'** (that is, it should be a **fair** commercial price).

(c)   The transfer price, if possible, should encourage profit centre managers to agree on the amount of goods and services to be transferred, which will also be at a level that is consistent with the organisation's aims as a whole such as **maximising company profits**.

In practice it is very difficult to achieve all three aims.

Question   Autonomy

(a)   What do you understand by the term 'divisional autonomy'?

(b)   What are the likely behavioural consequences of a head office continually imposing its own decisions on divisions?

Answer

(a)   The term refers to the right of a division to govern itself, that is, the freedom to make decisions without consulting a higher authority first and without interference from a higher body.

(b)   Decentralisation recognises that those closest to a job are the best equipped to say how it should be done and that people tend to perform to a higher standard if they are given responsibility. Centrally-imposed decisions are likely to make managers feel that they do not really have any authority and therefore that they cannot be held responsible for performance. They will therefore make less effort to perform well.

4 Transfers at market price

If an **external market** price exists for transferred goods or services, profit centre managers will be aware of the price they could charge or the price they would have to pay for their goods on the external market, and so will **compare** this price with the internal transfer price.

It might therefore be agreed that transfers at market price are 'fair' and appropriate.

4.1 Example: transferring goods at market value

A company has two profit centres, A and B. Centre A sells half of its output on the open market and transfers the other half to centre B. Costs and external revenues in an accounting period are as follows.

	Centre A	Centre B	Total
	$	$	$
External sales	8,000	24,000	32,000
Costs of production	12,000	10,000	22,000
Company profit			10,000

Required

What are the consequences of setting a transfer price at market value?

Solution

If the transfer price is at market price, centre A would be happy to sell the output to centre B for $8,000, which is what centre A would get by selling it externally instead of transferring it.

	A		B		Total
	$	$	$	$	$
Market sales		8,000		24,000	32,000
Transfer sales		8,000		–	
		16,000		24,000	
Transfer costs	–		8,000		
Own costs	12,000		10,000		22,000
		12,000		18,000	
Profit		4,000		6,000	10,000

The consequences, therefore, are as follows.

(a) Centre A earns the same profit on transfers as on external sales. Centre B must pay a commercial price for transferred goods, and both divisions will have their profit measured fairly.

(b) Centre A will be indifferent about selling externally or transferring goods to centre B because the profit is the same on both types of transaction. Centre B can therefore ask for and obtain as many units as it wants from centre A.

A **market-based** transfer price might therefore seem to be the **ideal** transfer price.

4.2 Adjusted market price

However, internal transfers are often **cheaper** than external sales, with **savings** in selling and administration costs, bad debt risks and possibly transport/delivery costs. It would therefore seem reasonable for the buying division to expect a **discount** on the external market price.

The transfer price might therefore be set at an amount slightly below market price, so that both profit centres can **share the cost savings** from internal transfers compared with external sales. It should be possible to reach agreement on this price and on output levels with a minimum of intervention from head office.

4.3 The disadvantages of market value transfer prices

Market value as a transfer price does have certain disadvantages.

(a) The division receiving the internal transfer might decide that an external supplier would be more convenient, or might do the job better or more quickly. There is **no incentive for the division to 'buy' the goods or services internally**, because it would be just as cheap to buy outside. From the point of view of the organisation as a whole, however, it might be very desirable that internal transfers should be preferred to external market purchases.

(b) The market price may be a **temporary** one, induced by adverse **economic conditions**, or dumping, or the market price might depend on the volume of output supplied to the external market by the profit centre.

(c) A transfer price at market value might, under some circumstances, act as a disincentive to use up any **spare capacity** in the divisions. A price based on incremental cost, in contrast, might provide an incentive to use up the spare resources in order to provide a marginal contribution to profit.

(d) Many products do not have an equivalent market price so that the price of a similar, but not identical, product might have to be chosen. In such circumstances, the option to sell or buy on the open market does not really exist.

5 Cost-based approaches to transfer pricing

FAST FORWARD

> **Fixed costs** in the supplying division can be accounted for in a number of ways to ensure that it at least breaks even.
>
> **Standard costs** should be used for transfer prices to avoid encouraging inefficiency in the supplying division.

Cost-based approaches to transfer pricing are often used in practice, particularly where the following conditions apply.

(a) There is **no external market** for the product that is being transferred.

(b) Alternatively, although there is an external market it is an **imperfect** one because the market price is affected by such factors as the amount that the company setting the transfer price supplies to it, or because there is only a limited external demand.

In either case there will not be a suitable market price upon which to base the transfer price.

5.1 Transfer prices based on full cost

Under this approach, the **full cost** (including fixed overheads absorbed) incurred by the supplying division in making the 'intermediate' product is charged to the receiving division. If a **full cost plus** approach is used, a **profit margin** is usually added to cost to reach the transfer price.

Key term

> An **intermediate product** is one that is used as a component of another product, for example car headlights or food additives.

5.2 Example: transfers at full cost (plus)

A company has two profit centres, P and Q. Centre P assembles a product which it then transfers to Centre Q. Centre Q does the finishing work on the product, after which it is sold on the external market. Budgeted production costs for the year are as follows.

	Centre P	Centre Q
Units produced	30,000	30,000
Variable cost per unit incurred	$5	$2
Fixed costs	$210,000	$180,000

The finished item sells for $25 per unit.

If a profit centre organisation did not exist, the budgeted profit would be as follows.

	$	$
Sales (30,000 × $25)		750,000
Variable costs (30,000 × $7)	210,000	
Fixed costs	390,000	
Total costs		600,000
Profit		150,000

If a profit centre structure were to operate, what would be the profits of centre P and centre Q if units were transferred between the divisions:

(a)   at full cost
(b)   at full cost plus a margin of 25%?

Solution

Transfer price at full cost

The full cost of output from centre P is the variable cost of $5 plus a fixed cost per unit of $7 ($210,000/30,000). If the transfer price is at full cost ($12), centre P would have sales to centre Q of $360,000 (30,000 units at $12), and the profits of each centre would be as follows.

	Centre P		Centre Q		Company	
	$	$	$	$		$
External market sales		–		750,000		750,000
Internal transfers		360,000		–		
Total sales		360,000		750,000		
Costs						
Transfers	–		360,000			
Own variable costs	150,000		60,000		210,000	
Own fixed costs	210,000		180,000		390,000	
Total costs		360,000		600,000		600,000
Profit		0		150,000		150,000

The transfer sales of centre P are self-cancelling with the transfer costs of centre Q so that total profits are unaffected by the transfer items. The transfer price simply spreads the total profit of $150,000 between P and Q. Since the transfers are at full cost, the budgeted profit of centre P is nil. The only ways in which centre P can make a profit would be:

(a)   to produce more units than budgeted, and so make a profit because fixed costs will remain unchanged, and a contribution of $7 per unit will be earned on every unit in excess of 30,000
(b)   keep actual costs below budget.

The obvious drawback to a transfer price at cost is that division P needs a profit on its transfers in order to be motivated to supply division Q; and transfer pricing at cost is therefore inconsistent with the use of a profit centre accounting system.

Transfer price at full cost plus

If the transfers are at cost plus a margin of 25%, transfers by division P to division Q will be at $12 plus 25%, i.e. $15 per unit, or $450,000 in total. Divisional profits will be as follows.

	Centre P		Centre Q		Company
	$	$	$	$	$
External market sales		–		750,000	750,000
Internal transfers	450,000		–		
Total sales		450,000		750,000	
Costs					
Transfers	–		450,000		
Own variable costs	150,000		60,000		210,000
Own fixed costs	210,000		180,000		390,000
Total costs		360,000		690,000	600,000
Profit		90,000		60,000	150,000

The total profit is now shared between the two divisions. However, the choice of 25% as a profit mark-up was arbitrary and unrelated to any external market conditions. If the profit centre managers cannot agree on the size of the mark-up, a transfer pricing decision would have to be imposed by head office. If this were to happen, the degree of autonomy enjoyed by the profit centres would be weakened.

A potential weakness with transfers at cost plus is that the division making the transfers might not be sufficiently motivated to control costs. On the contrary, if transfers are priced at actual cost plus, the transferring division would make bigger profits by spending more.

To provide an incentive to control costs, transfers at cost plus should therefore be at a budgeted cost plus or a standard cost plus.

Question
Transfer price

In the example above, what should be the transfer price, expressed in terms of cost plus, if centre P and centre Q were to have the same budgeted profit?

Answer

The total budgeted profit is $150,000. Divided equally, this would give a profit of $75,000 to each division. Centre P's budgeted costs are $360,000 in total, which means that to earn a profit of $75,000, it must transfer the 30,000 units for a total revenue of $435,000, or $14.50 per unit.

Divisional profitability would then be:

	Centre P		Centre Q		Company
	$	$	$	$	$
External market sales		–		750,000	750,000
Internal transfers	435,000		–		
Total sales		435,000		750,000	
Costs					
Transfers	–		435,000		
Own variable costs	150,000		60,000		210,000
Own fixed costs	210,000		180,000		390,000
Total costs		360,000		675,000	600,000
Profit		75,000		75,000	150,000

Both divisions can improve profitability by making and selling more units, and by keeping their costs below budgeted levels.

5.3 Transfer price at variable cost

A variable cost approach entails charging the variable cost that has been incurred by the supplying division to the receiving division, probably with a profit mark-up. In the above example, centre P might transfer its output to centre Q at variable cost plus, say, 200%. This would give a transfer price of $15 per unit ($5 plus 200%).

A problem with variable cost plus transfer prices is that unless a transfer price is sufficiently high (ie the mark-up is sufficiently large) the supplying division will not cover its fixed costs and make a profit.

There are ways in which this problem could be overcome.

(a) Each division can be given a **share** of the overall contribution earned by the organisation, but it would probably be necessary to decide what the shares should be centrally, thereby undermining **divisional autonomy**. Alternatively central management could impose a range within which the transfer price should fall, and allow divisional managers to **negotiate** what they felt was a fair price between themselves.

(b) An alternative method is to use a **two-part charging system**: transfer prices are set at variable cost (or variable cost plus some mark-up) and once a year there is a transfer of a fixed fee to the supplying division, representing an allowance for its fixed costs. Care is needed with this approach. It risks sending the message to the supplying division that it need not control its fixed costs because the company will **subsidise any inefficiencies**. On the other hand, if fixed costs are incurred because spare capacity is kept available for the needs of other divisions it is reasonable to expect those other divisions to pay a fee if they 'booked' that capacity in advance but later failed to utilise it. The main problem with this approach, once again, is that it is likely to conflict with **divisional autonomy**.

5.4 Standard cost versus actual cost

When a transfer price is based on cost, **standard cost** or **budgeted cost** should be used, not actual cost. A transfer of actual cost would give no incentive to **control costs**, because they could all be passed on. Actual cost-plus transfer prices might even encourage the manager of the transferring profit centre to overspend, because this would increase the divisional profit, even though the company as a whole (and the profit centre receiving the transfers) might suffer.

Question

Transfer prices again

Motivate has two profit centres, P and Q. P transfers *all* its output to Q. The variable cost of output from P is $5 per unit, and fixed costs are $1,200 per month. Additional processing costs in Q are $4 per unit for variable costs, plus fixed costs of $800 per month. Budgeted production is 400 units per month, and the output of Q sells for $15 per unit. The transfer price is to be based on standard full cost plus. From what *range* of prices should the transfer price be selected, in order to motivate the managers of both profit centres to both increase output and reduce costs?

Answer

Any transfer price based on **standard** cost plus will motivate managers to cut costs, because favourable differences between standard costs and actual costs will add to the division's profits. Managers of each division will also be willing to increase output above the budget of 400 units provided that it is profitable to do so; that is:

(a) in P, provided that the transfer price exceeds the variable cost of $5 per unit;

(b) in Q, provided that the transfer price is less than the difference between the fixed selling price ($15) and the variable costs in Q itself ($4). This amount of $11 ($15 – $4) is sometimes called **net marginal revenue**.

The range of prices is therefore between $5.01 and $10.99.

6 Opportunity cost and transfer pricing

If a **profit-maximising output** level has been established, the transfer price should be set such that there is **not a more profitable opportunity** for individual divisions. In other words transfer prices should include **opportunity costs** of transfer.

The problem with this approach is that it entails collecting all the relevant divisional **data** centrally and **imposing** a transfer price, undermining divisional autonomy.

Ideally, a transfer price should be set that enables the individual divisions to maximise their profits at a level of output that maximises profit for the company as a whole. The transfer price which achieves this is unlikely to be a market-based transfer price (if there is one) and is also unlikely to be a simple cost plus based price.

If optimum decisions are to be taken by profit centre managers, transfer prices should reflect **opportunity costs**.

(a)   If profit centre managers are given sufficient autonomy to make their own output and selling decisions, and at the same time their performance is judged by the company according to the profits they earn, they will be keenly aware of all the commercial opportunities.

(b)   If transfers are made for the good of the company as a whole, the commercial benefits to the company ought to be **shared** between the participating divisions.

Transfer prices can therefore be reached by:

(a)   recognising the levels of output, external sales and internal transfers that are best for the **company as a whole**; and

(b)   arriving at a transfer price that ensures that all divisions maximise their profits at this same level of output. The transfer price should therefore be such that there is **not a more profitable opportunity** for individual divisions. This in turn means that the opportunity costs of transfer should be covered by the transfer price.

6.1 Limiting factors and transfer pricing

When an intermediate resource is in short supply and acts as a limiting factor on production in the transferring division, the **cost of transferring** an item is the variable cost of production plus the contribution obtainable from using the scarce resource in its next most profitable way.

6.2 Example: scarce resources

Suppose, for example, that division A is a profit centre that produces three items, X, Y and Z. Each item has an external market.

	X	Y	Z
External market price, per unit	$48	$46	$40
Variable cost of production in division A	$33	$24	$28
Labour hours required per unit in division A	3	4	2

The maximum **external** sales are 800 units of X, 500 units of Y and 300 units of Z. In addition to the external sales, product Y can be transferred to division B, but the maximum quantity that might be required for transfer is 300 units of Y.

Instead of receiving transfers of product Y from division A at $46 per unit division B could buy similar units of product Y on the open market at a slightly cheaper price of $45 per unit.

What should the transfer price be for each unit if the total labour hours available in division A are 3,800 hours?

Solution

Hours required to meet maximum demand:

External sales:	Hours
X (3 × 800)	2,400
Y (4 × 500)	2,000
Z (2 × 300)	600
	5,000
Transfers of Y (4 × 300)	1,200
	6,200

Contribution from external sales:

	X	Y	Z
Contribution per unit	$15	$22	$12
Labour hours per unit	3 hrs	4 hrs	2 hrs
Contribution per labour hour	$5.00	$5.50	$6.00
Priority for selling	3rd	2nd	1st
Total hours needed	2,400	2,000	600

If only **3,800 hours** of labour are available, division A would choose, **ignoring transfers** to B, to sell:

	Hours
300 Z (maximum)	600
500 Y (maximum)	2,000
	2,600
400 X (balance)	1,200
	3,800

To transfer 300 units of Y to division B would take 1,200 hours (300 × 4 hrs) and involve forgoing the sale of 400 units of X which also would take 1,200 hours (400 × 3 hrs).

Opportunity cost of transferring units of Y, and the appropriate transfer price:

	$ per unit
Variable cost of making Y	24
Opportunity cost (contribution of $5 per hour	
available from selling X externally): benefit forgone (4 hours × $5)	20
Transfer price for Y	44

The transfer price for Y should, in this case, be less than the external market price.

7 The 'general rule'

We have studied several methods of calculating transfer prices and also the reasons for setting a transfer price (namely the need to reconcile the possibly conflicting objectives of decentralisation, divisional autonomy, goal congruence and managerial effort). These different objectives means that **there may be no one best transfer price** - for example, the senior management may place priority on say divisional autonomy ahead of goal congruence in the belief that this will motivate managers and lead to other benefits and profits that are not immediately quantifiable.

However, if the company is seeking a 'mathematical' best transfer price that will maximise profits in the short term, then the **'general rule'** is that the ideal transfer price should reflect the opportunity cost of sale to the supplying division and the opportunity cost to the buying division.

This leads to the following 'general rule':

Transfer price per unit = Standard variable cost in the producing division *plus* the opportunity cost to the company as a whole of supplying the unit internally

If there is no external market for the units produced, and no alternative use for the resources in the producing division, then the opportunity cost is zero, and the transfer price should be set as the standard variable cost in the producing division.

In the example in paragraph 6.2, the general rule can be applied to derive the appropriate transfer price for product Y from division A to division B.

Transfer price per unit = Standard variable cost in division A ($24)

+ Opportunity cost of supplying the unit internally (contribution forgone by not using the labour hours in their next best alternative use, 4 hours × $5 = $20 as described above)

So the transfer price = $24 + $20 = $44

8 Negotiated transfer prices

> In practice, **negotiated** transfer prices, **market-based** transfer prices and **full cost-based** transfer prices are the methods normally used.

A transfer price based on opportunity cost is often **difficult to identify**, for lack of suitable information about costs and revenues in individual divisions. In this case it is likely that transfer prices will be set by means of **negotiation**. The agreed price may be finalised from a mixture of accounting arithmetic, politics and compromise.

The process of negotiation will be improved if **adequate information** about each division's costs and revenues is made available to the other division involved in the negotiation. By having a free flow of cost and revenue information, it will be easier for divisional managers to identify opportunities for improving profits, to the benefit of both divisions involved in the transfer.

A negotiating system that might enable **goal congruent plans** to be agreed between profit centres is as follows.

(a) Profit centres **submit plans** for output and sales to head office, as a preliminary step in preparing the annual budget.

(b) Head office **reviews these plans**, together with any other information it may obtain. Amendments to divisional plans might be discussed with the divisional managers.

(c) Once divisional plans are acceptable to head office and **consistent** with each other, head office might let the divisional managers arrange budgeted transfers and transfer prices.

(d) Where divisional plans are **inconsistent** with each other, head office might try to establish a plan that would maximise the profits of the company as a whole. Divisional managers would then be asked to negotiate budgeted transfers and transfer prices on this basis.

(e) If divisional managers fail to agree a transfer price between themselves, a head office **'arbitration' manager** or team would be referred to for an opinion or a decision.

(f) Divisions **finalise their budgets** within the framework of agreed transfer prices and resource constraints.

(g) Head office **monitors the profit performance** of each division.

Key learning points

- Transfer prices are a way of promoting **divisional autonomy**, ideally without prejudicing the **divisional performance** measurement or discouraging overall **corporate profit maximisation**.

- They may be based on **market price** where there is a market.

- If not, problems arise with **cost-based** transfer prices because one party or the other is liable to perceive them as unfair.

- **Fixed costs** in the supplying division can be accounted for in a number of ways to ensure that it at least breaks even.

- **Standard costs** should be used for transfer prices to avoid encouraging inefficiency in the supplying division.

- If a **profit-maximising output** level has been established, the transfer price should be set such that there is **not a more profitable opportunity** for individual divisions. In other words transfer prices should include **opportunity costs** of transfer.

- The problem with this approach is that it entails collecting all the relevant divisional **data** centrally and **imposing** a transfer price, undermining divisional autonomy.

- In practice, **negotiated** transfer prices, **market-based** transfer prices and **full cost-based** transfer prices are the methods normally used.

Quick quiz

1   Why might an *adjusted* market price be used as a transfer price?
2   What are the disadvantages of market value transfer prices?
3   What is the drawback of setting a transfer price at full cost?
4   Why should actual costs not be used to set transfer prices?
5   Where there is no external market for an intermediate product, in what range should the transfer price be set?
6   Why should transfer prices reflect opportunity costs?

1   To give both the transferring division and the receiving division a share of the benefits from the lower costs of internal transfers compared with the cost of external sales (savings in sales and despatch costs, invoicing and debt collection, etc.)

2   The main disadvantage is that there is no incentive for the receiving division to 'buy' internally rather than buy from an external supplier. This would almost certainly be damaging to the organisation's profits. A further common problem is the absence of an easily-identifiable market price, particularly for non-standard items, or items with special features.

3   Without a mark-up, there is not much opportunity for the transferring division to make a profit, which could be de-motivating.

4   Standard costs, not actual costs, should be used to set cost-based transfer prices. If actual costs were used, cost inefficiencies in the transferring division would be passed on to the receiving division in the transfer price.

5   As a minimum, not less than the variable costs of production in the transferring division. As a maximum, not more than the sale value of the end product, minus the variable costs incurred in the receiving division.

6   So that profit centre managers will be motivated to achieve a level of output and sales that maximises the profits of the organisation as a whole.

Performance measurement

Introduction to performance measurement

Introduction

Performance measurement entails the setting of targets for achievement that are consistent with the organisation's goals and comparing actual results with the target, in order then to take any necessary action. This chapter introduces you to the ideas that are involved.

Learning objectives

On completion of this chapter you will be able to:

1 Performance measurement and the planning and control system

FAST FORWARD

Performance measures can be divided into two groups.
- **Financial** performance measures
- **Non-financial** performance measures.

Non-financial performance measures can be **quantitative** or **qualitative**.

Performance measurement is part of the planning and controls cycle of an organisation. Based on corporate objectives, expected levels of achievement – expressed in both financial and non-financial terms - are set for sectors of the organisation and for individuals and compared to actual achievement to aid future decisions.

A number of key points can be made on the topic of performance measurement:

- Performance measurement is an integral part of the management control system.
- The management control system includes planning and decision-making.
- Planning will be influenced by strategic decisions and organisational objectives.
- The management control system will influence behaviour.
- Performance measurement will compare actual performance against predefined and predetermined yardsticks.
- Performance measurement will be carried out at different levels within the organisation (corporate, division, section and individual).
- Resource allocation will be influenced by performance measurement.
- Both financial and non-financial measures will be used in performance measurement.

Exam focus point

The examiner wrote an article in Finance Matters in March 2007 on measuring performance. In this article he states that the definition of performance measurement above provides the context of a performance measurement within the DipFM syllabus.

In the syllabus there are numerous performance measurement techniques that may be examined. The examiner notes that regardless of the technique examined candidates should ensure that they understand the purpose, method of calculation, and application of that technique. He concludes his article with five key points for performance measurement:

- Consider the context
- Select measures related to objectives
- Justify your measures
- Specify your measures
- Include non-financial/qualitative measures.

Performance measurement was examined in December 2007.

1.1 Financial performance measures

Financial measures (or **monetary** measures) include the following.

Measure	Example
Profit	**Profit** is probably the most common measure of financial performance for companies. Profit may also be related to the amount of investment needed to earn the profit, and expressed in terms of **return on capital**.
Revenue	Financial performance might also be measured in terms of sales revenue, or sales revenue growth.
Costs	Most organisations have financial plans that include budgets for expenditure, and for the planned cost of products or services. Performance is commonly measured in terms of whether actual costs were higher or lower than budgeted, and so whether or not costs appear to be under control.
Share price	For companies whose shares are traded on a stock exchange, financial performance will also be measured in terms of the returns for shareholders. These include both dividend payments and any rise or fall in the share price.
Cash flow	As well as monitoring profit, companies should also monitor their cash flow, to ensure that the business is generating sufficient cash from its operations to meet its foreseeable liabilities. One measure of cash flow performance is the amount of 'free cash flow' earned by a company during a period. Free cash flow is the cash surplus available to the company's management to spend at their discretion, for example on dividends or non-essential capital expenditure.

1.2 Productivity measurements

Productivity is a measure of the quantity of the product or service produced **(output) in relation to** the resources put into producing them (**input**). Examples of productivity measurements are the number of units produced per labour hour or per machine hour, or per employee, or per tonne of material. Productivity measures **how efficiently resources are being used**.

1.3 Ratios and performance measurement

It is often useful to measure performance by means of ratios.

- It is **easier to look at changes over time** by comparing ratios in one time period with the corresponding ratios for other periods.
- Ratios **relate one item to another, and so help to put performance into context**. For example the profit/sales ratio sets profit in the context of how much has been earned per $1 of sales, and so shows how wide or narrow profit margins are.
- Ratios can be used as **targets,** for example for productivity. Managers will then take decisions that will enable them to achieve their targets.
- Ratios provide a way of **summarising** an organisation's results, and **comparing** them with other, similar organisations.

1.4 Percentages as performance measures

A percentage expresses one number as a proportion of another and **gives meaning to absolute numbers**. Market share, capacity levels, wastage and staff turnover are often expressed using percentages. For example, an organisation might work at 94% capacity during a month, compared to a target of 98%. Similarly, a company might experience a 25% turnover each year in skilled staff, when the maximum acceptable turnover rate is, say, 20%.

2 Disadvantages of financial performance indicators

Concentration on financial indicators means that important goals and factors may be ignored.

2.1 Concentration on too few variables

If performance measurement systems focus entirely on those items which can be expressed in monetary terms, managers will **concentrate on only those variables** and **ignore** other important variables that cannot be expressed in monetary terms.

For example, pressure from senior management to **cut costs and raise productivity** will produce **short-term benefits** in cost control but, in the **long term,** managerial performance and motivation is likely to be affected, labour turnover will increase and product quality will fall.

Reductions in cost can easily be measured and recorded in performance reports, employee morale cannot. **Performance reports** should therefore **include** not only costs and revenues but **other important variables**, to give an indication of expected future results from present activity.

2.2 Lack of information on quality

Traditional responsibility accounting systems also fail to provide **information on the quality or importance of operations**. Drury provides the following example.

> 'Consider a situation where a purchasing department regularly achieved the budget for all expense items. The responsibility performance reporting system therefore suggests that the department was well managed. However, the department provided a poor service to the production departments. Low-cost suppliers were selected who provided poor quality materials and frequently failed to meet delivery dates. This caused much wasted effort in chasing up orders and prejudiced the company's ability to deliver to its customers on time.'

2.3 Measuring success, not ensuring success

Financial performance indicators have been said to simply **measure success**. What organisations also require, however, are performance **indicators that ensure success**. Such indicators, **linked** to an organisation's **critical success factors** such as quality and flexibility, will be **non financial** in nature.

Exam focus point

In the examiner's report to the December 2007 exam the examiner commented on the question on performance measurement. He emphasised the importance of both the financial and non-financial: 'One key weakness which candidates for the Diploma must avoid is using only financial measures to assess performance. Non-financial measures can provide considerable insight into performance. However, establishing, defining and using non-financial measures is often far from simple. For a not for profit organisation, non-financial measures will have particular significance.'

3 Growing emphasis on NFPIs

Changes in cost structures, the competitive environment and the manufacturing environment have lead to an **increased use of non-financial performance indicators (NFPIs)**.

3.1 Impact of changes in cost structures and the manufacturing and competitive environments

These have led to a shift from treating financial figures as the foundation of performance measurement to treating them as one of a range of measures.

3.1.1 Changes in cost structures

Modern technology requires massive investment and product life cycles have got shorter. A greater proportion of costs are sunk and a large proportion of costs are planned, engineered or designed into a product/service before production/delivery. **At the time the product/service is produced/delivered, it is therefore too late to control costs.**

3.1.2 Changes in competitive environment

Financial measures do not convey the full picture of a company's performance, especially in a **modern business environment**.

> 'In today's worldwide competitive environment companies are competing in terms of product quality, delivery, reliability, after-sales service and customer satisfaction. None of these variables is directly measured by the traditional responsibility accounting system, despite the fact that they represent the major goals of world-class manufacturing companies.'

3.1.3 Changes in manufacturing environment

New manufacturing techniques and technologies focus on minimising throughput times, inventory levels and set-up times. But managers can reduce the costs for which they are responsible by increasing inventory levels through maximising output. If a performance measurement system **focuses principally on costs**, managers may **concentrate on cost reduction and ignore other important strategic manufacturing goals**.

3.2 Introducing NFPIs

Many companies are therefore discovering the usefulness of quantitative and qualitative **non-financial performance indicators (NFPIs)**. The following definition from CIMA's *Official Terminology* is useful because of the examples it provides.

Key term

Non-financial performance measures are 'measures of performance based on non-financial information which may originate in and be used by operating departments to monitor and control their activities without any accounting input.

Non-financial performance measures may give a more timely indication of the levels of performance achieved than do financial ratios, and may be less susceptible to distortion by factors such as uncontrollable variations in the effect of market forces on operations.

Examples of non-financial performance measures:

Area assessed	Performance measure
Service quality	Number of complaints
	Proportions of repeat bookings
	Customer waiting time
	On-time deliveries
Production performance	Set-up times
	Number of suppliers
	Days' inventory in hand
	Output per employee
	Material yield percentage
	Schedule adherence
	Proportion of output requiring rework
	Manufacturing lead times

Marketing effectiveness	Trend in market share
	Sales volume growth
	Customer visits per salesperson
	Client contact hours per salesperson
	Sales volume forecast v actual
	Number of customers
	Customer survey response information
Personnel	Number of complaints received
	Staff turnover
	Days lost through absenteeism
	Days lost through accidents/sickness
	Training time per employee.'

(CIMA Official Terminology)

4 The value of NFPIs

4.1 Ease of use

FAST FORWARD

> NFPIs do have advantages over financial indicators but a **combination** of both types of indicator is likely to be most successful.

Unlike traditional variance reports, NFPIs can be provided quickly for managers, per shift, **daily** or even **hourly** as required. They are likely to be easy to calculate, and easier for non-financial managers to understand and therefore to use effectively.

The beauty of non-financial indicators is that **anything can be compared** if it is **meaningful** to do so. The measures should be **tailored** to the circumstances so that, for example, number of coffee breaks per 20 pages of Study Text might indicate to you how hard you are studying!

Many suitable measures combine elements from the chart shown below. The chart is not intended to be prescriptive or exhaustive.

Note that the chart is not to be read across each horizontal row of cells – it does not for example suggest that you should measure 'defects per second'.

Errors/failure	Time	Quantity	People
Defects	Second	Range of products	Employees
Equipment failures	Minute	Parts/components	Employee skills
Warranty claims	Hour	Units produced	Customers
Complaints	Shift	Units sold	Competitors
Returns	Cycle	Services performed	Suppliers
Stockouts	Day	kg/litres/metres	
Lateness/waiting	Month	m²/m³	
Misinformation	Year	Documents	
Miscalculation		Deliveries	
Absenteeism		Enquiries	

Traditional measures derived from these lists like 'kg (of material) per unit produced' or 'units produced per hour' are fairly obvious, but what may at first seem a fairly **unlikely combination** may also be very revealing. 'Absenteeism per customer', for example, may be of no significance at all or it may reveal that a particularly difficult customer is being avoided, and hence that some action is needed.

There is clearly a need for the information provider to work more closely with the managers who will be using the information to make sure that their needs are properly understood. The measures used are likely to be **developed and refined over time**. It may be that some will serve the purpose of drawing attention to areas in need of improvement but will be of no further relevance once remedial action has been taken. A flexible, responsive approach is essential.

Question   NFPIs

Using the above chart make up five non-financial indicators and explain how each might be useful.

Answer

Here are five indicators, showing you how to use the chart, but there are many other possibilities.

(a)   Services performed late v total services performed
(b)   Total units sold v total units sold by competitors (indicating market share)
(c)   Warranty claims per month
(d)   Documents processed per employee
(e)   Equipment failures per 1,000 units produced

Don't forget to explain how the ones that you chose might be useful.

4.2 NFPIs and financial measures

Arguably, NFPIs are less likely to be **manipulated** than traditional profit-related measures and they should, therefore, offer a means of counteracting short-termism, since short-term profit at any (non-monetary) expense is rarely an advisable goal. The ultimate goal of commercial organisations in the long run is likely to remain the maximisation of **profit**, however, and so the financial aspect cannot be ignored.

There is a danger that too many such measures could be reported, leading to **information overload** for managers, providing information that is not truly useful, or that sends conflicting signals. A further danger of NFPIs is that they might lead managers to pursue detailed **operational goals** and become blind to the **overall strategy** in which those goals are set.

A **combination** of financial and non-financial indicators is therefore likely to be most successful.

4.2.1 The balanced scorecard

The need to **link financial and non-financial measures** of performance and to identify the **key performance measures** provided the impetus for the development of the balanced scorecard, which we look at in Chapter 12.

5 NFPIs in relation to employees

FAST FORWARD

NFPIs can usefully be applied to **employees** and product/service **quality**.

One of the many criticisms of **traditional accounting performance measurement systems** is that they **do not measure the skills, morale and training of the workforce**, which can be as **valuable to an organisation as its tangible assets**. For example if employees have not been trained in the manufacturing practices required to achieve the objectives of the new manufacturing environment, an organisation is unlikely to be successful.

Employee attitudes and morale can be measured by **surveying** employees. Education and skills levels, promotion and training, absenteeism and labour turnover for the employees for which each manager is responsible can also be monitored.

The **weighting** attached to employee-orientated NFPIs when assessing managerial performance should be high. High profitability or tight cost control should not be accompanied by 100% labour turnover.

6 NFPIs in relation to product/service quality

NFPIs are extremely useful when assessing **product/service quality.**

6.1 Performance measurement in a TQM environment

As you may already know (but will study further in Chapter 15), Total Quality Management is a highly significant trend in modern business thinking.

Because **TQM embraces every activity** of a business, performance measures cannot be confined to the production process but must also cover the work of sales and distribution departments and administration departments, the efforts of external suppliers, and the reaction of external customers.

In many cases the measures used will be non-financial ones. They may be divided into three types.

6.1.1 Measuring the quality of incoming supplies

The quality of output depends on the quality of input materials, and so **quality control** should include procedures for acceptance and inspection of goods inwards and measurement of rejects.

(a) **Inspection** will normally be based on statistical sampling techniques and the concept of an acceptance quality level (AQL).

(b) Another approach that can be used is to give each **supplier a 'rating'** for the quality of the goods they tend to supply, and give preference with purchase orders to well-rated suppliers.

(c) Where a **quality assurance scheme** is in place, the supplier guarantees the quality of goods supplied. This places the onus on the supplier to carry out the necessary quality checks, or face cancellation of the contract.

6.1.2 Monitoring work done as it proceeds

This will take place at various key stages in the production process. Inspection, based on random sampling and other statistical techniques, will provide a continual check that the production process is under control. The aim of inspection is not really to sort out the bad products from the good ones after the work has been done. The aim is to **satisfy management that quality control in production is being maintained.**

'In-process' controls include statistical process controls and random sampling, and measures such as the amount of scrap and reworking in relation to good production. Measurements can be made by product, by worker or work team, by machine or machine type, by department, or whatever is appropriate.

6.1.3 Measuring customer satisfaction

Some sub-standard items will inevitably be produced. In-process checks will identify some bad output, but other items will reach the customer who is the ultimate judge of quality. **'Complaints'** may be monitored in the form of letters of complaint, returned goods, penalty discounts, claims under guarantee, or requests for visits by service engineers.

Some companies adopt a more pro-active approach to monitoring customer satisfaction by surveying their customers on a regular basis. They use the feedback to obtain an index of customer satisfaction which is used to identify quality problems before they affect profits.

6.2 Quality of service

Service quality is measured principally by **qualitative measures**, as you might expect, although some quantitative measures are used by some businesses.

(a) If it were able to obtain the information, a retailer might use number of lost customers in a period as an indicator of service quality.

(b) Lawyers use the proportion of time spent with clients.

Fitzgerald *et al* identify 12 factors pertaining to service quality and the following table shows the measures used and the means of obtaining the information by British Airports Authority, a mass transport service.

Service quality factors	Measures	Mechanisms
Access	Walking distances	Customer survey and internal operational data
	Ease of finding way around	Customer survey
Aesthetics/appearance	Staff appearance	Customer survey
	Airport's appearance	Customer survey
	Quantity, quality, appearance of food	Management inspection
Availability	Equipment availability	Internal fault monitoring system and customer survey
		Customer survey and internal operational data
Cleanliness/tidiness	Cleanliness of environment and equipment	Customer survey and management inspection
Comfort	Crowdedness of airport	Customer survey and management inspection
Communication	Information clarity	Customer survey
	Clarity of labelling and pricing	Management inspection
Courtesy	Courtesy of staff	Customer survey and management inspection
Friendliness	Staff attitude and helpfulness	Customer survey and management inspection
Reliability	Number of equipment faults	Internal fault monitoring systems
Responsiveness	Staff responsiveness	Customer survey
Security	Efficiency of security checks	Customer survey
	Number of urgent safety reports	Internal operational data

Question

Measuring quality

What do you conclude are the two main means of measuring service quality at BAA (the British Airports Authority)?

6.3 Measures of customer satisfaction

You have probably filled in **questionnaires** in fast food restaurants or on aeroplanes without realising that you were completing a customer attitude survey for input to the organisation's management information system.

Case Study

Horngren cites the 'Customer Satisfaction Target' used by Holiday Inns, where information is measured by evaluating scores (A-F) on guest inspection cards and imposing a limit of 0.457 guest complaint letters per 1,000 room-nights sold.

Other possible measures of customer satisfaction include:

(a)   Market research information on customer preferences and customer satisfaction with specific product features

(b)   Number of defective units supplied to customers as a percentage of total units supplied

(c)   Number of customer complaints as a percentage of total sales volume

(d)   Percentage of products which fail early or excessively

(e)   On-time delivery rate

(f)   Average time to deal with customer queries

(g)   New customer accounts opened

(h)   Repeat business from existing customers

7 Qualitative issues

Qualitative factors are 'those that can be expressed in monetary terms only with much difficulty or imprecision'.

There will often be no conclusion that you can draw from qualitative information. Your job is to **be aware of its existence** and report it under the heading of **'other matters to be considered'**. In practice of course, many decisions are finally swayed by the strength of the qualitative arguments rather than the cold facts presented in the quantitative analysis, and rightly so.

Exam focus point

As a general guideline, if you are asked in the exam to comment on qualitative issues, you should consider matters such as the following.

(a)   The impact on or of human behaviour. What will be the reaction on the factory floor? How will managers feel? Will customers be attracted or deterred? Can suppliers be trusted?

(b)   The impact on or of the environment ('surroundings'). Is the country in a recession? Is government or legislation influential? Are there 'green' issues to be considered? What is the social impact? What action will competing companies take? Is changing technology a help or a hindrance?

(c)   The impact on or of ethics. Is the action in the public interest? Are we acting professionally? Are there conflicts of interest to be considered? Will fair dealing help to win business? Are we treating staff properly?

7.1 Branding

Brand identity conveys a lot of information very quickly and concisely. This helps customers to identify the goods or services and thus helps to **create customer loyalty** to the brand. It is therefore a means of increasing or maintaining sales.

Where a brand image promotes an idea of **quality**, a customer will be disappointed if his experience of a product fails to live up to his expectations. Quality control is therefore of utmost importance. It is essentially a problem for **service industries** such as hotels, airlines and retail stores, where there is **less possibility** than in the manufacturing sector of **detecting and rejecting the work of an operator before it reaches the customer**. Bad behaviour by an employee in a face-to-face encounter with a customer will **reflect on** the **entire company** and possibly deter the customer from using any of the company's services again.

Brand awareness is an **indicator of a product's/organisation's place in the market**. **Recall tests** can be used to assess the public's brand awareness.

7.2 Company profile

Company profile is **how an organisation is perceived by a range of stakeholders.** For example, stakeholders may have a negative attitude towards an organisation, perhaps as a result of an ethical issue or a crisis that has struck the organisation and the associated media comment. **Market research** can determine company profile and **marketing campaigns** can improve it if necessary.

8 Measuring profitability

Profitability can be measured by **return on investment (ROI)/return on capital employed (ROCE)**, **profit margin**, **gross profit margin** or **cost/sales ratios**.

Profitability is a key measure of financial performance. It can be expressed in a number of ways, in addition to a simple measurement of the actual amount of profit earned in a period.

8.1 Return on investment (ROI)

Key term

Return on investment (ROI) (also called **return on capital employed (ROCE)**) is a measurement of profit, expressed as a percentage of the investment required to earn the profit. It is calculated as (profit/capital employed) × 100% and shows how much profit has been made in relation to the amount of resources invested.

Profits alone do not show whether the return is sufficient, in view of the value of assets committed. Thus if company A and company B have the following results, company B would have the better performance.

	A	B
	$	$
Profit	5,000	5,000
Sales	100,000	100,000
Capital employed	50,000	25,000
ROI	10%	20%

The profit of each company is the same but company B only invested $25,000 to achieve that profit whereas company A invested $50,000.

What does the ROI tell us? What should we be looking for? There are three principal comparisons that can be made.

(a) actual ROI achieved against either a budget target or a longer-term financial target
(b) the change in ROI from one year to the next
(c) the ROI being earned by other organisations.

8.2 Profit margin

Key term

The **profit margin** (profit to sales ratio) is calculated as (profit ÷ sales) × 100%.

The profit margin provides a simple measure of performance for management. Investigation of unsatisfactory profit margins enables control action to be taken, either by reducing excessive costs or by raising selling prices.

8.3 Example: the profit to sales ratio

A company compares its year 2 results with year 1 results as follows.

	Year 2 $	Year 1 $
Sales	160,000	120,000
Cost of sales		
Direct materials	40,000	20,000
Direct labour	40,000	30,000
Production overhead	22,000	20,000
Marketing overhead	42,000	35,000
	144,000	105,000
Profit	16,000	15,000
Profit to sales ratio	10%	12½%

An analysis of this information shows that there has been a decline in profitability in year 2 compared with year 1, in spite of the $1,000 increase in profit, because the profit margin is less in year 2 than year 1. Looked at another way, an increase of $40,000 in sales revenue in year 2, compared with year 1, resulted in a rise in profit of only $1,000.

8.4 Cost/sales ratios

An organisation might measure its actual expenditures against budgeted costs, and report differences or 'variances' between actual costs and the budget. Another way of measuring costs is by expressing costs incurred as a percentage of total sales revenue, and monitoring changes in this ratio over time. Cost ratios that might be used are:

- production costs as a percentage of sales
- distribution and marketing costs as a percentage of sales
- administrative costs as a percentage of sales.

Cost/sales ratios can be taken to subsidiary levels of cost, such as:

- material costs as a percentage of the sales value of goods produced
- direct labour costs as a percentage of the sales value of goods produced
- production overheads as a percentage of the sales value of goods produced.

8.5 Example: cost/sales ratios

Look back to the example in Paragraph 8.3. An analysis of costs would show that higher direct materials are the probable cause of the decline in profitability.

	Year 2	Year 1
Material costs/sales	25%	16.7%

The other cost/sales ratios have remained the same or improved.

9 Responsibility accounting

FAST FORWARD

> At a departmental and divisional level within an organisation, financial performance is measured in terms of cost control (**cost centres**), profitability (**profit centres**) and return on investment or residual income (**investment centres**).

When performance at various levels within an organisation is measured in terms of accounting results the name given to the control reporting system is **responsibility accounting**.

Responsibility accounting is a system of accounting that segregates revenues and costs into areas of personal responsibility in order to monitor and assess the performance of each part of an organisation.

A **responsibility centre** is a unit or function of an organisation headed by a manager having direct responsibility for its performance.

Responsibility accounting aims to provide accounting reports that make every manager aware of all the items which are within his or her area of authority so that he or she is in a position to explain them and **judge their performance**.

Responsibility centre	Performance measure
Cost centres	Standard costs, variance reports, efficiency measures
Profit centres	Revenues, costs, output levels and, of course, profit
Investment centres	Return on investment (ROI) and subsidiary ratios, residual income (RI), costs, revenues, assets employed and liabilities

These financial reporting systems are explained in the following chapters.

9.1 Controllable costs and uncontrollable costs

Managers should only be held accountable for costs over which they have some influence. This may seem quite straightforward in theory, but it is not always so easy in practice to distinguish controllable from uncontrollable costs.

Controllable costs are items of expenditure which can be directly influenced by a given manager within a given time span.

(a)   A cost which is not controllable by a **junior manager** or supervisor might be controllable by a **senior manager**. For example, there may be high direct labour costs in a department caused by excessive overtime working. The supervisor may feel obliged to continue with the overtime in order to meet production schedules, but his senior may be able to reduce costs by deciding to hire extra full-time staff, thereby reducing the requirements for overtime.

(b)   A cost which is not controllable by a manager in **one department** may be controllable by a manager in **another department**. For example, an increase in material costs may be caused by buying at higher prices than expected (controllable by the purchasing department) or by excessive wastage and spoilage (controllable by the production department).

Some costs are **non-controllable**, such as increases in expenditure items due to inflation. Other costs are **only controllable in the long term** not in the short term. For example, production costs might be reduced by the introduction of new machinery and technology, but in the short term, management must attempt to do the best they can with the resources and machinery at their disposal.

Traditionally, performance has been measured in manufacturing by means of comparing actual results against budgeted results (budgetary control) and possibly by comparing actual costs against standard costs. Budgetary control is described in Chapter 10 and standard cost variances in Chapter 11. Other approaches to performance measurement are then considered in Chapters 12 and 13.

Key learning points

- Performance measures can be divided into two groups.

    - **Financial** performance measures
    - **Non-financial** performance measures.

- Non-financial performance measures can be **quantitative** or **qualitative**.

- Profitability can be measured by **return on investment (ROI)/return on capital employed (ROCE), profit margin**, **gross profit margin** or **cost/sales ratios**.

- At a departmental and divisional level within an organisation, financial performance is measured in terms of cost control (**cost centres**), profitability (**profit centres**) and return on investment or residual income (**investment centres**).

Quick quiz

1   List five possible financial performance measures.
2   Costs are down by 15% is an example of a qualitative performance measure. True or false?
3   How is ROI calculated?
4   What does the performance measure 'deliveries late: deliveries on schedule' indicate for a manufacturing organisation?
5   What is a cost centre? How does it differ from a profit centre?

Answers to quick quiz

1   Profit, revenue, costs, share price and cash flow. Of course there are others.
2   False. It is quantitative.
3   (Profit ÷ capital employed) × 100%
4   The efficiency of production and production scheduling.
5   A department or part of an organisation's activities for which the manager is responsible and accountable for costs incurred. In a profit centre, the manager is responsible for both costs incurred and revenues earned, ie for profit.

Comparing actual results with the budget

Introduction

A budget is a plan for the following period, expressed in money terms. Earlier in this text you saw how budgets are drawn up. The purpose of this chapter is to study how budgets can be used by management as a control device in their organisation.

Learning objective

On completion of this chapter you will be able to:

Syllabus reference

- calculate, explain and interpret variances recorded in flexible budgeting systems   12

1 Budgetary control

FAST FORWARD

Budgetary control is a system of financial performance measurement. Actual results are compared with what results should have been.

An important aspect of budgeting is the co-ordination of planning and decision making across an organisation, and the linking of strategic planning with operational plans.

A further use of budgets is as a control mechanism. Since a budget is a plan of what the organisation wants to achieve in the planning period, it can be used to judge actual performance. Actual results and achievements can be compared with the budget, and any differences between what has happened and what was planned might enable management to:

(a)   Identify reasons for either good or bad performance
(b)   Where appropriate, identify aspects of operations where control measures might be called for

Using the budget for a comparison with actual results, identifying reasons for differences, and taking appropriate management action to rectify any unsatisfactory aspects of performance, is known as **budgetary control**.

Measuring performance through budgetary control focuses on **financial performance**, in particular sales, costs and profits, although budgeted and actual cash flows can also be monitored.

2 Variances

FAST FORWARD

The differences between the components of the fixed budget and the actual results are known as **budget variances**.

A variance is the difference between an actual outcome and what should have been expected. Budgetary control measures performance by comparing actual results for each item of revenue or cost, comparing the actual result with what the outcome should have been, and reporting the difference as a variance.

(a)   When actual results are better than expected, the variance is **favourable**. A favourable variance is usually reported as an amount of money, followed by (F).

(b)   When actual results are worse than expected, the variance is **adverse** or **unfavourable**. An adverse or unfavourable variance is usually reported as an amount of money, followed by either (A) or (U).

The term **variance analysis** refers to the process of explaining the difference between budgeted and actual results as the sum of a number of sales variances and cost variances. The total sum of the variances adds up to the difference between the budgeted profit and the actual profit for the period.

3 Flexible budgets and budgetary control

FAST FORWARD

To obtain meaningful variances, actual results must be **compared with a flexible budget** for the same level of activity. The difference between the fixed budget profit and the flexible budget profit is explained as a sales volume variance.

Variances can be calculated for costs, revenues and profit, and also for cash flow.

> **Budgetary control** is the practice of establishing budgets which identify areas of responsibility for individual managers (for example production managers, purchasing managers and so on) and of regularly comparing actual results against expected results. The differences between actual results and expected results are called **variances** and these are used to provide a guideline for control action by individual managers.

Individual managers are held responsible for **investigating differences** between budgeted and actual results, and are then expected to **take corrective action** or amend the plan in the light of actual events.

3.1 The wrong approach to budgetary control

The **wrong approach** to budgetary control is to **compare actual results against a fixed budget**. Consider the following example.

Tree manufactures a single product, the widget. Budgeted results and actual results for June are shown below.

	Budget	Actual results	Variance
Production and sales of widgets (units)	2,000	3,000	
	$	$	$
Sales revenue (a)	20,000	30,000	10,000 (F)
Direct materials	6,000	8,500	2,500 (A)
Direct labour	4,000	4,500	500 (A)
Maintenance	1,000	1,400	400 (A)
Depreciation	2,000	2,200	200 (A)
Rent and rates	1,500	1,600	100 (A)
Other costs	3,600	5,000	1,400 (A)
Total costs (b)	18,100	23,200	5,100 (A)
Profit (a) – (b)	1,900	6,800	4,900 (F)

(a) In this example, **these variances are meaningless** for purposes of control. **Costs were higher than budget because the volume of output was also higher**. Expected variable costs will be higher than the variable costs in the fixed budget, given that output is higher.

(b) For control purposes, it is necessary to know:

   (i)   Were actual costs higher than they should have been to produce and sell **3,000** widgets, i.e. the **actual** number of units produced?

   (ii) Was actual sales revenue satisfactory from the sale of **3,000** widgets?

   (iii) Has the volume of units made and sold varied from the budget favourably or adversely, and what has been the effect on profit of this sales volume difference?

3.2 The correct approach to budgetary control: using a flexible budget

The **correct approach** to budgetary control is:

- Identify fixed and variable costs
- Produce a **flexible budget** for the actual volume of sales and production achieved, using marginal costing techniques

Actual results should then be compared by:

(a) Comparing actual costs with what costs should have been for the actual volume of production and sales (i.e. compare actual costs with costs in the flexed budget)

(b) Comparing actual sales revenue with what revenue should have been for the actual volume of sales (i.e. compare actual prices with prices in the flexed budget)

(c) Comparing the actual sales volume achieved with what was originally budgeted, and measuring the effect the sales volume difference has had on profit.

In the previous example of Tree, suppose the following information on cost behaviour is available.

(a) Direct materials and maintenance costs are variable.

(b) Although basic wages are a fixed cost, direct labour is regarded as variable in order to measure efficiency/productivity.

(c) Rent and rates and depreciation are fixed costs.

(d) 'Other costs' consist of fixed costs of $1,600 plus a variable cost of $1 per unit made and sold.

Now that the cost behaviour patterns are known, a budget cost allowance can be calculated for each item of expenditure. This allowance is shown in **a flexible budget** as the **expected expenditure on each item for the relevant level of activity**. The budget cost allowances are calculated as follows.

(a) Variable cost allowances = original budgets × (3,000 units/2,000 units)
     eg material cost allowance = $6,000 × ³/₂ = $9,000

(b) Fixed cost allowances = as original budget

(c) Semi-fixed cost allowances = original budgeted fixed costs + (3,000 units × variable cost per unit)
     eg other cost allowance = $1,600 + (3,000 × $1) = $4,600

The budgetary control analysis should be as follows.

	Fixed budget (a)	Flexible budget (b)	Actual results (c)	Budget variance (b) – (c)
Production & sales (units)	2,000	3,000	3,000	
	$	$	$	$
Sales revenue	20,000	30,000	30,000	0
Variable costs				
Direct materials	6,000	9,000	8,500	500 (F)
Direct labour	4,000	6,000	4,500	1,500 (F)
Maintenance	1,000	1,500	1,400	100 (F)
Semi-variable costs				
Other costs	3,600	4,600	5,000	400 (A)
Fixed costs				
Depreciation	2,000	2,000	2,200	200 (A)
Rent and rates	1,500	1,500	1,600	100 (A)
Total costs	18,100	24,600	23,200	1,400 (F)
Profit	1,900	5,400	6,800	1,400 (F)

Variances are favourable when actual results are better than what should have been expected, and adverse when they are worse than expected.

We can **analyse** the above variances as follows.

(a) In selling 3,000 units the expected profit should have been, not the fixed budget profit of $1,900, but the flexible budget profit of $5,400. Instead, actual profit was $6,800 i.e. $1,400 more than we should have expected. The reason for the improvement is that, **given actual output and sales** of 3,000 units, **costs were lower than expected** (and sales revenue exactly as expected).

	$
Direct materials cost variance	500 (F)
Direct labour cost variance	1,500 (F)
Maintenance cost variance	100 (F)
Other costs variance	400 (A)
Fixed cost variances	
Depreciation	200 (A)
Rent and rates	100 (A)
	1,400 (F)

Profit was therefore increased by $1,400 because costs were lower than anticipated.

(b) Another reason for the improvement in profit above the fixed budget profit is the **sales volume**. Tree sold 3,000 units instead of 2,000 units, with the following result.

	$	$
Sales revenue increased by		10,000
Variable costs would be expected to increase by:		
direct materials	3,000	
direct labour	2,000	
maintenance	500	
variable element of other costs	1,000	
		6,500
Profit increased by (contribution of $3.50 per unit)		3,500

Profit was therefore increased by $3,500 because sales volumes increased, thereby increasing contribution and profit.

(c) A full variance analysis statement, also called an **operating statement**, would be as follows.

	$	$
Fixed budget profit		1,900
Variances		
Sales volume	3,500 (F)	
Direct materials cost	500 (F)	
Direct labour cost	1,500 (F)	
Maintenance cost	100 (F)	
Other costs	400 (A)	
Depreciation	200 (A)	
Rent and rates	100 (A)	
		4,900 (F)
Actual profit		6,800

If management believes any variance is significant enough to warrant investigation, they will investigate to see whether any corrective action is necessary or whether the plan needs amending in the light of actual events.

Question   Budget and operating statement

The budgeted and actual results of Stint for September were as follows. The company uses a marginal costing system. There were no opening or closing inventories.

Sales and production	*Fixed budget* 2,000 units		*Actual* 1,800 units	
	$	$	$	$
Sales		194,000		166,000
Variable cost of sales				
Direct materials	46,000		34,500	
Direct labour	24,000		22,750	
Variable overhead	4,000		3,750	
		74,000		61,000
Contribution		120,000		105,000
Fixed costs		85,000		88,000
Profit/(loss)		35,000		17,000

Required

Prepare a budget that will be useful for management control purposes, and prepare an operating statement explaining the difference between the budgeted profit of $35,000 and the actual profit of $17,000.

Answer

We need to prepare a flexible budget for 1,800 units.

	Fixed budget	Flexed budget	Actual	Variance
Units of production and sales	2,000	1,800	1,800	
	$	$	$	$
Sales	194,000	174,600	166,000	8,600 (A)
Costs				
Direct materials	46,000	41,400	34,500	6,900 (F)
Direct labour	24,000	21,600	22,750	1,150 (A)
Variable overhead	4,000	3,600	3,750	150 (A)
Total variable costs	74,000	66,600	61,000	5,600 (F)
Contribution	120,000	108,000	105,000	3,000 (A)
Fixed costs	85,000	85,000	88,000	3,000 (A)
Profit	35,000	23,000	17,000	6,000 (A)

		$	$
Fixed budget profit			35,000
Variances			
Sales volume (35,000 – 23,000)		12,000 (A)	
Sales price		8,600 (A)	
Direct materials cost		6,900 (F)	
Direct labour cost		1,150 (A)	
Variable overhead cost		150 (A)	
Fixed overhead expenditure		3,000 (A)	
			18,000 (A)
Actual profit			17,000

4 Cash flow variances

A similar approach can be taken to analysing the difference between actual and budgeted cash flow, using a 'flexed' version of the cash budget for comparing with actual results.

4.1 Example

Brill, a retailing organisation, prepared a cash budget in the expectation that its sales in 20X4 would be a constant $100,000 each month and that its purchases of inventory would be a constant $30,000 each month. Its cash budget was also based on the following assumptions.

(a) All sales are on credit. Debtors would be given three months to pay.

(b) All purchases of goods are on credit, and the company takes one month's credit from suppliers.

(c) At the beginning of 20X4, there would be $275,000 of trade receivables and $28,000 of trade payables.

(d) Wages and salaries (fixed costs) would be $240,000 for the year, all paid in cash.

(e) Other fixed expenditures would be $220,000, all paid in cash with the exception of a depreciation charge of $15,000.

(f) Other variable costs would be $60,000, all paid in cash.

(g) A new non-current asset would be purchased during the year, at a cost of $150,000 (to be paid for in cash).

(h) The company would have $30,000 in cash at the start of the year.

(i) Wages and salaries and other costs would be incurred at a constant rate each month, and would be paid for in the month they are incurred.

The cash budget is as follows, allowing for receivables at the year end of $300,000 (three months' sales) and payables at the year end of $30,000 (one month's purchases).

	$	$
Cash receipts ($275,000 + $1,200,000 – $300,000)		1,175,000
Payments		
For materials purchased ($28,000 + $360,000 – $30,000)	358,000	
Wages and salaries	240,000	
Fixed overheads ($220,000 – $15,000 depreciation)	205,000	
Variable overheads	60,000	
Non-current asset purchase	150,000	
Total payments		1,013,000
Surplus of receipts over payments		162,000
Cash at start of year		30,000
Cash at end of year		192,000

Actual sales in 20X4 were only $900,000, and actual cash flows were as follows.

	$	$
Cash receipts		902,000
Payments		
For materials purchased	270,000	
Wages and salaries	238,000	
Fixed overheads	225,000	
Variable overheads	50,000	
Non-current asset purchase	138,000	
Total payments		921,000
Shortfall of receipts below payments		(19,000)
Cash at start of year		30,000
Cash at end of year		11,000

Required

A statement explaining the difference between the budgeted and the actual cash flow.

Solution

Actual sales were only $900,000, 75% of the original budget. If we can assume that purchases would therefore be 75% of budget, at $270,000 for the year, or $22,500 each month, we can construct a cash budget on the basis of a 75% activity level. In the flexed cash budget:

(a) Closing receivables should be $225,000 (three months' sales), therefore receipts from sales should be $(275,000 + 900,000 – 225,000) = $950,000.

(b) Closing payables should be $22,500 (one month's purchases), therefore payments for materials should be $(28,000 + 270,000 – 22,500) = $275,500.

The comparison of budget and actual is now as follows:

	Fixed budget $	Flexed budget $	Actual $	Variance $
Cash from sales	1,175,000	950,000	902,000	48,000 (A)
Payments				
For materials	358,000	275,500	270,000	5,500 (F)
Wages and salaries	240,000	240,000	238,000	2,000 (F)
Fixed overhead	205,000	205,000	225,000	20,000 (A)
Variable overhead	60,000	45,000	50,000	5,000 (A)
Purchase of non-current assets	150,000	150,000	138,000	12,000 (F)
Total payments	1,013,000	915,500	921,000	5,500 (A)
Receipts less payments	162,000	34,500	(19,000)	53,500 (A)
Cash at start of year	30,000	30,000	30,000	–
Cash at end of year	192,000	64,500	11,000	53,500 (A)

An operating statement reconciling the budgeted end-of-year cash position and the actual end-of-year cash position can be drawn up, as follows

	$	$
Budgeted end-of-year cash		192,000
Variances		
Sales volume ($192,000 – $64,500)	127,500 (A)	
Payments from debtors	48,000 (A)	
Payments for materials	5,500 (F)	
Payments of wages and salaries	2,000 (F)	
Payments for fixed overheads	20,000 (A)	
Payments for variable overheads	5,000 (A)	
Non-current asset purchase	12,000 (F)	
Total variances		181,000 (A)
Actual end-of-year cash		11,000

An analysis of the variances shows that the major reason for the difference between budgeted and actual cash flows was the shortfall in sales. However, poor control over debt collection has worsened the situation by a further $48,000.

Question

Cash flow variance

A company has the following cash budget for April:

	$'000	$'000
Operating profit before depreciation		120
Depreciation		40
		160
Increase in inventory	(25)	
Decrease in receivables	10	
Increase in payables	10	
		(5)
		155
Payment of interest	(8)	
Capital expenditure payments	(15)	
		(23)
Cash surplus for month		132
Opening cash		30
Closing cash		162

The company sells one standard unit at a price of $50 per unit, and unit variable costs of sales are $25. The budgeted sales for the month are 10,000 units. Budgeted fixed costs are $130,000 for the month, including depreciation of $40,000.

Actual results for the month were as follows.

	Start of the month $'000	End of the month $'000
Cash	30	133
Inventory	80	120
Receivables	60	65
Payables	35	25

	In the month $'000
Interest payments	8
Payments for capital expenditure	19

Actual sales in the month were 11,000 units, and the unit sales price, unit variable costs and monthly fixed costs were as budgeted. The depreciation for the month was also as budgeted.

Required

Produce a cash flow variance statement for the month, reconciling the opening cash balance of $30,000 with the closing cash balance of $133,000.

Answer

Working

The unit contribution is ($50 – $25) = $25, which means that the actual contribution from sales is 11,000 units x $25 = $275,000, and after deducting fixed costs of $130,000, the actual contribution was $145,000.

Cash flow variance statement for April

	Budget $'000	Actual $'000	Variance $'000	
Profit before depreciation	120	145	25 (F)	Sales volume variance
Depreciation	40	40		
	160	185		
(Increase)/decrease in inventory	(25)	(40)	15 (A)	Inventory level variance
(Increase)/decrease in receivables	10	(5)	15 (A)	Receivables level variance
Increase/(decrease) in payables ·	10	(10)	20 (A)	Payables level variance
Interest payment	(8)	(8)	–	
Capital expenditure	(15)	(19)	4 (A)	
Cash increase	132	103		
Opening cash	30	30		
Closing cash	162	133	29 (A)	

Key learning points

- Budgetary control is a system of financial performance measurement. Actual results are compared with what results should have been.

- The differences between the components of the fixed budget and the actual results are known as **budget variances**.

- To obtain meaningful variances, actual results must be **compared with a flexible budget** for the same level of activity. The difference between the fixed budget profit and the flexible budget profit is explained as a sales volume variance.

- Variances can be calculated for costs, revenues and profit, and also for cash flow.

BPP
LEARNING MEDIA

Quick quiz

1 What is a fixed budget?
2 Why is it necessary to compare actual results with a flexed budget, for the purpose of budgetary control?
3 What might be the benefit of cash flow variances, compared with calculating more 'traditional' sales and cost variances?
4 A company earns a mark-up on its sales of 25% on cost. Its monthly budgeted sales are $300,000. What would be the sales variance and the variable cost variance if actual sales in the month were $280,000 and variable costs were $240,000?

Answers to quick quiz

1 A budget for sales, costs and profits etc, at a given volume of sales/production. This volume is the planned sales/production volume.

2 In order to analyse variances between budgeted and actual profit. Changes in profit due to a higher or lower sales volume than planned can be separated from the variations due to the sales price or variable costs or fixed costs being higher or lower than planned.

3 Cash flow variances can highlight changes from the budget that a cost/sales revenue variance statement would not. In particular, items such as variances in working capital changes, variations in payments of interest and taxation, and payments for capital expenditure can be highlighted.

4 Budgeted contribution (25% on cost = 20% of revenue) $60,000.

Sales volume variance = 20% of ($300,000 - $280,000) = $4,000 (A).

Variable costs should be 80% of sales, i.e. 80% of $280,000 = $224,000. They were actually $240,000. Variable cost variance = $16,000 (A).

Actual contribution = $280,000 - $240,000 = $40,000.

The sales variance and the variable cost variance together explain the difference between the budgeted and actual contribution.

11

Standard costing

Introduction

Budgeting involves planning money amounts for an organisation in total for a period. By contrast, standard costing establishes predetermined costs for each item of product or service produced by the organisation, for example the standard amount and price of the materials and labour in each computer assembled by a computer manufacturer. Once again, management can investigate the variances arising between the standard amounts and the actual amounts in a period.

Learning Objectives

On completion of this chapter you will be able to:

Syllabus reference

- calculate standard cost variances   12
- prepare an operating statement that includes standard cost variances   12
- describe how standard cost variances may be used to appraise performance   12

1 Standard costs and standard costing

FAST FORWARD

A **standard cost** is an estimated unit cost.

A standard cost is built up of standards for each cost element (standard resource price and standard resource usage).

Standard costing variances are used to measure performance and provide a performance control system.

Standard costing is most suited to mass production and repetitive assembly work.

Key term

A **standard cost** is an estimated unit cost for a standard item of production, showing the component elements of cost.

A standard full cost of product 12345 is set out below on a **standard cost card.**

STANDARD COST CARD Product No 12345	Cost	Requirement	$	$
Direct materials				
A	$2.00 per kg	6 kgs	12.00	
B	$3.00 per kg	2 kgs	6.00	
C	$4.00 per litre	1 litre	4.00	
Others			2.00	
				24.00
Direct labour				
Grade I	$4.00 per hour	3 hrs	12.00	
Grade II	$5.40 per hour	5 hrs	27.00	
				39.00
Variable production overheads	$1.00 per hour	8 hrs		8.00
Fixed production overheads	$3.00 per hour	8 hrs		24.00
Standard full cost of production				95.00

A standard cost is built up from **standards for each cost element:** standard quantities of materials at standard prices, standard quantities of labour time at standard rates and so on. It is therefore determined by estimates of the following.

- The expected prices of materials, labour and expenses.
- Efficiency levels in the use of materials and labour.
- Budgeted overhead costs and budgeted volumes of activity.

1.1 The uses of standard costing

Standard costing has two principal uses.

- **To give a value to inventories** of finished goods and to give a cost to items of production for cost accounting purposes.
- **To act as a performance measure and control device**. Actual costs can be compared with the expected costs, thus highlighting areas of operations that might be out of control.

Since standard costs are made up of component elements of cost (direct materials usage and price, direct labour hours and wage rates, and so on), the variances that can be obtained from standard cost variance analysis are more detailed than the variances obtained from a flexed budget.

1.2 Standard costing as a control technique

Standard costing involves the establishment of predetermined estimates of the costs of products or services, the collection of actual costs and the comparison of the actual costs with the predetermined estimates. The predetermined costs are known as standard costs and the difference between standard and actual cost is known as a **variance**. The process by which the total difference between standard and actual results is analysed is known as **variance analysis**.

Standard costing is best suited to organisations that produce a range of standard items, or a range of standard services. It is not suitable to non-standard work, such as contract and jobbing work, or professional services.

Question

Standard costing

Can you think of a service organisation that could apply standard costing?

Answer

Just one example is standard recipes in a restaurant. If a large number of meals are produced, say, for conference delegates, mass production systems will apply. Standards may not be calculated with the same accuracy as in manufacturing environments, but the principles are still relevant. Other examples are equally valid.

2 Budgets and standard costs compared

FAST FORWARD

Budgets and standards are very similar and interrelated, but there are important differences between them.

The **responsibility** for setting standards should be shared between the managers able to provide the necessary information about levels of expected efficiency, prices and overhead costs.

A **budget** is a quantified monetary plan for a future period. It is used for communicating plans and co-ordinating activities within an organisation.

A **standard cost** is a carefully predetermined cost target that should be achievable in certain conditions.

Budgets and standards are **similar** in the following ways.

(a)   They both involve **looking to the future** and **forecasting** what is likely to happen given a certain set of circumstances.

(b)   They are both used for **control** purposes. Actual results are compared with the budget or standard and action is taken to correct any variances where necessary. A standard also achieves control by comparison of actual results against a predetermined target.

If an organisation uses standard costing, standard costs will be used to prepare the budget. In addition, the fixed overhead cost element in a standard full unit cost will be based on the budget for fixed overhead expenditure and the budgeted volume of activity.

There are, however, important **differences** between budgets and standards.

(a)   A budget gives the **planned total costs for a cost centre** such as production department A, whereas a standard cost shows the amount of **resource** that should be used for a **single task**, for example the standard labour hours for a single unit of production.

(b)   The use of standards is limited to situations where repetitive actions are performed and output can be measured. Budgets can be prepared for all functions (such as administration costs), even where output cannot be measured.

Question	Advantages of standard costing system

What are the possible advantages for the control function of an organisation of having a standard costing system?

Answer	

(a)   Carefully planned standards are an aid to more accurate budgeting.

(b)   Standard costs provide a yardstick against which actual costs can be measured.

(c)   The setting of standards involves determining the best materials and methods that may lead to economies.

(d)   A target of efficiency is set for employees to reach and cost-consciousness is stimulated.

(e)   Variances can be calculated which enable the principle of 'management by exception' to be operated. Only the variances that exceed acceptable tolerance limits need to be investigated by management with a view to control action.

(f)   Standard costs and variance analysis can provide a way of motivation to managers to achieve better performance. However, care must be taken to distinguish between controllable and non-controllable costs in variance reporting.

A significant difference between a standard cost and a budgeted cost is the detailed analysis of the component elements of cost that make up a standard cost. This detailed analysis enables an organisation to prepare more detailed and meaningful variances in budgetary control reports.

3 Ideal, attainable and current standards

FAST FORWARD   Standards may be **ideal**, **attainable** or **current**.

A standard cost includes an estimate of efficiency in using resources. There is a standard rate of usage of materials, and a standard efficiency rate for labour. There are differing ways in which a 'standard' efficiency rate may be set.

Key terms

An **ideal standard** is a standard that can be attained under perfect operating conditions, with no wastage of materials and no inefficiencies, idle time, or breakdowns.

An **attainable standard or target standard** is a standard that can be attained if production is carried out efficiently, machines are properly operated and/or materials are properly used. Some allowance is made for wastage and inefficiencies.

A **current standard** is a standard based on current working conditions (current wastage, current inefficiencies).

These different types of standard have a number of advantages and disadvantages.

(a)   Ideal standards can be seen as long-term (strategic) targets but are not very useful for day-to-day control purposes. Ideal standards cannot be achieved. It follows that if ideal standard costs are used for budgeting, an allowance will have to be included to make the budget realistic and attainable.

(b)   Attainable standards or target standards can be used for budgeting and performance measurement, but reflect a level of achievement that has not yet been reached. Attainable standards are probably the best type of standard for performance measurement and management.

(c)   Current standards do not seek to achieve any improvement in performance, and regard the current efficiency level as an adequate standard of performance. However, a current standard is possibly best suited for budgeting, since they are based on a known and realistic level of achievement.

4 Introduction to standard cost variances

You must be able to calculate all the **variances** described in this chapter.

Standard cost variances are similar in concept to variances calculated with a flexed budget, but go into greater in-depth analysis of differences between actual results and expected results ('standard').

(a)   The variance for **direct materials costs** is analysed into a materials usage variance and a materials price variance.

(b)   The variance for **direct labour costs** is analysed into an efficiency variance and a labour wage rate variance.

(c)   The variance for **variable production overhead costs** is analysed into an efficiency variance and an 'expenditure per hour' variance.

(d)   There is a sales price variance, reporting the effect on profit of the difference between the actual **selling price** for products and the planned standard selling price.

Standard cost variances may be based on either a standard full cost (absorption costing) or a standard marginal cost.

When standard costs are a standard full cost:

(a)   There are **fixed overhead variances** that together explain the total under- or over-absorbed fixed production overhead. These variances are called a fixed overhead expenditure variance and a fixed overhead volume variance.

(b)   There is a **sales volume variance**, but this is valued at the standard profit per unit, not in terms of contribution.

The inter-relationship between the different variances can be expressed in a diagram, which you may find easier to remember.

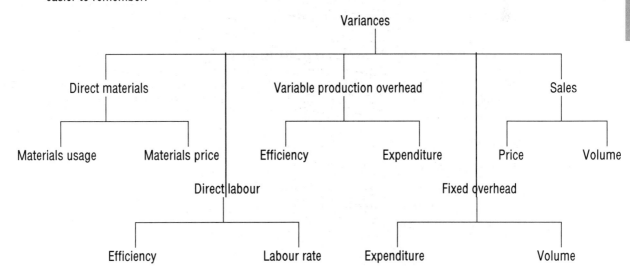

5 Direct materials variances

The **direct material total cost variance** is the difference between what the output actually cost and what it should have cost, in terms of material. It can be divided into the following two sub-variances.

The **direct material price variance** is the difference between what the materials did cost and what they should have cost.

The **direct material usage variance** is the difference between the quantity of the materials that should have been used and the standard quantity of the materials that should have been used, valued at the standard cost per unit of material.

5.1 Direct materials price variance

A materials price variance can be calculated by filling in the appropriate figures in the following table.

		$
[Quantity of materials purchased]	*should have cost*	(Quantity × Standard price per unit)
	but did cost	(Actual cost)
Materials price variance	=	Difference

The price variance is favourable if actual purchase costs were less than standard, and adverse if actual purchase costs exceeded the standard.

5.2 Direct materials usage variance

A materials price variance can be calculated by filling in the appropriate figures in the following table.

		Quantities
[Quantity of standard item produced]	*should have used*	(Quantity of product made × Standard materials usage per unit)
	but did use	(Actual usage)
Materials usage variance	*(in usage quantities)*	Difference
Materials usage variance	*(in money terms)*	Difference × Standard materials price per unit

The usage variance is favourable if the actual usage of materials in production was less than standard, and adverse if actual usage exceeded the standard.

5.3 Example: direct material variances

A unit of Product P has a standard direct material cost of 10 kilograms of material Y at $10 per kilogram (= $100 per unit of P). During period 4, 1,000 units of Product P were manufactured, using 11,700 kilograms of material Y which cost $98,600.

Required

Calculate the following variances.

(a)   The direct material total cost variance
(b)   The direct material price variance
(c)   The direct material usage variance

Solution

(a) **The direct material total cost variance**. This is the difference between what 1,000 units should have cost and what they did cost.

	$
1,000 units should have cost (× $100)	100,000
but did cost	98,600
Direct material total variance	1,400 (F)

The variance is favourable (F) because the units cost less than they should have cost. However, in practice, this variance would not be calculated, since it is analysed further into a materials price and a materials usage variance.

(b) **The direct material price variance**. This is the difference between what 11,700 kgs should have cost and what 11,700 kgs did cost.

	$
11,700 kgs of Y should have cost (× $10)	117,000
but did cost	98,600
Material Y price variance	18,400 (F)

The variance is favourable because the material cost less than it should have.

(c) **The direct material usage variance**. This is the difference between how many kilograms of Y should have been used to produce 1,000 units of Product P and how many kilograms were used, valued at the standard cost per kilogram.

1,000 units should have used (× 10 kgs)	10,000 kgs
but did use	11,700 kgs
Usage variance in kgs	1,700 kgs (A)
× standard cost per kilogram	× $10
Usage variance in $	$17,000 (A)

The variance is adverse (A) because more material than should have been used was used.

(d) **Summary**

	$
Price variance	18,400 (F)
Usage variance	17,000 (A)
Total variance	1,400 (F)

5.4 Alternative method of calculating materials variances

You may prefer to calculate materials variances using the following rote-learned formulae but it is unlikely that this approach will help you to understand the topic fully.

Let SQ = standard quantity of materials required for actual production
SP = standard price per unit of materials
QP = actual quantity of materials purchased
AQ = actual quantity of materials used
AP = actual price per unit of materials

Total materials cost variance = (SQ × SP) − (AQ × AP)

Materials price variance = (SP − AP) × QP

Materials usage variance = (SQ − AQ) × SP

6 Direct labour variances

Key terms

The **direct labour total variance** is the difference between what the output should have cost and what it did cost, in terms of labour. It can be divided into two sub-variances.

The **direct labour rate variance** is the difference between what the labour hours worked did cost and what they should have cost.

The **direct labour efficiency variance** is the difference between the hours that should have been worked and the hours that were actually worked, valued at the standard direct wage rate per hour.

The calculation of labour variances is very similar to the calculation of material variances. The calculation of the labour rate variance is similar to that for the material price variance while the calculation of the labour efficiency variance is similar to that for the material usage variance.

6.1 Direct labour rate variance

A labour rate variance can be calculated by filling in the appropriate figures in the following table.

		$
[Number of hours worked]	*should have cost*	(Quantity of hours × Standard wage rate per hour)
	but did cost	(Actual cost)
Labour rate variance	=	Difference

The rate variance is favourable if actual labour costs were less than standard for the hours worked, and adverse if actual costs exceeded the standard for the hours worked.

6.2 Direct labour efficiency variance

A labour efficiency variance can be calculated by filling in the appropriate figures in the following table.

		Hours
[Quantity of standard item produced]	*should have taken*	(Quantity of product made × Standard hours per unit)
	but did use	(Actual hours)
Labour efficiency variance	*(in hours)*	Difference
Labour efficiency variance	*(in money terms)*	Difference x Standard rate per hour

The efficiency variance is favourable if the actual time taken to produce the output was less than standard, and adverse if actual time taken exceeded the standard.

6.3 Example: direct labour variances

The standard direct labour cost of Product P is 2 hours of grade Z labour at $5 per hour (= $10 per unit of Product P). During period 4, 1,000 units of Product P were made, and the labour cost of grade Z labour was $8,900 for 2,300 hours of work.

Required

Calculate the following variances.

(a)   The direct labour total variance
(b)   The direct labour rate variance
(c)   The direct labour efficiency (productivity) variance

Solution

(a) **The direct labour total variance.** This is the difference between what 1,000 units should have cost and what they did cost.

	$
1,000 units should have cost (× $10)	10,000
but did cost	8,900
Direct labour total variance	1,100 (F)

The variance is favourable because the units cost less than they should have done. In practice, this total labour cost variance would not be calculated, because it can be analysed into its component elements of a rate variance and an efficiency variance.

(b) **The direct labour rate variance.** This is the difference between what 2,300 hours should have cost and what 2,300 hours did cost.

	$
2,300 hours of work should have cost (× $5 per hr)	11,500
but did cost	8,900
Direct labour rate variance	2,600 (F)

The variance is favourable because the labour cost less than it should have cost.

(c) **The direct labour efficiency variance.** This is the difference between the number of hours it should have taken to produce 1,000 units of P, and the number of hours it did take, valued at the standard rate per hour.

1,000 units of P should have taken (× 2 hrs)	2,000 hrs
but did take	2,300 hrs
Efficiency variance in hours	300 hrs (A)
× standard rate per hour	× $5
Efficiency variance in $	$1,500 (A)

The variance is adverse because more hours were worked than should have been worked.

(d) **Summary**

	$
Rate variance	2,600 (F)
Efficiency variance	1,500 (A)
Total variance	1,100 (F)

6.4 Alternative method of calculating labour variances

Labour variances can also be calculated using rote-learned formulae.

Let   SH = standard number of hours required for actual production
      SR = standard rate per hour
      AH = actual hours **worked**
      AR = actual rate per hour

Total direct labour cost variance = $(SH \times SR) - (AH \times AR)$

Direct labour rate variance = $(SR - AR) \times AH$

Direct labour efficiency variance = $(SH - AH) \times SR$

6.5 Idle time variance

A company may operate a costing system in which any **idle time** is recorded. Idle time may be caused by machine breakdowns or not having work to give to employees, perhaps because of bottlenecks in production or a shortage of orders from customers. When idle time occurs, the labour force is still paid wages for time at work, but no actual work is done. Time paid for without any work being done is unproductive and therefore inefficient. In variance analysis, idle time is an adverse efficiency variance.

When idle time is recorded separately, it is helpful to provide control information which identifies the cost of idle time separately and in variance analysis there will be an idle time variance as a separate part of the labour efficiency variance. The remaining efficiency variance will then relate only to the productivity of the labour force during the hours spent *actively* working.

6.6 Example: labour variances with idle time

The direct labour cost of product C is as follows.

3 hours of grade T labour at $2.50 per hour = $7.50 per unit of product C.

During June 20X3, 300 units of product C were made, and the cost of grade T labour was $2,200 for 910 hours. During the month, there was a machine breakdown, and 40 hours were recorded as idle time.

Required

Calculate the following variances.

(a)   The total direct labour cost variance
(b)   The direct labour rate variance
(c)   The idle time variance
(d)   The direct labour efficiency variance

Solution

(a)   *The total direct labour cost variance*

	$
300 units of product C should cost (× $7.50)	2,250
but did cost	2,200
Total direct labour cost variance	50 (F)

Actual cost is less than standard cost. The variance is therefore favourable.

(b)   *The direct labour rate variance*

The rate variance is a comparison of what the hours paid should have cost and what they did cost.

	$
910 hours of grade T labour should cost (× $2.50)	2,275
but did cost	2,200
Direct labour rate variance	75 (F)

Actual cost is less than standard cost. The variance is therefore favourable.

(c)   *The idle time variance*

The idle time variance is the hours of idle time, valued at the standard rate per hour.

Idle time variance = 40 hours (A) × $2.50 = $100 (A)
Idle time is always an adverse variance.

(d)   *The direct labour efficiency variance*

The efficiency variance considers the hours actively worked (the difference between hours paid for and idle time hours). In our example, there were (910 – 40) = 870 hours when the labour force was not idle. The variance is calculated by taking the amount of output produced (300 units of product C) and comparing the time it should have taken to make them, with the actual time spent *actively* making them (870 hours). Once again, the variance in hours is valued at the standard rate per labour hour.

300 units of product C should take (× 3 hrs)		900 hrs
but did take (910 – 40)		870 hrs
Direct labour efficiency variance in hours		30 hrs (F)
× standard rate per hour		× $2.50
Direct labour efficiency variance in $		$75 (F)

(e)   *Summary*

	$
Direct labour rate variance	75 (F)
Idle time variance	100 (A)
Direct labour efficiency variance	75 (F)
Total direct labour cost variance	50 (F)

Remember that, when idle time is recorded, the actual hours used in the efficiency variance calculation are the hours *worked* and not the hours paid for.

7 Variable production overhead variances

In standard costing, variable overhead expenditure is usually assumed to vary with the number of direct labour hours worked. A standard cost for variable overheads therefore consists of the number of labour hours per unit, multiplied by the standard expenditure per hour on variable overhead expenses.

Variable overhead variances are therefore calculated in a similar way to direct labour variances. The total cost variance for variable overheads is analysed into a **variable overhead expenditure variance** (similar to a materials price variance and a labour rate variance) and a **variable overhead efficiency variance**.

7.1 Example: variable production overhead variances

The variable production overhead cost of Product P is 2 hours at $1.50 (= $3 per unit). 400 units of Product P were made during the period. The labour force worked 760 hours. The variable overhead cost was $1,230.

Required

Calculate the following variances.

(a)   The variable production overhead total cost variance
(b)   The variable production overhead expenditure variance
(c)   The variable production overhead efficiency variance

Solution

	$
400 units of Product P should cost (× $3)	1,200
but did cost	1,230
Variable production overhead total variance	30 (A)

In some variance reporting systems, the variance analysis goes no further, and expenditure and efficiency variances are not calculated. However, the adverse variance of $30 may be explained as the sum of two factors.

(a)   The hourly rate of spending on variable production overheads was higher than it should have been, ie. there is an expenditure variance.

(b)   The labour force worked inefficiently, and took longer to make the output than it should have done. Since more hours were worked, and variable overhead spending increases as more hours are worked, spending on variable production overhead was higher than it should have been. In other words there is an efficiency (productivity) variance. The variable production overhead efficiency variance is exactly the same, in hours, as the direct labour efficiency variance, and occurs for the same reasons.

The **variable production overhead total variance** is the difference between what the output should have cost and what it did cost, in terms of variable production overhead. It can be divided into two sub-variances.

The **variable production overhead expenditure variance** is the difference between the amount of variable production overhead that should have been incurred in the actual hours actively worked, and the actual amount of variable production overhead incurred.

The **variable production overhead efficiency variance** is the difference between the standard cost of the hours that should have been worked for the number of units actually produced, and the standard cost of the actual number of hours worked.

In our example, the variable overhead expenditure and efficiency variances would be as follows.

		$
(a)	760 hours of variable production overhead should cost (× $1.50)	1,140
	but did cost	1,230
	Variable production overhead expenditure variance	90 (A)
(b)	400 units of Product P should take (× 2 hrs)	800 hrs
	but did take (active hours)	760 hrs
	Variable production overhead efficiency variance in hours	40 hrs (F)
	× standard rate per hour	× $1.50
	Variable production overhead efficiency variance in $	$60 (F)
(c)	*Summary*	$
	Variable production overhead expenditure variance	90 (A)
	Variable production overhead efficiency variance	60 (F)
	Variable production overhead total variance	30 (A)

7.2 Alternative method of calculating variable overhead variances

Variable overhead variances can also be calculated using rote-learned formulae.

Let   SH = standard number of hours required for actual production
      SVOR = standard variable overhead spending rate per hour
      AH = actual hours worked
      AVOR = actual variable overhead spending rate per hour

Total variable overhead cost variance = (SH × SVOR) − (AH × AVOR)

Variable overhead expenditure variance = (SVOR − AVOR) × AH

Variable overhead efficiency variance = (SH − AH) × SVOR

8 Fixed production overhead variances

You may have noticed that the method of calculating cost variances for variable cost items is essentially the same for direct materials, direct labour, and variable overheads. Fixed production overhead variances are very different. In an absorption costing system, they are simply an **attempt to explain the under- or over-absorption of fixed overheads.**

The fixed production overhead total variance may be broken down into two parts.

(a)   A fixed overhead **expenditure variance**
(b)   A fixed overhead **volume variance**.

The fixed production overhead volume variance sometimes causes confusion. The most important point is that the volume variance applies to *fixed* production overhead costs *only*, and not to variable production overheads.

(a) Variable production overhead spending will change with the volume of activity (hours worked). If the master budget is to work for 300 hours and variable production overheads are incurred and absorbed at a rate of $3 per hour, the variable production overhead budget will be $900. If only 200 hours are actually worked, the variable production overhead absorbed will be $600, but the expected expenditure will also be $600. This means that there will be no under- or over-absorption of variable production overhead because of volume changes.

(b) Fixed production overheads are different because the level of expenditure does not change as the number of hours worked varies. If the master budget is to work for 300 hours and fixed production overheads are budgeted to be $2,400, the fixed production overhead absorption rate will be $8 per hour. If actual hours worked are only 200 hours, the fixed production overhead absorbed will be $1,600, whereas expected expenditure will be unchanged at $2,400. There is an under-absorption of $800 because of the volume variance of 100 hours multiplied by the absorption rate of $8 per hour.

You may find it easier to calculate and understand fixed production overhead variances if you bear in mind the whole time that you are trying to explain the reasons for any under- or over-absorbed production overhead. Remember that the absorption rate is calculated as (budgeted fixed production overhead ÷ budgeted level of activity).

The total fixed overhead cost variance is the total amount by which actual fixed overhead costs have been under- or over-absorbed into the cost of production. This total variance has two causes.

(a) The fixed production overhead **expenditure variance** measures the under- or over-absorption caused by the actual production overhead expenditure being different from budget.

	$
Budgeted fixed overhead	X
Actual fixed overhead	Y
Fixed overhead expenditure variance	X – Y

The variance is favourable if actual expenditure is less than the budgeted expenditure, and adverse if actual spending exceeds the budget.

(b) The fixed production overhead **volume variance** measures the under- or over-absorption caused by the actual production volume being different from budget.

	Units
Budgeted production volume	A
Actual production volume	B
Fixed overhead volume variance, in units	A – B
× Standard fixed overhead rate per unit	R
Volume variance, in money terms	(A – B) × R

Over-absorption is 'favourable'. This is because too much overhead cost has been absorbed into the cost of the units produced. The cost of production has therefore been over-stated. To counter-balance this over-charging of cost, the profit for the period needs to be adjusted upwards.

If actual production volume exceeds the budgeted production volume, the variance is therefore favourable, and if actual volume is less than budgeted, the variance is adverse.

<table>
<tr><td>Key terms</td><td>

Fixed production overhead total variance is the difference between fixed production overhead incurred and fixed production overhead absorbed. In other words, it is the under- or over-absorbed fixed production overhead.

Fixed production overhead expenditure variance is the difference between the budgeted fixed production overhead expenditure and actual fixed production overhead expenditure.

Fixed production overhead volume variance is the difference between actual and budgeted production volume multiplied by the standard absorption rate per *unit*.

</td></tr>
</table>

8.1 Example: fixed production overhead variances

A company budgets to produce 1,000 units of product E during August. The expected time to produce a unit of E is five hours, and the budgeted fixed production overhead is $20,000. The standard fixed production overhead cost per unit of product E will therefore be 5 hours at $4 per hour (= $20 per unit). Actual fixed production overhead expenditure in August turns out to be $20,450. The labour force manages to produce 1,100 units of product E.

Required

Calculate the following variances.

(a) The fixed production overhead total variance
(b) The fixed production overhead expenditure variance
(c) The fixed production overhead volume variance

Solution

(a) **Fixed production overhead total variance**

	$
Fixed production overhead incurred	20,450
Fixed production overhead absorbed (1,100 units × $20 per unit)	22,000
Fixed production overhead expenditure variance	1,550 (F)
(= over-absorbed overhead)	

The variance is favourable because more overheads were absorbed than budgeted. In practice, this variance is not calculated, because it is further analysed into an expenditure and a volume variance.

(b) **Fixed production overhead expenditure variance**

	$
Budgeted fixed production overhead expenditure	20,000
Actual fixed production overhead expenditure	20,450
Fixed production overhead expenditure variance	450 (A)

The variance is adverse because actual expenditure was greater than budgeted.

(c) **Fixed production overhead volume variance**. The production volume achieved was greater than expected. The fixed production overhead volume variance measures the difference at the standard rate.

	$
Actual production at standard rate (1,100 × $20 per unit)	22,000
Budgeted production at standard rate (1,000 × $20 per unit)	20,000
Fixed production overhead volume variance	2,000 (F)

The variance is favourable because output was greater than expected.

8.2 Alternative method of calculating fixed overhead variances

Fixed overhead variances can also be calculated using rote-learned formulae.

Let BV = budgeted production volume
AV = actual production volume
BFOE = budgeted fixed overhead expenditure
AFOE = actual fixed overhead expenditure
SC = standard fixed overhead cost per unit
(SC = BFOE ÷ BV)

Total fixed overhead cost variance = (AV × SC) − AFOE

Fixed overhead expenditure variance = BFOE - AFOE

Fixed overhead volume variance = (BV − AV) × SC

Brain produces and sells one product only, the Blob, the standard cost for one unit being as follows.

	$
Direct material A – 10 kilograms at $20 per kg	200
Direct material B – 5 litres at $6 per litre	30
Direct wages – 5 hours at $6 per hour	30
Variable production overhead – 5 hours at $2 per hour	10
Fixed production overhead	50
Total standard cost	320

The fixed overhead included in the standard cost is based on an expected monthly output of 900 units.

During April the actual results were as follows.

Production	800 units
Material A	7,800 kg used, costing $159,900
Material B	4,300 litres used, costing $23,650
Direct wages	4,200 hours worked for $24,150
Variable production overhead	$8,600
Fixed production overhead	$47,000

Required

(a) Calculate price and usage variances for each material.
(b) Calculate labour rate and efficiency variances.
(c) Calculate variable overhead expenditure and efficiency variances.
(d) Calculate fixed production overhead expenditure and volume variances.

Answer

(a) *Price variance – A*

	$
7,800 kgs should have cost (× $20)	156,000
but did cost	159,900
Price variance	3,900 (A)

Usage variance – A

800 units should have used (× 10 kgs)	8,000 kgs
but did use	7,800 kgs
Usage variance in kgs	200 kgs (F)
× standard cost per kilogram	× $20
Usage variance in $	$4,000 (F)

Price variance – B

	$
4,300 litres should have cost (× $6)	25,800
but did cost	23,650
Price variance	2,150 (F)

Usage variance – B

	litres
800 units should have used (× 5 l)	4,000
but did use	4,300
Usage variance in litres	300 (A)
× standard cost per litre	× $6
Usage variance in $	$1,800 (A)

(b)   *Labour rate variance*

		$
4,200 hours should have cost (× $6)		25,200
but did cost		24,150
Rate variance		1,050 (F)

Labour efficiency variance

800 units should have taken (× 5 hrs)	4,000 hrs
but did take	4,200 hrs
Efficiency variance in hours	200 hrs (A)
× standard rate per hour	× $6
Efficiency variance in $	$1,200 (A)

(c)   *Variable overhead expenditure variance*

		$
4,200 hours should have cost (× $2)		8,400
but did cost		8,600
Rate variance		200 (A)

Variable overhead efficiency variance

Same in hours as labour efficiency, but valued at $2 per hour (the standard variable overhead spending rate).

200 hrs (b) x $2 per hour = $400 (A)

(d)   *Fixed overhead expenditure variance*

		$
Budgeted expenditure ($50 × 900)		45,000
Actual expenditure		47,000
Expenditure variance		2,000 (A)

Fixed overhead volume variance

		units
Budgeted production		900
Actual production		800
Volume variance, in units of production		100 (A)
Standard rate per unit		$50
Fixed overhead volume variance, in $		$5,000 (A)

9 Sales price and sales volume variances

9.1 Selling price variance

Key term

> The **selling price variance** is a measure of the effect on expected profit of a different selling price from standard selling price. It is calculated as the difference between what the sales revenue should have been for the actual quantity sold, and the actual sales revenue.

A sales price variance can be calculated by filling in the appropriate figures in the following table.

		$
[Quantity of units sold]	*should sell for*	(Quantity sold × Standard sales price per unit)
	but did sell for	(Actual revenue)
Sales price variance	=	Difference

The sales price variance is favourable if actual sales revenue exceeds the standard revenue, and adverse if actual revenue is less than standard for the units sold.

9.2 Sales volume variance

Key term

> The **sales volume variance** measures the increase or decrease in expected profit as a result of the sales volume being higher or lower than budgeted. In an **absorption costing** system, the **sales volume variance is valued at the standard profit per unit**, not the standard contribution.

A sales volume variance can be calculated by filling in the appropriate figures in the following table.

	Units of product
Budgeted sales quantity	X
Actual sales quantity	Y
Sales volume variance, in units	X – Y
× Standard profit per unit	
Sales volume variance, in $	(X – Y) × standard unit profit

The sales volume variance is favourable when actual sales volume exceeds the budget, and adverse when actual sales volume is less than budgeted.

9.3 Example: sales price variance

The standard selling price of Product P is $15. Actual sales in March were 2,000 units at $15.30 per unit. The selling price variance is calculated as follows.

	$
2,000 units should sell for (× $15)	30,000
but did sell for (× $15.30)	30,600
Sales price variance	600 (F)

The variance is favourable because the price was higher than expected.

9.4 Example: sales volume variance

A company budgets to sell 8,000 units of product J for $12 per unit. The standard full cost per unit is $7. Actual sales were 7,700 units, at $12.50 per unit. The sales volume variance is calculated as follows.

Budgeted sales volume	8,000 units
Actual sales volume	7,700 units
Sales volume variance in units	300 units (A)
× standard profit per unit ($(12–7))	× $5
Sales volume variance	$1,500 (A)

The variance is adverse because actual sales were less than budgeted.

9.5 Further Example: sales variances

Jasper has the following budget and actual figures for May.

	Budget	*Actual*
Sales units	600	620
Selling price per unit	$30	$29

Standard full cost of production = $28 per unit.

Required

Calculate the selling price variance and the sales volume variance.

Solution

(a)

	$
Sales revenue for 620 units should have been (× $30)	18,600
but was (× $29)	17,980
Selling price variance	620 (A)

(b)

Budgeted sales volume	600 units
Actual sales volume	620 units
Sales volume variance in units	20 units (F)
× standard profit per unit ($(30 – 28))	× $2
Sales volume variance	$40 (F)

9.6 Alternative method of calculating sales variances

Sales variances can also be calculated using rote-learned formulae.

Let BV = budgeted sales volume
AV = actual sales volume
SSP = standard selling price per unit
ASP = actual selling price per unit
SPft = standard profit per unit

Sales price variance = (ASP - SSP) x AV

Sales volume variance = (BV − AV) × SPft

10 The reasons for variances

Standard cost variances help management to assess actual performance, and to identify situations where actual results are significantly better or worse than planned. Variances might also provide clues as to why actual results have been better or worse than expected.

There are many possible reasons for cost variances arising, including efficiencies and inefficiencies of operations, errors in budgeting and standard setting and changes in exchange rates. There now follows a list of a few possible causes of cost variances. This is not an exhaustive list and in an examination question you should review the information given and use your imagination and common sense to suggest possible reasons for variances.

Variance	Favourable	Adverse
Material price	Unforeseen discounts received Greater care in purchasing Change in material quality standard Fall in market price of materials	Price increase Careless purchasing Change in material quality standard
Material usage	Material used of higher quality than standard More effective use made of material Errors in allocating material to jobs	Defective material Excessive waste Theft Stricter quality control Errors in allocating material to jobs
Labour rate	Use of workers at a rate of pay lower than standard	Wage rate increase

Variance	Favourable	Adverse
Labour efficiency	Output produced more quickly than expected, because of work motivation, better quality of equipment or materials Errors in allocating time to jobs	Lost time in excess of standard allowed Output lower than standard set because of lack of training, sub-standard material etc Efficiency standard set at an ideal level Errors in allocating time to jobs
Idle time	Idle time variances are always adverse	Bottlenecks in the production system Illness or injury to worker Problems with machines Non-availability of materials
Overhead expenditure	Savings in costs incurred More economical use of services	Increase in cost of services Excessive use of services Change in type of services used
Overhead volume	Production or level of activity greater than budgeted	Production or level of activity less than budgeted
Selling price	Unplanned price increase	Unplanned price reduction Discounts given to customers to win sales
Sales volume	Additional demand Low price offer attracting higher demand	Unexpected fall in demand Production difficulties

11 Investigating variances

FAST FORWARD

Materiality, controllability and **variance trend** should be considered before a decision about whether or not to investigate a variance is taken.

One way of deciding whether or not to investigate a variance is to only investigate those variances which exceed **pre-set tolerance limits**.

If the cause of a variance is **controllable**, action can be taken to bring the system back under control in future. If the variance is **uncontrollable**, but not simply due to chance, it will be necessary to review forecasts of expected results, and perhaps to revise the budget.

Before management decide whether or not to investigate the reasons for a particular variance, there are a number of factors to be considered.

Materiality. Because a standard cost is really only an *average* expected cost, small variations between actual and standard are bound to occur and are unlikely to be significant. Obtaining an 'explanation' of the reasons why they occurred is likely to be time consuming and irritating for the manager concerned. For such variations **further investigation is not worthwhile** since such variances are not controllable.

Controllability. The cause of some variances may be known, and due to reasons beyond the manager's control. Uncontrollable variances call for a change in the plan, not an investigation into the past.

The type of standard being used. The efficiency variance reported in any control period, whether for materials or labour, will depend on the efficiency level set. If, for example, an ideal standard is used, variances will always be adverse. However, adverse variances in excess of a certain amount should be investigated, even when the efficiency standard is an ideal one.

Variance trend. Although small variations in a single period are unlikely to be significant, small variations that occur consistently may need more attention. Cumulative trends in a variance are probably more important than a variance for one accounting period. The trend provides an indication of whether the variance is fluctuating within acceptable control limits or becoming out of control.

Interdependence between variances. Individual variances should not be looked at in isolation. One variance might be inter-related with another, and much of it might have occurred only because the other variance occurred too. **When two variances are interdependent (interrelated) one will usually be adverse and the other one favourable.** Here are some examples.

Interrelated variances	Explanation
Materials price and usage	If cheaper materials are purchased for a job in order to obtain a favourable price variance, materials wastage might be higher and an adverse usage variance may occur. If the cheaper materials are more difficult to handle, there might be an adverse labour efficiency variance too. If more expensive materials are purchased, the price variance will be adverse but the usage variance might be favourable if the material is easier to use or of a higher quality.
Labour rate and efficiency	If employees are paid higher rates for experience and skill, using a highly skilled team might lead to an adverse rate variance and a favourable efficiency variance (experienced staff are less likely to waste material, for example). In contrast, a favourable rate variance might indicate a larger-than-expected proportion of inexperienced workers, which could result in an adverse labour efficiency variance, and perhaps poor materials handling and high rates of rejects too (and hence an adverse materials usage variance).
Selling price and sales volume	A reduction in the selling price might stimulate bigger sales demand, so that an adverse selling price variance might be counterbalanced by a favourable sales volume variance. Similarly, a price rise would give a favourable price variance, but possibly cause an adverse sales volume variance.

12 Operating statements

An **operating statement** provides a reconciliation between budgeted and actual profit.

An operating statement or statement of variances is a report to management reconciling the difference between the budgeted profit for a period and the actual profit. This reconciliation is usually presented as a report to senior management at the end of each control period (e.g. at the end of each month).

Key term

An **operating statement** is a regular report for management which compares actual costs and revenues with budgeted figures and shows variances.

An extensive example will now be introduced, both to revise the variance calculations already described, and also to combine them into an operating statement.

12.1 Example: variances and operating statements

Armoured Kangaroo manufactures one product, and the entire product is sold as soon as it is produced. The company operates a standard costing system. The standard cost card for the product, a boomerang, is as follows.

STANDARD COST CARD – BOOMERANG

		$
Direct materials	0.5 kilos at $4 per kilo	2.00
Direct wages	2 hours at $5.00 per hour	10.00
Variable overheads	2 hours at $0.30 per hour	0.60
Fixed overhead	2 hours at $3.70 per hour	7.40
Standard cost		20.00
Standard profit		6.00
Standard selling price		26.00

Budgeted output for June was 5,100 units. Actual results for June were as follows.

Production of 4,850 units was sold for $124,280

Materials consumed in production amounted to 2,300 kilos at a total cost of $9,800

Labour hours paid for amounted to 8,000 hours at a cost of $42,000

Variable overheads amounted to $2,600

Fixed overheads amounted to $42,300

Required

Calculate all variances and prepare an operating statement for June.

Solution

Workings

(a)

	$
2,300 kg of material should cost (× $4)	9,200
but did cost	9,800
Material price variance	600 (A)

(b)

	kg
4,850 boomerangs should use (× 0.5 kg)	2,425
but did use	2,300
Material usage variance in kg	125 (F)
× Standard cost per kg	$4
Material usage variance in $	$500 (F)

(c)

	$
8,000 hours of labour should cost (× $5)	40,000
but did cost	42,000
Labour rate variance	2,000 (A)

(d)

	hours
4,850 boomerangs should take (× 2 hrs)	9,700
but did take	8,000
Labour efficiency variance in hours	1,700 (F)
× Standard cost per hour	$5
Labour efficiency variance in $	$8,500 (F)

(e)

	$
8,000 hours of variable overhead expenditure should cost (× $0.30)	2,400
but did cost	2,600
Variable overhead expenditure variance	200 (A)

(f)

	Hours
Variable overhead efficiency variance in hours (same as for labour)	1,700 (F)
× Standard cost per hour	$0.30
Variable overhead efficiency variance in $	$510 (F)

(g)

	$
Budgeted fixed overhead (5,100 units × $7.40)	37,740
Actual fixed overhead	42,300
Fixed overhead expenditure variance	4,560 (A)

(h)

	units
Budgeted production	5,100
Actual production	4,850
Volume variance, in units	250 (A)
× Fixed overhead cost per unit	$7.40
Fixed overhead volume variance, in $	$1,850 (A)

(i)

		$
4,850 boomerangs should have sold for (× $26)		126,100
but did sell for		124,280
Selling price variance		1,820 (A)

(j)

	units
Budgeted sales	5,100
Actual sales	4,850
Sales volume variance, in units	250 (A)
× Standard profit per unit	$6
Sales volume variance, in $	$1,500 (A)

There are several ways in which an operating statement may be presented. Perhaps the most common format is one which reconciles budgeted profit to actual profit. Sales variances are reported first, and the total of the budgeted profit and the two sales variances results in a figure for 'actual sales minus the standard cost of sales' as follows.

	$	$
Budgeted profit (5,100 units × profit of $6 per unit)		30,600
Selling price variance	1,820 (A)	
Sales volume variance	1,500 (A)	
		3,320 (A)
Actual sales less the standard cost of sales		27,280

The cost variances are then reported, and an actual profit calculated.

ARMOURED KANGAROO - OPERATING STATEMENT FOR JUNE

	$	$	$
Budgeted profit			30,600
Selling price variance		1,820 (A)	
Sales volume variance		1,500 (A)	
			3,320 (A)
Actual sales less the standard cost of sales			27,280
Cost variances	(F)	(A)	
Material price		600	
Material usage	500		
Labour rate		2,000	
Labour efficiency	8,500		
Variable overhead expenditure		200	
Variable overhead efficiency	510		
Fixed overhead expenditure		4,560	
Fixed overhead volume		1,850	
	9,510	9,210	
Total cost variances			300 (F)
Actual profit			27,580

Check: calculation of actual profit

	$	$
Sales		124,280
Materials	9,800	
Labour	42,000	
Variable overhead	2,600	
Fixed overhead	42,300	
Total costs		96,700
Profit		27,580

13 Variances in a standard marginal costing system

If an organisation uses standard marginal costing instead of standard absorption costing, there will be **two differences** in the way the standard costing variances are calculated.

(a) In marginal costing, fixed costs are not absorbed into product costs and so there are no fixed cost variances to explain any under- or over-absorption of overheads. There will, therefore, be *no* **fixed overhead volume variance**. There will be a fixed overhead expenditure variance, calculated in exactly the same way as for an absorption costing system.

(b) The **sales volume variance will be valued at standard contribution margin**, not standard profit margin (that is, sales price per unit minus variable costs of sale per unit).

13.1 Example: marginal costing operating statement

Returning to the example of Armoured Kangaroo, the variances in a system of standard marginal costing would be as follows.

(a) There is no fixed overhead volume variance.

(b) The standard contribution per unit of boomerang is $(26 – 12.60) = $13.40, therefore the sales volume variance of 250 units (A) is valued at (× $13.40) = $3,350 (A).

The other variances are unchanged, therefore an operating statement might appear as follows.

ARMOURED KANGAROO – OPERATING STATEMENT FOR JUNE

	$	$	$
Budgeted profit			30,600
Selling price variance		1,820 (A)	
Sales volume variance		3,350 (A)	
			5,170 (A)
Actual sales less the standard marginal cost of sales			25,430
Cost variances	(F)	(A)	
Material price		600	
Material usage	500		
Labour rate		2,000	
Labour efficiency	8,500		
Variable overhead expenditure		200	
Variable overhead efficiency	510		
Fixed overhead expenditure		4,560	
	9,510	7,360	
Total cost variances			2,150 (F)
Actual profit			27,580

Question	Operating statement

Hides of March manufacture a standard leather walking boot, model number M25, for which the standard unit cost and selling price are as follows.

		$
Direct materials		
Leather	3 units at $5 per unit	15
Other materials		3
		18
Direct labour	1½ hours at $4 per hour	6
Variable production overheads	1½ hours at $2 per hour	3
Fixed production overheads	1½ hours at $6 per hour	9
Standard cost		36
Selling price		48
Standard profit, before marketing and administrative expenses		12

Budgeted production and sales for period 7 of 20X3 were 3,000 units of M25.

During period 7 the actual results were as follows.

Production and sales of M25	3,200 units
Sales revenue	$150,000
Leather purchased and used: quantity	9,750 units
cost	$47,000
Other materials purchased and used	$9,500
Direct labour: hours paid for	5,850 hours
labour cost	$24,100
Variable production overheads	$10,650
Fixed production overheads	$31,500

A standard full costing system is in operation.

Required

Prepare an operating statement for period 7 reconciling budgeted and actual profit and specifying all the relevant variances. Ignore marketing and administration costs.

Answer

Workings

Budgeted profit. This is 3,000 units × standard profit of $12 per unit = $36,000.

(a)

	$
9,750 units of leather should cost (× $5)	48,750
but did cost	47,000
Material price variance, leather	1,750 (F)

(b)

	Units of leather
3,200 units of M25 should use (× 3)	9,600
but did use	9,750
Leather usage variance in units	150 (A)
× standard cost per unit	$5
Leather usage variance in $	750 (A)

Other materials. We are not given a breakdown into units of material and price per unit of material, and so the only materials variance we can calculate is the total cost variance.

(c)

	$
3,200 units of M25 should cost (× $3)	9,600
but did cost	9,500
Materials cost variance, other materials	100 (F)

(d)

	$
5,850 hours of labour should cost (× $4)	23,400
but did cost	24,100
Labour rate variance	700 (A)

(e)

	hours
3,200 units of M25 should take (× 1.5 hrs)	4,800
but did take	5,850
Labour efficiency variance in hours	1,050 (A)
× standard cost per hour	$4
Labour efficiency variance in $	$4,200 (A)

(f)

	$
5,850 hours of variable overhead expenditure should cost (× $2)	11,700
but did cost	10,650
Variable overhead expenditure variance	1,050 (F)

(g)

Variable overhead efficiency variance in hours (same as for labour)	1,050 (A)
standard cost per hour	$2
Variable overhead efficiency variance in $	$2,100 (A)

(h)

	$
Budgeted fixed overhead	27,000
Actual fixed overhead	31,500
Fixed overhead expenditure variance	4,500 (A)

(i)

	units
Budgeted production	3,000
Actual production	3,200
Volume variance, in units	200 (F)
× Fixed overhead cost per unit	$9
Fixed overhead volume variance, in $	$1,800 (F)

(j)

	$
3,200 units of M25 should have sold for (× $48)	153,600
but did sell for	150,000
Sales price variance	3,600 (A)

(k)

	units
Budgeted sales	3,000
Actual sales	3,200
Sales volume variance, in units	200 (F)
× Standard profit per unit	$12
Sales volume variance, in $	$2,400 (F)

HIDES OF MARCH – OPERATING STATEMENT FOR PERIOD 7

	$	$	$
Budgeted profit			36,000
Selling price variance		3,600 (A)	
Sales volume variance		2,400 (F)	
			1,200 (A)
Actual sales less the standard cost of sales			34,800
Cost variances	(F)	(A)	
Leather price	1,750		
Leather usage		750	
Other materials cost	100		
Labour rate		700	
Labour efficiency		4,200	
Variable overhead expenditure	1,050		
Variable overhead efficiency		2,100	
Fixed overhead expenditure		4,500	
Fixed overhead volume	1,800		
	4,700	12,250	
Total cost variances			7,550 (A)
Actual profit			27,250

Check: calculation of actual profit

	$	$
Sales		150,000
Leather	47,000	
Other materials	9,500	
Labour	24,100	
Variable overhead	10,650	
Fixed overhead	31,500	
Total costs		122,750
Profit		27,250

Exam focus point

Whilst you need to be able to compute variances in order to fully understand the information they provide about the operations of a business, the Examiner has said 'Diploma assessments are not likely to require the routine calculation of variances, but are more likely to provide the variances and require comments and analysis of the likely reasons for these'. Therefore you must be prepared to sit back and look at the number you have produced (or are given) and try to read the story they are telling you and identify issues for discussion.

In December 2002 a question required you first to summarise some detailed operating statements, which required the ability to assimilate a volume of data and think how best to present it. The question then asked you to comment on the data, both detailed and summarised, including suggesting possible causes for areas highlighted and what further information would be required. This written part took two thirds of the marks for the question. In December 2003 a question focused on the reasons for variances and variance investigation.

Key learning points

- A **standard cost** is an estimated unit cost.

- A standard cost is built up of standards for each cost element (standard resource price and standard resource usage).

- **Standard costing** variances are used to measure performance and provide a performance control system.

- Standard costing is most suited to mass production and repetitive assembly work.

- **Budgets** and standards are very similar and interrelated, but there are important differences between them.

- The **responsibility** for setting standards should be shared between the managers able to provide the necessary information about levels of expected efficiency, prices and overhead costs.

- Standards may be **ideal**, **attainable** or **current**.

- You must be able to calculate all the **variances** described in this chapter.

- **Materiality, controllability** and **variance trend** should be considered before a decision about whether or not to investigate a variance is taken.

- One way of deciding whether or not to investigate a variance is to only investigate those variances which exceed **pre-set tolerance limits**.

- If the cause of a variance is **controllable**, action can be taken to bring the system back under control in future. If the variance is **uncontrollable**, but not simply due to chance, it will be necessary to review forecasts of expected results, and perhaps to revise the budget.

- An **operating statement** provides a reconciliation between budgeted and actual profit.

Quick quiz

1 What is an operating statement?
2 Fixed production overhead volume variances do not occur in a standard absorption costing system. True or false?
3 What does the sales volume variance measure?
4 What does a materials usage variance measure?
5 Suppose that a company reports a favourable labour rate variance for the first half of the year and an adverse labour rate variance for the rest of the year. What might be the cause of the variances throughout the year?
6 Why is the variable overhead efficiency variance always the same, in hours, as the labour efficiency variance?

Answers to quick quiz

1 An operating statement provides a reconciliation between budgeted and actual profit.
2 False. They do not occur in standard marginal costing systems.
3 The effect on profit (standard full costing) or contribution (standard marginal costing) due to actual sales volume (in units) being higher or lower than the volume budgeted.
4 The effect on profit of using more or less materials in production than should have been expected, given the actual volume of production.
5 The standard labour rate per hour might be based on an estimated average pay rate for the year, and the work force might receive an annual pay increase mid-way through the year. If so, we should expect favourable labour rate variances before the pay increase and adverse rate variances afterwards.
6 Variable overhead spending is assumed to vary with actual labour hours worked. Labour efficiency or inefficiency will therefore affect both labour costs and variable overhead costs.

Other aspects of performance measurement

12

Topic list
1 Measures of shareholder value
2 Critical success factors and key performance indicators
3 Balanced scorecard
4 Benchmarking

Introduction

Traditional budgeting and standard costing are well-established techniques that are most useful in stable manufacturing environments. As modern economies turn increasingly away from manufacturing, and operate in volatile environments, new methods of performance measurement have been proposed. This chapter looks at these proposals.

Learning objectives

On completion of this chapter you will be able to:

Syllabus reference

- identify and explain measures of shareholder value   3 (a)
- explain the meaning of critical success factors and how key performance indicators should be set for these factors   3 (b)
- explain the balanced scorecard approach to setting targets and measuring performance   3 (d)
- explain a benchmarking approach to performance measurement   3 (e)

1 Measures of shareholder value

FAST FORWARD

The **shareholder value concept** is that a company should have as its main objective the aim of maximising shareholder value, and should therefore develop strategies for increasing shareholder value. Measures of shareholder value include profit, return on assets and economic value added.

Key term

Companies are owned by their ordinary shareholders, who invest in their company in the expectation of obtaining returns, in the form of dividends and a higher share value. The **shareholder value concept** is that the main objective of a company should be to maximise the wealth of its shareholders, and that all other objectives are subordinate to this.

This concept is not universally accepted. It can be argued that there are many different 'stakeholders' in a company, in addition to the shareholders. Stakeholder groups include the senior management, other employees, customers, suppliers and the general public. Each stakeholder group has expectations of what a company should provide for them. For example, employees might want to earn a good income, be rewarded for efforts made on behalf of the company and job satisfaction. Customers might expect a company to supply products or services that satisfy their needs at a reasonable price.

Even so, there is general acceptance that companies should aim to create **shareholder value**, and in doing so, other stakeholders are likely to benefit from the company's success. If a company earns bigger profits, it can afford better wages or salaries for the people it employs and reward individuals for their achievements. By providing better value to customers, in the form of improved products or lower prices, companies should be successful in their markets: customer satisfaction is essential for achieving commercial success.

If the shareholder value concept is accepted, it follows that performance measures should focus on the creation of shareholder value. Any of several different measures might be used as the main measure or measures of performance.

(a) **Profit**. Profit is either paid out to shareholders as a dividend, or reinvested in the business for future growth. A company might therefore establish a profit target as its key objective. Shareholders will have expectations of what the company's profits and dividends should be, and will be disappointed if actual profit turns out less than expected. Lower profits are likely to result in a fall in the share price, and a loss of shareholder value. Targets for profit will therefore normally include an element for *profit growth*.

(b) **Earnings per share**. A company might issue new shares to raise fresh capital, for investment in future growth. When new shares are issued for cash, total profits should increase, but the profit per share (i.e. earnings per share or EPS) might fall. If a company increases its share capital by 10% but profits increase only by 5%, it would be argued that existing shareholders have suffered some loss in value, due to a fall in the earnings per share. The main performance measure for a company might therefore be expressed in terms of a target for earnings per share and growth in earnings per share.

(c) **Return on assets**. To earn profits, capital has to be invested. A larger investment should provide a larger profit. For example, it can be argued that a return of $10,000 on an investment of $100,000 (10%) is much better than a return of $20,000 on an investment of $1 million (2%). Performance should therefore be judged in terms of the size of the profit relative to the size of the capital investment, and the main performance measure might be return on assets employed or return on investment (ROI).

(d) **Profit margin**. Some companies might measure overall performance in terms of their profit/sales ratio, or return on sales. However, although return on sales is a useful secondary measure, it is not a reliable guide to the creation of shareholder value. Return on sales might be improved, but sales volume might fall as a result. For example, a company might increase its profit/sales ratio from 5% to 7% by increasing its prices, but if sales volume falls substantially as a result of the price rise, the overall result could be a fall in total profit and a lower return on assets.

(e) **Economic value added** or EVA®. Profit and return on assets are based on accounting measurements of profitability and asset values. It can be argued that accounting measurements are unreliable guides to true economic value. Economic value added or EVA® is a measure of performance, developed by consultants Stern Stewart, that addresses this problem. Adjustments are made to items of expense and asset values, in order to convert reported accounting profits into a measure that represents the economic value created for shareholders during the period. EVA® is explained in more detail in a later chapter.

Performance measurement should consider the long-term rather than the short-term. Maximising shareholder value means having to achieve certain performance levels over a long period of time, not just over a 12-month time frame. Companies should therefore set targets over a time period longer than the budget period.

2 Critical success factors and key performance indicators

FAST FORWARD

> An organisation should identify **critical success factors**, and **key performance indicators** for measuring actual performance against these factors. Critical success factors can be both financial and non-financial in nature.

Having established its main objectives, in terms of creating shareholder value, a company should identify the factors that are essential for success in achieving those objectives. Critical success factors are those aspects of a business that must go right; otherwise the company will fail to achieve its objectives.

Key term

> **Critical success factors (CSFs)** are the few key areas of a business that must go right if success is to be achieved. They are of vital importance for achieving the organisation's objectives, and the organisation cannot afford non-achievement for any CSF.

There will usually be just a small number of critical success factors, and at a departmental level, they might be expressed in **financial** terms (e.g. keeping costs under control), and perhaps also in terms of **productivity** and **quality**. At the organisational level, critical success factors might be expressed in financial terms (e.g. growth in shareholders' wealth) but also in terms of market share or technological innovation.

Critical success factors might be identified, for example, in terms of:

(a) Profitability
(b) Market share
(c) Productivity
(d) Product leadership
(e) Personnel development
(f) Employee attitudes
(g) Public responsibility
(h) Balance between long-term and short-term goals

It might be a useful exercise to look at a specific example.

A food manufacturer has the crucial marketing tasks of persuading shops and supermarkets to stock their produce, and persuading customers to buy it. It has therefore been suggested that the critical success factors for a manufacturer of processed food products are:

(a) New product development
(b) Good distribution, and
(c) Effective advertising.

New product development is necessary to create products that customers want to buy. Good distribution is essential to persuade supermarket chains and other retailers to buy the goods of the manufacturer, rather than similar goods of rival producers. Effective advertising is essential to create demand from consumers, who will then expect to see the manufacturer's products in the places they buy their food. Good distribution provides marketing 'push' and effective advertising, by stimulating consumer demand, creates a marketing 'pull'.

2.1 Key performance indicators

Having established what its critical success factors are, the company must then identify targets and measures of performance. These are **key performance indicators**. For a food manufacturer, the key performance indicator might be:

(a) The *number* of new products developed during the period. For example, a target might be to launch four new products on the market, of which one should be an organic food product.

(b) The *amount of revenue* earned from sales of new products. For example, a target might be for 20% of annual sales to be achieved from new products launched since the previous year.

Key performance indicators for good distribution could be a target for the time from receipt of a customer's order to delivery. The target might be that distribution time should be no longer than, say, 24 hours, and actual performance can be measured against this target.

2.2 CSFs and non-profit-making organisations

Critical success factors can be used by non-profit-making institutions. For example, a university might see its objectives as to carry out academic research and to teach students to a high standard. The critical success factors for a university might be:

(a) The availability of funding, for both research and teaching
(b) Student recruitment, to obtain students of a suitable calibre
(c) The skills of the academic team, in both research and teaching
(d) Course design
(e) Responding to external needs, for example the needs of employers and the demand from other organisations (eg companies) for research
(f) The exploitation of technology.

For each critical success factor, targets and key performance indicators could be set.

An approach to establishing performance measures in both profit-making and non-profit making organisations might therefore be to:

(a) Identify the organisation's corporate objectives
(b) Determine the critical success factors, at the organisational level, and also at divisional, departmental or other operating level within the organisation
(c) Determine a small number of key performance indicators for each factor.

A sandwich shop in a large city is considering setting up a mobile delivery service to take sandwiches and other refreshments to customers in their offices. Identify three CSFs for this project and suggest a key performance indicator for each.

Answer

Three CSFs might be:

- Variety of sandwiches offered
- Speedy response to customer demand
- Rapid establishment of customer base

For which key performance indicators might be (respectively):

- Number of varieties offered in comparison with competitors, perhaps supplemented by the number of times a customer requests something not currently offered
- Percentage of orders delivered within 15 minutes of time order required by customer
- Growth in sales/number of deliveries.

3 Balanced scorecard

FAST FORWARD

> There could be a risk that short-term financial performance will take prominence over longer-term objectives, including non-financial objectives, and the organisation's strategy. One approach to linking performance target setting and performance measurement to strategy is the **balanced scorecard**.

Measures of shareholder value, and responsibility accounting measures of performance within an organisation, focus on financial issues. It has already been suggested that the objectives of an organisation, and targets for achievement, will be non-financial as well as financial.

Unless an organisation has clear targets for its non-financial objectives, and measures actual performance in achieving those objectives, there is a severe risk that an organisation's performance management systems will focus on financial targets, to the exclusion of non-financial factors.

An approach to target setting and performance measurement, developed by Kaplan and Norton in the 1990s, is the **balanced scorecard**.

Key term

A **balanced scorecard** establishes non-financial as well as financial targets, and measures actual performance in relation to all these targets. Areas covered include profitability, customer satisfaction, internal efficiency and innovation.

The balanced scorecard approach focuses on four different aspects of performance.

Perspective	The key question
Customer	What do existing customers and targeted new customers value from us? Focusing on this issue gives rise to targets that matter to customers, such as cost (value for money), quality or place of delivery.
Internal	What processes must we excel at to achieve our financial and customer objectives? Focusing on this issue should lead to improvements in internal processes and decision making.

Perspective	The key question
Innovation and learning	Can we continue to improve and create value? Focus on this issue draws attention to the ability of the business to maintain its competitive position, through the acquisition of new skills and the development of new products. Suitable measures of performance might include the percentage of sales derived from new products compared to the percentage derived from longer-established products, and the time required to bring a new product to market.
Financial	How do we create value for our shareholders? Financial measures of performance include share price growth, profitability and return on investment, and market value added.

For organisations that adopt a balanced scorecard approach, targets are set for a range of critical financial and non-financial areas, and the main monthly performance report for management is a balanced scorecard report, not budgetary control reports. In other words, with a balanced scorecard, the budget 'takes a back seat' to the balanced scorecard.

Typical measures of outcomes for each of the four aspects of performance are as follows.

Perspective	Outcome measures
Core financial measures	• Return on investment, or economic value added/market value added • Profitability • Revenue growth/ revenue mix • Cost reduction/ productivity • Cash flow
Core customer measures	• Market share • Customer profitability • Attracting new customers • Retaining existing customers • Customer satisfaction • On-time delivery
Internal business measures	These will vary according to the nature of the business, but might include: • Success rate in winning contract orders • Production cycle time • Level of re-works
Core learning and growth measures	• The percentage of total revenue generated by new products • Time to develop new products • Employee productivity • Employee satisfaction • Employee retention • Revenue per employee

Important benefits of a balanced scorecard approach are that:

(a)   It looks at both internal and external factors affecting the organisation

(b)   It is related to key elements of the organisation's strategy, and is a strategy-focused performance management system

(c)   Financial and non-financial measures are included, and (short-term) financial performance measures do not take precedence over the others.

Raffles & Co own a chain of ten medium-sized restaurants in the South East of England. These restaurants are aimed at the young professional market, and sell themselves as a place to meet, drink and eat at lunchtime, after work and into the evening. They are generally situated in the centre of towns, which makes rental of properties quite expensive. The directors are concerned about the impact of a new chain of modern restaurants that are starting to encroach on Raffles' restaurants' territory and feel that a balanced scorecard approach to evaluating performance will help to keep Raffles' business ahead in their market.

Suggest with reasons, one key measure for each of the main aspects of a balanced scorecard for Raffles' restaurant business.

Answer

Note: only one measure is required for each perspective.

Customer perspective – %age of revenues generated at different times of day/customer satisfaction (from surveys left on tables)/% capacity filled, benchmarked against competitors.

Internal perspective – Level of food wastage/cost effectiveness of menu design.

Innovation/learning perspective – frequency of menu changes/% of wine revenues derived from newly introduced lines/number of promotions and special offers.

Financial perspective – EVA® against budgeted EVA® for the chain as a whole/return on investment by unit/revenue growth.

3.1 Implementing a balanced scorecard approach

Robert Kaplan and David Norton, originators of the balanced scorecard approach in the 1990s, recommend that :

(a)   A firm should start by translating its strategy into a balanced set of key objectives. This will probably include setting a high-level financial objective, such as increasing the return on capital employed from its current level to a higher target level

(b)   These key objectives should then be converted into operational targets

(c)   These operational targets should be communicated to employees

The focus of attention is therefore on strategic objectives and the success factors necessary for achieving them.

A framework for adopting a balanced scorecard approach is given in the following table.

Identify the company's mission and vision. Establish the main objectives	
Identify strategies for achieving objectives.	Senior management decide which strategies to follow. *Examples* We must invest in modern technology. We must achieve cost efficiency and be cost leaders in the market. We must achieve a high quality of product.

Identify the critical success factors for achieving the strategic objectives.	CSFs can be structured along the balanced scorecard approach, with CSFs for customer, internal, innovation and learning and financial perspectives. *Examples* Financial CSFs: • profitability • cost efficiency Customer perspective CSFs: • on-time delivery • customer satisfaction Internal perspective CSFs: • use the right technology • fast production throughput Innovation and learning CSFs: • develop new products on time • innovation • employee attitudes • employee competences
Identify key performance measures for each CSF	For example, if a critical factor is on-time delivery of orders to customers, a key performance indicator will be the percentage of orders delivered on time, and the balanced scorecard should set a target of performance, such as at least 99.5% of deliveries to customers to be on time. Similarly, if a CSF is to achieve fast production throughput, a key performance indicator might be the average lead time for production (time from starting a job to completion). The balanced scorecard would then set a target for the average production lead time.
The balanced scorecard should be evaluated.	Management should check that achievement of targets selected should ensure that the company will achieve its objectives. The key question at this stage is: Are we measuring the right things?
Create action plans for achieving the balanced scorecard targets.	
Implement. Monitor performance against the scorecard.	

 Case Study

Mobil

An example of a balanced scorecard approach, described by Kaplan and Norton in their book *The Strategy-focused Organization*, is the case of Mobil in the US in the early 1990s. Mobil is a major supplier of petrol, and was competing with other suppliers on the basis of price and the location of petrol stations. The strategic focus was entirely on cost reduction and productivity. Even so, return on capital was not high enough.

The senior management of the company re-assessed the company's strategy, with a view to achieving growth in market share and greater differentiation for the Mobil brand name. They wanted the company to attract customers who bought more-than-average quantities of petrol at each visit to a petrol station, bought higher-priced blends of petrol, and who would also buy other goods from the petrol station stores.

The company re-assessed its high-level financial objective, and set a target of improving return on capital employed from its current level (about 6 – 7%) to 12% within three years.

From a financial perspective, it identified key success factors as productivity and sales growth.

(a)   Targets were set for productivity. These were to reduce costs (measured in terms of operating costs per gallon) so as to become the cost leader in the industry, and also to increase 'asset intensity' (i.e. to handle a larger volume of business without increasing the asset base of the company). Asset intensity targets were set in terms of operational cash flow.

(b)   Targets for growth were to achieve an above-average growth in revenues compared to the industry as a whole, and also to achieve a bigger volume growth in premium-priced products (measured in terms of the percentage of total sales coming from premium-priced products).

From a customer perspective, Mobil carried out market research into who its customers were and what factors influenced their buying decisions. It was able to group customers into five categories, of which three were buyers of higher-priced products (i.e. were not price-sensitive) and who tended to use the same petrol stations for all their petrol purchases. Targets were established for providing petrol to these categories in a way that would 'delight' the customer and differentiate Mobil's products from rival petrol suppliers. Basic issues were identified, such as having petrol stations that were both clean and safe, and offering a good quality product and a trusted brand. Targets were set for these. Targets were also identified and set for differentiating Mobil's products from those of rival suppliers: these included targets for a speedy service at petrol stations, friendly and helpful customer service and giving some recognition to customer loyalty.

Mobil also had to address the problem of improving the processes for delivering its products and services to customers. Since many petrol stations in North America were not owned by the petrol companies, but by independent owners, these processes had to be developed in collaboration with the owners.

For each aspect of its strategic planning, Mobil identified targets for achievement, and measured performance on the basis of these targets. All targets on the balanced scorecard were given due attention. These included short-term financial targets, but short-term financial targets did not take prominence over the other non-financial targets.

 ## Case Study

Analog Devices

Another interesting example is the experience of Analog Devices, a semi-conductor company in the US which was the first company to devise a balanced scorecard approach in the 1980s when preparing its five-year strategic plan for 1988 – 1992.

Analog Devices had a clearly-expressed corporate objective that set out its mission and vision. This provided a valuable reference for the development of non-financial performance measures in the balanced scorecard. The company's corporate objectives were summarised as follows: 'Achieving our goals for growth, profits, market share and quality creates the environment and economic means to satisfy the needs of our employees, stockholders, customers and others associated with the firm. Our success depends on people who understand the interdependence and congruence of their personal goals with those of the company and who are thus motivated to contribute towards the achievement of those goals.'

Three basic strategic objectives identified by the firm were market leadership, sales growth and profitability. The most critical problems appeared to be customer-related, and the company established three key targets:

(a)   Percentage of orders delivered on time. A target was set for the five-year period to increase the percentage of on-time deliveries from 85% to at least 99.8%.

(b)   Outgoing defect levels. The target was to reduce the number of defects in items leaving the company's premises for delivery to customers, from 500 per month to less than 10 per month.

(c)   Order lead time. Here, the target was to reduce the time between receiving a customer order to delivery from 10 weeks to less than three weeks.

The company also had a quality improvement programme, and used cross-functional problem-solving teams to identify ways of improving production methods and quality. From an internal process perspective, the drivers of success were seen as:

(a) Having products rated 'number one' by at least 50% of customers, based on their attitudes to whether the company was making the right products, performance, price, reliability, quality, delivery, lead time, customer support, responsiveness, willingness to co-operate and willingness to form partnerships.

(b) Eliminating waste in all parts and at all levels in the organisation.

The company therefore developed a number of targets with an internal perspective:

(a) Manufacturing cycle time. To reduce this from 15 weeks to 4 to 5 weeks over the five-year planning period.

(b) Defective items in production. The target was to reduce defects in production from 5,000 per month to less than 10 per month.

At the same time, the company committed itself to pursuing aggressively company-wide cost reductions. Targets were also set for improvements in employee productivity.

Learning and innovation targets were also set, for:

(a) The number of new products introduced to the market

(b) The amount of sales from new products

(c) The new product sales ratio. This was the percentage of total sales achieved by products introduced to the market within the previous six quarters.

(d) Average annual revenues for new products in their third year.

(e) Reducing the average time to bring new product ideas to market.

Financial targets were set for revenue, revenue growth, profit and return on assets.

Analog Devices succeeded, through its innovative balanced scorecard approach, in integrating financial and non-financial metrics into a single system, in which the various targets did not conflict or compete with each other, and were not in any way contradictory.

3.2 The need for care when adopting a balanced scorecard approach

Supporters of the balanced scorecard approach to performance measurement are amongst those who doubt the value of budgets and budgetary control as a system of planning and control and performance management.

However, implementing a balanced scorecard approach can have its problems. The argument originally put forward by Kaplan and Norton to support a balanced scorecard approach was that financial indicators of performance on their own were inadequate.

(a) Accounting figures are unreliable and can be manipulated.

(b) Changes in the business and in market conditions facing a company do not show up in the financial results until much later. Accounting results therefore do not provide early warning indicators of change.

Performance measures should ideally be difficult to manipulate, and should provide advance warning of what could happen in the future. They should also relate to factors that management can do something about. In other words, performance indicators should act as pointers to what should be done to improve matters.

3.3 Example

In an article in *Financial Management* (November 2001) Gering and Mntambo make a useful sporting analogy. In a football match, the manager of a team has the responsibility for winning the match. The ultimate measure of performance throughout the match is the score. However, the manager uses other indicators as the match progresses, to decide what he should do to improve the prospect of winning. During the first half, he will take note of how many scoring chances have been created, how much possession of the ball the team has had and which players appear to be out of form. He will use these indicators to make adjustments at half time, or to take decisions about substituting players or changing tactics. The aim is to win the match, but performance indicators about shots on goal, possession, the number of corner kicks for each side, and so on can help him to make decisions that will hopefully lead to eventual victory.

A balanced scorecard operates in the same way.

The ultimate objective is to maximise profits. However, other indicators of performance can help managers to make assessments and think about whether changes or adjustments are needed to make achievement of the objective more likely. Financial measures, customer measures, internal business measures and learning and growth measures can all be used. It is essential to remember, however, that they act as guides to achieving the key financial objective, but are not in themselves the main objective.

Returning to the football match analogy, a useful measure of performance is how many shots on goal the team has had, because this provides a guide to the likelihood of scoring. However, the number of shots on goal is not in itself the objective. It is scoring more goals than the other team that ultimately counts.

A difficulty with the balanced scorecard approach in practice can be that the targets for each item on the balanced scorecard might be seen as key objectives in their own right. The four categories of performance indicator each focus on one of the major stakeholders in the company (shareholders, customers, executive managers and employees). Each of these groups might use a balanced scorecard system to apply pressure on the company to have regard for their interests. Instead of supporting the main financial objective, balanced scorecard targets can become part of a political process for reconciling the interests of stakeholder groups. The risk is that each part of the balanced scorecard becomes an independent list of targets and measurements.

Exam focus point

The balanced scorecard was examined in December 2002 in the context of an engineering design company. It initially required a discussion of the importance of, and problems with, the use of non-financial performance measures in performance evaluation. It then moved on specifically to the balanced scorecard, requiring a description of its main features and its application to the company concerned.

The examiner wrote an article in Finance Matters in March 2007 on measuring performance. In this article he looks at, amongst other things, the balance scorecard and how it should be used appropriately. '.... it should be noted that it (the balanced scorecard) is not the technique itself which leads to improved performance. In fact it is the activities, analysis and behaviours that the balanced scorecard prompts that lead to improved performance. This is because introducing and using the balanced scorecard leads to an examination of how the organisation functions and what needs to be controlled to ensure success. The balanced scorecard might be described as communication and behavioural tool, rather than measurement tool.'

4 Benchmarking

FAST FORWARD

Another way of measuring performance, that should encourage strategic thinking, is **benchmarking** against the world's best.

Key term

Benchmarking has been described as 'the formalisation of the basic notion of comparing practices. It is a systematic analysis of one's own performance against that of another organisation .... The overall objective of benchmarking is to improve performance by learning from the experience of others' (Smith).

Benchmarking therefore aims to **achieve competitive advantage** by **learning from others' experiences and mistakes**, finding **best practice** and translating this best practice into **use in the organisation**.

4.1 Types of benchmarking

External benchmarking involves:

(a) Comparing the performance of an organisation with that of a **direct competitor** - ideally one that is acknowledged to be the 'best in class' (**competitive benchmarking**), or

(b) Comparing the performance of an internal function with those of the best **external practitioners of those functions**, regardless of the industry within which they operate (**functional benchmarking**).

Given that the benchmark is the 'best' in a particular field ('the world's best'), it provides a meaningful target towards which the organisation should aim.

Internal benchmarking, on the other hand, involves comparing the performance of **one part of a business with that of a different part of the same business** with the aim of establishing best practice throughout an organisation. Some external benchmarking is still required, however, in order to establish best practice.

Although any process can be benchmarked, studies indicate that the business functions most subjected to benchmarking are **customer services, manufacturing, human resources** and **information services.**

4.2 Why benchmark?

Performance measurements within an organisation should help it to achieve its aims and objectives. However, there is often a tendency for performance measurements to become an end in themselves, instead of a way of helping management to achieve their goals. Managers might even take measures that are harmful to the organisation, in order to produce good results 'on paper'.

'Perhaps performance measures, when done correctly, help everyone in the company focus on the right things in the right place at the right time. However ... there are many stories of dysfunctional behaviour - the telephone company which pledged to have at least 90% of payphones working, then achieving this figure by simply removing all public payphones from those areas most often vandalised. Or the bus operator which, plagued by delays, decided to pay bonuses to drivers who arrived at the terminus on time. As a result, most buses arrived at the terminus on time - however, drivers no longer tended to stop for passengers along the way!

Measuring performance by itself has no meaning. Meaning can only be achieved through comparison, either against poor performance, which usually provides no true indication of future or competitive position, or through benchmarking.' (*Management Accounting*, November 1996)

4.3 Limitations and advantages of benchmarking

Both approaches to benchmarking suffer from a number of **limitations**.

(a) **Limitations of external benchmarking**

- Deciding which activities to benchmark
- Identifying which organisation is the 'best in class' at an activity
- **Persuading that organisation to share information**
- Successful practices in one organisation may not transfer successfully to another.

(b) The principal limitation of internal benchmarking centres on the relevance of the other part of the business.

- The amount of resources devoted to the units may differ
- There may be local differences (use of different computer hardware)
- Inputs and outputs may be difficult to define.

Benchmarking **works**, it is claimed, for the following reasons.

(a) The comparisons are carried out by the managers who have to live with any changes implemented as a result of the exercise.

(b) Benchmarking focuses on improvement in key areas and sets **targets** which are **challenging but 'achievable'**. What is *really* achievable can be discovered by examining what others have achieved: managers are thus able to accept that they are not being asked to perform miracles.

Benchmarking can also provide **early warning of competitive disadvantage** (i.e. helps an organisation to identify key areas where competitors are performing better) and should lead to a greater incidence of **team-working** and **cross-functional learning** within an organisation, through joint efforts to achieve improvements in performance standards to 'world-class' levels.

4.4 Relationship between balanced scorecard and benchmarking

The balanced scorecard and benchmarking are similar in that they both involve identifying key areas of a business and the selection of performance measures to monitor how the areas are performing.

The balanced scorecard identifies four specific areas (financial, customer, internal and learning), whereas benchmarking is not so prescriptive and benchmarks any areas of the business but typically customer services, manufacturing, human resources and information systems.

Both techniques set targets against which to assess performance. The balanced scorecard will set a target that will typically be taken from the strategic plan for the business; benchmarking will usually take the targets either from external competitors or use comparisons from internal divisions.

One of the main differences between the two techniques is that the balanced scorecard (as its name suggests) does not rank any performance measure as more important than another eg it does not attribute more importance to financial measures than non-financial. The whole point of the system is the recognition that for long term growth a business has to move forward on all fronts – exceptional strength in one area may not compensate in the long run for a serious weakness in others. For example, a strong profit performance may not be sufficient to mask under-investment in skills training or research and development. A company using the balanced scorecard would consider that it was failing if the scores were unbalanced.

Benchmarking does not necessarily concern itself with balance, although the benchmarks may be interpreted to use the balanced scorecard concept to assess overall performance.

Key learning points

- The **shareholder value concept** is that a company should have as its main objective the aim of maximising shareholder value, and should therefore develop strategies for increasing shareholder value. Measures of shareholder value include profit, return on assets and economic value added.

- An organisation should identify **critical success factors**, and **key performance indicators** for measuring actual performance against these factors. Critical success factors can be both financial and non-financial in nature.

- There could be a risk that short-term financial performance will take prominence over longer-term objectives, including non-financial objectives, and the organisation's strategy. One approach to linking performance target setting and performance measurement to strategy is the **balanced scorecard**.

- Another way of measuring performance, that should encourage strategic thinking, is **benchmarking** against the world's best.

Quick quiz

1   What are the four perspectives of strategy and performance measurement addressed by a balanced scorecard approach?

2   A country's health service has a target for reductions in the waiting list for surgical operations. Its management achieves this target by directing most of its resources to handling relatively minor and non-critical operations, at the expense of the smaller numbers of serious and life-improving operations. How might this short-termist approach be overcome by benchmarking?

Answers to quick quiz

1   Customer, internal, innovation and learning, financial.

2   Comparisons with other national health services (the 'world's best') should reveal differences in patient treatment and the nature of the hospital waiting lists, and show up the health service in question in a bad light.

13

Divisional performance measurement

Topic list
1 Divisional organisation and responsibility accounting
2 Return on investment (ROI)
3 ROI and decision making
4 Residual income
5 Economic value added (EVA®)
6 Accounting profit and controllable profit
7 Measuring divisional performance by cash flows

Introduction

Typically, a large organisation is split up into a number of different business units, which may or may not be allowed to operate autonomously. This chapter considers a range of methods for measuring and managing the performance of the different business units.

Learning objectives

On completion of this chapter you will be able to:

Syllabus reference

- describe the various ways in which the performance of a division within an organisation might be measured — 3 (f)
- understand the limitations of accounting profit as a measure of divisional performance — 3 (f)
- understand the significance of controllable profit for performance measurement — 3 (f)
- describe how divisional performance might be measured by cash flows rather than profit — 3 (f)

1 Divisional organisation and responsibility accounting

FAST FORWARD

> Performance measurement may be based on a **divisional reporting system**, with major divisions regarded as autonomous investment centres. (Within investment centres, there may be a hierarchy of profit centres and cost centres).

Key terms

A **division** is a separately identifiable unit of an organisation, and might alternatively be called a subsidiary or a strategic business unit (SBU).

A **cost centre** is a production or service location, function, activity or item of equipment for which costs are accumulated. *(CIMA Official Terminology 2000)*

A **profit centre** is a part of a business accountable for both costs and revenues.
(CIMA Official Terminology 2000)

An **investment centre** is a profit centre with additional responsibilities for capital investment and possibly for financing. *(CIMA Official Terminology 2000)*

Responsibility accounting is a system of accounting that attributes costs and/or revenues to individual business units for which a particular manager is held responsible.

When the manager of a division is given a reasonable amount of autonomy, with the authority to make important decisions for the division, there should be a system of performance measurement providing a way of:

(a) Establishing targets for the division that are consistent with the strategic targets of the organisation as a whole

(b) Establishing budget targets for the division

(c) Measuring actual performance against those targets, and

(d) Holding the divisional management responsible and accountable for their division's performance.

1.1 Cost centres

If divisional managers are responsible for the costs incurred in the division, but are not responsible for revenue-earning activities, each division may be a **cost centre**, and the management will then be held responsible for the costs of the division. Performance reports might be a form of variance report.

1.2 Profit centres

If divisional managers are responsible for both the costs incurred by their division and for revenue-earning activities, each division may be a **profit centre**. The management will then be held responsible for the profits earned by the division, and performance reports might compare the actual and budgeted profits for the division. When divisions are established as profit centres, and carry out work for other divisions within the organisation, they will sell their products or services internally, at an internal sales price or **transfer price**. Transfer pricing was explained in an earlier chapter.

1.3 Investment centres

Divisional managers might be responsible, not only for the costs of their division and the revenue-earning activities, but also for capital expenditure decisions, inventory-holding, invoicing customers and debt collection and materials procurement. When this is the case, performance of the division should be measured in terms of both the profitability of the division, and also in terms of the investment of resources in the division. Each division should be an **investment centre**, and management should be held responsible for earning a sufficient return on the amount of capital invested.

When an organisation consists of several investment centres, each centre should have strategic goals that are consistent with the overall objectives of the organisation. The performance of each investment centre might be measured in a similar way to the measurement of performance of the organisation as a whole.

1.4 Responsibility accounting

Cost centres, profit centres and investment centres are all **responsibility centres**, and there may be a hierarchy of responsibility centres within the organisation. A large company or group of companies might consist of a number of investment centres, and within each investment centre there may be several profit centres. Within each profit centre, there might be several cost centres. Reporting the financial performance of a responsibility centre is known as **responsibility accounting**.

Divisional performance can be measured in **non-financial** terms, as well as financial terms. Non-financial performance measurements have been explained earlier in this text. This chapter deals exclusively with the **financial** performance measurement of investment centres, and more particularly with **profitability and return on capital**.

2 Return on investment (ROI)

FAST FORWARD

Return on investment is the main measure of divisional performance, but it has several limitations. The main problem lies in the fact that ROI might be used as a guide for investment decisions, whereas it is inappropriate to use accounting profits to make investment decisions. There is no generally agreed method of calculating ROI.

Return on investment (ROI), also known as **return on capital employed (ROCE)**, is generally regarded as the key financial performance ratio, both for an organisation as a whole and for investment centres within the organisation. The main reasons for its widespread use as a major financial objective and as a measure of performance are as follows.

(a) It ties in directly with the accounting process, and is identifiable from the income statement and statement of financial position of the division.

(b) Even more importantly, ROI is the **only** measure of performance available (apart from residual income or EVA®) by which the return on investment for a division or company **as a single entire unit** can be measured. It is not sufficient to measure the profits of an investment centre. It is also necessary to relate the size of the profit to the amount of capital that has been invested to earn it. The strategic financial goal of an organisation is often expressed in terms of increasing the ROI, and it is appropriate that investment centre performance should be measured in a consistent manner.

Key term

> **Return on investment (ROI)** shows how much profit has been made in relation to the amount of capital invested and is calculated as (profit ÷ capital employed) × 100%.

Suppose a company has two investment centres A and B, which achieve the following results.

	A	B	Total
	$	$	$
Profit	60,000	30,000	90,000
Capital employed	400,000	120,000	520,000
ROI	15%	25%	17.3%

Investment centre A has made double the profits of investment centre B, and in terms of profits alone has therefore been more 'successful'. However, B has achieved its profits with a much lower capital investment, and so has earned a much higher ROI. This suggests that B has been a more successful investment than A.

2.1 Measuring ROI

ROI can be measured in different ways.

(a)   The figure for profit is usually measured as the division's profit after charging depreciation on the non-current assets of the division.

(b)   Capital employed might consist of the non-current assets of the division only. However, capital employed might also include an amount for working capital. **Working capital** is generally measured as the total of the inventories and receivables of the division, minus the division's payables.

In dealing with an examination question, you might need to check the wording of the question carefully, to establish how ROI is measured.

2.2 Capital employed with non-current assets at net book value

The most common method of measuring ROI is 'profit after depreciation/non-current assets net of depreciation (at 'net book value') plus working capital'. However, there is a problem with this method of measurement. If an investment centre maintains the same annual profit, and keeps the same assets without a policy of regular non-current asset replacement, its ROI will increase year by year as the assets get older and their net book value declines. This can give a false impression of improving performance over time.

For example, the results of investment centre X, with a policy of straight-line depreciation of assets over a 5-year period, might be as follows.

Year	Non-current assets at cost $'000	Depreciation in the year $'000	Net book value (mid year) $'000	Working capital $'000	Capital employed $'000	Profit $'000	ROI %
0	100			10	110		
1	100	20	90	10	100	10	10
2	100	20	70	10	80	10	12.5
3	100	20	50	10	60	10	16.7
4	100	20	30	10	40	10	25
5	100	20	10	10	20	10	50

This table of figures is intended to show that an investment centre can improve its ROI year by year, simply by allowing its non-current assets to depreciate, and there could be a **disincentive** to investment centre managers to **reinvest** in new or replacement assets, because the centre's ROI would probably fall if new assets were bought.

Question

Divisional ROI

A newly-established investment centre in a company has non-current assets of $460,000 which will be depreciated to nil on a straight line basis over 10 years. Working capital will consistently be $75,000 every year, and annual profits will be $30,000 each year, after depreciation. Capital employed is measured as non-current assets at net book value as at the end of the year, plus working capital. ROI is measured as return on capital employed. What is the division's ROI in year 2 and year 6?

	Profit	Non-current assets at cost	Accumulated depreciation	Non-current assets at net book value	Working capital	Total capital employed	ROI
	$'000	$'000	$'000	$'000	$'000	$'000	%
Year 2	30	460	92	368	75	443	6.8
Year 6	30	460	276	184	75	259	11.6

A further disadvantage of measuring ROI as profit divided by net assets is that it is **not easy to compare** fairly the performance of **different investment centres**.

For example, suppose that we have two investment centres:

	Investment centre P		Investment centre Q	
	$	$	$	$
Working capital		20,000		20,000
Non-current assets at cost	230,000		230,000	
Accumulated depreciation	170,000		10,000	
Net book value		60,000		220,000
Capital employed		80,000		240,000
Profit		$24,000		$24,000
ROI		30%		10%

Investment centres P and Q have the same amount of working capital, the same value of non-current assets at cost, and the same profit. But P's non-current assets have been depreciated by a much bigger amount (presumably P's non-current assets are much older than Q's) and so P's ROI is three times the size of Q's ROI. The conclusion might be that P has performed much better than Q. This comparison, however, would not be 'fair', because the difference in performance might be entirely attributable to the age of their non-current assets.

The **arguments in favour** of using net book values for calculating ROI are these.

(a) It is the 'normally accepted' method of calculating ROI.

(b) In reality firms are continually buying new non-current assets to replace old ones that wear out, and so on the whole, the total net book value of all non-current assets together will remain fairly constant (assuming nil inflation and nil growth).

2.3 Capital employed with non-current assets at cost

Capital employed might be measured as non-current assets at cost (or at current value) plus working capital. ROI would then be measured as a return on gross assets. This would remove the problem of ROI increasing over time as non-current assets get older.

If a company acquired a non-current asset costing $40,000, which it intends to depreciate by $10,000 p.a. for 4 years, and if the asset earns a profit of $8,000 p.a. after depreciation, ROI might be calculated on the basis of either net book values or gross values, as follows.

Year	Profit	Net book value (mid-year value)	ROI based on NBV	Gross value	ROI based on gross value
	$	$	%	$	%
1	8,000	35,000	22.9	40,000	20
2	8,000	25,000	32.0	40,000	20
3	8,000	15,000	53.3	40,000	20
4	8,000	5,000	160.0	40,000	20

The ROI based on net book value shows an increasing trend over time, simply because the asset's value is falling as it is depreciated. The ROI based on gross book value suggests that the asset has performed consistently in each of the 4 years, which is probably a more valid conclusion.

Question

Repeat the last question (Divisional ROI), measuring ROI as return on gross assets.

Answer

	Profit	Non-current assets at cost	Working capital	Total capital employed	ROI
	$'000	$'000	$'000	$'000	%
Year 2	30	460	75	535	5.6
Year 6	30	460	75	535	5.6

However, valuing non-current assets at cost to measure ROI has its **disadvantages**. Most important of these is that measuring ROI as 'return on gross assets' ignores the age factor, and does not distinguish between old and new assets.

(a) Older non-current assets usually cost more to repair and maintain. An investment centre with old assets may therefore have its profitability reduced by repair costs, and its ROI might *fall* over time as its assets get older and repair costs get bigger.

(b) Inflation and technological change alter the cost of non-current assets. If one investment centre has fixed assets bought ten years ago with a gross cost of $1 million, and another investment centre, in the same area of business operations, has non-current assets bought very recently for $1 million, the quantity and technological character of the non-current assets of the two investment centres are likely to be very different.

3 ROI and decision making

3.1 New investment

If investment centre performance is judged by ROI, we should expect that the manager of an investment centre will probably decide to undertake **new capital investments** *only if* these new investments are likely to increase the ROI of his or her division.

Suppose that investment centre A currently makes a return of 40% on capital employed. The manager of centre A would probably only want to undertake new investments that promise to **yield a return of 40% or more**, otherwise the investment centre's overall ROI would fall. For example, if investment centre A currently has assets of $1,000,000 and expects to earn a profit of $400,000, how would the centre's manager view a new capital investment which would cost $250,000 and yield a profit of $75,000 pa?

	Without the new investment	With the new investment
Profit	$400,000	$475,000
Capital employed	$1,000,000	$1,250,000
ROI	40%	38%

The new investment would reduce the investment centre's ROI from 40% to 38%, and so the manager would probably decide not to undertake the new investment.

If the group of companies of which investment centre A is a part has a target ROI of, say, 25%, the new investment would presumably be seen as beneficial for the group as a whole. But even though it promises to yield a return of 75,000/250,000 = 30%, which is above the group's target ROI, it would still make investment centre A's results look worse. The manager of investment centre A, in these circumstances, might be motivated to do not what is best for the organisation as a whole, but what is best for his or her division.

3.2 Using a target ROI

If a group sets a **target return** for the group as a whole, it might be group policy that investment projects should only go ahead if they promise to earn at least the target return.

For example, it might be a company's policy that:

(a)   There should be **no new investment** by any investment centre unless it is expected to earn at least a 15% return

(b)   Similarly, no non-current asset should be disposed of if the asset is currently earning a return in excess of 15% of its disposal value

(c)   Investments which promise a return of 15% or more ought to be undertaken (provided that the degree of uncertainty or risk in the project is acceptable)

A problem with such a policy is that even if investment decisions are based on a target rate of return over the life of the investment, actual performance would be measured each year on the basis of the ROI for that year. Since investments often take some time before they start earning a return, there might be a fall in ROI in the short term, that the investment centre manager might be reluctant to tolerate. New investments might therefore be rejected because of their short-term impact on divisional profits and ROI. Suppose that an investment in a non-current asset would cost $100,000 and make a profit of $10,000 p.a. after depreciation. The asset would be depreciated by $25,000 p.a. for four years. It is group policy that investments must show a minimum average annual ROI of 15% over their life. Capital employed is taken as non-current assets at their net book value as at the middle of the year. The average annual ROI of this investment would exceed 15%, and so the investment ought to be approved if group policy is adhered to.

In the table below, the accumulated depreciation starts as $12,500 in Year 1, which is one half of the annual depreciation charge. Accumulated depreciation then rises by $25,000 each year.

	Profit $'000	Non-current assets at cost $'000	Accumulated depreciation $'000	Non-current assets at net book value $'000	ROI %
Year 1	10	100	12.5	87.5	11.4
Year 2	10	100	37.5	62.5	16.0
Year 3	10	100	62.5	37.5	26.7
Year 4	10	100	87.5	12.5	80.0
Average	10			50.0	20.0

In view of the low accounting ROI in year 1 and year 2, the investment centre manager might decide not to undertake the investment, even though in the longer term it would appear to be worthwhile.

(a)   Strictly speaking, investment decisions should be based on a discounted cash flow (DCF) evaluation, and should not be guided by short-term accounting ROI.

(b)   Even if accounting ROI is used as a guideline for investment decisions, ROI should be looked at **over the full life** of the investment, not just in the short term. In the short term (in the first year or so of a project's life) the accounting ROI is likely to be low because the net book value of the asset will still be high.

3.3 Example: ROI and decision making

At the end of 20X3, Division S (part of a group) had non-current assets with a cost of $300,000, net current assets (working capital) of $40,000 and net profit of $64,000.

The non-current assets of Division S consist of five separate items, each costing $60,000. Each of these assets is being depreciated over 5 years on a straight-line basis. For each of the past years on 31 December, the division has bought a replacement for an asset that has just been withdrawn from service, and it proposes to continue this policy. Because of technological advances the asset manufacturer has been able to keep his prices constant over time. The company's target ROI is 15%. Capital employed is measured as non-current assets at net book value as at the *end* of the year, plus net current assets.

Required

Division S has the opportunity of an investment costing $60,000, and yielding an annual profit of $10,000 after depreciation. This will be depreciated over four years. Calculate its new ROI if the investment is undertaken, and on the basis of ROI, state whether you think the division's manager will undertake the investment.

Solution

The gross cost of the five existing non-current asset items is 5 × $60,000 = $300,000.

	$
Net book value of asset just bought on 31.12.X3	60,000
NBV of asset bought 1 year earlier	48,000
NBV of asset bought 2 years earlier	36,000
NBV of asset bought 3 years earlier	24,000
NBV of asset bought 4 years earlier	12,000
NBV of all 5 non-current assets at 31.12.X3	180,000
Net current assets	40,000
Total capital employed, Division S	220,000

The existing ROI is ((64/220) × 100% =) 29.1%. This is presumably the typical ROI achieved each year under the current policy of asset replacement.

The ROI with the new investment is as follows.

	Profit $'000	Non-current assets at cost $'000	Accumulated depreciation $'000	Non-current assets at net book value $'000	Working capital $'000	Total capital employed $'000	ROI %
Year 1	74	360	132	228	40	268	27.6
Year 2	74	360	144	216	40	256	28.9
Year 3	74	360	156	204	40	244	30.3
Year 4	74	360	168	192	40	232	31.9
Year 5	74	360	180	180	40	220	33.6
Average	74					244	30.3

The accumulated depreciation is $180,000 each year, for the existing five items that are replaced on a five-year cycle. The accumulated depreciation on the new item would be $12,000 in year 1, rising to $60,000 in year 5. (Net book value is measured as at the end of the year.)

If the investment centre manager based the investment decisions on whether an investment would increase or reduce the division's ROI, he or she might not want to make the additional investment. This is because the division's ROI would fall in the first two years. Over the life of the new investment, however, the divisional ROI would increase. If the investment centre manager takes a longer-term view, he or she might decide to undertake the investment.

This example illustrates the weakness of ROI as a guide to investment decisions. An investment centre manager might want an investment to show a good ROI from year 1, when the new investment has a high net book value. In the case of Division S, the **average net book value** of the asset over its full life will be 50% of $60,000 = $30,000, and so the **average ROI on the investment over time** will be ($10,000/$30,000) × 100% = 33.3%. However, the Division S manager might not want to wait so long to earn a good ROI, and wants to protect the division's performance in the short run as well as the long run.

4 Residual income

FAST FORWARD

> **Residual income** is an alternative measure of divisional performance. Divisions are charged a notional interest cost. Residual income is accounting profit minus the notional interest charge.

An alternative way of measuring the performance of an investment centre, instead of using ROI, is residual income (RI).

Key term

> **Residual income** is a measure of a division's profits after deducting a notional or imputed interest cost. This interest charge is a cost of the capital invested in the division.
>
> • The divisional profit is after deducting depreciation on capital equipment.
>
> • The imputed cost of capital might be the organisation's cost of borrowing, a target rate of return on shareholders' capital, or an average cost of the company's various sources of finance (a 'weighted average cost of capital').

4.1 Example

A division with capital employed of $400,000 currently earns an ROI of 22%. It can make an additional investment of $50,000 with a 5-year life, after which the investment would have no value. The annual profit from this investment would be $12,000 after depreciation. The division's cost of capital is 14%. Calculate the residual income before and after the investment.

Solution

	Before investment $	After investment $
Divisional profit	88,000	100,000
Imputed interest (400,000 × 0.14)	56,000	
(450,000 × 0.14)		63,000
Residual income	32,000	37,000

On the basis of residual income, the divisional manager would undertake the investment because it would increase the residual income of the division. Residual income will rise because the additional profit before interest exceeds the additional interest cost.

4.2 Comparison of residual income and ROI

A characteristic of residual income as a measure of divisional performance is that, in contrast to ROI, it is more likely to motivate management to undertake new investments.

The **advantages** of using RI are as follows.

(a) Residual income will **increase** when investments earning above the cost of capital are undertaken and when investments earning below the cost of capital are eliminated.

(b) Residual income is **more flexible** since a different cost of capital can be applied to investments with different **risk** characteristics. A higher cost of capital can be charged for higher-risk investments.

The main **weaknesses** of residual income are that:

(a) It does not facilitate comparisons between investment centres, and
(b) It does not relate the size of a centre's income to the size of the investment.

4.3 RI versus ROI: marginally profitable investments

Residual income will increase if a new investment is undertaken which earns a profit in excess of the imputed interest charge on the value of the asset acquired. Residual income will go up even if the investment only just exceeds the imputed interest charge, and this means that **'marginally profitable' investments are likely to be undertaken** by the investment centre manager.

In contrast, when a manager is judged by ROI, a marginally profitable investment would be less likely to be undertaken because it would reduce the average ROI earned by the centre as a whole, at least in the short term.

4.4 Example: residual income and decision making

In the example in Paragraph 3.3, whereas ROI would have worsened with the new investment opportunity, in the short term, residual income would have increased. Whereas the division's manager might reject the investment if the division's performance were judged on ROI, he or she would undertake the investment if performance were judged on residual income.

Division S

	Without new investment $	Investment $	With new investment $
Profit before notional interest	64,000	10,000	74,000
Notional interest (15% of 340,000)	51,000	9,000*	60,000
	13,000	1,000	14,000

* 15% of $60,000

The investment would add $1,000 each year to residual income, and so would probably be undertaken.

Residual income does not **always** point to the right investment decision, because the true investment yield on an investment is not measured by charging notional interest on accounting capital employed. (In practice, new investment decisions ought to be taken on the basis of a discounted cash flow analysis.) However, residual income is more likely than ROI to improve when managers make correct investment decisions, and so is probably a 'safer' basis than ROI on which to measure performance.

Question

ROI and RI

Brampton evaluates its divisions using Return on Investment (ROI) and Residual Income (RI) measures. In the year to 31 March 20X4 the Pickle division earned profit before interest and tax of $8.64m, paid interest of $1.44m and had net assets of $57.6m at the year end. Brampton uses a cost of capital of 16% to evaluate Pickle's activities.

What are the ROI and RI measures for the Pickle division for the year ended 31 March 20X4?

Answer

ROI = $8.64m/$57.6m × 100% = 15%

RI = $8.64m − ($57.6m × 16%) = $0.576m

5 Economic value added (EVA®)

FAST FORWARD

EVA® (**economic value added**) is a measure of performance similar to residual income, but it attempts to measure economic profit, and to make a charge for the economic value of capital consumed. In practice, it is calculated by making adjustments to accounting profit and accounting asset values. It has been claimed that there is a strong correlation between EVA® and changes in shareholder value (market value added).

Another measure of divisional performance, similar to residual income, is economic value added or EVA®. It was developed by the US management consultancy, Stern Stewart.

Key term

Economic Value Added (EVA®) is a measure of the degree to which a business or business unit has added economic value to the organisation as a whole. It can be defined as

EVA® = Adjusted operating profits after tax − (adjusted invested capital × WACC)

where the adjustments to profits and capital are made to properly reflect the extent to which transactions in the period have helped to build value, without the constraints of accounting standards and principles.

The underlying concept is that the performance of a company as a whole, as well as investment centres within a company, should be measured on the basis of whether the company or investment centre has added to the **economic value** of the business during the period under review.

The measurement of EVA® is conceptually quite straightforward. In order to add to the economic value, an organisation must deliver more net operating profit after tax ('NOPAT') than it costs to have access to the total amount of capital that has been used to generate the profit.

EVA® = NOPAT minus Capital charge

The similarity between EVA® and residual income should be immediately apparent. The key difference between EVA® and residual income is that:

(a)   Residual income is calculated by taking the **accounting profit** for a period, and subtracting a notional interest charge based on the **accounting value of the assets** employed, whereas

(b)   Economic value added is calculated by taking the **economic profit** for a period, and subtracting a capital charge based on the **economic value of the assets** employed.

5.1 Why is economic value added better than accounting profit or residual income?

Stern Stewart have argued that when an organisation adds to its economic value, it should also add to its total market value. EVA® is therefore closely connected to changes in **shareholder value**.

Stern Stewart have reinforced this argument by claiming that between 60% and 85% of the changes affecting the market value of a business are explained by the EVA® for the period.

EVA® is a better measure of divisional and company performance than profits or residual income, because of this close correlation between EVA® and changes in shareholder value. EVA®, it is argued, provides a basis for measuring performance that is much more closely linked than accounting profits to the strategic objectives of a company. It shows whether an organisation has been adding to shareholder value in the period under review, or destroying it.

5.2 Measuring EVA®

The complexities of EVA® lie in the calculation of economic profit and the economic value of assets. The detailed methodology is beyond the scope of the examination syllabus, but it may be helpful to understand it in outline.

The calculation of economic profit and economic value of assets is made by converting accounting profit and accounting asset valuations. Stern Stewart make a large number of adjustments to accounting figures.

(a) **Depreciation of non-current assets** is deducted in arriving at NOPAT. This is because the accounting charge for depreciation is used as a proxy for economic depreciation, which is the fall in the economic value of a non-current asset during the period. Using the accounting charge for depreciation saves the time and expense of revaluing non-current assets to their current economic value each year, in order to calculate the loss in their economic value since the previous year.

(b) Accounting profits are based on the accruals concept of accounting, whereas EVA® is based on **cash flow principles**. Adjustments are made to convert accounting profit based on the accruals concept into cash operating profits.

(c) Where a company has written off **goodwill** in its accounts, the goodwill must be added back to the economic value of its assets. Goodwill, although an intangible item, is a valuable asset that has usually been paid for.

(d) Any spending by the company on **research and development** should not be charged in full against profits in the year it is incurred. Instead, it should be capitalised (ie treated as a non-current asset item) and amortised or depreciated over (normally) five years. The effect of this is that the whole R&D cost is capitalised and therefore added back to profit and then $1/_5$ of the capitalised amount is written off and deducted from profit for 5 years.

(e) All **leases** must also be capitalised and amortised over (normally) five years. The effect of this is the same as for R&D above.

(f) Other adjustments may be necessary, and these will vary according to the industry in which the company or division operates, and the specific circumstances of the case.

5.3 NOPAT

Net operating profit after tax is calculated, broadly speaking, as follows:

	$
Net operating profit before tax for the period, as reported in the accounts	X
Adjustments to convert from accruals-based profit to operating cash flows ((b) above)	X
Add back Any purchased goodwill written off in the accounts ((c) above)	X
Any R & D expenditure (which is capitalised per (d) above)	X
Any lease expenditure charged against profits (which is capitalised per (e) above)	X
Subtract Amortisation of R & D and leases (the amounts capitalised and added back above are amortised over 5 years per (d) and (e) above)	(X)
Taxation on operating profits	(X)
Equals NOPAT	X

5.4 Capital invested

The economic value of assets employed is calculated, broadly speaking, as follows.

	$
Total assets, as reported in the accounts (in the statement of financial position)	X
Subtract Non-interest bearing liabilities, such as trade payables, and taxation payable	(X)
Add The economic value (net book value) of capitalised R & D expenditure	X
The economic value (net book value) of capitalised lease expenditure	X
Cumulative amortised goodwill (per (c) above)	X
Any provision for doubtful debts (since the economic value of receivables is their gross value, before deduction of any provision for doubtful debts)	X
Equals Capital invested	X

Note. The 'economic value (net book value)' of R&D and lease expenditure is the capitalised amount that has been added back in calculating NOPAT less the cumulative amount that has been written off each year. Thus assume $50,000 of R&D was incurred on 1 January 20X7 and had been written off in the financial accounts on 31 December 20X7. If we are calculating economic value two years later at 31 December 20X9, the value will be ($50,000 – (3 × $10,000)) = $20,000 (ie the capitalised amount less three years' amortisation).

5.5 Cost of capital

The cost of capital to apply to the capital invested should be a cost that reflects the weighted average cost of the organisation's shareholder capital and debt capital. For example, suppose that a company is 75% financed by share capital and 25% by debt capital. If the cost of its share capital is 14% and the after-tax cost of its debt capital is 8%, the weighted average cost of capital (WACC) to apply for the calculation of EVA® is (75% of 14%) + (25% of 8%) = 12.5%.

5.6 Calculating EVA® – example

A division has a capital value, measured by EVA® techniques, of $400 million. Net operating profit after tax has been measured as $57 million for the year. The cost of capital for the division is 12%.

EVA® = $57 million - (12% of $400 million) = $9 million.

Question

EVA®

The Greenway Division's financial statements to 31 March 20X4 show a profit before tax of $56.4m. During the year, Greenway had incurred $12.6m costs in developing a new product, which is to be launched in the following year, with an expected market life of three years. These costs had been written off in full against the profits for the year. Taxation for the year is $17.2m. Greenway's statement of financial position shows net assets of $184m, with trade, taxation and other such payables standing at $32.5m, and receivables of $42.5m, after a provision for doubtful debts of $8.5m. Greenways have a loan of $10m upon which they are paying interest at 6.5% pa; the division's risk adjusted cost of capital is 13%.

Compute Greenway Division's EVA® as far as the information given will allow, ignoring the effects of taxation on adjustments made.

Answer

NOPAT = 56.4 + 12.6 – (12.6/3 + 17.2) = $47.6m

Capital invested = $184m + $10m + $(12.6 – 12.6/3)m + $8.5m = $210.9m

(note that you are given *net* assets, thus we just need to add back the loan capital; the other payables are already deducted)

EVA® = $47.6m – 13% × $210.9m = $20.18m

5.7 Uses of EVA®

EVA® can be used:

(a) To set targets for divisional and corporate performance
(b) To measure actual performance
(c) For investment decision-making. EVA® provides a clear benchmark for evaluating the effectiveness of capital investments.

Other 'EVA® projects' might include:

(a) Identifying products and services that create a high level of EVA®
(b) Giving greater emphasis to customer orders for high EVA® products
(c) Reducing excess capital that is not creating sufficient value to justify its cost; for example, reducing plant and machinery, floor space or working capital
(d) Eliminating all activities that are not contributing to the fulfilment of customer orders.

5.8 Implementing EVA® – the problems and solutions

There are four steps to implementing an EVA® system.

The first step is to develop a commitment among the managers to the EVA® process. The managers must understand the theory of EVA® and how it works in practice.

The second step is to identify the centres in the business for which individual EVAs® will be calculated and calculate the cost of capital that is applicable.

The third step is to develop remuneration packages for the employees that are based on the EVA® concept so that managers are rewarded in the same way that the shareholders are rewarded – if the company's share price increases because of the increased EVA® then both managers and shareholders reap the benefit.

The fourth step is to train the whole workforce in the EVA® technique.

The main problem of implementation is not the complexity of the process (because it is relatively straightforward and driven by software programs that assist the decision making process). The main problems are the time it takes to implement through the whole business (which can be reduced by using specialist consultants) and perhaps more seriously, the culture change needed to persuade the workforce to operate in the new way.

The required change in culture can be facilitated by the use of consultants to help explain the systems and motivate the workforce, but management cannot simply offload their responsibility for managing the changes to consultants and look the other way. **Change management** is one of the most important responsibilities of today's executive managers.

Academics have developed models of change to assist managers in managing the process of change and combating the resistance to change exhibited by many employees. For example, Kurt Lewin suggested a three-stage process of change implementation:

(a) **Unfreeze** – create the motivation to change. If there is currently no motivation, it must be induced, for example by educating stakeholders of the benefits of the change.

(b) **Change** – once the resisting forces have been minimised, the change can be implemented, either by a process of rational persuasion or forced by the use of legitimate authority.

(c) **Refreeze** – the new mindset must be crystallised across all participants, who must accept the new practices as routine.

Lewin's three-stage model of change can be used to assist the effective implementation of any change within an organisation; in considering Lewin's model in the possible adoption of the EVA® concept, managers can identify their responsibilities at each stage of the change process, and only then turn to external consultants for additional assistance if they wish.

5.9 EVA®: conclusion

The main benefits claimed for EVA® are:

(a) It is a measure of performance closely linked to changes in shareholder value (market value added) during a period. As such, it is a better measure of performance than accounting profits or accounting return on capital.

(b) It can be applied to the entire operating performance of a business, and at an investment centre level as well as at the company level.

(c) Like accounting return, it can be tracked over clearly-defined time periods.

(d) It is easily understood by non-accountants.

EVA® should not be used in isolation, but should complement other performance measurement techniques.

The examiner has emphasised that whilst candidates will be expected to perform simple calculations relating to performance measurement, such as preparing standard cost variances, basic EVA®, ROI and RI etc, in exam questions it will be typical for more marks to be awarded to the analysis and evaluation that uses these calculations, than for the actual calculations.

A question in the June 2002 exam required calculations of a return on investment and residual income, with a discursive part on the major features of EVA® and its use to improve performance measurement in a given situation.

6 Accounting profit and controllable profit

It was suggested, in the description of EVA® above, that accounting profit has certain weaknesses as a method of measuring performance. Specifically, there is no obvious link between annual profits and increases in shareholder value. It might therefore be unrealistic for an organisation to achieve its strategic objective of increasing shareholder value by setting targets based on accounting profits or return.

The great value of accounting profit, however, is that it is regularly measured by an organisation's accounting system, and performance reports can encourage managers to improve their performance, by cutting costs, improving efficiency, increasing revenues, switching resources from less profitable to more profitable items and controlling investment.

A system of responsibility accounting will not be effective, however, if managers are held accountable and responsible for costs that they cannot control. Performance reporting systems should ideally distinguish between controllable and uncontrollable costs.

Controllable costs are items of expenditure that the manager can affect by decisions of his or her own making. **Uncontrollable costs** are expenses that the manager can do nothing about, possibly because another manager has control over them.

The significance of the distinction between controllable and uncontrollable costs is that:

(a)   Divisional managers are often rewarded on the basis of the performance of their division.
(b)   They will therefore normally be motivated to do what they can to improve performance.
(c)   However, if they are unable to improve performance for reasons outside their control, they are likely to feel hard done by.
(d)   Giving recognition to controllable costs, profits and returns should provide a better incentive to divisional managers, as well as providing a more realistic assessment of performance.

7 Measuring divisional performance by cash flows

Divisional performance can also be measured in terms of operating cash flows, or possibly in terms of operating cash flows minus net capital expenditure. An alternative measure based on cash flows is **cash flow return on investment** (CFROI), which should exceed the company's cost of capital.

Accounting profits earned by a division are not the same as the cash earned by the division from its operations. This is largely because:

(a)   Accounting profits are calculated using the matching concept or accruals concept of accounting
(b)   Some accounting costs, notably non-current asset depreciation, do not affect cash flows
(c)   Some cash flows for a division, such as capital expenditures, are not expenses in the income statement

It has been argued that the performance of a division would be better measured on the basis of cash flows, rather than accounting profit.

7.1 Cash flow return on investment (CFROI)

Cash flow return on investment (CFROI) is a measure of performance devised by the Boston Consulting Group. It is a measure of the sustainable cash flow that a company (or a division) generates from its operations, expressed as a percentage of the cash invested in the assets of the business or division.

Cash flows are operational cash flows, before deducting cash spent on capital expenditures. CFROI should therefore be expected to exceed the company's cost of capital.

Key learning points

- Performance measurement may be based on a **divisional reporting system**, with major divisions regarded as autonomous investment centres. (Within investment centres, there may be a hierarchy of profit centres and cost centres).

- **Return on investment** is the main measure of divisional performance, but it has several limitations. The main problem lies in the fact that ROI might be used as a guide for investment decisions, whereas it is inappropriate to use accounting profits to make investment decisions. There is no generally agreed method of calculating ROI.

- **Residual income** is an alternative measure of divisional performance. Divisions are charged a notional interest cost. Residual income is accounting profit minus the notional interest charge.

- **EVA**® (**economic value added**) is a measure of performance similar to residual income, but it attempts to measure economic profit, and to make a charge for the economic value of capital consumed. In practice, it is calculated by making adjustments to accounting profit and accounting asset values. It has been claimed that there is a strong correlation between EVA® and changes in shareholder value (market value added).

- Divisional performance can also be measured in terms of operating cash flows, or possibly in terms of operating cash flows minus net capital expenditure. An alternative measure based on cash flows is **cash flow return on investment** (CFROI), which should exceed the company's cost of capital.

Quick quiz

1   What are the essential conditions for a performance measurement system based on investment centres?
2   What is the main argument in favour of using non-current assets at cost for calculating ROI?
3   What is the main argument in favour of using non-current assets at net book value for calculating ROI?
4   How is residual income calculated?
5   What is economic value added, and how is it calculated?

1   The divisional manager should have control over costs, revenues and investments of the division. Performance reports should ideally distinguish between controllable and uncontrollable costs.

2   When non-current assets are valued at cost, the ROI is unaffected by the ageing of non-current assets. In contrast, when non-current assets are valued at net book value, ROI will increase as the asset gets older (assuming constant annual profits).

3   Net book value recognises that a non-current asset loses value as it gets older. It is also likely to lose profit-generating capability with age.

4   Accounting profit minus a notional interest charge. The notional interest charge is calculated by applying a cost of capital to the accounting value of the division's net assets.

5   It is a measure of the amount by which an organisation has added to (or lost) economic value during a period. It is calculated as economic profit (net operating profit after tax) minus a charge for capital to reflect the consumption of economic value of the assets during the period. The charge for capital is calculated by applying the cost of capital to an estimate of the economic value of the organisation's or division's net assets.

Performance management

14

Performance in operations and production management

Introduction

This chapter looks at various modern methods of operations management, the process of managing the operations within a manufacturing organisation. Traditional budgeting and standard costing systems are giving way to newer, more relevant systems made possible by powerful computing resources.

Learning objective

On completion of this chapter you will be able to:

Syllabus reference

- understand the key elements of operations management, and some of the   18
  production issues to which performance management methods might be
  applied

1 Key elements of operations management

FAST FORWARD

Operations management is the management of procurement, production, logistics, quality and related aspects of business operations.

Operations management is a general term for managing the operations within a manufacturing organisation. Some operations management concepts can be applied to non-manufacturing organisations. The focus of operations management is on how to achieve standards of performance that will enable the company to succeed in highly-competitive global markets.

The main elements of operations management should be familiar to you.

(a) **Procurement**. An organisation buys many products and services from other suppliers. Procurement involves processing procurement orders, placing orders with suppliers and (if necessary) chasing up late deliveries. There have been significant developments in recent years in procurement over the internet ('e-commerce' or 'e-procurement'), with large reductions in the amount of paperwork needed to place orders.

(b) **Production**. Production management is concerned with how items are produced. An objective of production management should be to produce items more quickly and more cheaply, and to a higher quality. Flexibility in production methods, for example customising products to customer specifications, might also be an important objective.

(c) **Logistics**. Logistics is concerned with transportation and warehousing. Items purchased from suppliers have to be delivered to the buyer's premises and stored. Finished output might have to be held in a warehouse until it is delivered to a customer, and then delivered to the customer. The aim of logistics management should be to achieve a cost-efficient and reliable way of transporting and storing purchased items and finished goods.

(d) **Quality management**. Quality is not just a production issue. Quality issues arise in procurement and logistics operations. The aim of quality management is to improve the quality of operations and production, both as a way of increasing customer satisfaction and reducing costs.

2 Operational structures and process-based structures

Traditionally, operations within a manufacturing organisation have been organised on a functional basis, with a separate department for each major operational function. For example, there might be separate departments in a factory for making metal products, for machining, grinding, assembly and finishing. In an old-fashioned factory for making towels, there might have been departments for carding, dyeing, spinning, weaving and warehousing. Within an operational or functional structure, every product manufactured by the company goes through every department, and emerges as a finished product at the end of all the processes.

There are different types of manufacturing process.

(a) **Project processes** are production processes that usually deal with discrete, customised orders. The time to complete individual projects can be long, and the work is characterised by low volume and high variety. Examples of project processes include construction projects and the making of a film.

(b)   **Jobbing processes** also deal with low-volume and high-variety work. Jobs are essentially small projects. However, whereas in project processes, each individual project has its own dedicated resources, for example its own labour force and its own equipment, in jobbing processes, different jobs share the same resources.

(c)   A **batch process** is one in which products are made several at a time, in discrete batches, but are not made continuously.

(d)   **Mass processes** produce goods of a fairly standard type in large volumes. Some variations in product design are possible: for example, car production is a mass process, but it allows for cars to have different colours of paint and other differing features.

(e)   **Continuous processes** are an extreme form of mass production, in which the volumes of output are larger than in mass production, and product variety is less. Typically, output is in an endless, continuing flow, and the process is highly capital-intensive. Examples of continuous processes might be chemicals production and baked beans manufacture.

The most efficient methods of managing production are likely to vary according to the process type.

3 World-class manufacturing and the re-design of operations

FAST FORWARD

To be a **world class manufacturing business**, many companies have re-organised their operations, perhaps based on focus factories, flow production, work flow production or customising orders.

Operations management strategy for a company might be to become a **'lean' manufacturer**. Lean manufacturing is based on flow production, continuous improvement, the elimination of waste, inventory reduction, work cells etc.

Key term

> **World class manufacturing** is a position of international manufacturing excellence, achieved by developing a culture based on factors such as continuous improvement, problem prevention, zero defect tolerance, customer-driven JIT-based production and total quality management.
>
> *(CIMA Official Terminology 2000).*

The general term 'world class manufacturing' refers to manufacturing systems that achieve a high level of performance, allowing the manufacturer to compete on a global stage against rival producers. It is also associated with changes to manufacturing methods, away from traditional mass production and batch production systems.

There are a number of production concepts, many of them closely related and compatible with each other. Some are described below.

3.1 Focus factories

Key term

> A **focus factory** can be defined as a collection, within a large manufacturing plant, of a group of people and machines dedicated to the production and assembly of a specific product, often for a specific customer. Each focus factory has its own management team, which is responsible for output and performance.

In 'traditional' manufacturing systems, all the items produced within a single plant go through the same production departments. Each department deals with one stage in the overall production process (for example, machining, assembly, finishing). Production is often carried out in large batches, so that at each stage in the overall process, there are batches of part-finished items waiting to go into the next process. In practice, production delays occur regularly, and as a result, the overall production process is often slow, and the quantities – and cost – of part-finished work in process scattered around the factory floor is very high. Since items are produced in batches, some items are made in expectation of demand that does not yet exist, so that finished goods go into storage in a warehouse until a customer order materialises.

With focus factories, the manufacturing plant is divided into smaller units (known as focus factories) and each unit concentrates on the manufacture of a single product or product line, replacing the large all-purpose production departments. The entire production of an item goes through its focus factory, with the work carried out by 'work cells'.

Experience has shown that a focus factory based arrangement can lead to very large reductions in work-in-process, thereby saving inventory holding costs, including the interest cost of the working capital investment in the WIP.

3.2 Flow production

With traditional manufacturing, the emphasis is on making efficient use of plant and machinery. With flow production, the emphasis is on the responsiveness of the manufacturer to customer orders.

Flow manufacturing is a production methodology aimed at achieving fast response to customer demand, by pulling items from suppliers and taking it through a synchronised manufacturing process to make the item the customer has asked for. The terms *one-piece flow* and *continuous flow manufacturing* are also used.

One-piece flow means a flow of work one unit at a time through production, at a pace determined by the needs of customers and without the need for building up inventories of part-finished items at each stage in the production process.

Continuous flow manufacturing is similar to flow manufacturing, but refers to a manufacturing philosophy that is demand led such that its proponents talk of the manufacturing process being part of the 'demand chain' rather than the 'supply chain'.

The entire manufacturing operation is reconfigured and based on customer requirements. Rather than manufacturing quantities of products that are then pushed into the marketplace, the manufacturing process is pulled by the customers' requirements. Computer systems are in place to receive customer needs and organise the supply from external suppliers of the parts needed and also organise the company's manufacturing cells to produce the required parts and final goods. The system is a mixture of JIT and Kanban systems, with zero inventories and the customer as the ultimate 'pull' that initiates the production process.

3.3 Work cell production

Work cell production has similarities to focus factories. With this type of production, the factory is divided into a number of different work cells or units.

Key term

> A **work cell** is a group of equipment or workstations within the same small area of the factory floor, arranged in processing sequence. Each work cell is capable of making one or more products with similar characteristics, and is designed to support a smooth flow of production with minimal transportation of part-finished items and minimal delays. The team in the work cell has the entire production process under its control.

By putting into a work cell the employees and equipment needed to make similar products, it is possible to obtain some of the benefits of flow manufacturing (one-piece flow) – faster production, simpler production scheduling, reduced set-up times and lower inventories of work in progress.

Within a work cell, the machines and other equipment are operated by multi-skilled workers. Each person can work on any of the machines, and does not specialise in just one type. This allows for much greater flexibility than in traditional manufacturing systems, where each type of machine has its own specialist handlers.

Work cell production also makes possible high variety production, because it is a flexible and adaptable system of working. Members of the team are all in the same small area of the factory floor, and so can communicate easily. This allows them to adapt readily to variations in customer specifications, so that the production system is capable of *customising orders.* An ability to customise orders has become an essential factor for success in many product markets.

3.4 Flexible manufacturing systems

The reorganisation of manufacturing processes into smaller units – focus factories and work cells – can be accompanied by a high degree of computerisation. A flexible manufacturing system (FMS) is a cluster of machine tools, a robot to change the work pieces and a system of conveyor belts that shuttle them from one tool to another, all controlled by computers.

The system gets its name from its flexibility in being able to be programmed to produce a number of different ranges of machined parts, and to switch from one to another quickly and economically.

In addition to this flexibility, the other main benefits to be derived from such a system include:

(a) The ability to continuously repeat the same operations to the same accuracy and quality

(b) Reduced lead times from design to marketing

(c) Reduced labour costs

(d) Production stability even in the case of disruption, eg due to machine breakdown, as the unit can be reprogrammed to adapt to changes in work scheduling

3.5 Empowered work teams

The changes in operational process organisation and technology that modern manufacturing systems bring, along with a changing workforce profile, have led many businesses to consider moving from a traditional hierarchical management structure to a team-based organisation. Empowered work teams are groups of employees who work together to achieve a particular task or set of tasks, who will often interact with other groups to achieve the overall business plan.

Being competitive in a marketplace that values quality, flexibility and response times requires manufacturers to hire or develop employees who can demonstrate these same characteristics. It's no longer possible to take people off the street, train them in half an hour and expect them to make a profit, as it was in the days of mass production. Employees must be able to measure and manage the quality of their jobs to very high standards, be able to switch flexibly from one task or product to another, and to assist in product and process innovations that can keep their business at the cutting edge. And in addition to these high skill levels, the employee must also be able to interact and share information in a time efficient manner, as they will be operating in one area of the business that will be interdependent with others. Such communication is facilitated by the use of specialised work teams.

An additional motivator towards the team-based approach is the changing nature of today's workforce. Over the last forty years or so, the proportions of women and older people in the workplace have increased, bringing increased demand for more flexible working structures – flexi-time, job shares, career breaks etc. This requires employees to be able to support and fill in for each other, a need best fulfilled by the use of work teams. The workforce is also growing more slowly than in the past, which makes hiring new staff more difficult. New skills therefore need to be acquired by re-training existing employees, with cross training to provide flexibility. This is also best accomplished within a team environment.

The particular structure and characteristics of the teams will be dictated by the particular ends they are designed to achieve, with the underlying principle that a team should be organised in a way that will maximise its chances of goal attainment.

For example, **task forces** are teams that are organised as cross-functional units. They may come together around a single project, issue or problem, and disappear once the project has ended. **Work teams** are teams whose members rely on each other every day to meet production schedules.

Whatever their format, teams need some kind of organisation – a charter – to determine their roles and limits of responsibilities.

For example, it might be considered business sense to delegate the daily production scheduling responsibility to a work team to free up a manager for more important tasks.

When setting the charter, consideration must be made of the extent to which team members can, for example, rotate jobs, manage suppliers, redesign workflow, monitor quality, deal with substandard performance, remove team members etc.

Briefly discuss any problems you think may arise when empowered work teams are first introduced to a previously hierarchical management structure.

Answer

The key advantage offered by work teams is increased flexibility from the ability of each team's members to do a wide range of tasks and to swap tasks between each other as needed. This will require the ability and willingness on the part of the employees to undertake extensive retraining and be prepared to move from one task to another at short notice. Not all employees will be receptive to this, others will simply not be able to cope with the demands, and there is bound to be a significant degree of staff turnover in the early days.

In addition, front-line managers will find their traditional role subsumed within the work team, which will take over many of his/her previous responsibilities and decisions. This is likely to lead to redundancies for some and a radical change of role for others. Care must be taken to address this issue, with a clear definition of the new role of such managers in managing teams rather than individuals, or valuable managerial experience may be lost.

3.6 Lean manufacturing

The concept of lean manufacturing began in Japan after 1945, with a number of companies (notably Toyota) and subsequently found its way into the US. 'Lean' means using less human effort, a smaller investment of capital, less floor space, fewer materials and less time in production. Lean manufacturing also has a customer-oriented focus, concentrating on the production and delivery of items that a customer has asked for, rather than on large-scale batch production of standard items.

It applies a systematic approach to identifying and eliminating waste in production. Waste is any activity that does not add value for the customer, and costs more to perform than the value of any benefit it provides. Two aspects of lean manufacturing are:

(a) Achieving a flow of production in response to the demands of customers, and

(b) An embedded process of continuous improvement in manufacturing (known in Japanese as '**kaizen**'), in search of 'perfection'.

At the centre of lean production is an **attack on waste**. Several categories of waste can be identified.

(a) Over-production creates waste. Over-production means making more of an item than there is demand from customers. If the demand never materialises, the items will have to be discarded, or possibly sold at a heavily-discounted price. Even when the items are eventually sold, there will be a period of time during which they are held as inventory, for which there is a holding cost. Holding inventories of any kind is unnecessarily wasteful because it has a cost but adds no value.

(b) Part-finished work-in-process is also wasteful. This is work going through the production process, that has completed one stage of the overall process and is waiting to be taken through the next stage. Work-in-process tends to build up when production processes have a long lead time, so there can be a long delay for production items between completion of one process and starting the next.

(c) The transportation of material items does not add value. Any form of motion is waste, whether it involves the movement of people, materials, part-finished items or finished goods. The reduction of movement is one of the concepts underlying work cell production.

(d) There is often waste in the production process itself. Any activities within processing that do not add value should be eliminated.

(e) Time spent by workers waiting for a machine to complete processing is wasteful. The aim should be to maximise the use of the worker, not the machine.

(f)   The manufacture of defective items is wasteful. Defective items must be either scrapped or re-worked if they are identified before they leave the factory. After defective items have been delivered to a customer, there are costs of handling the complaint and making good to the customer. Poor-quality output also risks the loss of customer goodwill.

There follows a list of concepts commonly associated with lean production

- The elimination of waste
- Lower inventory levels
- Reducing defective output
- Continuous improvement (kaizen)
- A stop-the-line quality system, whereby any defect in production brings the entire production line to a halt
- Achieving a level production of items, rather than manufacturing in occasional large batches
- Continuous flow
- Point of use storage of materials and components, to reduce materials flow, rather than having a centralised storage area
- Reduction in production lead times and in set-up times
- Improvement in equipment reliability
- Teamwork within work cells

3.7 Continuous improvement – kaizen

Key term

> **Kaizen** is a Japanese term for the philosophy of continuous improvement in performance in all areas of a business's operations.

Continuous improvement, or **kaizen**, calls for ever-continuing efforts of finding ways to make small improvements in production, and is an integral part of the just-in-time philosophy. The concepts underlying continuous improvement are:

(a)   The organisation should always seek perfection. Since perfection is never achieved, there must always be scope for improving on the current methods.

(b)   The search for perfection should be ingrained into the culture and mindset of all employees. Improvements should be sought all the time.

(c)   Individual improvements identified by the work force will be small rather than far-reaching.

The philosophy of continual small-scale improvements is in stark contrast to business process re-engineering, which seeks to make radical one-off changes to improve an organisation's operations and processes.

4 Materials requirements planning (MRP I)

FAST FORWARD

> There are various systems for improving operations management. **Materials requirements planning (MRP I)** is a computerised system for planning and ordering materials, based on a master production schedule, bills of materials and inventory level records.

The concepts described above relate to manufacturing methods and the re-design of manufacturing systems. Another aspect of manufacturing is planning. Within traditional manufacturing systems, the planning process has been improved enormously by computerisation.

Key term

> **Materials requirements planning, or MRP I**, is a computerised system for planning the requirements for raw materials and components, sub-assemblies and finished items.

4.1 Example

The potential benefits of MRP I can perhaps be understood with a simple example. Suppose that a company manufactures product X, which consists of two units of sub-assembly A and one unit of sub-assembly B. The company makes the sub-assemblies. One unit of sub-assembly A needs six units of component C and three units of component D, and one unit of sub-assembly B needs four units of component D and five units of component E.

In a traditional materials procurement system, new orders are generated for finished goods, sub-assemblies, components or raw materials when the inventory level for the item falls to a re-order level. A new batch is then ordered. In the example above, the production of a new batch of product X could result in new production orders for sub-assembly A or B, and these in turn could generate new orders for any of the components, depending on inventory levels.

Where a manufacturing process uses many sub-assemblies, components and raw materials items, it could be difficult to keep check on materials requirements and the re-ordering process, and there would be a risk of stock-outs of key items, or possibly overstocking of key items to reduce the likelihood of stock-outs.

A further complication is that each sub-assembly, component or raw material item has its own production lead time (if manufactured in-house) or supply lead time (if purchased externally). The task in planning materials requirements is therefore not just a matter of what to order and in what quantities, but when to order to ensure that deliveries occur in time.

MRP I dates back to the 1960s, and the introduction of computers into business. It is a computerised information, planning and control system. It can be used in a traditional manufacturing environment as well as with advanced manufacturing technologies, but is most commonly used with batch manufacturing. The main advantage of MRP I is that it can process a large amount of data, and so simplifies what would otherwise be a complex and time-consuming operation.

The elements of an MRP I system are as follows.

(a)   The system has access to **inventory records**, for all items of inventory (finished goods, sub-assemblies, components, raw materials) and so is aware of current inventory levels. For each inventory item, there are also records for the production lead time or purchase lead time.

(b)   The system has access to a **bill of materials** for each item of production. A bill of materials is simply a detailed list of the sub-assemblies, components and raw materials, including the quantities of each, needed to make the item.

(c)   The system also has access to a **master production schedule**. This is a production schedule, detailing the quantities of each item that need to be produced, and the time by which completed output is required. The master production schedule is produced from firm sales orders and current estimates of future sales demand within the planning period.

(d)   Taking the production schedule, the bills of materials and inventory records, the system computes what quantities of materials are required, and by when. In the case of items purchased externally, the system will report when the purchase orders must be placed. Where items are produced in-house, the system will provide a schedule for the commencement of production for each item.

(e)   The system can produce works orders and materials plans and automatic purchase orders for use by the purchasing department.

(f)   As information about sales orders changes, the production schedule can be altered quickly, and a new materials procurement programme prepared automatically.

The aims of MRP I are to:

(a)   Minimise inventory levels by avoiding over-stocking and earlier-than-necessary materials requisitions

(b)   Avoid the costs of rush orders

(c)   Reduce the risk of stock-outs and resulting disruptions to the flow of production.

5 Manufacturing resource planning (MRP II)

FAST FORWARD

Manufacturing resource planning (MRP II) is an extension of MRP I, that integrates the manufacturing, materials requirements planning, engineering, finance and possibly marketing databases into a single planning control system database.

Manufacturing Resource Planning, known as MRP II, evolved out of MRP I in the 1970s.

Key term

MRP II is a computerised system for the planning of all resources in a manufacturing company, and materials requirements planning is a core element in MRP II.

The difference between MRP II and MRP I is principally that MRP II extends the computer system beyond manufacturing operations, and provides a common database for all functions in the organisation, such as sales and marketing, finance and distribution and transportation (logistics). It attempts to integrate materials requirement planning, factory capacity planning, shop floor control, production design, management accounting, purchasing and even marketing into a single complete (and computerised) control system.

Without an MRP II system, each separate function within the company would need its own stand-alone database, even though some of the information they use is common to each.

5.1 Example

The production engineering department needs information about bills of materials. If it makes a change to a product specification, the bill of materials for the product must be changed. In the absence of an MRP II system, the same changes would have to be made to the databases of both the production department and the production engineering department. There would also be the risk of one database being updated but not the other.

The finance department uses information from a production budget and bills of materials to produce budgets and reports on product costs and product profitability. When a bill of materials is changed, the accounts department needs to know so that product costs can be re-calculated. When the production schedule is amended, the accounts department needs to know in order to prepare revised production cost estimates. Without an MRP II system, any changes to the production schedule would have to be fed into the production database and the accounting database separately.

MRP II therefore offers the advantages of a common database – easier updating and a common set of data for all departments to use.

MRP I and MRP II systems have their critics, particularly from advocates of just-in-time production and lean production. A problem with the MRP approach is that it creates a model of what currently happens in the manufacturing plant, not what perhaps ought to happen. It builds in bad habits and waste. It allows for long lead times, bottlenecks in production, large batch sizes. Management will not be motivated to achieve improvements and eliminate waste when poor productivity and poor quality are built into the MRP II planning system.

Question   Modern manufacturing system

The major requirements of a modern manufacturing system are the flexibility to meet customer requirements, the cost-effective production of small batches of customised products and the maintenance of a high standard of quality with an underlying principle of continuous improvement. To what extent does this impact upon the traditional cost control techniques such as standard costing and variance analysis?

Cost behaviour patterns are different in a modern manufacturing environment; they no longer vary in response to cost units, or labour hours, but more to process activities. Traditional standard costing cannot be used in this context, as it tends to focus on a standard cost per unit. There are no longer large volumes of standardised units being produced, but small batches of customised products.

The traditional emphasis on labour measures, such as efficiency, becomes redundant for the highly mechanised and computerised manufacturer; indeed, an emphasis on efficiency can be detrimental, as it tends to lead to a desire for continuous production. No consideration is given to whether the inventories produced can actually be sold and, if not, what their holding/scrap costs might be. Similarly, a common way to improve an adverse price variance is to buy in bulk to take advantage of discounts; again, this ignores the additional inventory holding costs that will be incurred.

Traditional variance analysis, with its total concentration on cost, does not allow for quality issues, where costs incurred now (eg on preventative maintenance) may give improved long-term results in terms of minimisation of breakdowns, defective production etc.

As a result of these drawbacks of the traditional techniques of cost control, alternative models have been developed, such as activity based budgeting (ABB) and target costing.

6 Optimised production technology (OPT)

> An **optimised production technology (OPT)** system is another type of system for planning manufacturing and materials resource requirements. Whereas MRP plans requirements to a given production schedule, OPT plans production schedules to known capacity constraints in the production process. The OPT approach is based on the theory of constraints.

OPT is an alternative computer system to MRP II. Like MRP II, it can be used to plan manufacturing and materials requisition requirements. Unlike MRP II, however, it plans production schedules to known capacity constraints within the production process.

Key term

> **Optimised production technology (OPT)** has making money as its primary goal, progress towards which can be measured by three criteria: production rate (throughput), inventory and operating expenses. The aim of OPT is to maximise throughput whilst minimising inventory levels and operating expenses.

6.1 How OPT works

Essentially, an OPT system simulates the factory or workshop and its current workload.

A production process consists of a sequence of tasks, each carried out with a different group of workers and on a different group of machines. There are resources for each task (for example, a given number of workers or machines) and the volume of output achievable will be restricted by the quantity of those resources available. There will be one point in the process where output capacity is lower than at any other point in the process. In other words, there must always be a **bottleneck**. An OPT system identifies the bottleneck (or bottlenecks) in production. This could be a particular machine or group of machines, or available skilled labour time.

When a bottleneck has been identified, management can look for ways of overcoming it and reducing the limitation on output and optimising work flow. When one bottleneck has been alleviated, another stage in the production process will become the new bottleneck, and management can switch its attention to the new restriction on output. By focusing on the bottleneck, management should optimise production throughput.

Once a plan has been prepared for maximising work flow through the bottleneck, the remainder of the production facility should be organised for supplying parts to the bottleneck or for dealing with the production processes after the bottleneck point. The manufacturer might try to ensure that there is always some inventory (work in progress) waiting to go through the bottleneck operation, so that this operation is never brought to a halt by a stock-out. Management should also avoid any unnecessary build up of part-finished work in other parts of the manufacturing operation, which cannot be completed because of the bottleneck. A benefit of OPT, in addition to optimising throughput, should also be to reduce inventory levels in other parts of the operation, away from the bottleneck.

6.2 Rationale for OPT

Although OPT is a computer system, it had its origins in a 1992 love story thriller book, *The Goal*. This book was co-written by Eli Goldratt, who became a management consultant. The ideas of Goldratt led to the Theory of Constraints, which states that any system consists of multiple steps, where the output of one step depends on the output of one or more previous steps. The output of these previous steps will be limited (constrained) by the least productive of those steps.

The aim of a company should be to maximise profits. Higher profits can be achieved to some extent by reducing costs and reducing inventory levels. Goldratt suggested, however, that the greatest opportunities for improving profits will come from optimising the flow through the system. Optimum throughput is achieved by focusing on existing constraints, and:

(a)   Identifying what they are

(b)   Deciding how best to optimise the work flow, given the existing constraint

(c)   Seeking ways to overcome the constraint, for example by working overtime on the constraining operation, or buying more machines or hiring more labour.

Once one constraint has been 'elevated' (i.e. overcome, so that it is no longer a constraint) the next task is to identify the new constraint in the system and seek ways to overcome that.

Exam focus point

MRP I, MRP II and OPT were all tested in the same question in the June 2004 exam.

7 Enterprise resource planning (ERP) systems

FAST FORWARD

Enterprise Resource Planning (ERP) systems are software systems designed to support and automate the business processes such as manufacturing, distribution, personnel, project management, payroll and finances. They are accounting-oriented information systems for identifying and planning the enterprise-wide resources needed to **take**, **make**, **distribute**, and **account** for customer orders.

Enterprise Resource Planning (ERP) systems were introduced in Chapter 1. They were originally extensions of MRP II systems, but their scope has since been broadened.

An ERP system can be defined in its widest sense as any software system designed to support and automate the business processes of medium and large businesses. This may include manufacturing, distribution, personnel, project management, payroll and finances.

ERP systems are accounting-oriented information systems for identifying and planning the enterprise-wide resources needed to **take**, **make**, **distribute** and **account** for customer orders. For example, they help track the flow of raw materials into an organisation, the integration of those components into final products, the cost and processes associated with running the business, and the delivery of the products to the customer.

The benefits to be derived from this detailed and accurate tracking of such operational data include:

• Enabling informed business process decisions to reduce costs
• Speeding product delivery times through shortened cycle times
• Increasing customer satisfaction
• Increasing shareholder value

Twenty years ago these automated systems were custom projects which were only attempted at significant cost by large organisations. There are now a number of independent software vendors who have developed common underlying systems that can be adapted to each business's needs, enabling a larger number of organisations to automate ERP functions.

The central feature of any ERP system is a large and powerful database, that incorporates all the information systems necessary to plan and track resource utilisation throughout the business. ERP systems employ highly developed technology in both their software and hardware to achieve the aims of speedy and accurate processing of data to provide relevant up to date information for management control.

For example, one outcome of the ERP development has been the increased availability of up to date and accurate information to employees, management and customers wherever and whenever needed, by the use of hand held and pocket PCs. These bypass the traditional paper-based systems by the use of computerised forms on mobile PCs, allowing data to be entered directly into the system at its point of origin, resulting in faster and higher quality data entry (lines cannot be left blank, data can be pre-checked for validity etc).

Microsoft used such devices to track inventory of the company's products on store shelves, and saw a 50% reduction in the time it took to collect the data when paper forms were converted to electronic forms.

8 Conclusion

This chapter has introduced elements of operations management, and explained the objective of many manufacturing organisations to be 'world class' manufacturers. In the next chapter, a variety of different techniques and approaches to improving performance will be considered.

Key learning points

- **Operations management** is the management of procurement, production, logistics, quality and related aspects of business operations.

- To be a **world class manufacturing business**, many companies have re-organised their operations, perhaps based on focus factories, flow production, work flow production or customising orders.

- Operations management strategy for a company might be to become a '**lean' manufacturer**. Lean manufacturing is based on flow production, continuous improvement, the elimination of waste, inventory reduction, work cells etc.

- There are various systems for improving operations management. **Materials requirements planning (MRP I)** is a computerised system for planning and ordering materials, based on a master production schedule, bills of materials and inventory level records.

- **Manufacturing resource planning (MRP II)** is an extension of MRP I, that integrates the manufacturing, materials requirements planning, engineering, finance and possibly marketing databases into a single planning control system database.

- An **optimised production technology (OPT)** system is another type of system for planning manufacturing and materials resource requirements. Whereas MRP plans requirements to a given production schedule, OPT plans production schedules to known capacity constraints in the production process. The OPT approach is based on the theory of constraints.

- **Enterprise Resource Planning (ERP)** systems are software systems designed to support and automate the business processes such as manufacturing, distribution, personnel, project management, payroll and finances. They are accounting-oriented information systems for identifying and planning the enterprise-wide resources needed to **take**, **make**, **distribute**, and **account** for customer orders.

Quick quiz

1   What is logistics management for a chain of supermarkets?
2   What is a focus factory?
3   What is the connection between flow production and work cell layout?
4   List five concepts commonly associated with lean manufacturing.
5   What does Kaizen mean?
6   What is a bill of materials, and how are bills of materials used in an MRP I system?
7   How is optimum manufacturing throughput achieved with OPT?

Answers to quick quiz

1   Logistics in a supermarket chain is concerned with obtaining products for re-sale from the company's many different suppliers and delivering them on time and in good condition to each supermarket in the chain. The goods might be held in warehouses or at distribution points on their way to the supermarkets. With internet shopping, there is also the process of delivering goods purchased by internet buyers to their homes. Logistics management is the management of these operations.

2   A site or work cell dedicated to the production and assembly of a specific product.

3   Flow production is concerned with rapid response to customer orders without the need for holding finished inventory. Work cell organisation often facilitates the fast production of items in response to customer orders, and flow production is often based on work cell organisation.

4   Elimination of waste, low inventory levels, reduction in defective output, continuous improvement, level production flow, stop-the-line quality system, continuous production flow, point of use storage of materials, reducing production lead times and set-up times, improvement in equipment reliability, work cell organisation of production.

5   Continuous improvement in small steps.

6   A bill of materials is a detailed list of material items (components etc) required for the manufacture of a particular item. Bills of materials are used, together with a master production schedule, to plan the materials requirements for making all the items in the schedule, and initiating new purchase orders where necessary.

7   By focusing on production constraints. Identify the main constraint, plan how to optimise production given the constraint and seek ways of overcoming the constraint.

Improving performance

15

Introduction

Standing still is not an option for today's business in an ever more competitive and global market place. Managers must continually seek new and better ways of doing things. This chapter looks at several of the modern ideas by which business performance can be improved.

Learning objectives

On completion of this chapter you will be able to:

Syllabus reference

- explain management techniques for improving purchasing and process management, such as supply chain management, e-procurement, just-in-time purchasing and production, target costing and kaizen costing, outsourcing and joint ventures and partnerships   19, 20, 21, 22

- explain the aims of activity-based management and business process re-engineering   23, 24

- understand techniques for continuous improvement, including total quality management   22

- define value for money, and explain how VFM is achieved   26

1 Supply chain management

FAST FORWARD

> An organisation should try to achieve **continuous improvements**, particularly by reducing costs and improving quality.
>
> Improvements can be achieved in purchasing and process management through improvements in the supply chain, from suppliers through to the end customer. **Supply chain management** calls for close co-operation with key suppliers.

1.1 The supply chain

A **supply chain** is the network of suppliers, manufacturers and distributors that is involved in the process of moving goods for a customer order from the raw materials stage through the production and distribution stages to the customer. Every firm operates somewhere within a supply chain.

Key term

> A **supply chain** is a network of facilities and distribution options that performs the functions of procurement of materials, transformation of these materials into intermediate and finished products and the distribution of these finished products to customers. (Ganeshan and Harrison, *Supply Chain Management*).

Within a supply chain, many processes might take place between the origination of raw materials to the eventual delivery of the finished product or service to the end customer. For each firm inside a supply chain, some of the processes are carried out by the firm itself, and others are carried out by suppliers or by other firms further down the supply chain.

1.2 Example

For example, a company manufacturing motor vehicles might have a plant where the vehicles are assembled and finished. It might manufacture some parts itself and produce the car body work, but most sub-assemblies and the tyres will be purchased from outside suppliers. The suppliers of sub-assemblies might make some components themselves, but will also purchase many of their components from other suppliers. The manufacturer, suppliers and sub-suppliers might all purchase raw materials, such as steel, from other suppliers. The manufacturer will also purchase capital equipment from equipment suppliers, who are another part of the supply chain. The finished cars will not be sold directly to the end customer, but to distributors, and the distributors will sell to the end customer.

1.3 The concept of supply chain management

A commonly-held view by the management of a company is that to improve profitability, it is necessary to get the lowest prices from suppliers, and obtain the best prices from the customer next in line down the supply chain. If there is a given amount of profitability in a particular market for a finished product, this profit will be shared out between all the firms involved in the supply chain. In this sense, suppliers and their customers compete with each other for a bigger share of the available profit. This 'traditional' attitude is evident in negotiations between a firm and its suppliers, and efforts by the firm to get the best terms possible and the lowest prices in their purchasing negotiations.

This view of the supply chain is challenged by the concept of **supply chain management**. Supply chain management looks at the supply chain as a whole, and starts with the view that all firms in the supply chain collaborate to produce something of value for the end customer. By adding value within the supply chain, customer satisfaction will be improved and customers will pay more for what they buy. Firms can also benefit collectively by reducing waste and inefficiency. A lot of wasteful activity (activity that does not add any value to the final product) occurs at the interface between firms within the supply chain. For example, a supplier might spend money on checking outwards supplies for quality, and the same goods will be checked by the firm buying them when they are delivered. Inspection costs could be reduced by closer collaboration between the firms, both to improve quality and to reduce inspection activities.

By looking at the supply chain as a collaborative effort, managers can look for ways of enhancing the profitability of the supply chain as a whole, so that everyone, including the end customer, benefits.

The concept of supply chain management can be stated as follows.

Key term

> **Supply chain management** views all the buyers and sellers in this chain as part of a continuum, and the aim should be to look at the supply chain as a whole and seek to optimise the functioning of the entire chain. In other words, a company should look beyond its immediate suppliers and its immediate customers to add value, for example by improving efficiency and eliminating waste.

Supply chain management is also referred to as '**pipeline management**' and '**value stream management**'. The overall supply chain can be thought of as a sequence of operations, each of which should add value. An activity has **value** if it gives the customer something that the customer considers worth having (i.e. values), but an activity only **adds** value if the amount of value added exceeds the cost of creating it. Value is therefore added by making something worth more (in terms of the price the customer will pay, or the quality the customer perceives) or by reducing the cost of the operation (without sacrificing quality).

1.4 Elements of supply chain management

To apply the concept of supply chain management fully, there has to be close collaboration between firms within the supply chain. A company must be able to work constructively with its suppliers. At the same time, it should continually look for ways of improving the supply chain structure, and this could involve switching to different suppliers, or selling output through new channels. The Internet has opened up new possibilities for identifying new suppliers world-wide and for selling direct to customers instead of through distributors.

There is no single model for the ideal supply chain, and supply chain management can involve decisions about improving collaboration with suppliers by sharing information and through the joint development of new products, switching to new suppliers by purchasing on-line, or outsourcing some activities that were previously performed in-house. Effective supply chain management calls for the co-ordination of all the different processes in the chain as quickly as possible, without losing any quality or customer satisfaction, and at the same time trying to reduce costs.

Supply chain management is particularly associated with:

(a)   Eliminating waste (activities that do not add value) in the supply chain
(b)   Adding value through better commercial relationships with suppliers.

The table below sets out some of the issues facing supply chain managers.

Production	The customer often wants suppliers to respond to their particular requirements, and to customise orders to their specific needs. A supply chain that can respond quickly to individual customer requirements is known as an 'agile' supply chain. Issues for management include deciding what products or components to make, and where to make them. Should the production of components, sub-assemblies or even the final product be done in-house or by external suppliers? Management focus is on capacity, quality and order volume. Production has to be scheduled so as to provide a sufficient workload for the production resources, and to achieve work load balance (so as to avoid both production bottlenecks and under-utilisation of resources). The challenge is to meet customer orders immediately, without having to invest heavily in inventories of finished goods, which are wasteful and expensive. Quality control is also an issue, because producing poor-quality output has implications for both cost and customer dissatisfaction.
Supply	Most manufacturing companies cannot make everything themselves and still keep the quality of their output high. Decisions have to be made about how much should be purchased from 'outside'. Some companies have chosen to close in-house production facilities and switch to external suppliers, so that they can concentrate on their 'core competences' where they add most value. In choosing external suppliers, management need to consider the capabilities of the supplier, and the extent to which a close collaboration will be necessary. (Collaboration is much more important for key supplies, and much less important for low-cost general supplies that can be purchased from numerous sources.) The management focus should be on the speed, quality and flexibility of supply, as well as on cost.
Inventory	If a firm holds large amounts of inventory, it should be able to meet many customer orders immediately out of inventory and should not suffer hold-ups due to inventory shortages. However, holding inventory is expensive, and there is no certainty that finished goods inventories will ever find a customer, unless they have been made to satisfy specific customer orders. Ideally, inventory levels should be minimised, but without damaging the ability of the firm to meet customer orders quickly or holding up work flow due to a stock-out of key supplies.
Location	Decisions need to be made about where to locate production facilities and warehousing facilities. Cost and tax issues might result in production facilities being constructed in emerging market economies.
Transportation	Logistics management is another aspect of supply chain management. Supplies need to be delivered to a firm's premises and finished goods delivered to customers efficiently, reliably and at a low cost.
Information	Information resources throughout the supply chain need to be linked together, for speed of information exchange and to reduce wasteful paper work. Some firms link their computer networks, or share information through the Internet.

Managing the supply chain calls for an understanding of and knowledge about:

(a)   Customer demand patterns
(b)   Service level requirements (speed of delivery expectations, quality expectations, and so on)
(c)   Distance considerations (logistics)
(d)   Cost

A firm can share its information about expected customer demand and orders in the pipeline, so that the suppliers can get ready themselves for orders that might come to them from the firm. 'Modern' supply chain management uses the Internet to share information as soon as it is available. A firm might have an integrated enterprise resource planning system that is accessible via the Internet. The ERP runs the supply chain database, holding information about a wide range of items, such as customer orders, inventory levels, pricing structures and so on.

A critical issue for successful supply chain management is the speed with which activities can be carried out and customer demands met. If a firm, helped by its suppliers and sub-suppliers in the chain, can respond quickly and flexibly to customer requirements, the benefits will come from lower inventories, lower operating costs, better product availability and greater customer satisfaction.

Question

The concept of supply chain management has important implications for lean manufacturing, just-in-time manufacturing and total quality management. Suggest some of these.

Answer

The implications of the concept of supply chain management on other aspects of modern manufacturing include:

(a)   Just-in-time manufacturing cannot operate successfully unless a company can arrange just-in-time purchasing from its key suppliers.

(b)   It will be difficult to eliminate waste successfully if there is waste at other points in the supply chain. Suppliers should be encouraged to eliminate waste, so that lean management methods can be applied to the entire value chain.

(c)   A manufacturer cannot achieve total quality unless suppliers also deliver quality.

(d)   If a company carries out 'non-core' activities, it is quite probable that those activities do not add as much value as they should. Someone else should be able to perform the same activities more efficiently, and so should add more value to the supply chain. This is an argument, for example, that is used to justify the outsourcing of services.

Lean manufacturing could therefore involve outsourcing, buying from external suppliers rather than manufacturing in-house. In principle, a company could become a 'virtual company', outsourcing and buying everything externally, and having as its core activity the management of the supply chain.

Case Study

Supply chain management and customisation of orders

Personal computer production provides an interesting example of how supply chain management can be used to provide fast delivery of customised products, thereby creating a 'flexible' or 'agile' supply chain.

When customers expect fast delivery of their orders for personal computers, and at the same time want PCs produced to their individual specifications, the parts needed to deliver the item to the customer must exist somewhere within the supply chain. A PC manufacturer operating in a build-to-order market relies on suppliers keeping inventory available, so that the manufacturer can minimise its own inventories without compromising the time needed to deliver the order to the customer. In the case of Dell Computers (reported in a Financial Times supplement on supply chain management, 20th June 2001), Dell itself held about five days' supply and other firms in the supply chain held about ten days' inventory of supplier-owned items. Replenishment of inventories took between 12 hours and two days.

'Build-to-order involves balancing what is available with what the customers want and Dell has become expert in gently massaging both these factors. Any shortage in a particular component is immediately countered by offering other available products on promotion....' By monitoring component inventory availability in real time, Dell and its suppliers can quickly see problems with any particular part. A first step is to increase lead time, informing customers that their preferred configuration will take eight to 10 days to deliver rather than the usual five. If that does not slow up demand, then would-be customers are offered a more expensive upgrade for the same price. "Everyone wins," [says Dell's vice president in the US]. "Our customers get a better deal, the suppliers get business and we can satisfy demand."'

The efficiency of the Dell build-to-order system depends on data sharing between Dell and its suppliers, and the integrity of the information databases. All systems throughout the supply chain are integrated, with common parts numbers and automated order processing and parts management.

The June 2003 exam contained a question on supply chain management, Just–in–time purchasing and the use of IT for both. In June 2005 supply chain management was examined again. Candidates were required to discuss the concept and key elements of supply chain management and how it can lead to improvements, and also to discuss outsourcing.

2 E-procurement

FAST FORWARD

Improvements in purchasing can be achieved through **e-procurement**. This involves placing orders with suppliers electronically, and creating a data link between the organisation's computer systems and those of suppliers.

2.1 E-business

E-business is business carried out over the Internet. There are three aspects to e-business, all of which have relevance to supply chain management:

Key terms

E-commerce: the sale and purchase of items through the Internet, either **B2C** (business-to-customer) or **B2B** (business-to-business)

E-procurement: the purchasing from suppliers through the Internet

E-collaboration: the sharing of information between firms, typically a firm and its key suppliers, through the Internet.

(a) **E-commerce**. A firm can try to sell its goods or services to buyers by offering them on a web site. **B2C** (business-to-customer) e-commerce involves the sale of items to the end-customer, and examples of B2C operations are Internet banking and the selling operations of firms such as Amazon and eToys. **B2B** (business-to-business) e-commerce involves transactions between businesses.

(b) **E-procurement**. Whereas e-commerce has a selling focus, e-procurement looks at the operation from the buyer's perspective.

(c) **E-collaboration**. A firm might put information about customer orders on to the Internet and allow its suppliers access. This allows suppliers to see what orders are in the pipeline, so that they can schedule their own production accordingly. Suppliers can also post information about the progress of their own production operations, so that customer orders can be tracked. Management can also identify any problems in the supply chain as they arise and try to deal with them.

2.2 Electronic data interchange (EDI)

Key term

EDI is the exchange of data, in a structured form, between computer systems, without the need for any manual intervention.

Computerisation of purchasing can be taken to the point where an organisation's computer system links with the computer systems of its key suppliers, and there is 'electronic data interchange' (EDI) between the two organisations.

Purchase orders and delivery instructions can be generated automatically within an organisation's computer system, and transmitted electronically to the supplier over a network link (or possibly over the Internet). The communication process is two-way: the supplier can use the link to acknowledge orders, give notification of deliveries and send invoices for payment.

The data transferred between buyer and supplier has to be in a mutually-agreed form.

(a) It may be necessary to have a process for translating data sent by an organisation to a supplier (or by a supplier to its customer). The translations may be carried out by a third-party organisation, which takes the message from the sender, translates it and sends it on to the recipient. The term **'value added network services'** or **VANS** is used to describe this type of arrangement. An organisation can use this type of arrangement to communicate with many different suppliers.

(b) The direct exchange of data between buyers and suppliers has been made easier by the development of an internationally-recognised standard for sending electronic messages. This is known as EDIFACT, which stands for 'electronic data interchange for administration, commerce and transport.' It is now widely used for transferring standard messages, such as purchase orders and invoices.

EDI, although adopted by many larger firms, has failed to gain acceptance from small and medium-sized firms, largely due to the investment costs involved. However, a major impetus to e-procurement has been provided by the Internet and the development of XML, a language that enables business information to be shared irrespective of its original format.

2.3 E-procurement and the electronic market place

Web-based e-procurement software is now widely available to link firms to suppliers, and, apart from the physical delivery of the goods themselves, all stages of the procurement process can be automated, including payments to suppliers. E-procurement involves information-sharing between buyer and supplier, and in its most efficient form results in collaborative planning and even collaborative new product development. By sharing information about their purchase orders, sales orders, sales forecasts and replenishment plans, firms should be better able to match demand and supply across the whole supply chain.

Some industries have electronic market places. Companies can link to a public electronic market. Suppliers are able to list their prices for parts and components and firms can place orders with selected suppliers. The advantage of a public market place is that firms can see what prices are available, and keep costs down by purchasing at the best prices available.

 Case Study

Some firms have chosen not to use a public market place, but to establish their own 'private exchange'. An article in the *Financial Times* (15th October 2001) described the e-procurement system at Sun Microsystems, the US technology company. 'Whereas B2B (public) marketplaces were meant to be collaborative ventures, run usually by a third-party software company or an industry consortium, private exchanges exist only to handle a single company's procurement. Sun's reasons for rejecting B2B marketplaces offer clues to why the vast majority failed. "I was taking 30 calls a week from people trying to persuade us to join a B2B marketplace," recalls [Sun's director of procurement strategy], "But we could not see the advantage in sharing information with our competitors. Our ability to manage the supply chain and build supplier relationships is a source of competitive advantage." '

The article suggested that it is likely that the success or failure of large companies such as Sun or United Technologies in developing private exchanges for e-procurement will determine whether the Internet will really be able to squeeze big efficiencies for companies from their supply chain.

In Sun Microsystems' e-procurement system:

(a) Suppliers are invited to bid against each other for contracts to supply specified components. A number of suppliers are given, about two weeks in advance, detailed specifications of the components that Sun will want to buy over the Internet. These suppliers can therefore plan in advance the prices that they might be willing to submit in the auction.

(b) The 'window' for bidding is left open for 30 – 60 minutes. Bidders are free to revise their bids in that time.

(c) The bidding takes place over the Internet, and rival bids are shown on screen for all suppliers to see.

(d)   The lowest bid does not necessarily win the contract. The bids are weighted by Sun in accordance with its assessment of each supplier's quality control processes, security of supply and other factors.

(e)   A procurement team also carries out due diligence to check that the promised price is deliverable.

Sun's experience to date suggests that 'dynamic bidding' could result in significant purchase cost savings. 'Even so, the suspicion remains that the private exchange is a zero-sum game: every dollar in Sun's pocket comes out of the supplier's wallet. [Sun] is well aware of the danger that suppliers may in fact loathe the process. In the long run this would damage supply chain efficiency, whatever the short-term financial gains.'

2.4 The benefits and problems with e-procurement

The benefits of e-procurement include:

(a)   reductions in the cost of purchase order processing (for the buyer) and sales order processing (for the seller). There are savings in the time needed to place an order and the time needed to amend orders, as well as savings in stationery costs and postage

(b)   reductions in the lead time between placing an order and receiving delivery. Shorter supply lead times should help the buyer to reduce inventory holding levels, and so reduce inventory costs.

E-procurement is normally an element in 'just-in-time' purchasing.

E-procurement has its problems too:

(a)   To set up an integrated e-procurement system for an entire supply chain would be expensive and complex.

(b)   There is consequently an investment risk for firms that decide to become involved in developing e-procurement systems.

(c)   Intermediaries in the supply chain might be reluctant to collaborate, due to a fear that they might be eliminated from the chain if their suppliers start 'talking' directly to their customers.

(d)   Firms will not become involved in e-procurement and collaboration in supply chain management unless they can see the benefit for themselves. There is a problem of which firms will benefit most and which might lose out as a result.

(e)   Although larger firms might consider the investment in e-procurement systems worthwhile, smaller firms might decide that the investment is too expensive and risky. The larger firms will then have to decide whether to try to coerce their smaller suppliers to invest, or whether to invest money themselves in conversion by their small suppliers to e-procurement.

3 Just-in-time production and purchasing

FAST FORWARD

Just-in-time purchasing and production seek to minimise inventory levels, by acquiring raw materials or producing goods only when they are needed. JIT purchasing calls for close co-operation between an organisation and its suppliers.

Just-in-time is an approach to operations planning and control based on the idea that goods and services should be produced only when they are needed, and neither too early (so that inventories build up) nor too late (so that the customer has to wait). JIT is also known as 'lean operations', 'stockless production' and 'fast throughput manufacturing'. It contrasts with the 'traditional' approach to purchasing and production, in which an organisation seeks to maintain sufficient inventories of all key supply items and finished goods to meet foreseeable demand.

Definitions of JIT are:

(a)   'JIT aims to meet demand instantaneously, with perfect quality and no waste.' (Bicheno, *Implementing Just-in-time*)

(b)   'Just-in-time is a disciplined approach to improving overall productivity and eliminating waste. It provides for the cost-effective production and delivery of only the necessary quantity of parts at the right quality, at the right time and place, while using a minimum amount of facilities, equipment, materials and human resources. JIT is dependent on the balance between the supplier's flexibility and the user's flexibility. It is accomplished through the application of elements which require total employee involvement and teamwork. A key philosophy of JIT is simplification.' (Voss, *Just-in-Time Manufacture*).

> **Just-in-time (JIT)** is a system whose objective is to produce or to procure products or components as they are required (by a customer or for use) rather than for inventory. A just-in-time system is a 'pull' system, which responds to demand, in contrast to a 'push' system, in which inventories act as buffers between the different elements of the system, such as purchasing, production and sales.
>
> **Just-in-time production** is a production system which is driven by demand for finished products whereby each component on a production line is produced only when needed for the next stage.
>
> **Just-in-time purchasing** is a purchasing system in which material purchases are contracted so that the receipt and usage of material, to the maximum extent possible, coincide. (*CIMA Official Terminology*)

In 'traditional' manufacturing, where there is a production process with several stages, management seek to insulate each stage in the process from disruption to another stage, by means of producing for inventory and holding inventory. For example, a manufacturing process consists of four consecutive stages. In a traditional manufacturing system, there would be inventories of raw materials and finished goods, and also inventories of part-finished items between stage 1 and stage 2, between stage 2 and stage 3 and between stage 3 and stage 4. If there is disruption to production at, say, stage 2, the other stages would not be immediately affected. Stages 3 and 4 would continue to operate, using the inventories of part-finished items from stages 2 and 3. Stage 1 would also continue to operate, producing inventory for stage 2. The responsibility for resolving the disruption would fall mainly on the managers of the stage affected, which in this example would be the management of stage 2.

In contrast, in its extreme form, a JIT system seeks to hold zero inventories. In the same four-stage process described above, a disruption at any stage would immediately have an impact on all the other stages. For example, if a disruption occurs at stage 2, stages 3 and 4 will have to stop working because they have no output from stage 2. Stage 1 will also have to stop working, because it will only produce when stage 2 is ready to receive and use its output.

In JIT a disruption at any part of the system becomes a problem for the whole operation to resolve. Supporters of JIT management argue that this will improve the likelihood that the problem will be resolved, because it is in the interest of everyone to resolve it. They also argue that inventories are a 'blanket of obscurity' that help to hide problems within the system, so that problems go un-noticed for too long.

3.1 Requirements of JIT

The operational requirements for JIT are as follows.

(a)   High quality. Disruption in production due to errors in quality will reduce throughput and reduce the dependability of internal supply.

(b)   Speed. Throughput in the operation must be fast, so that customer orders can be met by production rather than out of inventory.

(c)   Reliability. Production must be reliable and not subject to hold-ups.

(d)   Flexibility. To respond immediately to customer orders, production must be flexible, and in small batch sizes.

(e)   Lower cost. As a consequence of high quality production, and with a faster throughput and the elimination of errors, costs will be reduced.

A consequence of JIT is that if there is no immediate demand for output, the operation should not produce goods for inventory. Average capacity utilisation could therefore be low (lower than in a 'traditional' manufacturing operation). However, with a traditional manufacturing system, a higher capacity utilisation would only be achieved by producing for inventory at different stages of the production process. Supporters of JIT argue that there is no value in producing for inventory, and, as suggested above, it could damage the overall efficiency of an operation.

3.2 The JIT philosophy

JIT can be regarded as an approach to management that encompasses a commitment to continuous improvement and the search for excellence in the design and operation of the production management system. Its aim is to streamline the flow of products through the production process and into the hands of customers.

The JIT philosophy originated in Japan in the 1970s, with companies such as Toyota. At its most basic, the philosophy is:

(a)   To do things well, and gradually do them better (continuous improvement), and

(b)   To squeeze waste out of the system.

Three key elements in the JIT philosophy are:

(a)   **Elimination of waste**. Waste is defined as any activity that does not add value. Examples of waste identified by Toyota were:

      1   Overproduction, i.e. producing more than was immediately needed by the next stage in the process

      2   Waiting time. Waiting time can be measured by labour efficiency and machine efficiency.

      3   Transport. Moving items around a plant does not add value. Waste can be reduced by changing the layout of the factory floor so as to minimise the movement of materials.

      4   Waste in the process. There could be waste in the process itself. Some activities might be carried out only because there are design defects in the product, or because of poor maintenance work.

      5   Inventory. Inventory is wasteful. The target should be to eliminate all inventory by tackling the things that cause it to build up.

      6   Simplification of work. An employee does not necessarily add value by working. Simplifying work is an important way of getting rid of waste in the system (the 'waste of motion') because it eliminates unnecessary actions.

      7   Defective goods are 'quality waste'. This is a significant cause of waste in many operations.

(b)   **The involvement of all staff in the operation**. JIT is a cultural issue, and its philosophy has to be embraced by everyone involved in the operation if it is to be applied successfully. Critics of JIT argue that management efforts to involve all staff can be patronising.

(c)   **Continuous improvement**. The ideal target is to meet demand immediately with perfect quality and no waste. In practice, this ideal is never achieved. However, the JIT philosophy is that an organisation should work towards the ideal, and continuous improvement is both possible and necessary. The Japanese term for continuous improvement is '**kaizen**'.

3.3 JIT techniques

JIT is not just a philosophy, it is also a collection of management techniques. Some of these techniques relate to basic working practices.

(a)   Work standards. Work standards should be established and followed by everyone at all times.

(b)   Flexibility in responsibilities. The organisation should provide for the possibility of expanding the responsibilities of any individual to the extent of his or her capabilities, regardless of the individual's position in the organisation. Grading structures and restrictive working practices should be abolished.

(c)   Equality of all people working in the organisation. Equality should exist and be visible. For example, there should be a single staff canteen for everyone, without a special executive dining area; and all staff including managers might be required to wear the same uniform.

(d)   Autonomy. Authority should be delegated to the individuals responsible directly in the activities of the operation. Management should support people on the shop floor, not direct them. For example, if a quality problem arises, an operative on the production line should have the authority to bring the line to a halt ('line stop authority'). Gathering data about performance should be delegated to the shop floor and the individuals who use it. Shop floor staff should also be given the first opportunity to solve problems affecting their work, and expert help should only be sought if it is needed.

(e)   Development of personnel. Individual workers should be developed and trained.

(f)   Quality of working life. The quality of working life should be improved, through better work area facilities, job security, involvement of everyone in job-related decision-making and so on.

(g)   Creativity. Employees should be encouraged to be creative in devising improvements to the way their work is done.

Exam focus point

The June 2006 exam contained a question focusing primarily on the impact that JIT will have on quality and the culture of the company.

E J Hay (*The Just-in-Time Breakthrough*) identified seven aspects of JIT.

Aspect	Explanation
JIT purchasing	Small, frequent deliveries, rather than bulk supply orders. This requires close integration of suppliers with the company's manufacturing process.
Machine cells	The grouping of machines or workers by product or component instead of by type of work performed. For example, instead of having a single machining department and a single assembly or finishing department for all products made by the organisation, there is a small area on the factory floor (a 'cell') for the machining and assembly or finishing for each product or group. The entire production process for the product is carried out within the cell.
Set-up time reduction	The recognition of machinery set-ups as non 'value-adding' activities, which should be reduced or even eliminated.
Uniform loading	The operating of all parts of the production process at a speed that matches the rate at which the customer demands the final product.
Pull system (Kanban)	The use of a Kanban, or signal, to ensure that products/components are only produced when needed by the next process. Nothing is produced for inventory, in anticipation of need.
Total quality	The design of products, processes and vendor quality assurance programmes to ensure that the correct product is made to the appropriate quality level on the first pass through production.
Employee involvement	JIT involves major cultural change throughout an organisation. This can only be achieved if all employees are involved in the process of change and continuous improvement inherent in the JIT philosophy.

There are other JIT techniques and methodologies.

(a)   *Design for manufacture.* In many industries, the way that a product is designed determines a large proportion of its eventual production costs. Production costs can therefore be significantly reduced at the design stage, for example by reducing the number of different components and sub-assemblies required in the product (i.e. achieving greater simplicity).

(b)   *Use several small, simple machines*, rather than a single large and more complex machine. Small machines can be moved around more easily, and so offer greater flexibility in shop floor layout. The risk of making a bad and costly investment decision is reduced, because relatively simple small machines usually cost much less than sophisticated large machines.

(c)   *Work floor layout and work flow.* Work can be laid out to promote the smooth flow of operations. Work flow is an important element in JIT, because the work needs to flow without interruption in order to avoid a build-up of inventory or unnecessary down-times. The movement of materials and part-finished work is wasteful because it does not add value, which means that waste can be reduced by laying out the work floor and designing the work flow so as to minimise movements.

(d)   *Total productive maintenance (TPM)*. Total productive maintenance seeks to eliminate unplanned breakdowns and the damage they cause to production and work flow. Staff operating on the production line are brought into the search for improvements in maintenance, and are encouraged to 'take ownership' of their machines and carry out simple repairs on them. This frees up maintenance specialists to use their expertise to look for 'higher level' ways of improving maintenance systems, instead of spending their time on 'fire fighting' repairs and maintenance jobs.

(e)   *Visibility*. The work place and the operations taking place in it are made more visible, through open plan work space, visual control systems (such as kanbans, described later), information displays in the work place showing performance achievements, and signal lights to show where a stoppage has occurred.

3.4 Value added and JIT

JIT aims to eliminate all **non-value-added costs**. Value is only added when a product is actually being processed. Whilst it is being inspected for quality, moving from one part of the factory to another, waiting for further processing and held in store, value is not being added. Non-value-added activities should therefore be minimised, and ideally eliminated.

Key term

> A **value-added** cost is an expense that cannot be eliminated without the customer perceiving a deterioration in the performance or quality of a product.
>
> The costs of those activities that can be eliminated without the customer perceiving deterioration in the performance or quality of a product are **non-value-added**.

As a simple example of the distinction between value-added and non-value-added:

(a)   the cost of the memory chips in a computer are value-added. The memory chips cannot be removed, or the memory capacity reduced, without the customer noticing a deterioration in quality

(b)   the cost of handling the components in assembling a computer may be non-value-added. Changes can be made in the assembly process and in materials handling that do not affect the performance or quality of the computer that is produced.

Question   Traditional vs JIT

Solo produces one product, the Potten. Parts for the product are quality inspected on arrival and stored in a warehouse until needed. They are then moved from the warehouse to the machine room where they are machined to the product specification. This work is then inspected and, if satisfactory, the machined parts are moved to the assembly area. Once this processing is complete, the finished product is inspected and tested. This is then passed to the despatch department, where employees pack it in an attractive box with a printed instruction sheet. Finished goods are stored back in the warehouse until despatched to customers.

List all the activities in order under the traditional manufacturing system. Then eliminate the non-value-added activities to produce the set of activities that would take place under a JIT approach. Comment upon your answer.

Answer

Traditional system activities
Parts received
Parts quality inspected
Parts stored in warehouse
Parts moved to machine room

Parts machined
Machined parts inspected
Machined parts moved to assembly area
Machined parts assembled
Finished product inspected and tested
Finished goods passed to despatch department
Finished goods packaged
Packed goods moved back to warehouse
Packed goods stored
Packed goods despatched to customer

JIT activities
Parts received
Parts machined
Machined parts assembled
Finished goods packaged
Packaged goods despatched to customers

Comment

The JIT approach has 5 value-added activities, compared with 14 activities under the traditional approach – 9 non-value-added activities have been eliminated.

Receipt of parts, their machining, assembly, packaging and despatch to the customer are essential activities that increase the saleability of the product.

Solo needs to negotiate with its suppliers to guarantee the delivery of high quality parts to eliminate the need for quality inspection on arrival.

Storage and movement of parts, work in progress and finished goods do not add value; rather they introduce unnecessary delays. The machining, assembly and packaging areas should be in close proximity to avoid excessive movement, and ordering and processing should be scheduled so that there is no need to store parts before they go into production. Similarly, production should be scheduled to finish goods just as they are needed for despatch to avoid storage of finished goods.

Proper maintenance of machinery and good staff training in quality production procedures should ensure finished goods of a consistently high quality, removing the need for inspection and testing.

Thus the JIT approach eliminates all wastage of time in the storage of goods, unnecessary movement of goods and all quality checks, resulting in one continuous string of value-added activities.

3.5 Kanban

Holding inventories is one source of waste in production. Not having materials or parts when they are needed is another. In other words, both having inventory in hand and having stock-outs is wasteful practice.

Key term

'**Kanban**' is the Japanese word for 'card' or 'signal'. A kanban control system is a system for controlling the flow of materials between one stage in a process and the next. In its simple form, a card is used by an 'internal customer' as a signal to an 'internal supplier' that the customer now requires more parts or materials. The card will contain details of the parts or materials required.

Kanbans are the only means of authorising a flow of materials or parts. The receipt of a card from an internal customer sets in motion the movement or production or supply of one unit of an item, or one standard container of the item. The receipt of two cards will trigger the movement, production or supply of two units or two standard containers, and so on.

There are variants on the basic kanban system. For example, a production system might use 'kanban squares'. A space is marked out on the work shop floor. When the space is empty, it acts as a signal for production to start at the previous stage. When it is full, it acts as a signal that production at the previous stage should be halted.

Colour-coded kanban cards might be used, with each colour representing a different part or item of materials, or a different degree of urgency.

3.6 JIT in service operations

The JIT philosophy can be applied to service operations as well as to manufacturing operations. Whereas JIT in manufacturing seeks to eliminate inventories, JIT in service operations seeks to remove queues of customers.

Queues of customers are wasteful because:

(a) They waste customers' time
(b) Queues require space for customers to wait in, and this space is not adding value
(c) Queuing lowers the customer's perception of the quality of the service.

The application of JIT to a service operation calls for the removal of specialisation of tasks, so that the work force can be used more flexibly and moved from one type of work to another, in response to demand and work flow requirements.

Where tasks are specialised, JIT can be achieved by outsourcing the function. For example, certain aspects of the Human Resources department such as employment law can be outsourced. Similarly, specialised maintenance can be outsourced in manufacturing operations.

3.7 Control of JIT purchasing: quality assurance

JIT usually requires some form of **quality assurance scheme**. Suppliers are required to guarantee not only reliable deliveries but also the quality of the goods or materials they supply. The effect of this should be to reduce returns, and reduce the costs of waste and re-working.

Against this, a JIT purchasing system might call for:

(a) long-term supply contracts with suppliers
(b) expenditure on operating a quality assurance scheme, and monitoring quality

3.8 Use of JIT

JIT might not be appropriate in all circumstances.

(a) It is not always easy to predict patterns of demand.
(b) JIT makes the organisation far more vulnerable to **disruptions in the supply chain**.
(c) JIT was originated by Toyota when all of Toyota's manufacturing was done within a 50 km radius of its headquarters. Wide geographical spread makes JIT difficult, particularly where key suppliers are in another country.
(d) Suppliers are likely to charge a premium price for contractually guaranteed frequent small deliveries.
(e) JIT purchasing does not make it easier to respond to changes in demand on its own: it must be accompanied by JIT production systems.

 Case Study

In October 1991 the workforce at Renault's gear-box production plant at Cléon went on strike. The *day afterwards* a British plant had to cease production. Within two weeks Renault was losing 60% of its usual daily output a day. The weaknesses were due to the following:

- Sourcing components from one plant only
- Heavy dependence on in-house components
- Low inventory
- The fact that Japanese-style management techniques depend on stability in labour relations, something that was not widespread in many European countries at the time.

3.9 Financial implications of JIT

(a) In the short term

- Inventory is eliminated so the cost of holding inventories is reduced to nil (warehouse costs and interest charges on the capital tied up in inventory).

- Cash flow may be affected. In a traditional purchasing system, payment to creditors for purchases may be delayed offering a source of working capital. It may be more difficult to do this with suppliers with JIT when much depends on them delivering goods on demand.

- If suppliers require immediate payment then both inventories and trade payables will be eliminated from the statement of financial position.

- There will be a considerable initial investment and cash flow as new systems, software and staff training are needed to implement the new ordering processes.

(b) In the medium term

- The first two points above will still be relevant.

- JIT is more than just quick inventory replenishment. It is rather a culture that benefits from lower wastage and mistakes, better procedures and plant layout, more flexible work procedures, better maintenance that reduces unplanned machine down time and generally better working practices and staff morale. All these tend to reduce costs, and the greater flexibility, quality and reliability may also increase sales and profits.

4 Target costing and kaizen costing

FAST FORWARD

An organisation might set targets for reducing costs. A programme of setting targets for continual cost reductions over time is known as **kaizen costing**.

Key terms

Target costing is the process of setting cost estimates for products by subtracting a desired profit margin from a target price. This may be less than original expectations of cost, but the aim will be to achieve this unit cost by the final production stage prior to launch.

Kaizen costing is a process of re-establishing new target costs after product launch, when operational improvements have been made, to ensure that the intended benefits of the improvements are obtained.

Target pricing is used in decision-making for new product design and development. When a new product idea is proposed, the attributes of the product should be considered, with a view to estimating what price customers might be willing to pay for the product if it is developed for the market. If a decision is taken to go ahead with the product development, the probable selling price can be established as a target price that the company will want to achieve.

Having established a target price, management can then decide what the size of the profit margin should be. A **target cost** can then be established by subtracting the desired profit from the target price. The target cost will usually be lower than can reasonably be achieved using current manufacturing methods and processes, and the design team has to find innovative ways of bringing costs down to the target level without sacrificing value. This process of reducing costs during product design without sacrificing value is known as **value engineering**.

In designing and developing the new product, the design team must then work within the constraint that the cost of the product that is eventually developed must not cost more to produce than the target cost. If it appears that the product will cost more than the target, the design team should consider ways of reducing costs without reducing the value of the product to the customer (i.e. without reducing the price that customers will be prepared to pay).

Target costing is therefore a technique for new product design, which ends when the product is launched on the market.

Kaizen costing, also known as enhancement estimation, is applied to a product after it has been launched on the market. The concept was developed by Yashuhiro Monden. It is connected to the management philosophy of kaizen, or continuous improvement.

When a continuous improvement philosophy is applied, a firm should find ways of making small improvements in the way that operations are carried out and products are made. Many of these small improvements should result in lower costs. Kaizen costing is a process of re-establishing new target costs when improvements have been made, to ensure that the intended benefits of the improvements are obtained.

Kaizen costing can be compared with more 'traditional' budgeted cost or standard costing systems.

(a) In a standard cost system, the expected cost is the standard. There is an assumption that existing production facilities and processes will be maintained unchanged. Management should therefore try to ensure that actual costs do not exceed the standard.

(b) In a kaizen costing system, the organisation seeks to reduce costs below the initial standard cost level, through continual small improvements. Cost reduction targets are set, to reflect the improvements that have been made. Management should try to ensure that actual costs are below standard costs, such that the cost reduction targets are met.

Question
Definitions

Match each of the following terms with its definition.

Terms

A Supply chain
C Kaizen
B ERP system
D FMS

Definitions

1. An accounting-oriented information system for identifying and planning the enterprise-wide resources needed to take, make, distribute and account for customer orders.

2. An integrated, computer-controlled production system, which is capable of producing any of a range of parts, and of switching quickly and economically between them.

3. A philosophy of continuous improvement in performance in all areas of an organisation's operations, incorporating benchmarks of excellent practice and instilling a sense of employee ownership of the process.

4. A network of facilities and distribution options that performs the functions of procurement of materials, transformation of these materials into intermediate and finished products and the distribution of these finished products to customers.

Answer

A – 4; B – 1; C – 3; D – 2

5 Outsourcing, joint ventures and partnerships

FAST FORWARD

Organisations might choose to focus on activities where they have core competences, and to outsource other functions to external organisations. **Outsourcing** of various services, such as information systems, facilities management, accounting functions and so on, is quite common.

Organisations can seek to obtain benefits of new product developments or new technology by entering into **joint ventures or partnerships** with other organisations.

5.1 The trend in outsourcing

A significant trend in the 1990s was for companies and government bodies to **concentrate on their core competences** – what they are really good at (or set up to achieve) – and **turn other functions over to specialist contractors.** A company that earns its profits from, say, manufacturing bicycles, does not also need to have expertise in, say, mass catering or office cleaning. **Facilities management companies** such as Rentokil have grown in response to this.

> **Outsourcing** is the use of external suppliers for finished products, components or services. This is also known as **contract manufacturing** or **sub-contracting.**

Reasons for this trend include:

(a)   Frequently the decision is made on the grounds that **specialist contractors** can offer **superior quality** and **efficiency**. If a contractor's main business is making a specific component it can invest in the specialist machinery and labour and knowledge skills needed to make that component. However, this component may be only one of many needed by the contractor's customer, and the complexity of components is now such that attempting to keep internal facilities up to the standard of specialists detracts from the main business of the customer.

(b)   Contracting out manufacturing **frees capital** that can then be invested in core activities such as market research, product definition, product planning, marketing and sales.

(c)   **Contractors** have the **capacity** and **flexibility** to start production very quickly to meet sudden **variations in demand**. In-house facilities may not be able to respond as quickly, because of the need to redirect resources from elsewhere.

5.1.1 Internal and external services

In administrative and support functions, too, companies are increasingly likely to use specialist companies. **Decisions** such as the following are now common.

(a)   Whether the **design and development of a new computer system** should be entrusted to in-house data processing staff or whether an external software house should be hired to do the work

(b)   Whether **maintenance and repairs** of certain items of equipment should be dealt with by in-house engineers, or whether a maintenance contract should be made with a specialist organisation

Even if you are not aware of specialist 'facilities management' companies such as Securicor, you will be familiar with the idea of office cleaning being done by contractors.

Question

Outsourcing

What do you think are the advantages and disadvantages of outsourcing? Try to think of at least four of each.

Answer

Advantages of outsourcing

(a)   It **frees up time**, both of the staff performing the functions, and also of those not directly involved in carrying out the function, but who spend some of their time supporting it – for example, the time of management and supervisors.

(b)   It allows the organisation to benefit from the **specialised expertise and equipment** of the external sub-contractor. It also avoids the requirement to have to employ similar staff and buy similar equipment, and run the risk of **under-utilising** them. If the sub-contractor is well-chosen it is likely that the service will be performed more quickly and to a higher standard than if the service is provided by in-house staff.

(c)   It may be **cheaper** in the long term, once time savings and opportunity costs are taken into account.

(d)   An organisation can **pay for the services it needs, and no more**. The amount of support provided by the external sub-contractor can be adjusted according to requirements.

Disadvantages of outsourcing

(a)   Without proper monitoring, there is no **assurance that the service will be performed to the required standard**. There may be a penalty clause in the contract with the sub-contractor, but financial compensation will not necessarily undo the damage caused by a sub-standard service. However, if a sub-contractor has to be closely monitored, this removes one of the arguments in favour of outsourcing in the first place.

(b)   There is a likelihood that outsourcing will be **more expensive**, at least in the short term, than doing the work in-house, although this is not always the case.

(c)   When any aspect of information-handling is outsourced, there is an increased **risk of commercially-sensitive data getting into the wrong hands**.

(d)   There will almost certainly be **opposition from the employees** affected by a decision to outsource.

5.2 Criteria for selecting functions to outsource

There are three main criteria for selecting functions for outsourcing.

(a)   **Whether or not the organisation sees the function as one that is part of its 'core business' or 'core competences'**. Functions that are not a part of core competences, such as office cleaning, are potential candidates for outsourcing.

(b)   **The relative costs and relative benefits** of outsourcing the function, compared with providing the service in-house.

(c)   **The consequences of mistakes**. If the sub-contractor makes mistakes in carrying out the work, what would be the consequences, and how (if at all) would they be remedied?

5.3 Exercising control over the cost of outsourced activities

Controls over the cost of outsourcing should be implemented at the planning and negotiation stage.

(a)   The organisation should document the details of the level and quality of the service it wants from the external organisation.

(b)   External organisations should then be invited to tender for the work. Ideally, the organisation should have a policy for its tendering processes, such as a specification of the number of bids required.

(c)   The organisation should confirm a price with the successful bidder.

The organisation should also give consideration to dealing with problems that could arise with the external provider.

(a)   How is the quality of the service provided to be judged, to assess whether or not it is acceptable?

(b)   A process should be established for approving costs in excess of those agreed in the contract.

(c)   The organisation might want to include a get-out clause in the contract, in the event that it becomes dissatisfied with the service provided.

(d)   A price increase clause should be included in the contract, to agree a procedure for increasing the price paid for the service at regular review intervals (e.g. annually).

(e)   A price reduction clause might be included in the contract, to apply if the level of service is lower than anticipated.

(f)   The potential failure of the external provider, or the external provider pulling out of the contract, leaving the organisation with, eg no cover for IT services.

When the outsourcing service has begun, there should be ongoing controls to ensure that the service delivered reaches the contracted standards for volume and quality.

5.4 Joint ventures and partnerships

In the continuous search for improvements, and for new products and services, an organisation might decide that it is unable to bear the full cost itself.

Joint ventures and partnerships are ways of carrying out an activity (for example, research and development work) in collaboration with one or more other organisations. The companies in a joint venture or partnership might even be competitors in other aspects of their operations.

An organisation might have a strategic objective of entering into partnerships, for example engineering partnerships, with customer organisations, as a means of establishing long-term relationships with those customers.

The main advantage of joint ventures or partnerships is to obtain the benefits of product developments or activities that the organisation would otherwise be unable to have. The main disadvantage is that the benefits are shared.

5.5 Preferred suppliers

A preferred supplier is one to whom a buyer gives advantages over other suppliers, usually in the form of regular purchases, perhaps for a guaranteed future period. In many cases such a relationship is likely to emerge as a result of long-standing good performance as a supplier in the past.

A buyer will enter into this sort of relationship if it wishes to be a **preferred customer** – a customer whom the supplier will favour over other customers. The major reason for choosing to have preferred suppliers is that they can provide the customer with a **competitive advantage** – they can provide a unique product or service, or a degree of quality or value that is not made available to the customer's competitors, or is not available from other suppliers.

Examples might include providing unique access to the supplier's most talented staff, first right of refusal on the supplier's time or manufacturing capacity, favourable intellectual property licensing or ownership rights, first rights to the supplier's new ideas and technology, in-country presence or expertise, or a supplier's willingness to forgo working on another customer's projects.

A number of matters need to be carefully considered if preferred supplier status is being sought with a customer. Many of these relate to the maintenance of a good relationship and good communication.

(a) Can the supplier afford to make this level of commitment to a particular customer? It may mean investing in new systems and new processes that would not otherwise be needed (for example to obtain ISO 9001:2000 certification). And this may not be a one-off expense: the supplier may be asked to invest in new equipment in the future at its own expense as a means of growing its own capabilities to match those required by the customer. The customer may also wish to influence personnel selection, how they work and what they focus on.

(b) Is the supplier in a position to offer a competitive advantage to a customer, and if so can it do so without compromising its own strategy or other business relationships? A good deal of existing business may be lost if other customers are always placed second in the supplier's priorities, or even if they just feel that they are placed second, despite the fact that they get the same level of service as before.

(c) Is there any danger that the customer in question will renege on the agreement, or go out of business, or be taken over by a third party who will not wish to continue the agreement? The supplier must beware of putting all its eggs in one basket. Too much commitment to one customer may make the supplier too inflexible, and unable to respond to changes in circumstances.

(d) Turnover of personnel on both sides may be a problem. If the relationship is too dependent on individuals buyers may move business from one firm to another to stay with a person who has provided good service in the past. It is important for suppliers to make sure that they meet the customer's needs via systemic approaches rather than through methods that are dependent on key persons.

(e)   Trust is a major issue. Both the customer and supplier need to be willing to share information with each other that they might not normally share with another customer or supplier. This may be difficult for some managers and employees to accept, especially at first.

(f)   Customers will often make the mistake of assuming that since they are outsourcing to an expert in the field, they can forget about having to manage that particular piece of their business. For day to day issues this may be true, but the effort required to understand each other's expectations and objectives, together with that required to build strong relationships, can far exceed the management effort required for in-house work.

(g)   The status of work needs to be communicated regularly and routinely. The customer should hear about problems as quickly as if it had performed the work in-house. Overspending by the supplier should not happen: if additional funds are required this should be discussed proactively with the customer. Again such methods of working may be difficult for some managers and employees to accept at first, if they are used to doing things differently.

(h)   Clear definitions of leadership and overall accountability for the work will need to be established from the outset. These may conflict with existing arrangements, and once again be difficult for managers and employees to accept. On the other hand, in a preferred customer-supplier relationship, the axiom 'the customer is always right' does not hold true. The customer depends upon the expertise that the supplier brings to the table. Thus, if the supplier does not understand why the customer wants the work done in a certain manner, or the supplier thinks it has a better approach, this should be discussed. If the customer's desires prevail, there should be mutual agreement as to why this is appropriate, as well as a clear delineation of the responsibilities and liabilities of each party.

(i)   The business ethics of the supplier should be the same as those of the customer. The supplier should understand the customer's principles and behave accordingly. However, in certain circumstances this may require a change of culture, which the supplier may find hard to achieve.

 Case Study

Preferred suppliers

For many businesses, streamlining the number of suppliers that need to be linked into the corporate systems is a mammoth task. Industrial gas supplier BOC spent over two years in the late 1990s paring down the number of companies in its supply chain from 200 to 10. Ted Dwyer, BOC materials manager, says the streamlining process is essential if a company is going to be in a position where it can strengthen links with its suppliers.

'By working together, defences go down and a desire to build on a relationship comes through,' he says. 'We can consolidate spend, put in place agreements and negotiate prices that can only be achieved when you have fewer suppliers.'

An extract from the BOC website emphasises many of the key points made in this section.

'BOC aims to work with suppliers who share our dedication and commitment to quality and continuous improvement. BOC aims to operate with suppliers and partners who operate within a legal and ethical framework. BOC will terminate relationships with suppliers that fail repeatedly to maintain or who show a gross disregard for the standards outlined in the ethical purchasing policy. Additionally, we seek to do business with those who can provide us with a competitive advantage and who can supply goods and services in a reliable and cost-effective manner. These business relationships are based on more than just price. The mutual lasting benefits to both parties come through innovation and improvements in specification, service, business process and a deeper understanding of each other's businesses. We will develop meaningful performance measurement together, along with a greater focus and understanding of our customers' needs and requirements.'

(www.boc.com/suppliers and partners/)

5.6 Measuring the outcomes of outsourcing

When a business outsources certain functions the business loses a certain amount of control over the performance of the function. Before the decision to outsource is taken, the business will have to consider two things.

(a) **Will the supplier perform the function better than or as well as the business itself (where better will include both a cost and a performance criterion?**

The answer to (a) will depend on the nature of the outsourced function. Most businesses consider outsourcing non-core activities to a specialist provider on the basis that the expertise and the economies of scale that are available to the provider will ensure that the outcome is satisfactory. Airlines often use external caterers, taking the attitude that 'we fly planes, we don't make sandwiches'. Before entering into the agreement the business would have to

- decide the performance targets that the supplier would have to meet
- obtain some indication (probably based on the past record of the supplier) that the supplier would meet those targets
- calculate the cost to the business of performing to that standard themselves, including the management time and the opportunity cost of that management time
- agree a price with the supplier that was acceptable.

(b) **Can the business identify and enforce performance measures on the supplier?**

Identifying performance should not present a problem for the business as it is likely that the business already has performance measures for the function which it will be performing itself.

The measures should be both quantitative and qualitative. The quantitative measures will depend on the function itself and must be easily measurable.

The qualitative measures will be very important to the business particularly if the function involves direct contact with the business's own customers. Differences in attitude and culture between the business and the supplier company have to be minimised or eliminated in case the customers do not receive the proper 'experience' that the business fosters in all its dealings.

5.7 Measuring the outcomes of joint ventures and partnerships

As with outsourcing, a business that is considering joint ventures or partnerships must assess whether the arrangements will improve overall performance and whether it can measure and control that improvement.

The difference from outsourcing is that the business may not be seeking external assistance because it is not itself specialised in the particular area, but rather because there may be some joint benefits or joint expertise that both parties may enjoy.

The decision whether the arrangement will offer improved performance will be made more difficult because the business will be sharing the results of the arrangement and will not have sole ownership or control.

As with outsourcing however, the same broad principles apply.

(a) The decision to enter into the arrangement will be based on calculations as to profitability, market share, brand perception and whatever other objectives the business is seeking. Even more importantly, the business will consider the culture of the proposed partner and whether it is similar enough to their own.

(b) The control of the outcome when the arrangement is in place will involve qualitative and quantitative measures as before.

6 Activity-based management and business process re-engineering

Activity-based management is an approach to management based on the study of major activities within an organisation. ABM seeks improvements in these activities, in terms of cost, quality, time to complete and innovation.

Business process re-engineering involves a radical re-assessment of processes within an organisation, and questions why activities are carried out, when, where and by whom. The aim is to overhaul processes, with a view to achieving improvements in performance.

6.1 Activity-based management (ABM)

Key term

Activity based management has connections with activity-based costing and activity-based budgeting. It is a system of management that uses activity-based cost information to improve performance, for example by reducing costs, or for cost-modelling or customer profitability analysis.

Whereas the emphasis of activity-based costing is to produce more accurate product costs and assessments of profitability, activity-based management is the application of activity cost analysis to the management of costs. ABM has been defined as 'a system-wide, integrated approach that focuses management's attention on activities with the object of improving customer value and the profit achieved by providing this value'. (Hansen and Mowen, *Cost Management Accounting and Control*).

The aim of ABM is to analyse the activities within an organisation, their cost drivers, and the resources they consume, with a view to reducing costs by improving the way in which the activities are carried out and managed. The aim is to question the purpose of activities, as well as how well they are performed. ABM analysis provides information about the costs of activities, including inefficient activities, and the potential benefits to be gained from improvements.

ABM information can support measures to introduce radical changes and improvements to business operations, through business process re-engineering, re-designing the layout of plants, or outsourcing some aspects of operations.

An activity-based approach to cost analysis is useful for studying cost trends, and for assessing whether improvements are being achieved.

6.2 Example

For example, a major area of 'overhead' in manufacturing organisations used to be known as 'warehousing', but is now commonly known as 'materials handling'. If the cost driver for materials handling is the number of production runs, a materials handling cost per production run can be measured, and trends in this cost monitored over time. Targets can also be set for reductions in this activity cost.

 Case Study

An example from the 1990s is the Dutch company Wavin, a manufacturer of plastic pipe systems. This company identified strong relationships between activities and costs.

Activity/cost pool	Cost drivers
Extrusion production	Product weights, number of production runs
Injection moulding	Cycle times, set-ups, number of pieces
Finishing	Standard times, number of pieces
Maintenance	Production volume, planned maintenance programme

Activity/cost pool	Cost drivers
Warehousing	Number of warehouse locations, number of lanes, number of products, demand levels
Order entry	Customer groups, number of customers/order lines
Selling costs	Number of sales representative's calls
Finance	Number of customers/suppliers/transactions

An ABM approach would consider ways of reducing costs in each of these areas, improving quality, reducing times to get work done and encouraging innovation. Each activity should be studied, together with the drivers that give rise to cost, and methods for improvements devised. In the example of Wavin, one approach to the management of warehousing might be to consider ways of reducing the number of warehouse locations, or re-designing the layout of warehouses. Similarly, an approach to managing selling costs would be to consider ways of reducing the number of sales representatives' calls that are necessary.

6.3 Activity-based approach to cost measurement

An activity-based approach to the management of costs is based on a number of different perceptions.

(a) **Organisation structure**. Traditionally, costs have been reported in a way that reflects the structure of an organisation (e.g. production costs, administration overheads, departmental costs). What businesses do, however, are processes or activities that cut across departmental boundaries. Activity costs should be studied, rather than departmental costs.

(b) **Overhead costs**. Overhead costs are a large proportion of total costs in many organisations. Management attention should therefore focus on these 'overhead' areas, in administration, selling and distribution, as well as in production.

(c) **Timing**. Traditional costing focuses on the costs of production for established products. However, the costs of a product are largely determined by their design. It is at the design stage that decisions are made about what materials will be used in a product, what features should be incorporated in the product, and what production methods will be used to make it. In the car industry, it has been estimated that 85% of all future product costs are largely determined by the end of the new model testing stage.

(d) **Controllable costs**. It has been argued that only a small percentage of direct costs are actually controllable, whereas a much larger proportion of overhead costs are controllable. Management should therefore give close attention to the management of these costs.

(e) **Many costs are driven by customers**; for example, order-handling costs, selling costs, after-sales service, finance costs, and so on. Companies might be trading at a loss with some of its customers, without being aware of this fact. An ABC approach to customer profitability analysis will show which customers are more profitable than others, and which customers make losses for the company. Improvement measures can then be devised from this analysis.

6.4 Elements of activity-based management

ABM is not just about cost reduction. There are four areas of activity-based management. These are:

(a) **Cost**. Addressing the problems of activity costs, and finding ways to reduce costs.
(b) **Quality**. Exploring factors that inhibit performance and restrict quality.
(c) **Time**. Exploring the causes of inflexibility, inertia and bottlenecks in work flow.
(d) **Innovation**. Exploring ways of enhancing innovation and process flexibility.

ABM, defined broadly, therefore encompasses a range of performance management methodologies, such as just-in-time, total quality management, business process re-engineering, and customer profitability analysis, as well as activity-based costing, activity-based cost management and activity-based budgeting.

The following comments have been made about ABM.

(a) 'True ABM involves the *use of activities* in planning, budgeting, costing, modelling and performance measurement.'

(b) 'ABM allows all activities to be linked to business processes and hence encourages managers to take a cross-functional view of the organisation.'

(c) 'ABM encourages people to focus on business processes and hence eliminate the need for complex management structures often associated with functional organisations.'

6.5 Activity-based management and activity-based costing compared

Activity-based management and activity-based costing are approaches to performance measurement and management based on an analysis of activities. An activity-based costing system might also be established as part of an activity-based management programme. However, it is also possible to have ABM without ABC, and ABC without ABM.

Activity-based costing is a costing system that can be introduced into an organisation to replace the traditional absorption costing system. It can be used to cost products, and can also be used as a basis for budgeting and for setting product prices (cost plus pricing).

In contrast, ABM is an approach to improving efficiency within the organisation by focusing on improvements in the activities that are carried out. Improvements include not just cost reduction, but also quality improvements, reduction in times and innovation. ABM applications are not concerned with the cost of end products, but with the cost of activities. Many ABM applications may be one-off exercises, whereas activity-based costing is a system of costing that will be used continually, for costing or for pricing products.

It has been suggested by some writers on management that an organisation can use ABM for decision-making, but should keep its traditional absorption costing system, without introducing ABC.

(a) ABM is an approach to improving performance, and does not need a formal ABC costing system to support it.

(b) The use of activity-based costing information should be flexible, and (like information on relevant costs and opportunity costs) does not need to be incorporated into the organisation's formal costing system.

(c) However, where organisations have introduced ABC as their costing system, an ABM approach to improving performance should make use of the ABC information available from the costing system.

6.6 Business process re-engineering (BPR)

Business process re-engineering can be regarded as an element of activity-based management.

Key term

> **Business process re-engineering (BPR)** is the 'selection of areas of business activity in which repeatable and repeated sets of activity are undertaken, and the development of improved understanding of how they operate and the scope for radical re-design, with a view to creating and delivering better customer value.' (*CIMA Official Terminology*)

There are three underlying themes in BPR.

(a) The need to make **radical changes** to the organisation. In effect, the approach in BPR is to start with a clean sheet of paper, and ask the question: 'If we were starting again from scratch, how would we do things?'. Other critical questions are:

What is done?	Why do it?
How is it done?	Why do it that way?
Where is it done?	Why do it there?
When is it done?	Why do it then?
Who does it?	Why that person?

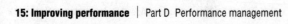

(b)   The need to **change functional hierarchies**. A traditional functional hierarchy within an organisation encourages functional excellence. However, the various functions often fail to work well together to meet customer needs. The interface between different functions is often a cause of major problem, resulting in inter-departmental rivalries, inefficiencies, excess costs, wasting of time and loss of quality.

(c)   The **need to address the problem of fragmented staff roles**. Many employees are now highly-specialised, with the result that they are only responsible for a small part of the overall task. This can result in loss of accountability for a finished task, and also a need for highly-complex scheduling and control systems.

Properly-implemented, BPR may help an organisation to reduce costs, improve service to customers, cut down on the complexity of the business and improve internal communications. At best, it might bring about new insight into the objectives of an organisation and how best to achieve them. At worst, BPR is a glorified term for squeezing costs (usually through redundancies).

6.7 Example: cellular manufacturing

An example of a development in manufacturing that might be described as BPR is cellular manufacturing.

Traditionally, manufacturing industries have fallen into a few broad groups according to the **nature of the production process** and **materials flow**.

Type of production	Description
Jobbing industries	**Items are produced individually** for a specific customer order or 'job'. Versatile equipment and highly-skilled workers are needed to give business the flexibility to do a variety of jobs. The jobbing factory is typically laid out on a **functional** basis with, say, a milling department, a cutting department and so on.
Batch processing	The manufacture of standard goods in batches. Batch production is often carried out using **functional** layouts but with a greater number of more **specialised machines**.
Mass production	Involves the **continuous production of standard items** from a sequence of continuous or repetitive operations. Often uses a **product-based** layout whereby Product A moves from its milling machine to its cutting machine to its paint-spraying machine, Product B moves from its sawing machine to its milling machine and so on. There is no separate 'milling department' or 'assembly department' to which all products must be sent to await their turn on the machines: **each product has its own dedicated machines**.

Cell manufacturing combines the flexibility of the functional layout with the speed and productivity of the product layout. It involves a **U-shaped production line** along which are arranged a number of different machines that are used to make products with similar machining requirements.

The machines are operated by workers who are **multi-skilled** rather than limited to one operation such as 'grinder', or whatever. The aim is to facilitate **just-in-time** production and obtain the associated improvements in **quality** and reductions in **costs**.

 Case Study

Dedicated cells

In January 1994 the *Financial Times* carried a good example of this approach in an article about the Paddy Hopkirk car accessory factory in Bedfordshire.

One morning the factory was just an untidy sprawl of production lines surrounded by piles of crates holding semi-finished components. Two days later, when the workforce came to work [after Christmas], the machines had been brought together in tightly grouped "cells". The piles of components had disappeared, and the newly-cleared floor space was neatly marked with colour-coded lines mapping out the flow of materials.

Overnight there were dramatic differences. In the first full day, productivity on some lines increased by up to 30%, the space needed for some processes had been halved, and work-in-progress had been cut considerably. The improved layout had allowed some jobs to be combined, freeing up operators for deployment elsewhere in the factory.

The new layout encourages 'one-piece production', with as many processes as possible being carried out on a single part consecutively rather than one process being done in a big batch. Parts are only delivered to the next stage of the production or assembly process when they are needed rather than piling up in huge storage bins, as before. Unnecessary walking and movements are eliminated by setting up production in a horseshoe shape rather than a straight line: 'in this way an operator doing a number of tasks will end up at the starting point for the next cycle'.

The advantages of cellular manufacturing are:

(a)   Increased **flexibility**, because staff are multi-skilled and will do any task necessary.

(b)   Reductions in **idle time,** because temporary lulls in activity will be filled by routine maintenance work rather than sitting waiting for production to pick up.

(c)   Reduction in **work-in-progress**, because products do not have to wait in a queue for a machine to be available. This frees up working capital for other uses.

(d)   Reduction in unnecessary **movement** of operatives and **handling** of materials (and associated **costs**), because of the horseshoe layout.

(e)   Reduction in process **losses** and **returns** of faulty goods, because ongoing **training** means that staff are more highly skilled and more careful, have more responsibility for the whole product, and are committed to producing high quality output.

(f)   **Rapid response** to sudden changes in demand or requirements, because of increased skills and the reduced likelihood of bottlenecks. **Late delivery** will be much reduced or eliminated, increasing **customer satisfaction**.

(g)   Better **motivation** amongst workers, partly because they will probably receive better rates of **pay** to allow for increased responsibilities, but also because the cultivation of a **team spirit** should increase levels of performance as employees take more pride in their work, and more account of each others' needs.

(h)   The improvement in the working environment and the support offered by team members should **reduce the level of staff turnover** and its associated costs.

Exam focus point

Business process re-engineering, and cellular manufacturing in particular, were examined in December 2005 in the context of a manufacturer of telecommunications equipment.

6.8 Problems caused by the technological interdependence between departments

The value chain describes a series of activities from input of raw materials to output of finished goods/services for the customers. These activities may be organised into departments even though the actual process of adding value may cross departmental boundaries.

The **links between different departments of a business can vary**, however, and hence the **need to manage the relationships between them**. **Interdependence** is the extent to which **different departments depend on each** other to accomplish their tasks. It is possible to identify three types of interdependence.

(a)   In **pooled interdependence**, each department/section works **independently** of the others, subject to achieving the overall goals of the organisation.

(b)   **Sequential interdependence** is when there is a sequence (or a **linked** chain of activities) with a **start** and **end** point. An example is an assembly line: raw materials are taken, moulded to the right sizes and shapes and are assembled into a product. The **outputs** of each stage sequence must be precisely tailored to the **inputs** of the next – standardisation of outputs might be one form of co-ordination used. The first activity must be performed correctly before the second can be tackled. **Management effort** is required to ensure that the **transfer of resources between departments is smooth**. They therefore need information about the process as a whole.

(c) **Reciprocal interdependence** exists when a **number of departments acquire inputs from and offer outputs to each other**. In other words, while resources have to be transferred, there is **no preset sequence**. The output of one department might be sent to another for processing, and then returned to the original department.

You should now have some idea as to the complexities of business processes overlapping different departments. **Some organisations have redesigned their structures on the lines of business processes**, adopting BPR to **avoid** all the co-ordination problems caused by reciprocal interdependence.

6.9 Changes that affect organisations which have adopted BPR

(a) **Work units change from functional departments to process teams, which replace the old functional structure.**

   (i) For example, within a functional framework, a sales order may be handled by many different people, in different departments or business functions. (One person takes the order in the department, and one person delivers).

   (ii) In process teams, the people are grouped together. A case team might combine to do all the work on a process and this applies not only to one-off projects but to recurring work.

   Multi-skilling also means that one individual does many of the tasks in a process.

(b) **Jobs change**. People do more, as team members are responsible for results. This ties in with **job enlargement** and **job enrichment**.

(c) **People's roles change**. They are empowered to make decisions relevant to the process.

(d) **Performance measures concentrate on results** rather than activities. Process teams create 'value' which is measurable.

(e) Organisation structures change from **hierarchical** to **flat** (ie delayered).

   (i) When a process becomes the work of a **whole team**, managing the process is the **team's responsibility**. Interdepartmental issues become matters the team resolves itself, rather than matters requiring managerial intervention.

   (ii) Companies require less managerial input. **Managers have less to do**, there are fewer of them and so fewer layers.

   (iii) Organisation structure determines lines of communication, and in many organisations is a weighty issue. This is not the case in process organisations, as **lines of communication 'naturally' develop around business processes**.

7 Further aspects of ABM and BPR

The aim of activity-based management (ABM) is to provide management with a method of introducing and managing process and organisational change.

It focuses on activities within a process, decision-making and planning relative to those activities and the need for continuous improvement of all organisational activity. Management and staff must determine which activities are critical to success and decide how these are to be clearly defined across all functions.

Everyone must co-operate in defining:

- Cost pools
- Cost drivers
- Key performance indicators

They must be trained and empowered to act; all must be fairly treated and success recognised.

Clearly, ABM and employee empowerment take a critical step forward beyond ABC by recognising the contribution that people make as the key resource in any organisation's success.

- It nurtures good communication and team work
- It develops quality decision-making
- It leads to quality control and continuous improvement

Some accountants do not appear to understand that ABM provides an essential link to total quality management (TQM) and its concepts of 'continuous improvement'.

ABM helps deliver:

- Improved quality
- Increased customer satisfaction
- Lower costs
- Increased profitability

It provides accountants and other technical managers with a meaningful path into the business management team.

Perhaps the clearest and most concise definition is offered by Kaplan *et al* in *Management Accounting*.

Key term

> **Activity based management (ABM)** is '…the management processes that use the information provided by an activity-based cost analysis to improve organisational profitability. Activity-based management (ABM) includes performing activities more efficiently, eliminating the need to perform certain activities that do not add value for customers, improving the design of products, and developing better relationships with customers and suppliers. The goal of ABM is to enable customer needs to be satisfied while making fewer demands on organisational resources.'

7.1 Cost reduction and process improvement

Traditional cost analysis analyses costs by types of expense for each responsibility centre. ABM, on the other hand, analyses costs on the basis of cross-departmental activities and therefore provides management information on why costs are incurred and on the output of the activity in terms of cost drivers. **By controlling or reducing the incidence of the cost driver, the associated cost can be controlled or reduced**.

This difference is illustrated in the example below of a customer order processing activity.

Traditional analysis

	$
Salaries	5,700
Stationery	350
Travel	1,290
Telephone	980
Equipment depreciation	680
	9,000

ABC analysis

	$
Preparation of quotations	4,200
Receipt of customer orders	900
Assessment of customer creditworthiness	1,100
Expedition of orders	1,300
Resolution of customer problems	1,500
	9,000

Suppose that the analysis above showed that it cost $250 to process a customer's order. This would indicate to sales staff that it may not be worthwhile chasing orders with a low sales value. By eliminating lots of small orders and focusing on those with a larger value, demand for the activities associated with customer order processing should fall, with spending decreasing as a consequence.

7.1.1 Problems associated with cost reduction and ABM

(a) The extent to which activity based approaches can be applied is very dependent on an organisation's ability to identify its main activities and their associated cost drivers.

(b) If a system of 'conventional' responsibility centres has been carefully designed, this may already be a reflection of the key organisational activities. For example, a despatch department might be a cost centre, but despatch might also be a key activity.

(c) In some circumstances, the 'pooling' of activity based costs and the identification of a single cost driver for every cost pool may even hamper effective control if the cost driver is not completely applicable to every cost within that cost pool. For example, suppose the cost of materials handling was allocated to a cost pool for which the cost driver was the number of production runs. Logically, to control the cost of materials handling the number of production runs should be controlled. If the cost is actually driven by the weight of materials being handled, however, it can only be controlled if efforts are made to use lighter materials where possible.

7.2 Activity analysis

The activity based analysis above provides information not available from a traditional cost analysis. Why was $1,500 spent on resolving customer problems, for example. An **activity analysis** usually **surprises managers** who had not realised the amount being spent on certain activities. This leads to **questions** about the **necessity for particular activities** and, if an activity is required, whether it can be carried out more effectively and efficiently.

Such questions can be answered by classifying activities as value added or non-value added (or as core/primary, support or diversionary/discretionary).

7.2.1 Value-added and non-value-added activities

Key term

An activity may increase the worth of a product or service to the customer; in this case the customer is willing to pay for that activity and it is considered **value-added.** Some activities, though, simply increase the time spent on a product or service but do not increase its worth to the customer; these activities are **non-value-added.** *(Rayborn, Barfield and Kinney, Managerial Accounting)*

As an example, **getting luggage on the proper flight is a value-added activity** for airlines, **dealing with the complaints from customers whose luggage gets lost is not**.

The **time** spent on **non-value-added activities** creates additional costs that are unnecessary. If such activities were **eliminated, costs** would **decrease without affecting the market value or quality of the product or service**.

The processing **time** of an organisation is made up of four types.

(a) **Production** or **performance time** is the actual time that it takes to perform the functions necessary to manufacture the product or perform the service.

(b) Performing quality control results in **inspection time.**

(c) Moving products or components from one place to another is **transfer time**.

(d) Storage time and time spent waiting at the production operation for processing are **idle time**.

Production time is value added. The other three are not. The time from receipt of an order to completion of a product or performance of a service equals production time plus non-value-added time.

JIT would of course eliminate a significant proportion of the idle time occurring from storage and wait processes but it is important to realise that **very few organisations can completely eliminate all quality**

control functions and all transfer time. If managers understand the non-value-added nature of these functions, however, they should be able to **minimise** such activities as much as possible.

Sometimes non-value-added activities arise because of inadequacies in existing processes and so they cannot be eliminated unless these inadequacies are addressed.

(a) The UK's National Health Service (NHS) is a classic example of this. Some heart patients on the NHS wait up to four months for critical heart surgery. During this time they are likely to be severely ill on a number of occasions and have to be taken to hospital where they spend the day receiving treatment that will temporarily relieve the problem. This non-value-added activity is totally unnecessary and is dependent on an inadequate process: that of providing operations when required.

(b) Customer complaints services can be viewed in the same way: eliminate the source of complaints and the need for the department greatly reduces.

(c) Setting up machinery for a new production run is a non-value-added cost. If the number of components per product can be reduced the number of different components made will reduce and therefore set-up time will also reduce.

One of the **costliest** things an organisation can do is to **invest in equipment and people to make non-value-added activities more efficient**. The objective is to eliminate them altogether or subject them to a major overhaul, not make them more efficient. For example, if a supplier of raw materials makes a commitment to supply high-quality materials, inspection is no longer required, and buying testing equipment and hiring more staff to inspect incoming raw material would waste time and money. **Non-value-added activities are not necessary for an organisation to stay in business.**

7.2.2 Core/primary, support and diversionary/discretionary activities

This is an alternative classification of activities.

Key terms

> A **core activity** or **primary activity** is one that adds value to a product, for example cutting and drilling materials and assembling them.
>
> A **secondary activity** is one that supports a core activity, but does not add value in itself. For example setting up a machine so that it drills holes of a certain size is a secondary activity.
>
> **Diversionary activities** or **discretionary activities** do not add value and are symptoms of failure within an organisation. For instance repairing faulty production work is such an activity because the production should not have been faulty in the first place.

The aim of ABM is to try to eliminate as far as possible the diversionary activities but, as with non-value-added activities, experience has shown that it is usually impossible to eliminate them all, although the time and cost associated with them can be greatly reduced.

7.3 Performance evaluation

ABM encourages and rewards employees for developing new skills, accepting greater responsibilities, and making suggestions for improvements in plant layout, product design, and staff utilisation. Each of these improvements reduces non-value-added time and cost. In addition, by focusing on activities and costs, ABM is better able to provide more appropriate measures of performance than are found in more traditional systems.

To monitor the effectiveness and efficiency of activities, performance measures relating to volume, time, quality and costs are needed.

(a) Activity **volume** measures provide an indication of the throughput and capacity utilisation of activities. For example reporting the number of times an activity such as setting-up is undertaken focuses attention on the need to investigate ways of reducing the volume of the activity and hence future costs.

(b) To increase customer satisfaction, organisations must provide a speedy response to customer requests and reduce the time taken to develop and bring a new product to the market.

Organisations must therefore focus on the **time** taken to complete an activity or sequence of activities. This time can be reduced by eliminating (as far as is possible) the time spent on non-value-added activities.

(c)   A focus on value chain analysis is a means of enhancing customer satisfaction. The value chain is the linked set of activities from basic raw material acquisition all the way through to the end-use product or service delivered to the customer. By viewing each of the activities in the value chain as a supplier-customer relationship, the opinions of the customers can be used to provide useful feedback on the **quality** of the service provided by the supplying activity. For example the quality of the service provided by the processing of purchase orders activity can be evaluated by users of the activity in terms of the speed of processing orders and the quality of the service provided by the supplier chosen by the purchasing activity. Such qualitative evaluations can be supported by quantitative measures such as percentage of deliveries that are late.

(d)   **Cost** driver rates (such as cost per set-up) can be communicated in a format that is easily understood by all staff and can be used to motivate managers to reduce the cost of performing activities (given that cost driver rate × activity level = cost of activity). Their use as a measure of performance can induce dysfunctional behaviour, however. By splitting production runs and therefore having more set-ups, the cost per set-up can be reduced. Workload will be increased, however, and so in the long run costs could increase.

7.4 Problems with ABM

ABM is not a panacea, however.

(a)   The **amount of work** in setting up the system and in data collection must be considered.

(b)   **Organisational and behavioural consequences**. Selected activity cost pools may not correspond to the formal structure of cost responsibilities within the organisation (the purchasing activity may spread across purchasing, production, stores, administrative and finance departments) and so determining 'ownership' of the activity and its costs may be problematic.

7.5 Comparing ABM and BPR

We have already said that business process re-engineering can be regarded as an element of activity based management.

BPR is concerned with analysing the business processes across the whole company (not just the engineering process part of a manufacturing company) and studying in particular the areas where repeated activities are undertaken. This may be an activity that is repeated in a given process (for example materials handling) such that the process may be reorganised to reduce the number of materials movements. Alternatively it may be an activity that occurs only once in a process but is repeated in different processes such that the activity may perhaps be reorganised to satisfy both processes at the same time. This could again be materials handling where two processes are serviced by internal deliveries at different times of the day – rescheduling the deliveries and the processes may remove the need for the second delivery.

ABM concentrates more on the major activities within the organisation and seeks improvements in these activities in terms of cost, quality, time to complete and innovation. It is a more complete 'overhaul' of the business than BPR and encompasses such techniques as JIT, TQM, customer profitability analysis and BPR.

8 Total quality management (TQM)

Total quality management is an approach to quality improvements that seeks to eliminate waste entirely and to achieve perfect quality standards.

Quality means 'the degree of excellence of a thing' – how well it is made, or how well it is performed (if it is a service), how well it serves its purpose, and how it measures up against its rivals.

The **management** of quality is the process of:

(a) Establishing **standards of quality** for a product or service

(b) Establishing **procedures or production methods** which ought to ensure that these required standards of quality are met in a suitably high proportion of cases

(c) **Monitoring** actual quality

(d) Taking **control action** when actual quality falls below standard

Quality management becomes **total** when it is applied to everything a business does.

Key term

> **TQM** is 'An integrated and comprehensive system of planning and controlling all business functions so that products or services are produced which meet or exceed customer expectations. TQM is a philosophy of business behaviour, embracing principles such as employee involvement, continuous improvement at all levels and customer focus, as well as being a collection of related techniques aimed at improving quality such as full documentation of activities, clear goal setting and performance measurement from the customer perspective.' (CIMA, *Official Terminology*).

TQM has been described as a 'natural extension' of previous approaches to quality management, which were:

(a) Inspection, i.e. inspecting output in order to detect and rectify errors.

(b) Quality control, i.e. using statistical techniques to establish quality standards and monitor process performance.

(c) Quality assurance. This extended quality management to areas other than direct operations, and uses concepts such as quality costing, quality planning and problem solving.

8.1 Get it right first time

One of the basic principles of TQM is that the cost of **preventing** mistakes is less than the cost of **correcting** them once they occur. The aim should therefore be **to get things right first time**.

'Every mistake, every delay and misunderstanding directly costs a company money through **wasted time and effort**, including time taken in pacifying customers. Whilst this cost is important, the impact of poor customer service in terms of **lost potential for future sales** has also to be taken into account'.

8.2 Continuous improvement

A second basic principle of TQM is dissatisfaction with the *status quo*: the belief that it is **always possible to improve** and so the aim should be to 'get it **more** right next time'.

 Case Study

In an average factory only one second is spent adding value - like drilling holes or packing - for every 1,000 seconds spent not adding value. Experts say that they have never seen a factory cut this ratio to less than 1:200. This nevertheless indicates the extent to which continuous improvement is possible and how workers should continuously be seeking ways to reduce time-wasting effort.

8.3 The requirements of quality

There are nine elements in a TQM approach.

(a) Accept that the only thing that matters is the **customer**.

(b) Recognise the all-pervasive nature of the **customer-supplier relationship**, including internal customers: passing sub-standard material to another division is not satisfactory or acceptable.

(c) Move from relying on inspecting to a predefined level of quality to **preventing the cause** of the defect in the first place.

(d) Each operative or group of operatives must be **personally responsible** for defect-free production or service in their domain. TQM requires an awareness by **all personnel** of the quality requirements compatible with supplying the customer with products of the agreed design specification.

(e) Move away from 'acceptable' quality levels. **Any** level of defects is **unacceptable.** TQM aims towards an environment of **zero defects** at minimum cost.

(f) It also aims towards the **elimination of waste**, where waste is defined as anything other than the minimum essential amount of equipment, materials, space and workers' time.

(g) **All departments** should try obsessively to get things right first time: this applies to misdirected telephone calls and typing errors as much as to production.

(h) **Quality certification** programmes should be introduced.

(i) The **cost of poor quality** should be emphasised: good quality generates savings.

When quality improvements are achieved by introducing **new technology** or **new practices**, then **training** to show people how to use the new technology or implement the new practices will be required.

However, workers themselves are frequently the best source of information about how (or how not) to improve quality. 'Training' means training workers to **want** to improve things: it is matter of **changing attitudes**.

(a) Workers can be **motivated** by a positive approach to quality: producing quality work is a tangible and worthwhile objective. Where responsibility for quality checking has been given to the worker (encouraging self-supervision), job satisfaction may be increased: it is a kind of job enrichment, and also a sign of trust and respect, because imposed controls have been removed.

(b) **Cultural** orientation (the deep 'belief' in quality, filtered down to all operatives) and work group norms and influence can be used. Competition to meet and beat quality standards, for example, might be encouraged. Quality circles may be set up, perhaps with responsibility for implementing improvements which they identify.

8.4 Involvement of all parts of the organisation: internal customers and internal suppliers

In a TQM approach, all parts of the organisation are involved in quality issues, and need to work together. Every person and every activity in the organisation affects the work done by others.

TQM promotes the concept of the **internal customer** and **internal supplier**. The work done by an internal supplier for an internal customer will eventually affect the quality of the product or service to the external customer. In order to satisfy the expectations of the external customer, it is therefore also necessary to satisfy the expectations of the internal customer at each stage of the overall operation. Internal customers are therefore linked in **quality chains**. Internal customer A can satisfy internal customer B who can satisfy internal customer C who in turn can satisfy the external customer.

The management of each 'micro operation' within an overall operation has the responsibility for managing its internal supplier and internal customer relationships. They should do this by specifying the requirements of their internal customers, for example in terms of quality, speed, dependability and flexibility, and the requirements for the operation itself (for example, in terms of cost).

The concept of internal supplier-customer relationships in a series of micro-operations helps to focus attention on the 'up-stream' activities in an operation, several stages removed from the external customer. Failure at an early stage on the operation, for example in new product design, has an adverse impact on all the supplier-customer relationships down the line to the external customer. The cost of rectifying an error becomes more expensive the further it goes down the 'supply chain' without rectification.

Some organisations formalise the internal supplier-internal customer concept by requiring each internal supplier to make a *service level agreement* with its internal customer. A service level agreement is a statement of the standard of service and supply that will be provided to the internal customer and will cover issues such as the range of services supplied, response times, dependability and so on. Boundaries of responsibility and performance standards might also be included in the agreement.

Service level agreements have been criticised, however, for over-formalising the relationship between the internal supplier and internal customer, and so creating barriers to the development of a constructive relationship and genuine co-operation between them.

8.5 Empowerment

Empowerment has a vital place in the quality control process: 'the people lower down the organisation possess the knowledge of what is going wrong within a process but lack the authority to make changes. Those further up the structure have the authority to make changes but lack the profound knowledge required to identify the right solutions. The only solution is to **change the culture** of the organisation so that everyone can become involved in the process of improvement and work together to make the changes'. (Max Hand)

Empowerment has two key aspects.

(a)   Allowing workers to **decide how to do** the necessary work, using the skills they possess and acquiring new skills as necessary to be an effective team member.

(b)   Making those workers personally **responsible** for achieving production targets and for quality control. (The French word for empowerment is 'responsibilisation'.)

8.6 Quality circles

A quality circle consists of a group of employees who meet regularly to discuss **problems of quality** and **quality control** in their area of work, and perhaps to suggest ways of improving quality. The quality circle has a leader who directs discussions and possibly also helps to train other members of the circle. It is also a way to encourage **innovation**.

8.7 Design for quality

Quality control happens at various stages in the process of **designing** a product or service.

(a)   At the **product design stage**, quality control means trying to design a product or service so that its specifications provide a suitable balance between price and quality (of sales and delivery, as well as manufacture) which will make the product or service competitive.

Modern manufacturing businesses use Computer Aided Design (CAD) to identify or rectify design features such as the following.

(i)   Opportunities to reduce the **number of parts** in a product overall. The fewer the number of parts, the less parts there are to go wrong.

(ii)   Opportunities to use parts or materials that are **already used** (or could be used) by other products. The more common parts overall, the less chance there is of a product failing to meet quality standards due to a rogue supplier of just one of many components. For example if a car with electric windows can be designed to use the same *glass* as a cheaper model with manually-wound windows, there will only be one glass supplier to keep a check on.

(iii)   Opportunities to improve **physical characteristics** such as shape, size or positioning of controls and so on to make the product more user-friendly.

(b)   **Production engineering** is the process of designing the **methods** for making a product (or service) to the design specification. It sets out to make production methods as efficient as possible, and to avoid the manufacture of sub-standard items.

(c)   **Administration: information systems** should be designed to get the required information to the right person at the right time; **distribution systems** should be designed to get the right item to the right person at the right time; and so on.

8.8 Quality control and inspection

A distinction should be made between **quality control** and **inspection**.

(a) **Quality control** involves setting controls for the **process** of manufacture or service delivery. It is aimed at **preventing** the manufacture of defective items or the provision of defective services.

(b) **Inspection** is concerned with looking at products made, supplies delivered and services provided, to establish whether they are up to specification. It is a technique of **identifying** when defective items are being produced at an unacceptable level. Inspection is usually carried out at three main points.

  (i)   Receiving inspection - for raw materials and purchased components
  (ii) Floor or process inspection for WIP
  (iii) Final inspection or testing for finished goods

8.9 Quality costs

Key term

> The **cost of quality** is defined as: 'The difference between the actual cost of producing, selling and supporting products or services and the equivalent costs if there were no failures during production or usage.'   (CIMA, *Official Terminology*).

Quality costs are therefore incurred because the quality of production or a service is not perfect. There are four categories of quality costs.

(a) **Prevention cost**. This is a cost incurred prior to making the product or delivering the service, in order to prevent substandard quality or defective product being delivered.

(b) **Appraisal cost or inspection cost**. This is a cost incurred after a product has been made, to ensure that the output meets the required quality standard.

(c) **Internal failure cost**. This is a cost arising from inadequate quality, where the problem is identified before the transfer of the item from the organisation to the customer.

(d) **External failure cost**. This is a cost arising from inadequate quality, where the problem is identified after the transfer of the item from the organisation to the customer.

8.10 Example

The different categories of quality cost can be illustrated in the context of a manufacturing operation.

(a) *Prevention costs*

  The cost of building quality into the product design.
  The cost of training staff in quality improvement and error prevention.
  The cost of prevention devices (e.g. fail-safe features).

(b) *Appraisal/inspection costs*

  The cost of inspecting finished goods or services, and other checking devices such as supplier vetting.

  Cost of inspecting goods inwards.

(c) *Internal failure costs*

  Cost of materials scrapped due to inefficiencies in the procedures for goods received and stores control.

  Cost of materials and components lost during production.
  Cost of units rejected during the inspection process.
  Cost of re-working faulty output.
  Cost of reviewing product specifications after failures.
  Losses due to having to sell faulty output at lower prices.

(d)   *External failure costs*

   Cost of product liability claims from customers.
   Cost of repairing products returned by customers.
   Cost of replacing sub-standard products.
   Delivery costs of returned units.
   Cost of the customer services section and its operations.
   Loss of customer goodwill and loss of future sales.

A 'traditional' approach to quality management is that there is an optimal level of quality effort, that minimises total quality costs, and there is a point beyond which spending more on quality yields a benefit that is less than the additional cost incurred. Diminishing returns set in beyond the optimal quality level.

The TQM philosophy is different. It takes the view that:

(a)   Failure and poor quality are unacceptable. It is inappropriate to think of an optimal level of quality at which some failures will occur, and the inevitability of errors is not something that an organisation should accept. The target should be zero defects.

(b)   Quality costs are difficult to measure, and failure costs in particular are often seriously under-estimated. The real costs of failure include not just the cost of scrapped items and re-working faulty items, but also all the management time spent sorting out problems and the loss of confidence between different parts of the organisation whenever faults occur.

(c)   A TQM approach does not accept that the prevention costs of achieving zero defects becomes unacceptably high as the quality standard improves and goes above a certain level. In other words, diminishing returns do not necessarily set in. If everyone in the organisation is involved in improving quality, the cost of continuous improvement need not be high.

(d)   If an organisation accepts an optimal quality level that it believes will minimise total quality costs, there will be no further challenge to management to improve quality further.

The TQM quality cost model is based on the view that:

(a)   Prevention costs and appraisal costs are subject to management influence or control. It is better to spend money on prevention, before failures occur, than on inspection to detect failures after they have happened.

(b)   Internal failure costs and external failure costs are the consequences of the efforts spent on prevention and appraisal. Extra effort on prevention will reduce internal failure costs and this in turn will have a knock-on effect, reducing external failure costs as well.

In other words, higher spending on prevention will eventually lead to lower total quality costs, because appraisal costs, internal failure costs and external failure costs will all be reduced. The emphasis should be on 'getting things right first time' and 'designing in quality' to the product or service.

8.11 Quality systems and procedures

TQM is a management philosophy. However, implementing TQM is not simply a matter of involving employees and encouraging a quality culture. There is also a need for systems and procedures for ensuring quality. Quality systems should be documented thoroughly, in the form of:

(a)   A company quality manual, summarising the quality management policy and system

(b)   A procedures manual, setting out the functions, structures and responsibilities for quality in each department, and

(c)   Detailed work instructions and specifications for how work should be carried out, to achieve the desired quality standards.

'ISO 9000' is shorthand for a family of standards for quality management systems, which has been adopted by organisations world-wide. A company registering for ISO 9001:2000 certification is required to submit its quality standards and procedures to external inspection. If it receives a certificate, it will be subjected to continuing audit. The aim of an ISO 9001:2000 certificate is to provide an assurance to customers (and suppliers) of the organisation that its products are made or its services are delivered in a way that meets certain standards for quality.

Adopting the ISO 9000 family of standards can also give a company the discipline to focus on quality issues and to implement a quality management system.

Despite revisions that bring it more into line with TQM thinking, ISO 9000 has been criticised for encouraging a culture of 'management by manual'. The requirement to document all procedures and to conduct internal audits of the system and its procedures, is also both time consuming and expensive.

9 Value for money (VFM)

FAST FORWARD

Performance in some organisations, particularly in not-for-profit organisations, can be managed through **value for money**. There are three elements to VFM: economy, efficiency and effectiveness. A VFM approach to performance involves setting targets for achievement (effectiveness) and seeking to achieve those targets economically and efficiently.

Value for money (VFM), as the term suggests, means giving or getting good value for the money spent. The management of VFM means trying to ensure that value for money is obtained, or improved.

There are three elements in getting value for money, sometimes called the 'three Es'.

(a) Economy
(b) Efficiency
(c) Effectiveness

Key terms

Economy. Economy means obtaining the appropriate quantity and quality of input resources (labour, materials, machinery and equipment, finance, etc.) at the lowest cost.

Efficiency. Efficiency describes the relationship between the utilisation of resources (inputs) and the output produced with those resources. Improving efficiency means getting more output from each unit of input, or getting the same amount of output with fewer input resources.

Effectiveness. Effectiveness is concerned with whether an activity or output succeeds in fulfilling the purpose for which it was intended.

VFM management can be applied in any organisation, but VFM is more usually associated with **not-for-profit organisations**. The results of a not-for-profit organisation cannot be measured in terms of profits or return on investment. Instead, results can be measured in terms of whether the organisation has succeeded in achieving what it intended (effectiveness) at the lowest cost, through economic purchasing and efficient use of resources.

9.1 Studying and measuring the three Es

Economy, efficiency and effectiveness can be studied and measured with reference to inputs, outputs and impacts.

(a) **Inputs**. Inputs are resources used by an organisation or activity. Resources are labour, materials and supplies, capital equipment and money. In a school, for example, inputs include the teaching staff and administrative staff, the school buildings, teaching equipment and books.

(b) **Outputs**. Outputs are the results of an activity, which are measurable as the services actually provided, and the quality of those services. In a school, outputs would include the number of pupils taught, the number of subjects taught per pupil, the number of examinations taken by pupils, the number of examinations passed and the grades obtained, the number of sixth-form pupils going on to higher education, and so on.

(c) **Impacts**. Impacts are the effect that the outputs of an activity or programme have in terms of achieving policy objectives. For example, in a school system, policy objectives might include providing a minimum level of education up to the age of sixteen, and for a target percentage of sixteen year olds to continue with their education and then go on to further education.

Economy is concerned with the cost of inputs, and obtaining the desired quality of resources at the lowest cost. Economy does not mean straightforward cost-cutting, because resources must be of a suitable quality to provide the service to the desired standard. However, economy is an important element in performance in not-for-profit organisations, such as government services.

Efficiency is concerned with maximising output with a given quantity of resources, or achieving a target output with the minimum quantity of resources. Examples of improving efficiency might be to increase the number of cases handled by members of the police force or a hospital service.

Effectiveness means ensuring that the outputs of an activity or programme succeed in achieving the policy objectives. For example, if the government has a policy of eliminating the incidence of a particular disease, the effectiveness of the programme of elimination will be judged on whether it succeeds, and how quickly.

Question
Economy, efficiency or effectiveness

State whether each of the following events in a hospital service are examples of economy, efficiency or effectiveness.

(a)   The average waiting time for individuals requiring minor surgery has been reduced to 14 weeks. The government's target is 15 weeks or less.

(b)   A regional health authority recruited several hundred qualified nurses from the Philippines, to be paid at standard rates of pay for nurses. This will reduce the requirement for overtime working by the current nursing staff in hospitals and for the need to hire agency nurses.

(c)   The average length of stay for patients in hospital beds in a particular area is reduced from 10 days to 8 days.

(d)   Fewer drugs are now needed to treat patients for a particular condition than was previously the case.

Answer

(a)   Effectiveness

(b)   Economy

(c)   Efficiency. If the government has a policy target for average stay, effectiveness would also be involved.

(d)   Efficiency

9.2 Example

Examples of VFM in the police force have included:

(a)   Civilianisation of duties. Some tasks for which police training is unnecessary, previously carried out by uniformed officers or detectives, are now carried out by civilian staff, at a lower cost. This also frees up more time for uniformed staff and detectives to do work for which they are trained ('put more bobbies on the beat').

(b)   Life cycle costing techniques have been used to optimise the policy for managing the fleet of police cars and other vehicles (optimal servicing policy, life cycle for cars before their replacement, optimum use of the vehicles available, proper specifications of requirements prior to purchasing, etc.)

9.3 VFM audits

A value for money audit is an investigation into whether proper arrangements have been made for securing economy, efficiency and effectiveness in the use of resources. A VFM audit in the public sector can be seen as an attempt to provide an independent verification that management has not spent wastefully, unnecessarily or excessively.

VFM: schools management

An illustrative example of applying VFM is in schools management in the UK. Since 1998, a larger proportion of control over funding and spending decisions has been devolved to the managers of individual schools. The UK government, through the Department for Children, Schools and Families (DCSF), wants to ensure that schools management focus on the need to achieve value for money and has issued a number of guidelines.

Examples of economy, efficiency and effectiveness in schools management are:

(a) Economy. Are costs being minimised having regard to the quality required? For example, are schools supplies of the quality specified being purchased at the best available price? Would it be cheaper to buy books via the Internet rather than through a bookshop or direct from the publisher?

(b) Efficiency. Have the costs of school meals been minimised, whilst at the same time enhancing the nutritional quality of the food given to pupils? Would it be more efficient to hire a temporary secretary to key examination data into the school's database instead of expecting a staff member to do the work? Using a temp will release the staff member to do more appropriate professional work, and the work should be completed in less time. Similarly, would it be more efficient to hire a full-time information and computer technology engineer instead of expecting staff members to deal with all problems in the school's computer systems?

(c) Effectiveness. Have the school's educational programmes improved examination success rates? Did the external provider of the school care-taking service improve the standard of care-taking?

The DCSF recommends that when they look at VFM, school managers should look at the answers to three questions.

(a) Are we spending money properly, and are we sure that our financial procedures are sound?

(b) Are we making wise decisions about spending money? Does our spending properly reflect the school's priorities? Are we choosing the right things to spend our money on? (For example, if the school has prioritised the need to improve standards of education at years 10 and 11, it should not be spending a larger part of its budget on new equipment for the infants' department.)

(c) Are we making sure that the money we spend is spent well, and do we know whether it achieves the desired results?

To deliver VFM, schools need to have in place:

(a) Sound financial management for the control of resources and proper accounting

(b) A system for organising the school's resources so as to maximise the effectiveness of those resources

(c) Strategic management skills that allow the school to respond to changes in its environment, and to innovate by introducing new initiatives.

Applying VFM to supply teacher decisions

The DCSF has suggested guidelines for how VFM should be applied to decisions about using 'supply teachers' to cover for full-time teaching staff absent through illness or on training days. Research has shown that schools make frequent use of supply teachers to cover for absences of full-time staff, but that even with good supply teachers, children do not seem to learn much in the lessons they deliver. In some areas, schools have great difficulty in finding supply teachers and a large number of supply teacher agencies have opened up to meet the growing demand.

VFM suggestions are to:

(a) Limit the use of supply teachers, to improve teaching quality without increasing costs. It might be better to employ a full-time 'floating' teacher to cover for the absences of colleagues. Smaller schools might pool their budgets and share a full time 'floating' member of staff. Measures might also be taken to reduce the absences of staff during term on training courses, by encouraging them to go on courses during holidays, or to use distance learning programmes.

(b)   Make better use of supply teachers. The inefficiency of supply teachers is probably due largely to their lack of familiarity with the school, the way it operates, and its teaching programmes for each term. Supply teachers might be used more efficiently and effectively if they are given an induction to the school and better support from the full-time staff. A school might consider introducing a formal system for evaluating their supply teachers, and to identify and deal with any weaknesses and shortcomings revealed by the evaluation. There should also be strategic absence policies, so that when full-time staff are absent, it is clear what the supply teacher should be teaching in each particular lesson.

9.4 VFM and best value

In the UK, local government authorities are required to achieve 'best value' in the functions they carry out. Best value has similarities to VFM, although the 3 Es of VFM are replaced by the 4 Cs of best practice.

(a)   Challenge. Challenge why, how and by whom each service is provided.

(b)   Comparison. Compare the performance with the performance of other local authorities. Seek to identify and apply good practice.

(c)   Consultation. Consult with the users of local government services and with the community at large.

(d)   Competition. Use fair competition, where practicable, to obtain efficient and effective local government services.

10 Problems with value for money

10.1 Evaluation of VFM

When a value for money programme is established, an important element in the system should be review and evaluation. Managers need to know whether the intended value for money has actually been achieved. There are various ways of assessing VFM.

(a)   Through benchmarking an activity against similar activities in other organisations. For example, hospitals can compare what they do with practices in other hospitals.

(b)   Through performance indicators. Actual performance can be monitored against targets.

(c)   By seeking out recognised good practice and seeing whether this can be applied to the organisation's own situation.

(d)   Internal audit.

(e)   By retaining documentation to show how an operation or activity has been planned, as evidence that good practice has been adopted.

(f)   By examining the results or outcomes of an activity or operation.

Economy, efficiency and effectiveness should seem desirable targets for management to achieve, but in practice, there can be problems in performance measurement, particularly in the public sector. These problems relate to:

(a)   How to identify objectives, and then state them in quantifiable terms
(b)   How to measure outputs and impacts.

A further problem is that there may be several totally different ways of meeting the service needs of the public. If so, a government cannot easily compare the alternatives using VFM. For example, suppose that the government's transport ministry is considering ways of easing congestion on the roads.

(a)   It could build more roads.

(b)   It could encourage the public to switch from using cars to other forms of transport, by increasing the tax on petrol or imposing motorway tolls.

These alternatives cannot be compared in quantifiable terms, and so VFM could not be used as a technique for reaching a policy decision.

To bring the problems of measuring value for money into sharper focus, think about how you might assess VFM in the following situations.

(a)   A government's decision to spend $600 million in the next five years on controls to curb emissions of sulphur dioxide from power stations, with a view to reducing acid rain in Europe.

(b)   A manifesto from the Royal College of Nursing, criticising the government for a deep malaise in nurses' training.

(c)   Fluoride in water – a long campaign for dental health care through prevention rather than cure.

Answer

(a)   The input costs are measurable in money terms ($600 million), and the outputs can be measured in non-monetary terms (emissions of sulphur dioxide). The problem is that the impact of any reduction in the emissions on acid rain in Europe cannot be measured in a reliable way.

(b)   The suggestion is that nurses' training should be improved, presumably by spending more money on training, so that nurses will be able to do their work better, or carry out a wider range of tasks and take some work load from doctors. Some outputs are measurable in non-financial terms, such as numbers trained and courses provided. However, there could be a problem in measuring other outputs, such as the improvement, if any, in the quality of the work done by nurses, and so the effects on the quality or practices of the health service.

(c)   The costs of providing fluoride in the water supply (inputs) can be measured, but again, there is a problem in establishing a link between cause and effect. Just what impact is the programme having on dental health in the longer term, and what health benefits and cost benefits (from a reduced need for dental treatment) will there be? Are resources being used economically and efficiently? For example, could the same results be achieved by putting less fluoride into water?

10.2 Barriers to value for money

Value for money is improved by making changes that reduce costs, increase efficiency or make an operation more effective in achieving its desired target. However, a willingness to make changes calls for:

(a)   Management that is willing to innovate and take serious steps to improve performance

(b)   Generating ideas for improving VFM, and the ability to evaluate these ideas and put them into practice

(c)   The co-operation of employees, and a general motivation to improve VFM.

10.3 Effectiveness audit

An effectiveness audit is a technique for assessing the effectiveness of a project by carrying out an ongoing review of the working of the project to assess whether it is working according to the original intention. The performance measures that are examined are both financial and non-financial.

There are various ways in which the audit can take place but an example of the Public Finance Initiative (PFI) in the UK National Health Service will illustrate the manner in which the audit is conducted.

The starting point is the design of a post-decision project evaluation system (PPE system). This is a system for assessing how a PFI has functioned after the decision to implement it has been taken and the project (say the building and running of a hospital) has been running for a period of time.

The PPE system should concentrate on the key features of the project, should cover all the risks of the project and should engage with all stakeholders as to how they perceive the project is working.

The effectiveness audit should take place at about five yearly intervals and its function is to consider the PPE system and assess how effectively the operation of the project satisfies the expectations set down before the project started.

10.4 Programme budgeting

Programme budgeting and marginal analysis is a technique for allocating resources within the UK Health Service. The system uses the notion of opportunity cost to determine where the marginal resource should be spent – if the marginal pound spent in project A delivers more value than the marginal pound spent in B then the resource should be diverted to A. Thus if treating smoking addiction offers greater benefits than knee joint surgery then resources should be diverted to curing the former.

The system is based on five questions. The first two relate to programme budgeting and are designed to identify how the current budget is spent. The next three relate to the marginal analysis and are designed to assess how resources should be moved to different procedures.

Key learning points

- An organisation should try to achieve **continuous improvements**, particularly by reducing costs and improving quality.

- Improvements can be achieved in purchasing and process management through improvements in the supply chain, from suppliers through to the end customer. **Supply chain management** calls for close co-operation with key suppliers.

- Improvements in purchasing can be achieved through **e-procurement**. This involves placing orders with suppliers electronically, and creating a data link between the organisation's computer systems and those of suppliers.

- **Just-in-time purchasing and production** seek to minimise inventory levels, by acquiring raw materials or producing goods only when they are needed. JIT purchasing calls for close co-operation between an organisation and its suppliers.

- An organisation might set targets for reducing costs. A programme of setting targets for continual cost reductions over time is known as **kaizen costing**.

- Organisations might choose to focus on activities where they have core competences, and to outsource other functions to external organisations. **Outsourcing** of various services, such as information systems, facilities management, accounting functions and so on, is quite common.

- Organisations can seek to obtain benefits of new product developments or new technology by entering into **joint ventures or partnerships** with other organisations.

- **Activity-based management** is an approach to management based on the study of major activities within an organisation. ABM seeks improvements in these activities, in terms of cost, quality, time to complete and innovation.

- **Business process re-engineering** involves a radical re-assessment of processes within an organisation, and questions why activities are carried out, when, where and by whom. The aim is to overhaul processes, with a view to achieving improvements in performance.

- **Total quality management** is an approach to quality improvements that seeks to eliminate waste entirely and to achieve perfect quality standards.

- Performance in some organisations, particularly in not-for-profit organisations, can be managed through **value for money**. There are three elements to VFM: economy, efficiency and effectiveness. A VFM approach to performance involves setting targets for achievement (effectiveness) and seeking to achieve those targets economically and efficiently.

Quick quiz

1   What is just-in-time production?
2   How does EDIFACT make e-procurement simpler?
3   What is a non-value-added activity?
4   How might VFM be measured?

Answers to quick quiz

1   The objective of just-in-time production is to manufacture products as they are required by a customer, rather than to produce finished goods for inventory. A just-in-time system is a 'pull' system, which responds to demand, in contrast to a 'push' system, in which inventories act as buffers between the different elements of the system, such as purchasing, production and sales. **Just-in-time production** is a production system which is driven by demand for finished products whereby each component on a production line is produced only when needed for the next stage.

2   The electronic exchange of data between a buying organisation and its suppliers calls for a method of exchanging data in a form that the computer systems of the buyer and all its suppliers can handle, i.e. the data transferred between buyer and supplier has to be in a mutually-agreed form. EDIFACT provides an internationally-accepted format for the transfer of standard messages such as purchase orders and invoices. Direct message exchanges can take place between organisations that use EDIFACT.

3   An activity that does not add to the customer's perception of the value of a product or service. In theory, non-value-added services should be eliminated.

4   Each element of VFM should be monitored. Effectiveness should be monitored by comparing actual achievements against performance targets. Economy and efficiency should be measured by comparing actual costs against expected costs (budgeted costs). Variance reports could be used to identify significant areas of difference between budget and actual costs. The causes of significant variances can be identified and (where appropriate) remedial action can be taken.

Performance measurement and management

Introduction

This final chapter links together the ideas of performance measurement and performance management. By **measuring** actual performance against targets, managers are able to take appropriate decisions to manage the process under review.

Learning objectives

On completion of this chapter you will be able to:

Syllabus reference

- explain how performance measures are used to manage performance — 25
- explain how divisional performance might be managed, and the problems of transfer pricing for performance management — 9, 17, 25
- explain the behavioural aspects of financial planning, particularly budgeting, and the consequences of behavioural issues for performance management — 25
- describe various types of incentive scheme and explain how incentive schemes can motivate managers to improve performance — 28
- describe various external events that might affect the ability of an organisation to manage its performance effectively — 27

1 Using performance measures to manage performance

Performance measures are used to provide a target for achievement. They are also used to compare actual performance against target, and to identify areas where performance needs to be improved.

The purpose of a system of performance measures is to set targets for achievement, and then to compare actual results against the target. Performance is managed because:

(a) Managers have clearly-defined targets that they are required to achieve

(b) Providing managers with information about actual performance allows them to monitor their progress towards the targets, and to take control action where this seems appropriate

An individual manager should be given **responsibility** for trying to achieve one or more particular targets, and should be accountable for the actual performance achieved (i.e. for 'success or failure'). Targets will be ignored unless someone is given the task of reaching them.

The individual responsible for achieving a particular target needs to have the authority to make decisions that could affect whether or not the targets are achieved. In other words, managers should only be made responsible and accountable for results over which they have some control. The significance of **controllable costs** in responsibility accounting systems has been mentioned in an earlier chapter.

Setting targets for which individual managers are responsible and accountable should be done at all levels of management within the organisation structure. Management implies having some authority, and managers should be made responsible for performance within their area of authority. The measures of performance selected for each manager should be appropriate for that manager's responsibilities.

A system of setting performance targets and measuring actual results against performance is more likely to be effective when managers (and other employees) are **motivated** to work towards achievement of those targets. Motivation can be enhanced by reward/incentive systems.

1.1 Financial and non-financial targets

Each manager might be given just one performance target, or might have several different targets, both financial and non-financial. The performance measures chosen for an individual manager should be consistent with the goals of the organisation.

There will usually be at least one financial target for managers. At a senior level within the organisation, or at divisional level, the main financial target might be ROI, residual income or economic value added. At other levels of management, performance might be measured in terms of profitability, cost variances, cost reduction, progress towards a target cost, or achieving sales revenue growth.

Various non-financial targets might be set for individual managers. The balanced scorecard approach is useful in this respect, because it suggests how strategic targets can be set for non-financial goals, and how these can be converted into operational goals for individual managers throughout the organisation.

As an alternative to the balanced scorecard approach, it might be useful to note that as long ago as 1952, General Electric undertook a performance measurement project and concluded that there were eight key results areas or critical success factors that should be measured.

These were:

(a)   Profitability
(b)   Market position
(c)   Productivity
(d)   Product leadership
(e)   Personnel development
(f)   Employee attitudes
(g)   Public responsibility
(h)   Short- versus long-term balance

1.2 The danger of short-termism

Short-termism is the tendency to place greater significance on short-term performance than on the long-run.

An organisation might focus its attention on short-term performance, particularly profitability or return on capital employed in the current financial year. When attention is focused on short-term financial returns, the danger is that other objectives, both non-financial and longer-term goals, will be ignored. Decisions might even be taken that will improve profits in the short-term, but at the expense of strategic objectives and longer-term interests.

2 Divisional performance and transfer pricing

Divisional financial performance is measured by profitability. Transfer pricing issues can result in sub-optimal decision making.

Many organisations are organised on a divisional basis, with the managers of each division having the authority to make decisions affecting costs, revenues and capital expenditures.

Multiple performance measures might be set for each divisional manager, based on a number of critical success factors, and possibly using a balanced scorecard approach.

Typically, the divisional manager is rewarded on the basis of success in achieving the performance targets.

2.1 The problem of transfer pricing

The main financial target for a division is usually return on investment, residual income or possibly economic value added. A major problem with measuring the financial performance of divisions is accounting for the transactions that are carried out between different divisions within the organisation. Some divisions will supply goods or services to other divisions, and are paid for these internal transfers. The price paid for internal transfers is a **transfer price**.

Internal transfers do not affect the profitability of the organisation as a whole, but do affect the profitability of individual divisions. A high transfer price means that the supplying division will earn a larger profit than if the transfer price is set lower. Equally, a high transfer price means that the 'buying' division will make a lower profit than if the transfer price were set lower. The nature of transfer pricing means that divisional profitability depends on the level at which transfer prices are set, even though transfer prices are totally irrelevant when it comes to measuring the profitability of the organisation.

The various ways in which transfer prices might be set were explained in an earlier chapter.

(a)   A transfer price might be set at the **market price** for the product or service. However, a market price does not always exist. A further problem is that when a market price does exist for the transferred item, and the transfer price is set at the market price, the buying division has no incentive to 'buy' the item from the supplying division. It would be just as cheap to buy the item from an external supplier. For example, suppose that an organisation has an IT department that sells its services to other divisions in the company, charging a market price for its services. A division that uses IT services might decide that it is more convenient to use the services of an external IT company, or might be able to negotiate a cheaper price from an outside supplier, or get a faster or better quality service from the outside supplier. If so, the division might refuse to buy IT services internally. Such a decision is unlikely to benefit the organisation as a whole, because it will usually be cheaper to do the work internally than to buy it externally at market price.

(b)   A transfer price might be set at **cost**. The drawback to using cost is that the supplying division has no motivation to supply items on which it makes no profit. If there is an external market for the item, the supplying division would make more profit by selling its output externally rather than supplying to other divisions within the company. Any decisions to sell externally rather than internally, or any reluctance to supply internally, are likely to be damaging to the company as a whole.

(c)   A transfer price might be set at **cost plus a fixed margin for profit**. This will be necessary if there is no external market for the transferred item, and so no market price. Where transfer prices are set at cost plus, there is a serious risk of disputes between divisions about what the transfer price should be.

(d)   Transfer prices might be **negotiated**, at a level somewhere above the marginal cost of supply to the supplying division and somewhere below market price. Even so, setting transfer prices can be a very contentious issue.

A major risk with transfer prices is that prices may be set badly, in a way that results in sub-optimal profits for the respective divisions.

2.2 Example

Suppose for example that an organisation has two divisions, Division A and Division B, and that Division A supplies two products to Division B, Product 1 and Product 2. Suppose also that:

(a)   At the current transfer prices for the two products, Division A makes a contribution of $6 per unit from Product 1, which needs two labour hours, and a contribution of $4 per unit from Product 2, which needs one labour hour. Labour hours in Division A are restricted by a shortage of skilled labour.

(b)   At the current transfer prices, Division B makes a contribution of $14 per unit from Product 1 and $8 per unit from Product 2. It can sell whatever quantities of each product that Division A supplies.

In this situation, the organisation as a whole will earn a larger profit from selling Product 2 than Product 1. This is because Division A labour is in short supply (a limiting factor), and the organisation earns a larger contribution per labour hour from Product 2 than Product 1.

	Product 1	Product 2
Contribution per unit	$(6 + 14) $20	$(4 + 8) $12
Division A labour hours	2 hours	1 hour
Contribution per labour hour	$10	$12
Profitability ranking	2nd	1st

Making more of Product 2 and less of Product 1 would benefit the organisation as a whole. It would also be more profitable for Division A, because Division A would earn a contribution of $4 per hour from Product 2 but only $3 per hour from Product 1, and labour is in short supply. Division B, however, might argue for higher volumes of Product 1, because this earns it a higher unit contribution.

The difficulty with transfer pricing is to establish a transfer price that motivates the managers of every division to organise operations in such a way as to maximise the profits of the company as a whole. When divisional managers are given the authority to negotiate transfer prices, they might put their self-interest (i.e. the division's profits) ahead of the interests of the company.

If transfer prices are imposed on divisions by senior managers, or if senior management dictates what each division should sell to or buy from other divisions, many of the advantages of divisional performance measurements (local autonomy and motivation of managers) will be lost.

3 Behavioural consequences of performance measures

Setting financial targets can act as a **motivation** to management, who will try to achieve or exceed those targets.

Motivation can be improved through **participation**.

Extensive research has been carried out into the behavioural aspects of performance measurement. The aim of setting targets for performance, and then measuring actual results against the targets, is to encourage management to work towards the achievement of these targets.

Two important questions, however, are:

(a)   Does setting performance targets motivate managers to achieve targets?
(b)   What can be done to improve the motivation of managers to achieve performance targets?

3.1 Human behaviour and budgeting

Interest in the behavioural factors at work in the budgeting and budgetary control process was stimulated by Chris Argyris in the 1950s. He identified four behavioural problems with budgeting and budgetary control.

Issue	Comment
Pressure device	The budget might be seen as a pressure device, used by management to force 'lazy' employees to work harder. The intention of pressure by management is to improve performance, but employees react adversely to it.
'Budget men' want to see failure	The accounting department is usually responsible for putting the budget figures together, and then for preparing variance reports or other financial performance reports. The accountants are seen as 'successful' if they report significant adverse variances, and identifying the managers responsible. The success of the 'budget man' is the failure of another manager. A tension exists between the information providers (the accountants) and management, and management might lose interest in the budget and their performance.
Targets and goal congruence	The budget usually sets targets for each division or department. Achieving the divisional target is of paramount importance, regardless of the effect this may have on other departments or on the overall performance of the company. This is the problem of lack of goal congruence.
Management style	Budgets are used by managers to express their character and style of leadership over subordinates. Subordinates resentful of the manager's style might blame the budget rather than the manager.

These issues in budgeting are reasons why a budget might fail to motivate managers and employees.

3.2 Can budgets motivate?

Despite the potential behavioural problems, there is evidence to suggest that budgets and other performance targets can motivate managers and other employees to achieve those targets.

There is less evidence, however, to suggest that greater motivation will translate itself into better performance!

To provide motivation, performance targets should be:

(a) Clear and specific. Individuals must know exactly what is expected of them

(b) Challenging, but realistic. If targets are too easily achieved, there will be no particular motivation to improve performance. However, if targets are unrealistic, they too are likely to fail to motivate, because 'failure' is certain.

Motivation can also be improved by incentive schemes (discussed later), and might possibly be improved by allowing subordinates to participate in the budget-setting (or target-setting) process, rather than having the targets imposed on them.

3.3 The effect of participation on motivation

There has been considerable debate about whether involving managers and other employees in the budget-setting or target-setting process will improve their motivation and performance.

The general argument in favour of participation in setting targets is that the individual will be more willing to accept the targets, having been involved in setting them. Identifying personally with targets is more likely to make the individual want to achieve them. However, participation needs to be 'real'. It will not be effective if senior managers pay lip service to participation, and having discussed targets with their subordinates, then impose entirely different ones on them. This would be 'pseudo-participation' only, and ineffective as a motivator.

It has also been argued that the effectiveness of participation will depend on the nature of the task being undertaken.

(a) In a highly-programmed and well-established area of operations, where performance standards are well-established, participation might have little to offer by way of motivation.

(b) In contrast, when the work involves high-levels of uncertainty, and calls for a flexible approach, innovation and the ability to deal with unexpected problems, participation in target setting and decision making can be very effective in motivating staff.

Other writers have drawn attention to the importance of the organisation structure. It has been found that where an organisation has decentralised authority, managers perceive themselves to be more closely-involved in the budget-setting process and to be more motivated by their performance targets than managers in a highly-centralised organisation.

There is also some evidence to suggest that personality has some effect on whether participation improves motivation. Some individuals are stimulated by participation in target-setting, whereas others prefer to be told what they need to do.

Question   Problems setting budgets

What do you think would be some of the potential *problems* with managers participating in setting their own budgets?

Answer

There are several problems that could arise when managers participate in setting their own budgets.

(a) **Lack of commitment**. Some individuals do not like 'number crunching'. Whereas they would like to have their views listened to, they do not want to do the detailed planning themselves. They might argue that they are 'too busy' to spend time on figures. Other managers might like the idea of being involved in target-setting, but dislike the formality and constraints of the formal budgeting process.

(b) **Lack of expertise**. Managers should be given adequate training in the skills required for planning and target-setting.

(c) **Budget slack**. There might be a temptation for managers to build in some 'comfort' into their budget, by over-estimating expected costs, or under-estimating likely revenues. Their performance will then seem good, when actual costs are below budget, or actual revenues exceed the budget. Building in 'budget slack' also provides a safety margin, in the event of unexpected costs or an unexpected shortfall in revenue.

3.4 Practical problems with participation in budgeting

The effectiveness of participation in budgeting as a motivator might also depend on the general management philosophy within the organisation. In an organisation that promotes '**employee empowerment**' and '**team work**', participation in budgeting would be just one example of the philosophy applied in practice.

4 Incentive schemes

FAST FORWARD

Incentive schemes are also designed to motivate managers and employees to achieve performance targets.

In most companies, managers are not the owners. The shareholders might have no day-to-day involvement in their company at all. The overall objective of the company might be expressed in terms of adding to shareholder value, but what will motivate management to show any concern for shareholder value?

A well-established method of linking the concerns of managers for their company's performance with the interests of their shareholders is to provide incentive schemes. Arguably, incentives can be a powerful motivator to managers to improve performance – but only those aspects of performance for which incentives are provided.

Rewards are most obviously thought of in terms of monetary reward or something with a monetary value. Alternatively, reward might take the form of promotion to a higher level within the organisation.

4.1 How to link performance to rewards

A good reward system should have the following characteristics.

(a) It should offer **real incentives**, sufficiently high to make it worthwhile for the individual to make a big effort.

(b) It should relate payments to performance over which the individual has **control**. If performance is not controllable, there is no point in offering incentives.

(c) There should be **clear rules** for the calculation of the incentive payments, and a clear understanding of the conditions that apply. This is to enable the individual to decide whether the reward is worth the extra effort.

(d) It should be sufficiently **flexible** to allow differing rewards for different levels of achievement. The payments should not be 'all or nothing'.

(e) It should be **cost-effective** for the organisation.

It might also be argued that:

(a) There should be a minimum level of performance, below which no incentive payments should be made. It is inappropriate to give rewards for mediocrity

(b) There should also be a cap on incentive payments for an individual, partly because excessive incentives might not be deserved and partly because of the risk that a manager might take short-term measures to maximise the reward. High incentive payments to one or two individuals, that are far in excess of rewards paid to other managers in the organisation, will almost inevitably create a sense of 'unfairness' and resentment within the organisation.

Care should be taken to ensure that the incentive scheme results in the desired outcome, for example if the desired outcome is improved product quality then an incentive scheme may be based around reducing the level of rework, whereas an incentive scheme based on, say, production volume may have the reverse effect.

4.2 Types of incentive scheme

There are four common types of scheme.

(a)   A scheme in which **bonuses** are paid for the achievement of a **range of financial and non-financial performance targets**. For example, a manager might receive a bonus for achieving a particular financial target (such as a target ROI or target profit), and further bonuses for achieving other non-financial targets (related to other critical success factors for the organisation, or balanced scorecard targets).

(b)   A **profit-related pay scheme**, in which the bonus is tied specifically to profitability.

(c)   A **profit-sharing scheme**, in which managers receive a reward, possibly in the form of share options in the company, in proportion to the profits earned by the company.

(d)   A **group bonus scheme**, in which a group of managers and employees are paid a bonus in relation to the size of the profits earned by their division. The achievement of non-financial targets might also determine the total size of the group bonus. Group bonus schemes are appropriate in situations where performance cannot be attributed to any individual, but is the result of team work.

Although incentives are commonly cash payments or share options, other incentives might be offered. For example, successful sales staff might be rewarded not just with higher sales commission, but also with holidays paid for by the company.

4.3 Problems with incentive schemes

Short-termism. A significant problem with many incentive schemes is their focus on short-term performance, to the exclusion of longer-term objectives. Incentives for longer-term achievements might be ineffective, partly because of the length of time before performance can be assessed, and partly because an individual manager might not be in the same position long enough to benefit from longer-term achievement.

Problems of measurement. There are three major problems with deciding on performance measurements on which to base rewards.

(a)   Performance targets for individual managers might encourage decision making that is not in the best interests of the organisation as a whole. For example, when the performance of divisional managers is assessed on the basis of profitability, **transfer prices** might be set badly, and **discourage goal congruence** in decision making. It is also questionable whether any set of performance measures can provide a comprehensive assessment of an individual's performance during a period.

(b)   When performance is measured by **non-financial targets**, there may be practical difficulties in measuring achievements. For example, if a manager's targets include improving customer satisfaction, how should customer satisfaction be measured?

(c)   It may be difficult to segregate the **controllable** elements of performance from the elements over which an individual has no control.

Problems of motivation. Incentive schemes will only work if they motivate individuals to make a greater effort to improve their performance, or achieve their targets. Money acts as a motivator, but is more of an incentive to some individuals than to others. There is also evidence to suggest that the motivational effect of a bonus scheme might wear off over time, as bonus payments become the norm. When this happens, there is a risk that failure to pay a sufficient bonus in any year might create dissatisfaction amongst the staff affected.

Problems in the public sector. There are further difficulties with any incentive scheme that might be set for managers in the public sector.

(a) Effective performance can often only be judged over the longer-term; for example initiatives in health or education can take many years to implement fully.

(b) The political dimension. A change of government could result in a change in policy objectives. A new government will not want to reward managers for achieving policy objectives that it opposes, and intends to scrap.

Question

Bonuses or other incentives for managers might be market-based, earnings-based or based on internal measures. What do you think is meant by each of these terms? Give an example of each.

Answer

(a) A market-based incentive is one that ties the bonus to a change in the market value of the shareholders' investment. This might be **total shareholder return** over a period of time, measured as the dividend payments and the increase in the share price in the period, expressed as a percentage of the share price.

(b) An earnings-based incentive is one that ties the bonus to the company's earnings. Examples of earnings-based incentives are bonuses for achieving (or exceeding) a target **growth in operating profit before interest and tax**, or a target **growth in total earnings** or a target **growth in earnings per share**.

(c) An internal measure is any measure of performance that can be calculated or assessed, and reported internally to management. Examples are achieving or exceeding a target for the increase in the number of clients during a period, or a target for unit cost reduction, or a target for improvement in product or service quality.

Exam focus point

Incentive schemes were examined in December 2004, when candidates were asked to consider the validity of reported profit as a criterion for a bonus and the benefits and problems associated with incentive schemes, and again in December 2005.

5 External influences on performance

FAST FORWARD

External events can disrupt the plans and targets of an organisation. When these are serious or long-lasting, an organisation might have to re-assess its longer-term strategies.

An organisation cannot control all the aspects of its business. External events might arise that prevent performance targets from being achieved. Any such events might also undermine the incentive schemes operated by the organisation.

A variety of external events might affect an organisation's performance. Some examples are as follows.

Actions of competitors. Competitors might take an action that forces an organisation to respond, or to re-assess its own objectives. For example, in a market where rival firms compete on the basis of price, a price-reduction initiative by another firm might call for an immediate response. When a 'price war' occurs, the profits of all the firms in the market are likely to suffer.

Price movements. Unexpected changes in the prices of resources (materials, labour, equipment, finance) will affect performance, particularly if the price increases cannot be passed onto the customer in the form of higher prices. An organisation might be able to respond to changes in prices, but only after a time delay. For example:

(a) An unexpected price rise in labour costs will reduce short-term profits. In the longer-term, the organisation can think about increasing automation and the use of technology, and reducing the need for labour.

(b)   If there is an unexpected price rise in a key raw material, short-term profits will be affected. In the longer-term, the organisation can reassess what materials it should use in its products or services, and consider whether a change to a cheaper material might be possible.

Foreign exchange movements. Many organisations are involved in international trade, buying or selling abroad. Some organisations have subsidiary companies in other countries. A significant change in foreign exchange rates can seriously affect performance.

5.1 Examples

(a)   Suppose that a UK company exports a large proportion of its goods to the US, and prices its goods in sterling. If the dollar falls in value against sterling, the company's goods would become more expensive to US buyers, and demand in the US is likely to fall. To counter a fall in demand, the company might have to reduce its prices.

(b)   Suppose that a UK company exports a large proportion of its goods to the US, and prices its goods in dollars. If the dollar falls in value against sterling, the company will earn less from its sales to the US, because the dollar revenue will convert into a smaller amount of sterling. To counter this problem, the company might have to raise its prices, but demand in the US would then fall.

(c)   Similar problems face importers. For example a UK company buying a large proportion of its goods from the euro-zone of the European Community might pay for these goods in euros. A rise in the value of the euro against sterling (i.e. a fall in the value of sterling) would make the cost of the imports higher.

A long-term shift in exchange rates, such as a long-term shift in the value of sterling against the US dollar, might force a company to reconsider its strategy for business location. For example, a long-term fall in the value of the US dollar against sterling might force a company to consider moving its production facilities out of the UK and into another country in the 'dollar zone'.

Labour disputes. An organisation may have an industrial dispute that disrupts its output. Equally, a labour dispute in a supplier organisation, or even a national strike in a key industry, might affect output. When a dispute is prolonged, short-term performance will be adversely affected.

Supply problems. Many organisations rely on just one or two suppliers for several of their key raw materials or components. This is a feature, for example, of just-in-time purchasing systems. Supply problems can have a knock-on effect, and prevent an organisation from meeting the demands of its customers. Supply problems could be due to a world-wide shortage of a raw material, local problems with the supply of power (electricity) or water, a strike at the supplier's organisation or a failure by a supplier to meet promised supply dates.

6 Cultural factors

Key term

> Charles Handy sums up **culture** as 'that's the way we do things round here'. It is the sum total of the beliefs, knowledge, attitudes of mind and customs to which people are exposed.

There are many **factors which influence an organisation's culture**.

Influencing factor	Detail
Economic conditions and strategy	In prosperous times organisations will either be complacent or adventurous, full of new ideas and initiatives. In recession they may be depressed, or challenged. The struggle against a main competitor may take on 'heroic' dimensions.
The nature of the business and its tasks	The types of technology used in different forms of business create the pace and priorities associated with different forms of work. Task also influences work environment to an extent.

Influencing factor	Detail
Leadership style	The approach used in exercising authority will determine the extent to which subordinates feel alienated and uninterested or involved and important. Leaders are also the creators and 'sellers' of organisational culture: it is up to them to put across the vision.
Policies and practices	The level of trust and understanding which exists between members of an organisation can often be seen in the way policies and objectives are achieved, for example the extent to which they are imposed by tight written rules and procedures or implied through custom and understanding.
Structure	The way in which work is organised, authority exercised and people rewarded will reflect an emphasis on freedom or formal control, flexibility or rigidity.
Characteristics of the work force	Organisation culture will be affected by the demographic nature of the workforce, for example its typical manual/clerical division, age, sex and personality.

6.1 The value of culture

'Positive' organisational culture may therefore be important in its **influence** on the following.

(a) The **motivation and satisfaction of employees** (and possibly therefore their performance) by encouraging commitment to the organisation's values and objectives, making employees feel valued and trusted, fostering satisfying team relationships, and using 'guiding values' instead of rules and controls.

(b) The **adaptability of the organisation**, by encouraging innovation, risk-taking, customer care, willingness to embrace new methods and technologies etc.

(c) The **image of the organisation**. The cultural attributes of an organisation (attractive or unattractive) will affect its appeal to potential employees and customers.

6.2 Cultural problems

The symptoms of a negative, unhealthy or failing culture (and possibly organisation as a whole) might be as follows.

(a) **No 'visionary' element:** no articulated beliefs or values widely shared, nor any sense of the future.

(b) **No sense of unity** – because no central driving force. Hostility and lack of co-ordination may be evident.

(c) **No shared norms of dress, habits or ways of addressing others**. Sub-cultures may compete with each other for cultural 'superiority'.

(d) **Political conflict and rivalry**, as individuals and groups vie for power and resources and their own interests.

(e) **Focus on the internal workings of the organisation** rather than opportunities and changes in the environment. In particular, disinterest in the customer.

(f) **Preoccupation with the short term.**

(g) **Low employee morale**, expressed in low productivity, high absenteeism and labour turnover, 'grumbling'.

(h) **Abdication by management of the responsibility** for doing anything about the above – perhaps because of apathy or hopelessness.

(i) **No innovation or welcoming of change:** change is a threat and a problem.

(j) **Rigorous control and disciplinary systems** have to be applied, because nothing else brings employees into line with the aims of the business.

(k) **Lacklustre marketing**, company literature and so on.

6.3 Changing a culture

It may be possible to 'turn round' a negative culture, or to change the culture into a new direction.

(a) The **beliefs expressed by managers and staff** can be used to 'condition' people, to sell a new culture to the organisation by promoting a new sense of corporate mission, or a new image. **Slogans, mottos** ('we're getting there'), **myths** and so on can be used to energise people and to promote particular values which the organisation wishes to instil in its members.

(b) **Leadership** provides an impetus for cultural change: attitudes to trust, control, formality or informality, participation, innovation and so on will have to come from the top – especially where changes in structure, authority relationships or work methods are also involved. The first step in deliberate cultural change will need to be a **'vision'** and a **sense of 'mission'** on the part of a powerful individual or group in the organisation.

(c) The **reward system** can be used to encourage and reinforce new attitudes and behaviour, while those who do not commit themselves to the change miss out or are punished, or pressured to 'buy in or get out'.

(d) The **recruitment and selection policies** should reflect the qualities desired of employees in the new culture. To an extent these qualities may also be encouraged through induction and training.

(e) Visible **emblems** of the culture – for example design of the work place and public areas, dress code, status symbols – can be used to reflect the new 'style'.

7 Conclusion: effective performance management

Performance management is concerned with improving performance, by identifying goals and setting targets for achievement. Performance is then controlled by measurements of actual achievement and comparisons with the targets.

There are various ways of setting performance targets and monitoring performance. None are perfect, and all of them have weaknesses. However, an effective performance management system should include the following elements.

(a) Targets for achievement that are consistent with the strategic objectives of the organisation, and that will enable the organisation to achieve its goals in a manner consistent with its purpose (mission).

(b) Information systems and costing systems to provide information for setting targets and monitoring performance.

(c) The use of appropriate techniques for financial planning and decision making.

(d) Giving recognition to non-financial objectives as well as financial objectives.

(e) A commitment to improving performance.

(f) The use of performance measures to provide a control system for the achievement of targets, and an incentive to management.

It has been said that 'what you measure is what you get', or alternatively 'what you measure is what you manage'. The two cryptic comments amount to much the same thing. The fact that you bother to establish a performance measure and then measure the relevant activities or results is half the battle. Having measured something, you will naturally want to do something about it – you will manage it, change it, improve it and finally you will get it, ie you will get the target figure that the performance measure is aimed at.

Question	Bonuses

(a) A group of employees is paid a collective bonus for achieving six different targets, three financial and three non-financial. How might the amount of the bonus be decided, for example if four targets are achieved but two are not?

(b) What are the main benefits and drawbacks to paying a bonus on the basis of long-term results?

(a)   A bonus can be set for each of the six targets, so that the group receive a bonus for achieving four of the six targets. Alternatively, the bonus can be paid on a sliding scale, with $A payable for achieving just one target, $B for achieving two targets, $C for achieving three targets, and so on up to six targets.

(b)   The benefits are that (a) a long-term bonus scheme will be based on achieving the long-term objectives of the company, thereby avoiding short-termism, and (b) the scheme should also persuade employees to remain with the company, at least until the bonus is earned. The main disadvantage is that employees will not necessarily be willing to wait a long time before earning a bonus for their efforts. (The solution might be to base the bonus on achieving internal targets that ought to lead on to improved company performance in the longer term.)

Key learning points

- **Performance measures** are used to provide a target for achievement. They are also used to compare actual performance against target, and to identify areas where performance needs to be improved.

- **Divisional financial performance** is measured by profitability. Transfer pricing issues can result in sub-optimal decision making.

- Setting financial targets can act as a **motivation** to management, who will try to achieve or exceed those targets.

- Motivation can be improved through **participation**.

- **Incentive schemes** are also designed to motivate managers and employees to achieve performance targets.

- **External events** can disrupt the plans and targets of an organisation. When these are serious or long-lasting, an organisation might have to re-assess its longer-term strategies.

Quick quiz

1   What were the eight critical success factors identified by General Electric in the 1950s?
2   What is short-termism?
3   What is goal congruence?
4   What is the potential problem with transfer pricing?
5   What conditions are necessary for budgets to motivate managers to achieve their targets?
6   What broad types of incentive scheme are there?
7   List five external events that might affect performance management within an organisation.

Answers to quick quiz

1   Profitability, market share, productivity, product leadership, personnel development, employee attitudes, public responsibility, short versus long-term balance.

2   Focusing on one or more short-term objectives to the exclusion of longer-term considerations.

3   A situation in which all managers have targets they are trying to achieve that are consistent with each other, and with the goals of the organisation as a whole.

4   Transfer prices might be set at a level whereby one or more divisional managers will want to do something to maximise divisional profits, but which might be against the interests of the organisation as a whole. The potential problem is therefore sub-optimal decision-making and lack of goal congruence.

5   Targets should be clear and specific. Targets should be challenging but realistic and achievable. Possibly, there should be participation by managers in the setting of their targets. Motivation is also likely to be improved by a suitable incentive scheme.

6   A scheme in which bonuses are linked to the achievement of a number of targets, both financial and non-financial. A profit-related pay scheme. A profit-sharing scheme (for a group of managers). A group bonus scheme (for a group of managers and employees).

7   Competitor actions, price movements, foreign exchange movements, labour dispute, supply problems, economic downturn. Others could be listed.

List of key terms and index

REVIEW FORM

BPP Learning Media always appreciates feedback from the students who use our books. We would be very grateful if you would take the time to complete this feedback form, and return it to the address below.

Name: _____   Address: _____

_____

How have you used this Text?
(Tick one box only)

☐ Home study (book only)

☐ On a course: college _____

☐ With 'correspondence' package

☐ Other _____

Why did you decide to purchase this Text?
(Tick one box only)

☐ Have used complementary Study Text

☐ Have used BPP Texts in the past

☐ Recommendation by friend/colleague

☐ Recommendation by a lecturer at college

☐ Saw advertising

☐ Other _____

During the past six months do you recall seeing/receiving any of the following?
(Tick as many boxes as are relevant)

☐ Our advertisement in *ACCA Finance Matters*

☐ Our brochure with a letter through the post

Which (if any) aspects of our advertising do you find useful?
(Tick as many boxes as are relevant)

☐ Prices and publication dates of new editions

☐ Information on Text content

☐ Facility to order books off-the-page

☐ None of the above

What BPP Learning Media products have you used?

☑ Text   ☐ Kit   ☐ Passcards

☐ i-Pass   ☐ Home Study package

Your ratings, comments and suggestions would be appreciated on the following areas

	Very useful	Useful	Not useful
Introductory section	☐	☐	☐
Chapter introductions	☐	☐	☐
Key terms	☐	☐	☐
Quality of explanations	☐	☐	☐
Case examples and other examples	☐	☐	☐
Questions and answers in each chapter	☐	☐	☐
Key learning points	☐	☐	☐
Quick quizzes	☐	☐	☐
List of key terms and index	☐	☐	☐

	Excellent	Good	Adequate	Poor
Overall opinion of this Study Text	☐	☐	☐	☐

Do you intend to continue using BPP Products?   ☐ Yes   ☐ No

Please note any further comments and suggestions/errors on the reverse of this page

Please return to: Pippa Riley, BPP Learning Media Ltd, FREEPOST, London, W12 8BR or e-mail pippariley@bpp.com

Review Form (continued)

TELL US WHAT YOU THINK

Please note any further comments and suggestions/errors below.